UNIX® Desktop Guide to Tools

Peter Holsberg

SAMS

A Division of Prentice Hall Computer Publishing

11711 North College, Carmel, Indiana 46032 USA

I dedicate this book to my wife, Cathy Ann Vandegrift, whose patience with me while I was closeted with this book had no bounds and is dearly appreciated. Thanks, Cathy.

Publisher
Richard K. Swadley

Publishing Manager
Joseph B. Wikert

Managing Editor
Neweleen A. Trebnik

Acquisitions Editor
Linda Sanning

Development Editors
Jennifer Flynn
Paula Northam Grady
Ted Moore

Production Editor
Andy Saff

Editors
Anne Clarke
Becky Freeman
Jodi Jensen
Rich Limacher

Technical Editor
Andrew Rieger

Editorial Assistants
Rosemarie Graham
San Dee Phillips

Art Director
Tim Amrhein

Cover Artist
Polly McNeal

Production Analyst
Mary Beth Wakefield

Book Designer
Michele Laseau

Indexer
John Sleeva
Tina Trettin

Production
Paula Carroll
Michelle Cleary
Mark Enochs
Brook Farling
Laurie Lee
Jay Lesandrini
Anne Owen
Caroline Roop
M. Louise Shinault
Suzanne Tully
Susan VandeWalle
Phil Worthington

*Composed in ITC Garamond and MCPdigital by
Prentice Hall Computer Publishing*

Printed in the United States of America

Overview

Contents

Acknowledgments

Many people have contributed to this book, both knowingly and otherwise. It's just not possible to name them all but I would be remiss in not thanking the following people:

- Bill Holliker started this book but was unable to complete it because of the pressures of a growing business. Bill allowed me to use and edit his material and examples, and, of course, any errors that remain are mine.

- My daughter, Lisa Holsberg, and her fiance, Dave Shevett, read all of what I wrote at the beginning and were both brave and knowledgeable enough to help me convert my early ramblings into what we hope you will think is worthwhile.

- Jon LaBadie, my local UNIX guru, and my friends on the UNIX Forum of CompuServe Information Services—Jean-Pierre Radley, Michael McConaghy, and Bob Stockler—provided examples of tools and necessary criticisms to keep this book technically valid.

- Many people at SAMS helped. Linda Sanning, the acquisitions editor, started me on this and was a joy to work with. Andy Saff's edits were so painstaking and detailed that he saw errors that everyone else had missed. Nice going, Andy! And the other editors—Jennifer Flynn, Paula Grady, Pat Wood, and Andrew Rieger— were no less thorough. Any errors that remain must lie on my shoulders.

- The last group is the hardest to acknowledge because there are so many of them: the readers on the USENET network who answered all my questions about esoteric and trivial aspects of UNIX tools, who tried my scripts to see whether they would break, and who offered suggestions when I was stuck. The irony is that all of these people are so much more expert in UNIX that they would have no need to buy this book and will probably never see my expression of gratitude! But, just in case—thank you, my friends.

Trademarks

All terms mentioned in this book that are known to be trademarks or service marks are listed below. In addition, terms suspected of being trademarks or service marks have been appropriately capitalized. SAMS cannot attest to the accuracy of this information. Use of a term in this book should not be regarded as affecting the validity of any trademark or service mark.

AT&T is a registered trademark of AT&T.

BSD is a trademark of University of California, Berkeley.

DEC is a registered trademark, and PDP-7 and ULTRIX are trademarks of Digital Equipment Corporation.

Microsoft, MS-DOS, and XENIX are registered trademarks of Microsoft Corporation.

Motorola is a registered trademark of Motorola, Inc.

UNIX is a registered trademark of UNIX System Laboratories, Inc.

Introduction

Most UNIX systems, including AT&T's System V (SV), XENIX, Berkeley Software Distribution (BSD), Ultrix, and SunOS, are distributed with over 200 programs, commonly called *commands* or *utilities*. By combining two or more of these utilities with some of the features of the *shell* (one of the 200 programs), UNIX users can create their own programs of commands. These can perform almost any kind of task, from the relatively simple one of enabling the user to use an oft-repeated group of commands by typing just one command, to handling the complex functions of a database management system. Thus UNIX users can write programs without being programmers.

The UNIX shell provides a simple but powerful mechanism that enables nonprogrammers to write programs: the *shell script*. A shell script is a text file that consists of UNIX commands, possibly used with such programming constructs as loops, if statements, and variables. The constructs are actually quite simple—the power of the shell script comes from the UNIX commands, because each command is a program in its own right. When you create a shell script that does a particular task, you are creating a custom *tool* for your own use—a tool that saves you from having to remember complicated sequences of commands, helps prevent typing errors, and automates frequently used tasks. (People in the UNIX world frequently share their tools with coworkers and others by electronically mailing copies to requestors and by sending copies to "archive" sites where they may be downloaded.)

To become proficient in writing your own tools, you have to know a little about the shell's programming constructs and a lot about the individual commands supplied with your system.

Many books have been written on shell programming, and a few on the utilities. This book contains a tutorial on using the commands of AT&T UNIX System V Release 4, and a reference section for those commands. The emphasis, of course, is on the commands that are most useful in shell scripts. I provide abundant examples and give a number of helpful hints.

The book is divided into three sections: Part I provides an overview of UNIX and its user environment, Part II is the tutorial, and Part III is the reference section. I discuss shell programming only as needed to illustrate the use of the commands. SAMS has, as part of the UNIX Desktop Guide series, a very fine book on Korn shell programming by an excellent writer, John Valley. If you want to get more deeply involved in shell programming, Valley's *UNIX Desktop Guide to the Korn Shell* is the book for you.

Assumptions

I've talked about the book; now it's time to talk about you! I'm assuming that you can do the following:

- Log in and log out of a UNIX system, either from a terminal or via a modem and terminal emulator.

- Explain what's meant by the *current working directory*, *your home directory*, a *parent directory*, an *absolute* or *full pathname*, and a *relative pathname*. This implies a knowledge of the UNIX hierarchical file organization.

- Use date, ls, cat, cd, ps, pwd, who, cp, mv, rm, and vi in their simplest forms.

- Understand what a *decision* (that is, an *if* statement) does and how a loop works.

- Find all the "funny" UNIX characters on your keyboard: the exclamation mark (!), the dollar sign ($), the circumflex (^), the ampersand (&), the asterisk (*), the period (.), the slash (/), the backslash (\), the vertical bar (¦), the equal sign (=), the subtraction sign (-), the plus sign (+), the single quotation mark (´), the double quotation marks ("), and the back quote or grave accent (`).

- Recognize a UNIX *prompt*.

  If you can do these few things, you'll learn much from this book.

  Good reading!

> **Note:** The UNIX system I used to create the examples in this book is System V Release 4. If you are using a different system, some of the commands may not work exactly as described in this book.

How to Contact the Author

If you have any questions or suggestions, or want to report any errors you find, please feel free to contact me via electronic mail. Here are some addresses you can use:

- Internet Address

  `pjh@mccc.edu`

- UUCP Address ("bangpath")

  `<backbone_site>!princeton!mccc!pjh`

- CompuServe

  `70240,334`

  or

  `>INTERNET:pjh@mccc.edu`

- MCIMAIL

  `EMS: INTERNET`
  `MBX: pjh@mccc.edu`

Please do not phone me directly. I respond much more promptly to electronic mail.

If you do not have access to electronic mail, please write to me at

P.C.L.A.B. Computing
44 Lopatcong Drive
Trenton, New Jersey 08638-1326

How to Get the Files Used in This Book

There are several ways for you to save yourself the chore of typing all the data files I use to illustrate UNIX tools.

Via Anonymous FTP

If you have an account on a computer that is connected to the Internet, or on one that can mail to the site decwrl.dec.com, you can download a file that is a collection of all the data files in the book.

Here are the steps for anonymous ftp from an Internet computer:

```
$ ftp pilot.njin.net
```

Login as "anonymous" and give your email address as the password:

```
$ cd /pub/TCF/UDGT
```

```
$ hash
```

```
$ get book
```

When the file transfer has completed, log off:

```
$ quit
```

On your own system, enter

```
$ sh book
```

This will create subdirectories that correspond to chapters, and copy the appropriate data files into each subdirectory.

To retrieve the file via the server at decwrl.dec.com, send email with the following contents to ftpmail@decwrl.dec.com:

```
reply <your electronic mail address>
connect pilot.njin.net
chdir /pub/TCF/UDGT
get book
quit
```

Your electronic mail address should be the same "bangpath" that you would use for UUCP email.

Some time later, a copy of the file will be mailed to you. Save it into an appropriate directory and enter

```
$ sh book
```

If the file is sent in two or more mail messages, save each with a different name, cat them into a file called book and then enter

```
$ sh book
```

On Disk

Send the order blank at the back of the book to the aforementioned mailing address and I will send you an MS-DOS disk with the book file on it. Enclose $20 (money order or check in U.S. funds drawn on a U.S. bank, please) and the desired MS-DOS disk type/size. Payment must accompany your order.

Part

Overview

## Chapter 1

Overview of UNIX

I n the past few years, UNIX has emerged from the university computer science research laboratories and the engineering development departments to become a viable operating system that supports a great variety of user-oriented applications. Where did UNIX come from? What makes it useful to end-users? Why was it "hidden" for so long? What features does it have? I'll try to answer these and other questions in this chapter.

The History of UNIX

In the late 1960s MIT, AT&T Bell Laboratories, and General Electric were jointly developing an interactive operating system, MULTICS, for the GE 645 mainframe computer. (MULTICS is an acronym for Multiplexed Information and Computing System.) This development effort was not truly successful, as MULTICS was complex, ran quite slowly, and required enormous (for that time) amounts of memory. For various reasons, Bell Labs ended its participation around 1968.

In 1969, however, one of the Bell Labs people who worked on the MULTICS project, Ken Thompson, wrote a program that simulated a spaceship traveling through

1

the solar system. The program originally ran on the MULTICS computer but then was translated to run on a GECOS (General Electric Computer Operating System) computer. GECOS so influenced UNIX that, even today, the fifth field in the password file is called the GECOS (sometimes, GCOS) field. He later ported it to an unused DEC PDP-7 that he "found" somewhere in Bell Labs. To make his program more efficient, Thompson wrote a new operating system, based on MULTICS, for the PDP-7.

Thompson's colleague, Brian Kernighan, made the first of the thousands and thousands of UNIX puns and dubbed Thompson's small, elegant operating system the Uniplexed Information and Computing System, or UNICS. The name was changed to *UNIX* in 1970.

Bell Labs liked UNIX, so Thompson and Dennis Ritchie rewrote it for the PDP-11/20, and UNIX became the operating system for text processing in the patent department of Bell Labs. They later rewrote UNIX in the C programming language, a step that made UNIX easy to "port" to other computers, and licensed the source code to colleges and universities for a nominal fee. Since then, UNIX has been ported to computers using microprocessors, such as the Motorola 68000 family and the Intel 80x86 family, to minicomputers and mainframes, and even to the Cray supercomputers.

The University of California at Berkeley became involved with UNIX in 1975 when Ken Thompson spent a sabbatical year there. He and two of his graduate students, Bill Joy and Chuck Haley, created the Berkeley version of UNIX by making a number of enhancements and changes to AT&T UNIX. In 1978, they provided 2BSD (the second Berkeley Software Distribution), followed in 1979 by 3BSD. The United States Department of Defense's Advanced Research Projects Agency (DARPA) adopted BSD UNIX and funded 4.1BSD, 4.2BSD, and, in 1987, 4.3BSD. Many computer vendors use BSD UNIX as the foundation for their versions of UNIX. These include Sun Microsystems, a company cofounded by the aforementioned Bill Joy.

Before 1980, UNIX was a minicomputer operating system. Then Microsoft developed XENIX, based on both AT&T UNIX and BSD UNIX. XENIX was intended for microprocessor-based desktop computers.

In 1982, AT&T went into the commercial computer business and released UNIX System III as its first software product. UNIX System V was released in 1983. (System IV was never released outside of Bell Labs.) Subreleases of UNIX System V became available: Release 2 in 1985, and Release 3.0 in 1987. The latter was followed by Releases 3.1 and 3.2, and in 1990, AT&T made available System V Release 4 (SVR4).

In a gigantic departure from all previous versions of AT&T UNIX, SVR4 attempts to unify System V UNIX, XENIX, and BSD UNIX into a single environment. One of the problems that arose was the conflict between the different versions of certain commands. Such commands were not merged into SVR4, but were placed into *compatibility packages*. Users accustomed to the XENIX or BSD versions of those commands can select the appropriate compatibility package for their own use without affecting other users.

Note: This book covers the standard SVR4 commands. Be advised that if you are using SVR3 or any of the BSD variants, your commands may not behave exactly as the ones covered here.

The Tool Philosophy

UNIX owes its longevity to the programming philosophy of Ken Thompson. He built into UNIX a high degree of support for programmers, and provided them with many resources. Because he was working on a computer that had a limited amount of memory, he developed utility programs that were small and efficient. This led to the building block or tool philosophy.

The underlying philosophy in UNIX is this: small is beautiful. Specifically, this means that each program (i.e., each command, utility, or tool) should do just one task, but do it well. Rather than rewrite an existing program to add new features, the UNIX programmer is directed to develop a new tool from existing tools. That is the topic of this book.

UNIX programmers usually follow these maxims:

- Expect the output of the program you're writing to be used as the input to another program.

- Don't clutter the output of your program with extraneous information, such as table headings or congratulatory messages.

- Accept simple, character-oriented inputs rather than binary values or values formatted into lists or tables.

- Avoid writing programs that require interaction with the user.

Programs written according to these rules are called *filters* and are the backbone of all UNIX tools. Almost all of the 200 or so commands distributed with UNIX are filters; UNIX programmers have done their job well. Although many of these programs may seem to do merely trivial things when used alone, you can combine them with other similar programs to create general and useful tools.

The UNIX System Environment

1

Before you can begin to build tools, you must examine the underlying system and the "raw materials" that you will build tools with.

The UNIX operating system consists of a *kernel*, a *shell*, and hundreds of commands or utilities. The kernel is the part of UNIX that interacts directly with the computer hardware. It manages memory, controls access to the computer, performs input and output, and provides services for programmers to use in their programs. You do not use the kernel directly in building tools, but do all work through the shell. The shell interacts with the kernel in a manner transparent to the user: it is a *command interpreter* program that "reads" what you have entered at the keyboard and translates your command into equivalent instructions that the computer can execute. The shell also provides a simple but powerful programming language. The combination of the kernel, the shell, the commands, and the hardware is the UNIX system. The UNIX system provides an *environment* for you to work in.

To become fully proficient in using and building tools, you must first understand the workings of the system environment. The UNIX system environment consists of two major subsystems:

- The file system—the physical and conceptual definition and organization of files. You should understand how files are used for input and output.

- The process control system—the relationship between a program (especially the shell) and the program's corresponding process. You should understand how these two things interact with the rest of the environment.

Understanding these two subsystems will help you grasp the relationships that exist between the system, the user environment, and the programs. With this understanding you can relate commands to each other and to the system. This is an important skill for the development of useful tools in UNIX.

The File System

UNIX people use the phrase *file system* in two quite different ways. One meaning is "an organized structure pertaining to how and where files and directories are stored on disks and in memory"—what is called the *physical* file system. The other is "the organization of files and directories in an inverted tree hierarchy"—what is called the *conceptual* or *logical* file system. This section looks briefly at the physical file system.

The hardware of a computer system includes a place to store programs and data while they're not being used, and a place to put each when it is being used. The former is called *secondary storage* or *mass storage*, the latter *main memory*. Most computers today use the hard disk as the instrument for implementing mass storage.

As it comes from the manufacturer, a hard disk consists of some electronics, one or more *platters* (like audio records) permanently mounted inside an airtight enclosure, a motor to spin the platters, and one or more *read/write heads* for retrieving and writing information. A platter is like a blank piece of paper: you can write anywhere on a blank piece of paper, but when the paper fills up, it often is hard to retrieve a particular piece of information. Computer systems therefore use the equivalent of a preprinted *form* that forces information to be written on the correct "lines" and in the proper "boxes." The disk is not formatted by drawing actual lines and boxes, of course—but each system does have a *formatting program* that does the equivalent to the magnetic surfaces of the platters.

The UNIX file system divides a hard disk into three major pieces, which are subdivided further into *blocks* (see Figure 1.1). (A block is an area on the disk that contains a fixed number of bytes, usually 512 or 1024.) The first two blocks at the beginning of the disk contain the code for *bootstrapping* the system (that is, starting it operating from a *power-off* condition) and the *superblock*. The superblock contains information about the resources on the disk—in particular, the location of the list of available data blocks. Next comes a structure of control blocks and *pointers* that describe how and where files are stored. This structure is called the *i-nodes* (described in the "Directory Files" section). The remainder of the disk contains the data blocks where data is stored. These control blocks and pointers may pertain to an entire hard disk or to a single section (or *partition*) of a hard disk. The blocks are analogous to the boxes on a printed form.

The system administrator (using the login ID root) has privileges that go far beyond those of ordinary users. The system administrator can build several file systems on one hard disk. This is similar to the situation in MS-DOS in which you might create a C: "drive," a D: "drive," and an E: "drive" on a single, large hard disk. Although MS-DOS requires that you know which disk a file is stored on, UNIX requires only that you know the file's name. A UNIX computer must have at least one file system (the *root* file system, or simply the *root*), although most UNIX systems have multiple file systems for easy organization and maintenance of information. The second file system is attached to, or *mounted* on, an unused directory—a *mount point*—anywhere in the root file system structure. Additional file systems can be mounted on other mount points. Mounting usually takes place automatically during bootstrap, although the system administrator can mount and unmount as needed for maintenance. Mounting is discussed further in the "Mountable File Systems" section.

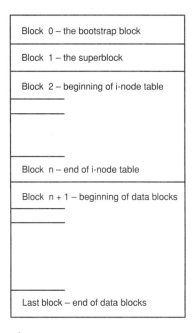

Block 0 – the bootstrap block

Block 1 – the superblock

Block 2 – beginning of i-node table

Block n – end of i-node table

Block n + 1 – beginning of data blocks

Last block – end of data blocks

Figure 1.1. File system layout.

The UNIX file system implementation has a number of features:

- Dynamic file expansion—No disk-space quotas are imposed by UNIX. However, the system administrator may limit the maximum size of each individual file.

- Structureless files—UNIX does not require that an ordinary file have a particular structure: a file consists of a stream of bytes. A programmer may write a program that creates a file with a particular structure, but the responsibility for dealing with that structure lies with the programs that use the file.

- Security—Access to files and directories can be controlled on individual files and directories.

- File and device independence—Programs on UNIX both read from and write to files. A file, however, can be associated with a device other than a disk, such as a terminal, printer, or tape. Therefore, programs do not know (nor do they have to know) where their input is coming from or where their output is going.

The Hierarchical (Logical) File System

A user rarely is concerned with the physical file system, because the physical file system model is directly related to hardware. Users want to know how to store and retrieve information without having to know about the underlying hardware. The UNIX kernel takes care of that for you, and presents a picture of how and where files are stored that is quite different from how the data blocks are actually stored on the platters.

The *hierarchical file system* consists of a set of directories and files. (Note: On UNIX, directories are considered files, too.) Some of the directories and files are created when the system administrator installs the UNIX system on the computer. Others are created manually by the system administrator, and yet others are created by users. Figure 1.2 shows a typical hierarchical file-system structure as distributed for UNIX System V Release 4.

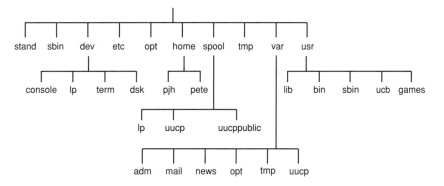

Figure 1.2. The top layers of a System V Release 4 file system.

Figure 1.2 shows the top layers of a typical System V Release 4 file system, as follows:

- The topmost directory is the *root directory* (/). This is the main directory of the file system; everything else branches off from the root.

- The directory /stand contains the standard data files that the system uses when it bootstraps itself into operation.

- /sbin contains the programs that bootstrap the system.

- /dev contains *special files* (also called *device files*) that refer to the hardware devices connected to the system:

  /dev/console refers to the system operator's console.

  /dev/lp refers to the printer.

1

/dev/term is a directory of user terminal files.

/dev/dsk is a directory of the system's disk partitions.

- /etc is a directory of system administration data.

- /opt is a directory of directories of add-on or optional software, usually applications programs.

- /home is a directory of directories of user files. The directories shown are /home/pjh and /home/pete.

- /spool is a directory of directories of

  Temporary files destined for the printer (/spool/lp)

  File transfers that are queued for the *UUCP* (UNIX to UNIX Copy Program) system (/spool/uucp)

  Files received from other systems that were transferred in via UUCP (/spool/uucppublic)

- The directory /tmp is used to store other temporary files.

- /var contains directories of files that vary from system to system, and files that vary in size that need to be checked and truncated:

  /var/adm contains log files created and maintained by various logging programs, including data for accounting purposes.

  /var/mail is where the electronic mail programs put incoming mail messages.

  /var/news contains messages that can be read by any user on the system, usually announcements of some sort.

  /var/tmp is another place to put temporary files.

  /var/opt is another place to put optional software.

  /var/uucp contains log files and status files for the UUCP system.

- The /usr hierarchy provides a place to put binaries (executable programs) and libraries:

  /usr/lib contains libraries that programmers use when creating programs.

  /usr/bin contains many of the UNIX command program binaries.

  /usr/sbin contains binaries that perform system administration.

  /usr/ucb contains the BSD compatibility packages.

/usr/games contains binaries and data for a number of games (although some System V Release 4 distributors leave this directory empty).

Every file has two *pathnames*. The *absolute* pathname is the name of the file beginning with root and showing all the directories that lie between root and the file in question. For example, /usr/bin/vi is the absolute, or *full*, pathname of the UNIX screen editor. The first slash (/) represents the root directory; other slashes are merely punctuation marks that separate names of files from one another. The other kind of pathname is called a *relative* pathname. Every file has one unique full pathname but many relative pathnames. The relative pathname of a file depends on two things: where the user is and where the file is in relation to the user's position. For example, in Figure 1.2, a file named joe.tmp residing in the /home/pjh directory would be joe.tmp to a user in the /home/pjh directory, but ../pjh/joe.tmp to a user in the /home/pete directory. Note: The .. means "move up to the parent of the current directory."

There are three kinds of files: ordinary files, directory files, and special files. These are discussed in the following subsections.

Ordinary Files

An *ordinary file* (also referred to as a *regular* file, with puzzling inconsistency!) consists of a stream of bytes that can represent

- ASCII text

- Program instructions in source form or in binary form

- Other data, such as a telephone directory, a list of all the users on your system, or a list of all the mountable file systems

Directory Files

A *directory*, more properly called a *directory file*, contains two-part entries:

- The first part of a directory entry is the *i-number*. Each i-number is a 16-bit number that refers to an *i-node* (short for *information-node*) stored in a special place on a hard disk (mentioned earlier). The i-node (sometimes written *inode*) contains information describing the particular file, including where the contents of that file can be found on the disk.

- The second part of a directory entry is the filename associated with the i-node. The maximum number of characters in a filename depends on which of the several types of file systems available with SVR4 the system administrator has chosen to use. Filenames on AT&T System V UNIX file systems are limited to 14 characters, while file systems based on Berkeley UNIX allow filenames of 255 characters. Filenames are used in commands, but UNIX uses the equivalent i-number. Every file in a file system has a unique i-number.

When a directory is created, two special entries are automatically created at the same time, named . ("dot") and .. ("dot dot"). Dot is used as a shorthand reference to the current directory. The i-number for dot is the same as the i-number of the current directory. "Dot dot" refers to the parent of the current directory. Table 1.1 shows the layout of one of the directories on my computer. The i-numbers shown are those that existed at the moment I created the table, and their values have no special significance.

Table 1.1. Layout of a UNIX directory.

I-Number (2 bytes)	Filename (14 bytes)
7225	.
3124	..
4990	gettydefs
4289	inittab
4656	Devices.tty
4715	Devices
4636	Dialers..TB
4307	Dialers
4306	gettydefs.tty
4322	Systems
4316	inittab.tty
0	Systems.cico
0	Systems.cu

Directories can grow but cannot shrink. The example directory is 208 bytes long: it has 13 entries—including the two erased files with i-number 0—of 16 bytes each. When a file is removed from a directory, the command that removes it merely changes its i-number to zero. When a file or directory is added, an entry with i-number zero is replaced by the new file's i-number and name.

For example, if you created a new file in the directory shown in Table 1.1, the new file's entry in the directory file would replace the entry for Systems.cico. However, the directory file size would not change; it would still be 208 bytes. If you created an additional new file, this new file would replace Systems.cu and the directory file size would still not change. Now, because there are no zero entries, the next new file's i-node number and name are added at the bottom of the directory, making the directory file 16 bytes bigger (224 bytes). When a program attempts to open a file, the entire directory must be searched from the first entry down, potentially slowing performance. Therefore, you should keep your directories small.

Special Files

Special files (also called *device files*) refer to hardware devices—the keyboard, the screen, the disks, the tape backup unit, the terminals, the printers, and so on—attached to the UNIX computer. They enable a programmer to write application programs that are not hardware-specific; the application need only read from and write to a file, even if the file is a keyboard or a floppy disk drive!

Manufacturers of peripheral devices—such as disk controllers, backup tape units, and multiple-port I/O specials—usually supply special programs called *device drivers* with their hardware products. The device driver is what enables UNIX to "talk" to the hardware device. (The programmer need only talk to the device file, and UNIX and the driver take care of the details.) The system administrator installs the hardware and then the device drivers, so that UNIX becomes aware of the new devices.

Through the use of special files, programs can be written so that they need only the information on how to access a file. The mapping between a filename and a hardware device is done by the operating system through special files. An operating system that receives a request for I/O activates the appropriate hardware device associated with the particular special file. For example, the special file for the terminal you logged in on is /dev/TTY. If a friend logged in on /dev/tty03, and you wanted to send him a message, you could copy a file you created to /dev/tty03. If you have *permission* to write to /dev/tty03, your friend would see your file on his screen. (See the section on "File Modes" in this chapter for more about permissions.)

Special files usually are located in the /dev directory and its subdirectories.

The Physical File System

The physical file system is the underlying structure that implements the hierarchical file system (see Figure 1.1). Recall that the physical file system consisted of a number of blocks—the superblock, the i-nodes, and the data blocks—and that each entry in a directory in the hierarchical file system contained an i-number and a filename. Each i-number refers to a specific i-node. I-nodes are maintained by the operating system and are used to access files. Each i-node contains the following information about a file:

mode	The file access permissions (discussed in the "File Modes" section).
nlink	The number of links to the file. The link count for a directory is the number of directories that the directory contains as subdirectories, plus 2 (for itself and its parent). Because a newly created directory refers only to itself and its parent, its initial link count is 2.
uid	The ID of the person who owns the file.
gid	The ID of the group the file belongs to.
size	The size of the file in bytes.
atime	The date and time the file was last accessed. (Note: A file is considered to be *accessed* when it is created, when its atime is changed directly by a program, and when its contents are read.)
mtime	The date and time the contents of the file were last modified. (Note: A file's contents are considered to be *modified* when the file is created, when its mtime is changed directly by a program, and when something is added to or deleted from the file.)
ctime	The date and time the file's i-node was last modified. (Note: An i-node is considered *modified* when it is created or when someone or something changes either the contents of the file, or its owner or group, its permissions, or its link count.)

When a program creates a file, UNIX allocates an i-node and supplies information about permissions, links, user ID, group ID, and time. As data is entered in the file, data blocks are allocated as needed (as the file grows by 1024 bytes). The following is an example of the kind of information contained in an i-node:

```
owner: pjh
group: root
type: regular file
permissions: rwxr-xr-x
last access: Sep 7 1991 5:50 P.M.
last modified: Sep 7 1991 1:32 P.M.
i-node modified: Sep 1 1991 9:15 A.M.
size: 1289 bytes
disk addresses: 40, 41
```

File Creation, Removal, Renaming, and Linking

When a file is created, the following actions occur:

1. A unique i-node is allocated, and the `mode`, `uid`, `gid`, `link`, `size`, and `time` information is filled in.

2. One data block is allocated (if data is written at the time of creation).

3. An entry—i-number and filename—is made in the directory.

When a file with just one *link* is removed, the following actions occur:

1. The directory entry associated with the file has its i-number set to zero.

2. The data blocks are made available.

3. The i-node is released.

If a file has more than one link and one of the links is removed, only step 1 is taken. The i-node and the data blocks must remain committed to the existing file. This demonstrates that a link is merely a reference to an existing file. Every link to a given file has the same i-number but a different name. In strict UNIX terminology, a file is itself a link.

When a file is renamed or moved, one of the following actions occurs:

• If the file is moved to a directory on the same file system, a new directory entry is created with the old filename (if no new one is given in the move command) and old i-number. The i-number for the file in the old directory is set to zero.

• If the file is moved to another file system, the file is first copied as a brand new file (thus a new i-number is assigned) to the directory of the destination file system and then the old file is removed.

A file can be linked to another file. As mentioned, creating a link creates a virtual copy of the original file without increasing the amount of disk storage. Compare this to copying, which creates an actual copy by doubling the amount of disk storage used.

Two schemes of linking are used: *direct*, used on all versions of UNIX, and *symbolic*, available only on BSD versions of UNIX and UNIX System V Release 4.

- A direct link can be made only to a file on the same file system as the target. A direct link consists of an entry in a directory that simply has the same i-number as an existing file. The existing file can be in the same directory, in which case the link must have a different name, or in a different directory, in which case the new file can have the same name.

  For example, consider the file /usr/pjh/phone.numbers. One possible link is /usr/pjh/rolodex, while another might be /usr/smith/phone.numbers. A file can have virtually an unlimited number of links.

- A symbolic link is a special type of file that contains the pathname of another file. Symbolic links can be made across file systems and across machines connected by a network, removing the "same file system" constraint of the direct link.

In both cases, the `ln` command is used to create the links. Chapter 3 shows some examples of creating direct ("hard") and symbolic links.

Mountable File Systems

Each file system appears to UNIX as if it were an independent device: each file system has its own boot block, superblock, list of unique i-nodes, and data blocks. However, merely creating a file system—something the system administrator does with the `mkfs` (*make file system*) command—does not make it available to UNIX; it must be *mounted*.

Mounting grafts an unmounted file system onto the current hierarchical tree. The administrator selects a *mount point* by creating a new directory—frequently but not necessarily in the root directory—and then issuing the mount command. This attaches the new file system to the mount point and makes an entry in the /etc/mnttab file. If you have three file systems on your computer, you will have three files with i-number 2, three with i-number 3, and so on. This explains why files cannot be direct-linked across file systems.

The Process Control System

A *process* is a program in execution. That is, UNIX generates a process when you tell it to execute a command.

Programs and Processes

A *program* is the list of machine code instructions and data required to carry out a certain task. When you tell UNIX to execute a certain program, it loads the program into memory from a file on a disk and creates a process that carries out the instructions of your program. Another term used for process is *task*.

Each process has a unique *process ID* (PID), a number assigned to a process when the process is created.

A *file descriptor* is a small, unique integer returned when the system opens the file. For a program file, the system automatically associates three file descriptors (each of which refers to a special file, by default) to its process:

0   Standard input (stdin)

1   Standard output (stdout)

2   Standard error output (stderr)

As many as 57 additional files can be opened.

For example, when you invoke the editor program on your UNIX system, it gets input from the keyboard (stdin), sends ordinary output to the screen (stdout), writes error messages to the screen (stderr), and permits you to manipulate the file(s) of your choice. Each file you edit has a unique file descriptor.

To redirect output, for example, the system simply closes the screen special file and opens a regular file, associating the named file with file descriptor 1. That is, the following "phrase" appearing on a UNIX command line

```
> mydata
```

associates 1 with the file mydata. Thus, output from the process now goes to mydata rather than to the screen.

1

Process Invocation and Execution

A process is created through the `fork` *system call*, made from inside a program, or by the UNIX shell. (A system call is a subroutine for a service that the kernel provides.) When a `fork` system call is made, a new process, almost identical to the process that called on `fork`, is created. Execution of the new process begins at the program statement immediately following the `fork`, and the caller process usually waits (the program includes a call to the `wait` system call) for the new process to terminate.

A parent/child relationship is established between the two processes. The caller is the parent and the new process is the child. The child inherits from the parent. The only difference between them is that each has a unique PID.

When you cause a program to be executed, it takes on your user ID and group ID, and therefore has the same reading and writing privileges that you have. Thus the program has an *effective uid* (*euid*) and an *effective gid* (*egid*) that match your IDs. Thus if you execute a program owned by the root, it won't be able to access files that only the root can access because it will be effectively owned by you during execution. This is done deliberately so that ordinary users are prevented from gaining root privileges merely by executing a program that root owns.

However, sometimes an ordinary user needs to have permission to read from or write to files that they ordinarily are excluded from. One example of this is the `passwd` command. When you change your password by issuing this command, you actually are changing the contents of a file that you ordinarily do not have permission to write to. The `passwd` program has its *setuid flag* on. This means that even though you are executing the program, its effective uid is still that of root. This gives you permission to change the contents of a file that is writable only by root. Only the owner of a program—and root—can set the `setuid` flag.

Scheduling and Priority

Process scheduling allows many processes to share one CPU. When you understand the fundamentals of process scheduling, you can appreciate the value of running programs in the background and the importance of troubleshooting your tools.

When a process recognizes that a certain resource it needs is unavailable, it waits for an event that indicates that the resource is available. Frequently, the resource it's waiting for is the CPU and the event is some sort of timer signal indicating that the current process has used up its allotted time and the next process can be executed. Each process has a priority value used by the *scheduler* (the part of the operating system kernel that schedules the use of system resources, including the CPU). When a resource becomes available, all processes awaiting the resource are placed on the run queue. The scheduler selects the process with the highest priority and begins executing it. If other processes are on the run queue waiting for the same resource, they are put to sleep until the resource becomes available.

Interprocess Communications

Processes can communicate with each other through the *interprocess* communication facilities. A pipe special file—a first in, first out queue set up in memory that allows passing information back and forth between two processes that are running concurrently—is used to establish the communications path in memory, rather than on the disk. A pipe looks much like an ordinary file except that the `pipe` system call returns two file descriptors: one for the input to the pipe and one for the output. Processes invoked in a *pipeline* operate in parallel (execute simultaneously), but the data read by the pipe is made available at the output in the same order in which it was read. Pipes that are created with the pipe system call are given names and affect all three types of the files they connect. You can create an unnamed pipe by using a special symbol on the command line.

For example, here's a simple `pipe` command, which is illustrated in Figure 1.3:

```
$ who ¦ wc -l
```

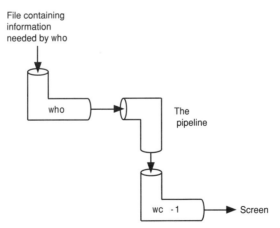

Figure 1.3. A pipeline.

The shell examines the command line, sees the pipe symbol (|), and determines that it must create two processes: one for the who command and one for the wc command. The who command outputs a list of users and other information, one per line. The wc command with the -1 option counts the number of lines as its input. Thus, this example command produces a number equal to the number of users logged in at the instant of its execution.

First, the shell opens both "ends" of the pipe. Next, the first child is created and executes who, with the pipe file descriptor as the output file. The second child is created and executes wc, with the pipe file descriptor as its input file. Because the who command is writing on the pipe and the wc command is reading from the pipe, the two processes can communicate through the pipe.

The UNIX Shell and the User

The shell is one of the programs distributed with UNIX systems. It interprets the commands that you type at the keyboard and translates them into system activities. The shell also functions as a programming language interpreter— it has the ability to recognize and act on such programming constructs as loops, if statements, and variables.

Not only does the shell execute commands typed at the keyboard, it also has the ability to read commands from a text file called a *shell script* and execute them.

The Three Shells

UNIX System V Release 4 is distributed with three shell programs: the traditional Bourne shell (sh), the compatible Korn shell (ksh), and the Berkeley UNIX C shell (csh). The Bourne shell is the shell most widely used with AT&T UNIX, and most shell scripts are written to conform to Bourne shell programming conventions. The Korn shell eventually will replace the Bourne shell and essentially is an enhanced version of it. The C shell programming language mimics the C language and is distributed with BSD-based UNIX systems.

The User Environment

When you log in to a UNIX computer, the `login` process invokes a shell program (either the Bourne shell, the Korn shell, or the C shell, depending on the system and what you and your system administrator have negotiated). The shell establishes and maintains an environment for you by defining and initializing a set of *environment variables*. The environment contains information about you and your preferences—that is, your home directory, any files you've opened, variables you've set, parameters defined by the system, and so on. The initial values of this information come from

- System parameters set by the system administrator during installation of the UNIX software

- The `login` program

- The commands in the system-wide /etc/profile (Bourne and Korn shells) or /etc/login (C shell) file

- The commands in your personal .profile or .login and .cshrc files contained in your home directory

You can change some of these environment variables to customize your working environment and make it more suitable for your working style.

Typically, the following parameters and variables are initialized during login:

umask   Establishes the default directory or file permissions that are set when a new file is created. This chapter's "File Modes" section investigates the ins and outs of permissions.

ulimit   Sets the maximum file size you can create. Only the system administrator can raise the value of your `ulimit`; all other users can only lower their values.

IFS   The Internal Field Separator, used by the shell to separate command words, options, and arguments. IFS usually is set to space bar, Tab, and newline; that is, you can separate command words with either a space, a tab, or (in some cases) a newline. Users frequently change this setting temporarily to help them process command files that have words separated by something other than a space, a tab, or a newline.

1

HOME	This value is the absolute pathname of the directory you "land" in when you log in. You shouldn't change this value.
LOGNAME	Your user ID. Don't change this value, either.
MAIL	If this parameter is set to the name of a mail file *and* you have not set the MAILPATH value (the usual case), the shell notifies you when mail arrives in the specified file.
MAILCHECK	Specifies how often, in seconds, the shell checks for changes in the modification time of any of the files specified by the MAILPATH or MAIL parameters. By default, MAILCHECK is set to 600 seconds (10 minutes). If MAILCHECK is set to zero, the shell checks before each prompt.
PATH	The search path for commands. By default, PATH is set to :/bin:/usr/bin, but each user can override the default. This PATH value means that when you type the name of a command, UNIX looks for it first in the current directory, then in /bin, and finally in /usr/bin.
PS1	The value of this parameter defines the primary prompt string that by default is $. If PS1 contains other shell variables, these variables are *expanded* before the prompt is displayed. Thus you can customize the prompt. Expanding a shell variable means to replace its name with its value. This chapter's "Shell Variables and Metacharacters" section discusses expanding variables in detail.
PS2	The secondary prompt string—by default, >.
SHELL	The pathname of the current shell you're using.

The system gives default values to IFS, HOME, MAIL, MAILCHECK, PATH, PS1, PS2, LOGNAME and SHELL.

When a program executes on a UNIX system, these environment values are inherited by the new program's process. The new program may change these values for its own use, but any changes are lost when the new program terminates. The new program gets only a copy of the environment and does not have access to the actual environment. In other words, a child process inherits from its parent but does not return anything to it.

You can take advantage of this in a number of ways. First, execute a new shell by entering

`$ `**`sh`**

This command starts a new Bourne shell with all the properties of the previous shell, including all environment variables with the values that exist at the moment you execute the command. You then change the values of any environment variables in this shell to customize the environment of this shell. When you exit using the command

```
^d
```

you return to your previous shell and previous environment values. The ones you used in the second shell have disappeared.

Here's an exercise you can try just after you log in (assuming you're using the Korn shell):

1. Enter set. This gives you a list of all currently defined shell variables and their values.

2. Enter sh.

3. Enter set again. This shows you the names and values of all variables that the second shell has inherited.

4. Choose one and change it. For example, enter

   ```
   PS1="Yes, dear?"
   ```

   Do you see the new prompt?

5. Try a few commands, such as set, date, ls, and echo *. Do you have the new prompt each time?

6. Now log out by entering ^d or exit.

   What prompt do you see now?

   What happens when you type set now?

Within shell programs you can change any of these environment values. The changes are in effect only while the shell program is running. For example, to limit a search path (or to improve performance) in a shell program, set the PATH variable as follows:

```
PATH=:/usr/local:/usr/project:/usr/bin:/bin
```

This helps the shell program find local and project programs first and therefore, may improve performance.

Issuing Commands

There are a number of ways to issue commands to the shell at the command line: singly, sequentially, in the background, concurrently, and in groups.

Issuing a single command is what you're already familiar with. It takes the usual form

```
$ command -option[s] arguments
```

The shell expands any unquoted *metacharacters* in the arguments and options and then passes the expanded list of words to the command. (Metacharacters are discussed in this chapter's "Shell Variables and Metacharacters" section.) Issuing single commands is the most fundamental use of UNIX, and UNIX reference manuals and books discuss each command in this form.

You can issue a set of sequential commands at a single prompt by separating them with semicolons. For example

```
$ ls; cd ..; ls
```

lists the files in the current directory, then changes to the parent directory and lists the files there. Then it remains in the parent and issues a shell prompt.

By appending an ampersand (&) to a command, you cause the shell to run it in the *background* and return a prompt immediately, without waiting for the command to terminate. For example

```
$ ls > myfiles &
```

creates a file containing the names of all files in the current directory, but does it in the background. This can be quite a time saver if your current directory has many files, because the shell returns control of the terminal to you just as soon as you press the Enter key after typing the command.

An interesting situation occurs when you run multiple commands in the background, launched from the same command line, such as

```
$ ls & ls .. &
```

These commands write to stdout. The fact that they execute *asynchronously* means that your screen will be a mess! It usually is much better to redirect both the stdout and stderr of commands running in the background to ordinary files. Asynchronous operation means simply that UNIX executes the first command for an appropriate amount of time, suspends it, executes the second for an appropriate amount of time, suspends it, resumes executing the first process, suspends it, resumes the second process, and so on, until both processes have terminated. Of course, any other processes that are running at the time you issued this command also get slices of the processor's time, so concurrency is more an illusion than a fact. It is an illusion that is aided by a fast processor.

Grouping commands is somewhat different from what I just discussed, because each group of commands runs under its own subshell. Consider the following example:

```
$ ( cd /usr/pjh ; tar cf - . ) ¦ ( cd /backup ; tar xvf - )
```

The `tar` command copies files either from a directory into an *archive* (a file that physically contains other files) or from an archive into a directory. The command shown consists of two groups of commands:

- The first group temporarily changes to the `/usr/pjh` directory and then archives all the files therein. In this case, the archive is not an ordinary file but is instead a pipe! When the first group completes, it returns to the original working directory and executes the second group.

- The second group changes temporarily to `/backup`, then takes all the files coming through the pipe "archive" and writes them to the new destination.

The reason I chose this approach rather than a simple

```
$ cd /usr/pjh; cp * /backup
```

is twofold. First, the grouped commands leave me in my original working directory when they terminate. Second, `tar` traverses subdirectories automatically—that is, tar archives all files in the current directory and its subdirectories. Thus my group command has copied a directory hierarchy from one place to another.

Relationship of the System, the Shell, and Programs

The UNIX philosophy is to provide small programs that help you write other programs. These smaller programs are used as building blocks for more complex programs. UNIX also provides mechanisms for you to "connect" these programs to each other or the system. These mechanisms are implemented through I/O *redirection* and pipes. (Redirection is described in this section.)

The common link between the UNIX system, the shell, and programs is the ordinary file. Because most programs read from the standard input and write to the standard output (that are, by definition, files), it's easy to see the relationship that can be established.

UNIX considers all devices—that is, disks, terminals, printers, and so on—to be files. Although they may be implemented as special files, a program on UNIX does not know (nor does it necessarily care) whether the file is associated with a device. For example, if the output of a program (who) can be redirected to an ordinary file (log):

```
$ who > log
```

Then the output can be redirected to a *device special file* (a file that represents a hardware device, such as a terminal or printer) as follows:

```
$ who > /dev/tty02
```

provided the user has permission to write to the device special file. (Notice the > for output redirection.) In the first example, the output of the who command was redirected to the ordinary file log. In the second example, the output was redirected to the terminal associated with the special file /dev/tty02, where it appears on its screen.

The pipe mechanism helps a stream of data to pass directly between two processes. One process writes to the pipe and the other reads from it. In the following example the who command is writing to a pipe (identified by the vertical bar, ¦) and the sort command is reading from it:

```
$ who ¦ sort
```

The output of the sort command can be redirected to a file or sent to another pipe. The processes do not have to know where the output is going; they work whether their standard output is a device, an ordinary file, or a pipe. The who command outputs the login name and other information of each logged-in user, one per line. The sort command, as used in the example, sorts the list of users into alphabetical order.

These two mechanisms, I/O redirection and piping, help you establish a relationship between the system, the shell, and programs: the system maintains control over the file systems, processes, and I/O devices; programs typically read input and write output; and the shell has the redirection and pipe mechanisms that simplify how a program (process) gets its input (from stdin, a file, or a pipe) and delivers its output (to stdout, a file, or a pipe).

Two factors govern whether you should output directly to a special device by output redirection:

- Is the device writable? For example, some devices, such as hard drive partitions, never should be directly writable by user processes and usually are not writable by an ordinary user. If they are, redirection of output to the device could cause extensive system damage.

1

- If the device is writable, what effect does writing directly to the device have? For example, if you're working in vi and someone writes directly to your terminal, their "message" appears on your screen, temporarily messing up your editing session. (If that happens, press ^L to redraw the screen and restore it to its previous condition.) If you write directly to a printer (without going through the spooling mechanism), you could write on top of another user's print job.

When a program is executed, three files are automatically opened:

Standard input (stdin)   This file gives the program its input, usually from the keyboard.

Standard output (stdout)   Output from the program is written to this file, usually the screen.

Standard error (stderr)   Error messages are written to this file, usually the screen.

Most programs running on a UNIX system write to their standard output. (Other special programs are silent when they execute successfully but write error messages to stderr.) Some programs do not read from stdin. For example, commands simply providing status information, such as ls, who, and ps, do not read from their standard input.

Many programs can open files if the filename is given as a command-line option, such as cat datafile or vi myfile. A small number of programs, such as tr, crypt, and xargs, are not designed to open files because filenames may conflict with their options and arguments. This happens because these programs cannot distinguish between filenames and other arguments. However, these programs can read information on their standard input, as supplied by a pipe or input redirection. Part II of this book looks at all the programs mentioned—except the vi editor.

If a program can open a file and the filename is not given, that program uses standard input (the keyboard) by default. In some programs, the - option by itself indicates you want the program to read from standard input.

The cat program is a good example. By default, cat reads from standard input (the keyboard) and writes to standard output (the screen). If you enter cat by itself, it reads what you type and, after you press the Enter key, prints on your screen what you type on your keyboard. cat also accepts a filename (or names) on the command line, opens the files, and prints the contents on your screen. If the filename is -, cat reads from the standard input. Therefore, the command:

```
$ echo foo ¦ cat names - addresses
```

does the following, in order:

1. Opens and prints the filenames.

2. Reads and prints the output of the echo command: the string foo.

3. Opens and prints the file addresses.

As you read this book you'll notice many examples showing input to a command coming from a file, from the standard input, or from both. If a command reads from standard input, the input may be supplied from a pipe, by input redirection, or typed at the keyboard.

Shell Variables and Metacharacters

Many commands supplied with the system depend on the values of one or more environment variables to point them to input files, output files, default conditions, and so on. You must understand how the shell treats variables, especially when it's evaluating one. The discussion that follows assumes that you're using either the Bourne or Korn shell, although the C shell is very similar.

When you assign a value to a shell variable, you use an *assignment statement* that looks like this:

```
VAR_NAM=character_string
```

For example

```
PATH=/usr/local/bin:/bin:/usr/bin
```

and

```
MAILCHECK=10
```

are assignment statements. The value of MAILCHECK appears to be a number but in fact is just the two characters 1 and 0. Any program that uses the value of MAILCHECK must somehow interpret them as the number 10.

To retrieve the value of a variable, you must prepend a $ to the beginning of the name, as in $PATH and $MAILCHECK. The values can be printed (displayed at stdout) using echo. For example

```
echo $PATH
```

would produce

```
/usr/local/bin:/bin:/usr/bin
```

on your screen. One common application of this assignment statement is to give to a variable a value that depended on its current value, as in

```
PATH=$PATH:/usr/local/games
```

This would cause PATH to have the following new value:

```
/usr/local/bin:/bin:/usr/bin:/usr/local/games
```

The PATH variable's value now is a longer string because of the assignment.

The shell has some other mechanisms and some special characters and operations that deal with variables and commands. You may already be familiar with some of them, but I'll discuss them all in the following sections.

Filename Completion

When you refer to a single file, you usually have to type its entire name. If you want to refer to several files in one command line, however, the shell gives you some shortcuts. These shortcuts depend on how the shell interprets certain characters: the asterisk (*), the question mark (?), the open square bracket ([), and the close square bracket (]). You've already seen that the shell has special interpretations for the right angle bracket (>, used for output redirection), the left angle bracket (<, used for input redirection), the vertical bar (¦, used for piping), the equal sign (=, used for value assignment), and the dollar sign ($, used to retrieve the value of the appended variable). All these characters, along with some you have not yet met, are called *shell metacharacters*.

The ? Metacharacter

The question mark (?) stands for any one character. Thus, if you write

```
ls ab?de
```

the shell lists all files in the current directory that have five-character names where the first two are ab and the last two are de. If there are no files that match that description, the shell simply echoes

```
ab?de: No such file or directory
```

or a similar message. You can use as many ? characters as you want. For example, ab??e? represents all files that have six-character names beginning with ab, followed by any two characters, followed by an e, followed by any character. Thus, abxxes, abcdef, and ab00e4 all match the description, but baxxex, abxex, and ab00e45 do not.

The * Metacharacter

The asterisk (*), also known as the star or splat, stands for zero or more characters. For example, ch*zz would match any files with names beginning with ch and ending with zz. Thus, it would match the following filenames (as long as they were in the current directory):

```
chzz
ch.....zz
ch123ABCzz
```

and so on. The period (.) isn't special to the shell unless it's the first character in a filename. The period is just another character that can be used in a filename.

Like the ?, there can be more than one * in a filename description; for example, ch*zz*1.

One interesting fact about * used by itself (as in ls *): the asterisk describes the names of all of the files in the current directory (except those that begin with a period)!

The [. . .] Pattern

A pattern within square brackets ([. . .]) matches any of the characters listed inside the brackets. You can abbreviate a range of consecutive letters or digits by using a dash (·). For example:

```
ls ch[0-4]
```

lists the names of all files having three character names beginning with ch and ending in one of the digits 0 through 4. (Note: You are not permitted to write [4-0]; the range must be written in ascending numeric order.)

The pattern [0-9a-zA-Z] matches any digit or upper- or lowercase letter.

Combining Patterns

You can make up your own patterns by combining any or all of the three types of metacharacters. For the following examples, assume you have these files in your current directory:

```
b bb bby betty c cc d dd letter1 letter2 letter3
```

Use the `ls -m` command to get the filenames printed as a horizontal list separated by commas. The command

```
ls -m *
```

would produce

```
b, bb, bby, betty, c, cc, d, dd, letter1, letter2, letter3
```

Here are some example commands and their results:

$ ls -m [abcd]

```
b, c, d
```

This matches any one-character filename beginning with the letter A, B, C, or D.

$ ls -m letter[13]

```
letter1, letter3
```

This matches any seven-character filename beginning with `letter` followed by either a 1 or a 3.

$ ls -m [bc]*

```
b, bb, bby, betty, c, cc
```

This matches any filename beginning with the letter B or C.

$ ls -m *[0-9]

```
letter1, letter2, letter3
```

This last example matches any filename ending in a digit.

Making Metacharacters Ordinary: Quoting

Sometimes you don't want the shell to expand the following metacharacters:

*	[ ]
?	$
>	Tab
<	Space
¦	Newline

and others you've not met yet. The shell provides a mechanism, *quoting*, to help you achieve that goal. There are several kinds of quoting characters: the single quotation mark (´), the double quotation marks ("), and the backslash (\). These quoting characters are special to the shell and are among the ones referred to in the first sentence as "others you've not met."

If you place a backslash immediately before a metacharacter, the shell does not recognize the special properties of that character and treats it as "just another character." For example, using the previously defined current directory, if you entered

```
$ ls \*
```

the result would be

```
*: No such file or directory
```

instead of a list filenames.

You can achieve the same end with a little more typing by using a pair of single quotation marks:

```
$ ls ´*´
```

Single quotation marks are useful when you have more than one character to quote. For example

```
$ ls ´ch???´
```

would match the one five-character filename beginning with the letters ch and ending with three question marks. The shell attributes no special meaning to any character found between a pair of single quotation marks; the shell ignores all special characters between single quotation marks.

What would happen if a \ were enclosed in single quotation marks? For example, if you were again using the sample directory, entering

```
$ ls -m ´\*´
```

would result in

```
\*: No such file or directory
```

The shell considers the backslash to be just an ordinary character because of the single quotation marks. The single quotation marks also removed the special meaning of the asterisk. To prove this, try entering the following:

```
$ ls -m ´*\´
```

A more revealing example shows the quoting mechanism with environment variables. Suppose your LOGNAME has the value pjh. Consider the following commands and their results:

```
$ echo $LOGNAME
```

pjh

```
$ echo \$LOGNAME
```

$LOGNAME

```
$ echo '$LOGNAME'
```

$LOGNAME

```
$ echo "$LOGNAME"
```

pjh

Notice that both the backslash and the single quotation marks remove the special meaning of the dollar sign ($), but the double quotation marks do not.

The double quotation marks are very much like the single quotation marks, except that double quotation marks are a little limited. A single quotation mark removes the special meaning of any shell special characters it encounters up to the next single quotation mark; that is, the shell does not interpret any of the characters between a pair of single quotation marks. The same is true for double quotation marks *except* for the dollar sign ($), the backslash (\), and the *back quotation mark* (`). (The back quote is new. I'll explain it shortly.) These three are still special even when found between pairs of double quotation marks.

A common use of double quotation marks is to enclose two or more words separated by whitespace characters on a command line so that the shell treats them as a single word. For example, if you entered

```
$ vi file1 file2 file3
```

vi would look for three files to edit. But if you had entered

```
$ vi 'file1 file2 file3'
```

vi would look for just one.

Quoting is needed for seemingly innocent situations involving a shell variable. For example, if you wanted to assign the phrase

```
this is fun
```

to a shell variable and you entered

```
$ phrase=this is fun
```

the shell would protest

```
is: not found
```

and dump you back to the prompt. Your attempt at assignment failed because of the space after the word this. Recall that the shell uses whitespace to separate words on the command line, so you need a way to make the shell think that this is fun is a single entity. One way to do this is to precede each space with a backslash; the space metacharacter is then matched by the space character itself. That is, the space character is no longer the separator between command-line words. Removing the special meaning of a metacharacter is called *escaping* the metacharacter. Another way of escaping spaces is to enclose the entire phrase in quotation marks; either double quotation marks or single quotation marks will do.

```
$ phrase="this is fun"
```

```
$ phrase='this is fun'
```

```
$ phrase=this\ is\ fun
```

In all cases, the variable phrase is assigned the entire string this is fun.

Back quotes (or grave accents) are placed *around* commands, such as `date`. One major reason for the back quote mechanism is to permit the output of a command to be assigned as the value of a variable. For example, suppose that, in the sample directory used before, you enter

```
$ xx=`ls`
```

and then

```
$ echo $xx
```

The result is

```
b bb bby betty c cc d dd letter1 letter2 letter3
```

That is, the first command assigned the output of the ls command to the variable xx, and the second command printed the value. Notice that echo interprets all the newlines that ls outputs as word separators (thanks to the environment variable IFS) and outputs them as spaces.

The echo command gives special meaning to certain ordinary characters that are preceded by a backslash:

- \n means "move to the beginning of the next line."

- \c means "do not move off this line."

However, the shell sees these backslashed characters before echo does and tries to interpret them as if they were shell special characters. For example:

```
$ echo this\nis\nfun
```

doesn't print the words on three different lines. The actual output is

```
thisnisnfun
```

The shell simply drops the backslashes and outputs the n! To get the shell to ignore these so that echo gets them, you must quote them as follows:

```
$ echo "this\nis\nfun"
```

```
$ echo 'this\nis\nfun'
```

```
$ echo this\\nis\\nfun
```

Shell Scripts, Functions, and Aliases

After you use a UNIX system for a few weeks, you'll find yourself typing the same sequences of commands over and over again. UNIX lets you store the commands in an ordinary text file and execute them from that file. The file is called a *shell procedure* or *shell script*.

A text file is not a program; even a text file that contains commands is not automatically executable. However, there are several ways to execute the commands in the script without typing them at the prompt:

- Make the script executable by using the chmod command. Simply add execute permission (x) for each class of user you like. To execute the program, enter its name as if it were a command. A new shell is invoked to execute your script:

  ```
  $ chmod +x myscript
  ```

- Directly invoke a new shell to execute your script by entering:

  ```
  $ sh myscript
  ```

- Execute your script in the current shell by using the dot command (.):

  ```
  $ . myscript
  ```

Recall that a child process cannot alter the parent's environment. If you use the cd command in your script and invoke the script with either of the first two methods, the change is valid only while the child is executing. When the script terminates, your current working directory reverts to the one you started from.

On the other hand, if you use the cd command with dot execution, the change is not discarded.

The shell script is a useful item in the tool building catalog, and you'll create some simple but powerful ones. A side benefit of scripts is that, as files, they can be copied and mailed to other users. The Bourne and Korn shells have a way to create more "personal" tools: the *function*. You define a function by typing its name followed by a pair of parentheses, followed by a left brace ({), a list of commands (each of which is terminated with a semicolon), and a right brace (}). For example, the following defines a function called l that prints a long listing of all files in the current directory:

```
l() { ls -al; }
```

Execute the function as if it were an ordinary command. The major advantage of functions is speed. For example, if you put all your function definitions in the file myfuns and then enter

```
$ . myfuns
```

or, alternatively, put them all into your .profile file, they are loaded into memory and remain there until you log out. That's quite an advantage over having an executable disk file for each of the equivalent commands.

Shell functions execute in the current shell and cannot be accessed by subshells. Shell functions can modify the environment of the current shell.

The Korn and C shells have an additional feature called *aliases*. An alias is a shorthand notation for a command, defined with this syntax:

```
alias name=value
```

For example

```
alias ll='ls -al'
```

lets you type ll when you want the shell to execute ls -al. The Korn shell lets you define an "environment file" by giving its name to the Korn shell variable ENV. Every time you invoke ksh (at login and any subsequent times), the shell executes the commands in the environment file. This file is a good place to keep your alias and function definitions.

File Modes

UNIX provides each user and the system with some measure of security by dividing the people who have login IDs on a system into three categories: you, people who belong to the same group (as assigned by the system administrator when your login account is created), and everyone else. The exception to this is the system administrator (the person using the root login ID). Root

1

ignores the security you set on your files. However, you can designate files you own as unaccessible to others. The modes of any file—except files having a dot as the first character of their names—are shown if you issue the following command:

```
$ ls -l filename
```

The modes appear at the left of the screen, in columns 2 through 10. UNIX uses nine columns because it recognizes three categories of users—you, others in your group, and everyone else—and three types of permissions—read, write, and execute. The UNIX terms for the categories of users are *owner* (or *user*), *group*, and *other* (or *all*). Thus there are nine *permission flags*, shown in Table 1.2.

Table 1.2. Permission flags.

Permission	Flag
Owner has permission to read from	r - - - - - - - -
Owner has permission to write to	- w - - - - - - -
Owner has permission to execute*	- - x - - - - - -
Every member of owner's group has permission to read from	- - r - - - - -
Group members have permission to write to	- - - - w - - - -
Group members have permission to execute	- - - - x - - -
Others have permission to read from	- - - - - - r - -
Others have permission to write to	- - - - - - w -
Others have permission to execute	- - - - - - - - x

> * By giving execute permission to a text file containing commands, you convert it to a shell script. Other executable files are those produced by a compiler or similar program.

All combinations are permitted. For example, a file that is readable and writable by everyone has a permission of rw-rw-rw-.

The chmod Command

The chmod command enables the owner (and only the owner and root can change a file's permissions) of a file to set its permissions (or *mode*), and can be used in either *symbolic* or *absolute* mode.

Symbolic Mode

The symbolic mode uses letters to represent the categories of users:

u   Owner or user

g   Group

o   Others (NOT owner!)

a   All

In addition to r, w, and x permissions, System V Release 4 also recognizes these modes:

s   User or group set-ID (that is, setuid and setguid)

t   "Sticky bit" (described in this section)

l   Mandatory locking (described in this section)

Finally, chmod also uses the following symbols:

+   Add permissions

-    Remove permissions

=   Assign permissions (must specify
     all permissions)

Some examples are in order:

```
$ chmod a=rw myfile
```

causes the file myfile to have rw-rw-rw- permissions.

```
$ chmod +x myfile
```

adds execute permission for all users to myfile.

```
$ chmod o-w myfile
```

removes write permission from others.

The *sticky bit* has two interpretations:

- When the sticky bit is set on an executable file, an executable its image of the program's process is stored in the swap area of memory when the program is not being executed. The next time this command is invoked, the system will be able to retrieve and execute it in much less time than it would take to fetch it from its file on the disk. Only root can set this bit on a nondirectory file.

- When the sticky bit is set on a directory, only the owner of the directory or the owner of a file in that directory is able to delete or rename that file; having write permission on the directory is not enough.

If a file has the *mandatory locking* flag set, only one program at a time can access it. This mode is useful, for example, for a database data file that can be updated by any number of users. For example, only one agent can sell the last seat on the flight from Philadelphia to Chicago if the "seat file" has its l flag set.

Absolute Mode

Absolute mode uses a numerical interpretation of the permissions, where r is interpreted as 4, w as 2, and x as 1. To use this mode you must specify a three-digit number. The first digit represents permissions for the owner, the second is for the owner's group, and the third is for everyone else. As shown in Table 1.3, eight values are possible for each digit.

Table 1.3. Absolute mode values and digits.

Value	Digit
Read, write, and execute permissions are enabled	7
Read and write are enabled; execute is disabled	6
Read and execute are enabled; write is disabled	5
Read is enabled; write and execute are disabled	4
Write and execute are enabled; read is disabled	3
Write is enabled; read and execute are disabled	2
Execute is enabled; read and write are disabled	1
Nothing is enabled; everything is disabled	0

For example:

```
$ chmod 644 myfile
```

assigns rw-r--r-- permissions to myfile:

- rw- is 4 plus 2, resulting in 6

- r-- is 4

Add 4000 for the setuid flag, 2000 for the setgid flag (if the group permission is an odd number), and 1000 for any sticky bit flag.

The umask Command

The *user mask*, or *umask*, determines the permissions that a file has when created. Entering umask at any time prints the current value of the user mask.

The umask value is logically opposite of the chmod value. For example, although a chmod 002 command would create a file with write permission for others, a umask 002 command creates files *without* write permission for others. Similarly, a umask value of 022 creates files without write permission for group and for others. To determine what permissions a file will have when created, subtract the umask value from 666 for regular files or from 777 for directory files.

The default umask value is set for the system by the system administrator in the /etc/profile file. You can set your own umask, perhaps to disable some default permissions that members of your group or others have, by inserting the command into your .profile file. Never set your own umask to less than the system default value.

Table 1.4 lists typical values for umask.

Table 1.4. Typical values for umask.

umask *Value*	*Level of Access Granted*
umask 002	Creates files without write permission for others
umask 022	Creates files without write permission for group and others
umask 006	Creates files without read/write for others
umask 026	Creates files without read/write for others and without write for group
umask 007	Creates files without read/write/execute for others
umask 027	Creates files without read/write/execute for others and without write for group
umask 077	Creates files without read/write/execute for others and group

File Permissions

When a new file is created by shell redirection (>) or by an application program, its permissions are set to 666 minus your umask value. If the umask value is 002, the file will be created with permissions 664 (rw-rw-r--: read enabled for all users, write enabled for you and members of your group, execute disabled for everyone). The user and group ID of the file are the same as those of the person running the command that creates the file.

Execute Permission

If you create the file by using cp, mv, or ln, the new file will have the same permissions as the old file. The user and group ID of the file are the same as those of the person using copy, move, or link, or executing a program that executes one of these commands.

Directory File Permissions

Directories have access permissions similar to files. You must have read (r) permission to list the contents of a directory (to read the directory file), write (w) permission to create and delete files in a directory (to edit the contents of a directory file), and *search* (x) permission to cd down through a directory structure, or *directory tree*, that includes that directory. (For directories, x permission is called *search* permission rather than *execute* permission because it doesn't make any sense to execute a directory file and because it controls who may and may not search through the directory.) To use any file in a directory tree, you must set the proper permissions for all directories in the path to the file.

For example, here is a listing of a couple of levels of directories on my computer. (Note: I use the Korn shell and my prompt shows the name of my computer and my current directory.) Pay careful attention to the permissions of the directories book, ch01, and ch02, and the file priv.user.

```
mccc [pjh] /home/pjh/tools> ls -l

total 60
-rw-r--r--   1 pjh      root          1605 Sep  9 16:17 awk
drwxr-xr-x   4 pjh      root            64 Sep 14 15:16 book
-rw-r--r--   1 pjh      root          1989 Sep  9 16:17 cmd.line
-rw-r--r--   1 pjh      root           430 Sep  9 11:39 diff
-rw-r--r--   1 pjh      root          4814 Sep  9 16:17 ksh.prompt
-rw-r--r--   1 pjh      root         11044 Sep  9 16:17 ksh.prompts
-rw-------   1 pjh      root          1879 Sep 11 08:24 priv.user
-rw-r--r--   1 pjh      root          1174 Sep  9 16:17 pwd
-rw-r--r--   1 pjh      root          4471 Sep 12 10:27 raw-cooked
-rw-r--r--   1 pjh      root           493 Sep  9 16:17 sed

mccc [pjh] /home/pjh/tools> cd book

mccc [pjh] /home/pjh/tools/book> ls -l
```

```
total 2
drwxr--r--    3 pjh        root              64 Sep 14 15:24 ch01
drwxr-xr-x    2 pjh        root              48 Sep 14 15:19 ch02

mccc [pjh] /home/pjh/tools/book> cd ch01

mccc [pjh] /home/pjh/tools/book/ch01> ls -l

total 2
-rw-r--r--    1 pjh        root              48 Sep 14 15:17 sect01
drwxr-xr-x    2 pjh        root              48 Sep 14 15:24 xyzzy

mccc [pjh] /home/pjh/tools/book/ch01> cat sect01

This is the first sentence of Ch 1 of the book.

mccc [pjh] /home/pjh/tools/book/ch01> cd xyzzy

mccc [pjh] /home/pjh/tools/book/ch01/xyzzy> ls -l

total 1
-rw-r--r--    1 pjh        root              11 Sep 14 15:24 dummy

mccc [pjh] /home/pjh/tools/book/ch01/xyzzy> cat dummy

dummy file

mccc [pjh] /home/pjh/tools/book/ch01/xyzzy> cd ../../ch02

mccc [pjh] /home/pjh/tools/book/ch02> ls -l

total 1
-rw-r--r--    1 pjh        root              48 Sep 14 15:19 sect01

mccc [pjh] /home/pjh/tools/book/ch02> cat sect01

This is the first sentence of Ch 2 of the book.

mccc [pjh] /home/pjh/tools/book/ch02>
```

Now, another user, pete, logs in and attempts to access some of my files and directories. (pete and I do not belong to the same group.)

```
$ pwd

/home/pete

$ cd /home/pjh/tools

$ ls -l
```

```
total 60
-rw-r--r--   1 pjh      root         1605 Sep  9 16:17 awk
drwxr-xr-x   4 pjh      root           64 Sep 14 15:16 book
-rw-r--r--   1 pjh      root         1989 Sep  9 16:17 cmd.line
-rw-r--r--   1 pjh      root          430 Sep  9 11:39 diff
-rw-r--r--   1 pjh      root         4814 Sep  9 16:17 ksh.prompt
-rw-r--r--   1 pjh      root        11044 Sep  9 16:17 ksh.prompts
-rw-------   1 pjh      root         1879 Sep 11 08:24 priv.user
-rw-r--r--   1 pjh      root         1174 Sep  9 16:17 pwd
-rw-r--r--   1 pjh      root         4471 Sep 12 10:27 raw-cooked
-rw-r--r--   1 pjh      root          493 Sep  9 16:17 sed
```

$ **pg priv.user**

```
priv.user: Permission denied
```

priv.user has 600 permissions!

$ **cd book**

$ **ls -l**

```
total 2
drwxr--r--   2 pjh      root           48 Sep 14 15:17 ch01
drwxr-xr-x   2 pjh      root           48 Sep 14 15:19 ch02
```

$ **cd ch01**

```
ksh: ch01: permission denied
```

ch01 does not have search/execute permission for others:

$ **ls ch01**

```
sect01
```

but it does have read permission for everyone!

$ **ls -l ch01**

```
ch01/sect01: Permission denied
total 0
```

To display the "long" listing, pete would need access to the i-node of sect01 but doesn't have it:

$ **pg ch01/sect01**

```
ch01/sect01: Permission denied
```

And, since he doesn't have search/execute permission in ch01, he can't use it in a pathname:

```
$ cp ../sed ch01
```

```
cp: cannot create ch01/sed
cp: Permission denied
```

Without write permission in ch01, pete is not permitted to copy a file into ch01:

```
$ cd ch02
```

```
$ ls -l
```

```
total 1
-rw-r--r--   1 pjh      root            48 Sep 14 15:19 sect01
```

```
$ cat sect01
```

```
This is the first sentence of Ch 2 of the book.
```

But pete has search/execute permission for ch02 and read permission for sect01:

```
$ cd /home/pete
```

Now pete tries full pathnames:

```
$ ls /home/pjh/tools
```

```
awk
book
cmd.line
diff
ksh.prompt
ksh.prompts
priv.user
pwd
raw-cooked
sed
```

```
$ ls /home/pjh/tools/book
```

```
ch01
ch02
```

```
$ ls /home/pjh/tools/book/ch01
```

```
sect01
```

```
$ cat /home/pjh/tools/book/ch01/sect01
```

```
cat: cannot open /home/pjh/tools/book/ch01/sect01
```

Using full pathnames makes no difference:

```
$ cat /home/pjh/tools/book/ch02/sect01
```

```
This is the first sentence of Ch 2 of the book.

$
```

When a directory is created using the `mkdir` command, its permissions are set to 777 minus the user's `umask` value. The user and group ID of the directory are the same as those of the person creating the directory. For example, user `joe`—who belongs to group `personnel`—wants to create a subdirectory called engineering under his HOME directory. The `umask` value is 022. `joe` logs in and enters

$ mkdir engineering

If `joe` then does a long listing of his HOME directory, one of the lines he sees shows a directory named engineering with permissions 755 (`rwxr-xr-x`).

To list the contents of a directory, you must have permission to open the directory file and read its contents. To copy or move a file into a directory, you must be able to change the contents of the directory file; that is, you must have write permission for the directory.

Search permissions help you "search" a directory's contents (this permission allows access to the i-nodes). If you have search permission on a given directory—even without read/write permissions—you can perform the following as long as you know the names of files in the directory:

- Create a long listing of a specific file:

  $ ls -[nd]l *PathnameOfFile*

- Edit a file in the directory:

  $ vi *PathnameOfFile*

- Look at the contents of a file:

  $ cat *PathnameOfFile*

- Execute a command contained in the directory:

  $ *PathnameToCommand*

- Change to a subdirectory:

  $ cd *PathnameToSubdirectory*

Some of the preceding commands assume the subdirectories have correct permissions on them (read, write, search, or all three, as appropriate). The rules for search, however, apply to all subdirectories in a tree.

A user with read permission can read the contents of the directory. That is, the user can perform the following:

1

- List the contents of the directory:

  ```
  $ ls dir
  ```

- Echo the names of the files in the directory:

  ```
  $ echo dir/[A-Za-z]0-9]*
  ```

Read permission also enables a user to look at the contents of the directory file. It does not give access to the i-node information for files and subdirectories. Therefore, without the search flag (x) set, the user *cannot* successfully execute ls with a number of options. Chapter 2 discusses these options. As you read Chapter 2, think about what each option means and how it relates to the search permission flag on a directory.

- View the names of the files in that directory:

  ```
  $ ls dir/[A-Za-z0-9]*
  ```

- Change directories:

  ```
  $ cd dir
  ```

Write permission in conjunction with search permission helps create, move, and remove directory entries. With a directory permission of at least 333, you can perform the following:

- Create a file with output redirection:

  ```
  $ cmd > dir/file
  ```

- Copy a file into the directory:

  ```
  $ cp file1 dir/file2
  ```

- Create a new subdirectory:

  ```
  $ mkdir dir/subdir
  ```

- Rename a file in the directory:

  ```
  $ mv dir/file /dir/newfile
  ```

- Move a file out of the directory:

  ```
  $ mv dir/file /tmp/file
  ```

- Move a file into the directory:

  ```
  $ mv /tmp/file dir/file
  ```

- Remove a file from the directory:

  ```
  $ rm dir/file
  ```

- Remove a subdirectory:

  ```
  $ rmdir dir/subdir
  (if subdir is empty)
  ```

Correct directory permissions are important for security. Set permissions for the members of your group and others so that they can at the most read your files but are prevented from changing or deleting them.

Therefore, give careful attention to shell programs and utilities that create directories.

Summary

From its modest beginnings on a cast-off PDP-7, UNIX has evolved into a widely used, commercial operating system that is portable to almost any computer. System V Release 4 is an effort to bring together the diverging developments in AT&T UNIX, Berkeley UNIX, and XENIX.

UNIX supports a tool-building philosophy wherein simple commands are combined to create more powerful ones. Many of the simple commands are *filters*. They are the backbone of most of the tools that UNIX users build.

UNIX has a hierarchical organization of files: ordinary or regular files, directory files, and special files. In UNIX, everything is a file, so UNIX is called a device-independent operating system. UNIX achieves this independence through device special files and device driver software.

Some of the other key points discussed in this chapter are the following:

- File systems are hierarchical organizations of ordinary (also called regular), directory, and special files, as well as physical organizations of i-nodes and data blocks.

- UNIX programs are called processes when they're being executed. At any instant, it appears that many processes are running simultaneously, but actually a scheduler allots each process a period of time during which that process has exclusive use of the CPU.

- Pipes and redirection are UNIX facilities that enhance your ability to build tools.

- System V Release 4 comes with three shells. The shell maintains the user's work environment, interprets what the user types at the keyboard, and serves as a programming language for scripts. The shell is able to recognize certain metacharacters and has a "quoting" mechanism that lets you designate any instance of any metacharacter as an ordinary character.

- Files have permissions for security protection against certain other users.

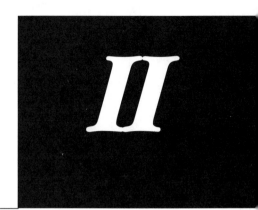

Part

Tutorial

## Chapter 2

Regular Expressions

A *regular expression* is a sequence of ordinary characters plus a set of special regular expression operators. Ordinary characters include the set of all uppercase and lowercase letters, digits, and other characters, such as the tilde (~), the back quote (`), the exclamation mark (!), the "at" sign (@), the pound sign (#), the underscore (_), the dash (-), the equals sign (=), the colon (:), the semicolon (;), the comma (,) and the slash (/). The metacharacters are all the rest. Some of the metacharacters may remind you of the special characters used in file name matching, but be forewarned: in general, regular expression operators have different meanings from the shell metacharacters discussed in Chapter 1.

A number of UNIX commands use regular expressions to find text in files. Regular expressions are also used to make changes to files without having to do each one interactively with an editor such as vi. Generally, you supply a regular expression to a command to tell that command what to search for. Most regular expressions match more than one text string.

The simplest form of a regular expression includes only ordinary characters. For example, the is a regular expression that matches only the three-letter sequence t, h, e. This pattern is found in the following words: the, therefore, bother (and in many more, of course). In other words, wherever the regular expression pattern is found— even if it's surrounded by other characters—it is matched.

The regular expression pattern-matching mechanism is its own language, and approximately 20 UNIX programs use it. Even though it takes some time and effort to learn the language of regular expressions, you'll find that it pays large dividends when you start building your own tools in UNIX.

2   Where Are Regular Expressions Used?

Some of the UNIX utilities that use regular expressions are as follows:

- The vi screen editor and its underlying line editor, ex

- The ed editor

- The sed stream editor

- The grep and egrep pattern-matching commands

- The more and pg file browsing commands

- The awk pattern scanning and processing language

- The expr expression evaluator command

The examples that follow use the utilities grep, egrep, and sed to illustrate matching with regular expressions. Here's a brief introduction to those three commands. They are discussed in detail later in this section, and they also appear in the reference in Part III.

grep
: The name means *globally* (throughout the entire file) search for a *regular expression* and *print* the line that contains it). In its simplest form, grep is called like this:

    grep *regular_expression filename*

    When grep finds a match to the regular expression, it displays the line of the file that contains it, and then goes on searching for a subsequent match. Thus, grep displays every line of a file that contains a text string that matches the regular expression.

egrep
: egrep is called exactly the same way as grep but uses an *extended* set of regular expression operators.

sed   The *stream editor* applies one or more editing commands—
usually "search and substitute" (also called "search and
replace")—to each line of a file. sed is frequently called like
this:

```
sed 'editing command' filename
```

Although it isn't always necessary to enclose the command
in single quotation marks, there are many times when you'll
want to "protect" some of the characters in it from the shell
(recall that some regular expression operators are the same
characters as certain of the shell metacharacters), so you
should always use quotation marks.

Be aware that none of these commands alter the original file! Output
goes to stdout (by default, stdout is the screen). To save the results, you must
redirect the output to a file.

Here are the contents of the file I'll use to demonstrate regular
expressions:

$ cat REfile

```
A regular expression is a sequence of characters taken
from the set of uppercase and lowercase letters, digits,
punctuation marks, etc., plus a set of special regular
expression operators. Some of these operators may remind
you of file name matching, but be forewarned: in general,
regular expression operators are different from the
shell metacharacters we discussed in Chapter 1.

The simplest form of a regular expression is one that
includes only letters. For example, the would match only
the three-letter sequence t, h, e. This pattern is found
in the following words: the, therefore, bother. In other
words, wherever the regular expression pattern is found
-- even if it is surrounded by other characters --, it will
be matched.
```

Regular Expression Characters

Regular expressions match patterns. They consist of a combination of
ordinary characters, such as letters, digits, and various metacharacters. A
character's use often determines its meaning in a regular expression. All

programs using regular expressions have a *search pattern*. The editor family
of programs (vi, ex, ed, sed) also has a *replacement pattern*. In some cases,
a metacharacter has a different meaning depending on whether it's used as
part of the search pattern or in the replacement pattern.

Here's an example of a simple search for an regular expression. This
regular expression is a character string with no metacharacters in it.

```
$ grep only REfile
```

prints

```
includes only letters. For example, the would match only
```

The first occurrence of only satisfied grep's search, so grep printed the
matching line.

There are two kinds of regular expressions: *limited* and *full* (sometimes
called *extended*). Limited regular expressions are a subset of full regular
expressions, but UNIX commands are inconsistent in the extended operations they permit. At the end of this discussion, you'll find a table illustrating
some of the common commands in UNIX System V Release 4 that use regular
expressions, along with the operations they can perform.

Certain characters have special meanings when used in regular expressions, and some of them have special meanings depending on their position
in the regular expression:

- The *dot* (.), *asterisk* (*), *left square bracket* ([) and *backslash* (\)
  are special except when they appear between a left-right pair of
  square brackets ([]).

- A *circumflex* or *caret* (^) is special when it's the first character of a
  regular expression, and also when it's the first character after the left
  square bracket in a left-right pair of square brackets.

- A *dollar sign* ($) is special when it's the last character of a regular
  expression.

- A pair of delimiters, usually a pair of *slash* characters (/), is special
  because it delimits the regular expression.

> **Note:** Any character not used in the current regular expression may
> be used as the delimiter, but the slash is traditional.

- A metacharacter preceded by a backslash is matched by the character itself. This is called *escaping*. When a metacharacter is escaped, the command recognizes it as a *literal*—the actual character with no special meaning. In other words, as in file name matching, the backslash removes the special meaning of the character that follows it.

Now let's look at each character in detail.

The dot matches any one character except a *newline*. For example, consider the following:

```
$ grep ´w.r´ REfile
```

prints

```
from the set of uppercase and lowercase letters, digits,
you of file name matching, but be forewarned: in general,
in the following words: the, therefore, bother. In other
words, wherever the regular expression pattern is found
```

The pattern w.r was matched by "wer" in "lowercase" on line 1, by "war" in "forewarned" on line 2, by "wor" in "words" on line 3, and by "wor" in "words" on line 4. This command can be expressed in English as "find all lines that match the pattern: w followed by any character except a newline followed by r."

A one-character regular expression can be formed by enclosing a list of characters in a left-right pair of square brackets. For example:

```
[aei135XYZ]
```

matches any one of the characters a, e, i, 1, 3, 5, X, Y, or Z. Consider the following:

```
$ grep ´w[fhmkz]´ REfile
```

```
words, wherever the regular expression pattern is found
```

This time, the match was satisfied only by the "wh" in "wherever," matching the pattern: "w followed by either f, h, m, k, or z."

If the first character in the list is a circumflex (also called a caret), the match occurs on any character that is *not* in the list. If the first character in the list is a right square bracket (]), it does not terminate the list—that would make the list empty and that's not permitted. Instead,] itself becomes one of the possible characters in the search pattern. For example:

```
[]a]
```

matches either] or a.

```
$ grep ´w[^fhmkz]´ REfile
```

```
from the set of uppercase and lowercase letters, digits,
you of file name matching, but be forewarned: in general,
shell metacharacters we discussed in Chapter 1.
includes only letters. For example, the would match only
in the following words: the, therefore, bother. In other
words, wherever the regular expression pattern is found
-- even if it is surrounded by other characters --, it will
```

There are many matches for the pattern "w followed by anything *except* f, h, m, k, or z!" On line 1, "we" in "lowercase" is a "w followed by anything except an f, an h, an m, a k, or a z." On line 2, "wa" in "forewarned" is a match, as is the word "we" on line 3. Line 4 contains "wo" in "would" while line 5 contains "wo" in words. Line 6 has "wo" in "words" as its match; the other possible matches on line 6 are ignored because the match was satisfied at the beginning of the line. Finally, at the end of line 7 "wi" matches "will."

You can use a minus sign (-) inside the left-right pair of square brackets to indicate a range of letters or digits. For example:

```
[a-z]
```

matches any lowercase letter.

Note: You are not permitted to write the range "backwards"; that is, [z-a] is illegal.

Consider the following example:

```
$ grep ´w[a-f]´ Refile
```

```
from the set of uppercase and lowercase letters, digits,
you of file name matching, but be forewarned: in general,
shell metacharacters we discussed in Chapter 1.
```

The matches are "we" on line 1, "wa" on line 2, and "we" on line 3. Look at REfile again and note how many potential matches were omitted because the character following the "w" was not one of the group "a through f."

Furthermore, you may include several ranges in one set of brackets:

```
[a-zA-Z]
```

matches any letter.

If you wish to specify precisely how many of a given character you want the regular expression to match, you may use the *escaped left-right curly brace pair* (\{____\}). For example:

```
X\{2,5\}
```

will match at least two, but not more than five, Xs: XX, XXX, XXXX, or XXXXX. The minimum number of matches is written immediately after the escaped left curly brace, followed by a comma (,), and then the maximum value. If you omit the maximum value (but not the comma), you're specifying that the match should occur for *at least* two Xs. That is,

```
X\{2,\}
```

If you write just a single value, omitting the comma, you're specifying the exact number of matches: no more, no less. For example:

```
X\{4\}
```

matches only XXXX. Here are some examples of this kind of regular expression:

```
$ grep ´p\{2\}´ REfile
```

```
from the set of uppercase and lowercase letters, digits,
```

This is the only line that contains "pp."

```
$ grep ´p\{1\}´ REfile
```

```
A regular expression is a sequence of characters taken
from the set of uppercase and lowercase letters, digits,
punctuation marks, etc., plus a set of special regular
expression operators. Some of these operators may remind
regular expression operators are different from the
shell metacharacters we discussed in Chapter 1.
The simplest form of a regular expression is one that
includes only letters. For example, the would match only
the three-letter sequence t, h, e. This pattern is found
words, wherever the regular expression pattern is found
```

Notice that on the second line, the first "p" in "uppercase" satisfies the search. grep doesn't even see the second "p" in the word because it stops searching as soon as it finds one "p"!

The asterisk matches zero or more of the *preceding regular expression*. Thus

```
X*
```

will match zero or more Xs: nothing, X, XX, XXX, and so on. To be sure you get at least one character in the match, use

```
XX*
```

For example,

```
$ grep 'p*' REfile
```

will display the entire file because every line can match "zero or more instances of the letter p." However

```
$ grep 'pp*' REfile
```

produces

```
A regular expression is a sequence of characters taken
from the set of uppercase and lowercase letters, digits,
punctuation marks, etc., plus a set of special regular
expression operators. Some of these operators may remind
regular expression operators are different from the
shell metacharacters we discussed in Chapter 1.
The simplest form of a regular expression is one that
includes only letters. For example, the would match only
the three-letter sequence t, h, e. This pattern is found
words, wherever the regular expression pattern is found
```

and

```
$ grep 'ppp*' REfile
```

produces

```
from the set of uppercase and lowercase letters, digits,
```

The regular expression ppp* matches "pp followed by zero or more instances of the letter p." Another way of stating this is "two or more instances of the letter p."

In the extended set of regular expressions, you'll find two additional operators used like the asterisk. They are the *plus sign*, or *plus* (+) and the *question mark* (?). Plus is used to match *one* or more occurrences of the preceding character, while question mark is used to match *zero or one* occurrences. For example:

```
$ egrep 'p?' REfile
```

outputs the entire file, whereas

```
$ egrep 'p+' REfile
```

produces

```
A regular expression is a sequence of characters taken
from the set of uppercase and lowercase letters, digits,
punctuation marks, etc., plus a set of special regular
expression operators. Some of these operators may remind
regular expression operators are different from the
shell metacharacters we discussed in Chapter 1.
```

```
The simplest form of a regular expression is one that
includes only letters. For example, the would match only
the three-letter sequence t, h, e. This pattern is found
words, wherever the regular expression pattern is found
```

A circumflex used outside the square brackets "anchors" the regular expression to the beginning of the line. That is

```
^[Tt]he
```

matches a line that has either The or the at the beginning, but does not match a line that has a The or the inside the line. For example:

$ grep ´[Tt]he´ REfile

produces

```
from the set of uppercase and lowercase letters, digits,
expression operators. Some of these operators may remind
regular expression operators are different from the
The simplest form of a regular expression is one that
includes only letters. For example, the would match only
the three-letter sequence t, h, e. This pattern is found
in the following words: the, therefore, bother. In other
words, wherever the regular expression pattern is found
-- even if it is surrounded by other characters --, it is
```

but

$ grep ´^[Tt]he´ REfile

prints

```
The simplest form of a regular expression is one that
the three-letter sequence t, h, e. This pattern is found
```

A dollar sign anchors the regular expression to the end of the line. For example:

```
digits$
```

will match

```
shell metacharacters we discussed in Chapter 1.
```

because the line ends in something that matches the regular expression. The period in the regular expression is preceded by a backslash so that the program "knows" that it's looking for a period and not just any character. Here's another example that uses REfile:

$ grep ´[Tt]he$´ REfile

```
regular expression operators are different from the
```

2

The regular expression .* is an idiom that is used to match zero or more occurrences of any characters. A multicharacter regular expression always matches the longest string of characters that fits the regular expression description. Consequently, .* used as the entire regular expression always will match an entire line of text. Therefore

```
$ grep '^.*$' REfile
```

would print the entire file.

When used as part of an "unanchored" regular expression, that idiomatic regular expression will match the longest string that fits the description. For example:

```
$ grep 'C.*1' REfile
```

```
shell metacharacters we discussed in Chapter 1.
```

The regular expression C.*1 matches the longest string that begins with a C and ends with a 1. The regular expression d.*d matches the longest string that begins and ends with a d. On each matched line in the following, the matched string is highlighted in boldface type:

```
$ grep 'd.*d' REfile
```

```
from the set of uppercase and lowercase letters, digits,
shell metacharacters we discussed in Chapter 1.
includes only letters. For example, the would match only
words, wherever the regular expression pattern is found
-- even if it is surrounded by other characters --, it is
```

You've seen that a regular expression command like grep will find a match even if the regular expression is surrounded by other characters. For example:

```
[Tt]he
```

matches

```
the, The, there, There, other, oTher
```

(even if this last is unlikely). Suppose you're looking for the word The or the and do not want to match other. In a few of the commands that use full regular expresions, you may surround the regular expression with *escaped angle brackets* (\<___\>). For example:

```
\<the\>
```

says "match the string the where t follows a character that is not a letter, digit or underscore, and where e is followed by a character that is not a letter, digit or underscore." The angle brackets can be used singly in cases where complete isolation from letters, digits, and underscores is not a necessity.

You can tell `egrep` to search for either of two regular expressions like this:

```
$ egrep 'regular expression-1 ¦ regular expression-2' filename
```

Finally, a regular expression may be enclosed in *escaped parentheses* (\(\)) to save it in a *hold space* for further processing. The following discussion of *replacement* will provide some examples of this approach.

The editor family of programs lets you do more than just locate patterns that match regular expressions—it enables you to change them. You give a command to an editor that says, in effect, "look for the following regular expression and when you find a text string that matches it, replace that text string with the following replacement string." I'll use `sed` with the *search and substitute* command examples. Because `sed` normally echos each line it reads, it has an option, `-n`, to make it work silently. Normally, however, you'd like to get some output from `sed`, so you're permitted to append `p` after the replacement string. The `p` tells `sed` to output all lines on which it performs a substitution. For example:

```
$ sed -n 's/regular_expression/text/p' filename
```

will cause `sed` to look for the specified regular expression on each line of the file, replace it with the replacement text, and print only the lines that have been altered. Of course, the original file is not changed at all; the changed text is written to stdout. More specifically:

```
$ sed -n 's/the/THE/p' REfile
```

```
from THE set of uppercase and lowercase letters, digits,
expression operators. Some of THEse operators may remind
regular expression operators are different from THE
includes only letters. For example, THE would match only
THE three-letter sequence t, h, e. This pattern is found
in THE following words: the, therefore, bother. In other
words, wherever THE regular expression pattern is found
-- even if it is surrounded by oTHEr characters --, it is
```

Notice on the third line from the bottom that only the first occurrence of "the" is changed to "THE." If you want to make the changes on all strings in the file, you must add the *line global* command `g` after the replacement string but before the `p`:

```
$ sed -n 's/the/THE/gp' REfile
```

```
from THE set of uppercase and lowercase letters, digits,
expression operators. Some of THEse operators may remind
regular expression operators are different from THE
includes only letters. For example, THE would match only
THE three-letter sequence t, h, e. This pattern is found
```

```
in THE following words: THE, THErefore, boTHEr. In oTHEr
words, wherever THE regular expression pattern is found
-- even if it is surrounded by oTHEr characters --, it is
```

Certain characters in a replacement string have special meanings. This is illustrated with a file called names:

```
$ cat names
```

```
allen christopher
babinchak david
best betty
bloom dennis
boelhower joseph
bose anita
cacossa ray
chang liang
crawford patricia
crowley charles
cuddy michael
czyzewski sharon
delucia joseph
```

The *ampersand* (&) in a replacement string is shorthand for "the string that matches the regular expression." Here's a sed command that adds the text " DP168" to the end of each line of the names file. (The -n and p have been omitted because the command will act on every line of the file.)

```
$ sed 's/^.*$/& DP168/' names
```

```
allen christopher DP168
babinchak david DP168
best betty DP168
bloom dennis DP168
boelhower joseph DP168
bose anita DP168
cacossa ray DP168
chang liang DP168
crawford patricia DP168
crowley charles DP168
cuddy michael DP168
czyzewski sharon DP168
delucia joseph DP168
```

The & was replaced by the string that the regular expression matched: "the entire line."

Previously I mentioned that the operators \(and \) are used to isolate portions of the search regular expression and place the isolated portion in a hold space. Suppose you want to process each line of the names file like this: extract all characters from the beginning of the line to the first space.

```
$ sed ´s/^\(.*\) .*/\1/´ names
```

```
allen
babinchak
best
bloom
boelhower
bose
cacossa
chang
crawford
crowley
cuddy
czyzewski
delucia
```

The search regular expression is "from the beginning of the line, all characters, a space, all the rest of the characters." This might seem strange because
a space is a legitimate character. The space is stated explicitly in the regular
expression because I wanted to group all characters to the left of the first
space. The hold space gets a subset of those characters: all the characters from
the beginning of the line up to but not including the first space. The
replacement string \1 doesn't do any replacements at all; it merely echos the
contents of the hold space.

You can isolate both character strings—the characters before the first
space and the ones that follow it—with a slightly different command:

```
$ sed ´s/^\(.*\) \(.*\)/\2/´ names
```

```
christopher
david
betty
dennis
joseph
anita
ray
liang
patricia
charles
michael
sharon
joseph
```

This command isolates what we recognize as the last name and the first
name of each person listed in the names file. The last name goes into the first
hold space, and the first name into the second hold space. Now let's display
both names but in "first name first, last name last" order:

```
$ sed ´s/^\(.*\) \(.*\)/\2 \1/´ names
```

```
christopher allen
david babinchak
betty best
dennis bloom
joseph boelhower
anita bose
ray cacossa
liang chang
patricia crawford
charles crowley
michael cuddy
sharon czyzewski
joseph delucia
```

There are many neat things you can do with regular expressions.

Regular Expression Examples

When you first look at the metacharacters list used with regular expressions, it seems that constructing search-and-replacement patterns is a complex process. A few examples and exercises using sed, however, can make them easier to understand.

Example 1: Changing the home directories of users in /etc/passwd.

In the passwd file, change the location of the home directories of all users having dp270 in their passwd file entries from file system u1 to file system u2. Here's the original passwd file, followed by the sed command accomplishing this goal, and the resulting output file. Note that I have highlighted the lines in both files that are affected by this command.

```
allen:x:278:20:allen christopher r:/u1/fall91/dp168/allen:/bin/ksh
babinch:x:271:20:babinchak david j:/u1/fall91/dp270/babinch:/bin/ksh
best:x:312:20:best betty:/u1/fall91/dp163/best:/bin/ksh
bloom:x:279:20:bloom dennis m:/u1/fall91/dp168/bloom:/bin/ksh
boelhow:x:314:20:boelhower joseph j:/u1/fall91/dp163/boelhow:/bin/ksh
bose:x:298:20:bose anita:/u1/fall91/dp168/bose:/bin/ksh
cacossa:x:259:20:cacossa ray:/u1/fall91/dp270/cacossa:/bin/ksh
chang:x:280:20:chang liang:/u1/fall91/dp168/chang:/bin/ksh
crawfor:x:317:20:crawford patricia a:/u1/fall91/dp163/crawfor:/bin/ksh
crowley:x:318:20:crowley charles j:/u1/fall91/dp163/crowley:/bin/ksh
cuddy:x:260:20:cuddy michael s:/u1/fall91/dp270/cuddy:/bin/ksh
czyzews:x:299:20:czyzewski sharon r:/u1/fall91/dp168/czyzews:/bin/ksh
delucia:x:300:20:delucia joseph:/u1/fall91/dp168/delucia:/bin/ksh
diesso:x:261:20:diesso michael d:/u1/fall91/dp270/diesso:/bin/ksh
dimemmo:x:301:20:dimemmo guy j:/u1/fall91/dp168/dimemmo:/bin/ksh
dintron:x:281:20:dintrone joseph e:/u1/fall91/dp168/dintron:/bin/ksh
```

```
$ sed '/dp270/s/u1/u2' passwd > passwd.1
```

```
$ cat passwd.1
```

```
allen:x:278:20:allen christopher r:/u1/fall91/dp168/allen:/bin/ksh
babinch:x:271:20:babinchak david j:/u2/fall91/dp270/babinch:/bin/ksh
best:x:312:20:best betty:/u1/fall91/dp163/best:/bin/ksh
bloom:x:279:20:bloom dennis m:/u1/fall91/dp168/bloom:/bin/ksh
boelhow:x:314:20:boelhower joseph j:/u1/fall91/dp163/boelhow:/bin/ksh
bose:x:298:20:bose anita:/u1/fall91/dp168/bose:/bin/ksh
cacossa:x:259:20:cacossa ray:/u2/fall91/dp270/cacossa:/bin/ksh
chang:x:280:20:chang liang:/u1/fall91/dp168/chang:/bin/ksh
crawfor:x:317:20:crawford patricia a:/u1/fall91/dp163/crawfor:/bin/ksh
crowley:x:318:20:crowley charles j:/u1/fall91/dp163/crowley:/bin/ksh
cuddy:x:260:20:cuddy michael s:/u2/fall91/dp270/cuddy:/bin/ksh
czyzews:x:299:20:czyzewski sharon r:/u1/fall91/dp168/czyzews:/bin/ksh
delucia:x:300:20:delucia joseph:/u1/fall91/dp168/delucia:/bin/ksh
diesso:x:261:20:diesso michael d:/u2/fall91/dp270/diesso:/bin/ksh
dimemmo:x:301:20:dimemmo guy j:/u1/fall91/dp168/dimemmo:/bin/ksh
dintron:x:281:20:dintrone joseph e:/u1/fall91/dp168/dintron:/bin/ksh
```

The sed command means: "Find all lines that contain the pattern dp270, and on these lines substitute u2 for u1."

Example 2: Changing some directories in the passwd file.

Suppose you want to change the original passwd file so that all fall91/dp168 directories were changed to spr92/dp269:

```
$ sed '/fall91\/dp168/s//spr92\/dp269' passwd > passwd.2
```

```
$ cat passwd.2
```

```
allen:x:278:20:allen christopher r:/u1/spr92/dp269/allen:/bin/ksh
babinch:x:271:20:babinchak david j:/u1/fall91/dp270/babinch:/bin/ksh
best:x:312:20:best betty:/u1/fall91/dp163/best:/bin/ksh
bloom:x:279:20:bloom dennis m:/u1/spr92/dp269/bloom:/bin/ksh
boelhow:x:314:20:boelhower joseph j:/u1/fall91/dp163/boelhow:/bin/ksh
bose:x:298:20:bose anita:/u1/spr92/dp269/bose:/bin/ksh
cacossa:x:259:20:cacossa ray:/u1/fall91/dp270/cacossa:/bin/ksh
chang:x:280:20:chang liang:/u1/spr92/dp269/chang:/bin/ksh
crawfor:x:317:20:crawford patricia a:/u1/fall91/dp163/crawfor:/bin/ksh
crowley:x:318:20:crowley charles j:/u1/fall91/dp163/crowley:/bin/ksh
cuddy:x:260:20:cuddy michael s:/u1/fall91/dp270/cuddy:/bin/ksh
czyzews:x:299:20:czyzewski sharon r:/u1/spr92/dp269/czyzews:/bin/ksh
delucia:x:300:20:delucia joseph:/u1/spr92/dp269/delucia:/bin/ksh
diesso:x:261:20:diesso michael d:/u1/fall91/dp270/diesso:/bin/ksh
dimemmo:x:301:20:dimemmo guy j:/u1/spr92/dp269/dimemmo:/bin/ksh
dintron:x:281:20:dintrone joseph e:/u1/spr92/dp269/dintron:/bin/ksh
```

There a couple of interesting things in this sed command:

- Notice that the / that occurs in both fall91/dp168 and in spr92/dp269 had to be escaped so that sed wouldn't think it was the regular expression delimiter.

- The pattern was not repeated in the "search" portion of the command. I simply used `s//spr92\/dp269` because the substitute part recalls the previous search. If the substitute and the previous search are the same, it is not necessary to repeat the search pattern.

There's another possibility for this command in case you don't like escaping the `/`: change the delimiter.

```
$ sed '\Xfall91/dp168XsXXspr92/dp269' passwd > passwd.2
```

By escaping the first X, you tell sed to use it as the delimiter. This permits you to avoid escaping the `/`.

Example 3: Eliminating duplicate spaces.

You can remove duplicate adjacent spaces in a file with the command:

```
$ sed 's/  //g' file > file.1
```

The g at the end of the command tells sed to search the entire line. You may recall that sed usually is happy enough to change the first thing it finds and then goes to the next line. For example,

```
$ cat file
```

```
A regular            expression   is a sequence   of   characters  taken
from    the set            of  uppercase and lowercase  letters and  digits.
```

```
$ sed 's/  //g' file > file.1
```

```
$ cat file.1
```

```
Aregularexpressionis a sequence of characterstaken
fromtheset ofuppercase and lowercaseletters anddigits.
```

Wherever there were two or more spaces, there now are none. That's not terribly useful; usually, changing multiple spaces to single spaces is preferable. Here's a possible solution:

```
$ sed 's/  / /g' file > file.2
```

```
$ cat file.2
```

```
A regular       expression  is a sequence   of   characters taken
from   the set      of uppercase and lowercase letters and digits.
```

That didn't work! sed looked for a pair of spaces and replaced it with a space. Then it looked for the next pair and replaced it with a space. So if there were four spaces in a row, there are now two. sed will not go back and see that there is a new set of two spaces. You need a different command:

```
$ sed ´s/  */ /g´ file > file.3
```

```
$ cat file.3
```

```
A regular expression is a sequence of characters taken
from the set of uppercase and lowercase letters and digits.
```

Ah, that one worked. Remember that an asterisk following any character matches zero or more instances of the character. Therefore, I specified two spaces followed by an asterisk so that one or more spaces (one plus zero or more) would be replaced by one space.

Example 4: Deleting all spaces at the end of lines.

Use the following regular expression to delete all spaces at the end of a line:

```
sed ´s/  *$//´ filename
```

This command replaces one or more spaces at the end of the line with nothing, that is, it removes them.

There's another way to delete the spaces at the end of a line that's worth examining. This method saves the part you want to save rather than removing the part you don't want to keep. Use the -ve option of cat so that you can see exactly where the end of each line is.

```
$ cat -ve names
```

```
allen christopher                 $
babinchak david        $
best betty                    $
bloom dennis                        $
boelhower joseph      $
bose anita                 $
cacossa ray                   $
chang liang        $
crawford patricia      $
crowley charles          $
cuddy michael          $
czyzewski sharon     $
delucia joseph  $
```

```
$ sed ´s/\(.*[^ ]\)/\1/´ names > names.1
```

In this case, you want to match the longest string that contains any characters followed by a character that is not a space, and you want to save all the matched characters. Let's take that a little at a time:

- The \(and \) surround the regular expression that represents the string you want to save in a hold space.

- .* is an idiom meaning "one or more characters," with no restrictions. That is, the characters may be all different from each other, and they can be any characters at all.

- [^] means "not a space character."

Thus, the string that went into the hold space terminates at the first space character.

In the replacement string, use \1, which is simply the string that got saved during the search:

```
$ cat -ve names.1

allen christopher$
babinchak david$
best betty$
bloom dennis$
boelhower joseph$
bose anita$
cacossa ray$
chang liang$
crawford patricia$
crowley charles$
cuddy michael$
czyzewski sharon$
delucia joseph$
```

Example 5: Using word matching and replacement.

To replace all occurrences of the word cal with calendar, a simple global replacement of

```
s/cal/calendar/g
```

is necessary:

```
$ cat cal

The cal command in UNIX is
very useful. It prints a
calendar of the month you
specify.
```

```
$ sed 's/cal/calendar' cal > cal.1
```

```
$ cat cal.1

The calendar command in UNIX is
very useful. It prints a
calendarendar of the month you
specify.
```

This worked on the first line, but notice that on the third line the word calendar was changed to calendarendar. sed saw the cal at the beginning of that word and changed it to `calendar`. Then it printed the rest of the characters on that line, including the original `endar`. You need to find a way to tell `sed` to ignore every occurence of `cal` that is contained in another word:

```
$ sed ´s/cal[ .,$]/calendar/g´ cal > cat.2
```

The `sed` command means: "For every occurrence of `cal` followed by a space, a period, a comma, or the end-of-line, replace it with the pattern `calendar`."

```
$ cat cal.2
```

```
The calendarcommand in UNIX is
very useful. It prints a
calendar of the month you
specify.
```

Oops! I fixed the "calendarendar" problem but introduced a new one: there's no longer a space between "calendar" and "command" on the first line. Here's a better version:

```
$ sed ´s/cal\([ .,$]\)/calendar\1/g´ cal > cal.3
```

```
$ cat cal.3
```

```
The calendar command in UNIX is
very useful. It prints a
calendar of the month you
specify.
```

Of course, the previous command will not prevent the incorrect replacement on the word "hysterical" in the next example file, but devising a new command for `sed`—one that solves this new problem—is not difficult.

```
$ cat cal1
```

```
The student became hysterical when confronted with the
many options to the calligraphy program.
```

```
$ sed ´s/cal\([ .,$]\)/calendar\1/g´ cal1 > cal1.1
```

```
$ cat cal1.1
```

```
The student became hystericalendar when confronted with the
many options to the calligraphy program.
```

It isn't difficult to create a new command for `sed`:

```
$ sed ´s/\([ .,$]\)cal\([ .,$]\)/\1calendar\2/g´ cal1 > cal1.2
```

```
$ cat cal1.2
```

```
The student became hysterical when confronted with the
many options to the calligraphy program.
```

2

Example 6: Changing all occurrences of and *to* &.

Remember that an ampersand (&) in a replacement string represents the original search string. Therefore, if you want to replace something with the actual & character, you must "escape" it by preceding it with the \ character. Look at the following example:

```
$ cat and
```

```
Have you ever seen a laddie go
this way and that way and this
way and that way?
```

```
-Traditional song
```

```
$ sed ´s/ and / \& /g´ and > and.1
```

```
$ cat and.1
```

```
Have you ever seen a laddie go
this way & that way and this
way & that way?
```

```
-Traditional song
```

It's too bad that sed doesn't recognize \< and \>.

Example 7: Deleting all blank lines.

If you wanted to delete all the blank lines from a file, you might try the following command:

```
$ sed ´s/^$//´ file
```

That is: "find a line that has nothing between its beginning (^) and its end ($) and delete it." But sed doesn't work like that. The s command is a character string substitution command and does not recognize the end-of-line character (line feed/newline in UNIX). Instead, you need to use the "delete" command:

```
$ sed ´/^$/d´ file
```

This command means: "Find the beginning of a line (^) that is followed immediately by the end of a line ($), and delete that line."

```
$ sed ´/^$/d´ REfile > re.1
```

```
$ cat re.1
```

A regular expression is a sequence of characters taken
from the set of uppercase and lowercase letters, digits,
punctuation marks, etc., plus a set of special regular
expression operators. Some of these operators may remind
you of file name matching, but be forewarned: in general,
regular expression operators are different from the
shell metacharacters we discussed in Chapter 1.
The simplest form of a regular expression is one that
includes only letters. For example, the would match only
the three-letter sequence t, h, e. This pattern is found
in the following words: the, therefore, bother. In other
words, wherever the regular expression pattern is found
-- even if it is surrounded by other characters --, it is
be matched.

Example 8: Deleting all lines that start with a period.

A period has special meaning when used in the search string: it represents any
one character. To search for a literal period, the period must be escaped:

$ **cat period**

```
.This file has a
period at the
.beginning of
every other line
.begining with
the first one and
.ending with the last.
```

$ **sed ´/^\./d´ period > period.1**

$ **cat period.1**

```
period at the
every other line
the first one and
```

The command says: "Delete every line that begins (^) with an actual period
(\.)."

Example 9: Matching lines that contain a date.

Consider that a standard USA date consists of a pattern that includes the
capitalized name of a month, a space, a one- or two-digit number representing the day, a comma, a space, and a four-digit number representing the year.
You could write that pattern as a regular expression:

```
[A-Z][a-z]* [0-9]\{1,2\}, [0-9]\{4\}
```

which could be improved a little by recognizing that May—the month with the
shortest name—has three letters and September has nine:

```
[A-Z][a-z]\{3,9\} [0-9]\{1,2\}, [0-9]\{4\}
```

Example 10: Matching Social Security Numbers

Social Security numbers also are highly structured: three digits, a dash, two digits, a dash, and four digits:

```
[0-9]\{3\}-[0-9]\{\2\}-[0-9]\{4\}
```

Example 11: Matching Telephone Numbers

Another structured pattern is found in telephone numbers, for example:

> 1-800-555-1212

A regular expression to match that pattern is

```
1-[0-9]\{3\}-[0-9]\{3\}-[0-9]\{4\}
```

Regular Expressions and Commands

Table 2.1 lists all the regular expression search and replace metacharacters and the programs that use regular expressions. The table also indicates which programs use which metacharacters and uses *RE* as an abbreviation for regular expression.

Note: Unfortunately, different implementations of each command may not comply with this table because of the propensity of software people to add "bells and whistles" to their products. Table 2.1 is accurate for the commands in UNIX System V Release 4.

Table 2.1. Regular expression metacharacters and programs.

RE	*ed*	*ex*	*grep*	*egrep*	*awk*	*sed*
.	yes	yes	yes	yes	yes	yes
\	yes	yes	yes	yes	yes	yes
RE*	yes	yes	yes	yes	yes	yes
[ ]	yes	yes	yes	yes	yes	yes
^	yes	yes	yes	yes	yes	yes
$	yes	yes	yes	yes	yes	yes
\(RE\)	yes	yes	yes	no	no	yes
(RE)	no	no	no	yes	yes	yes
&	yes	yes	yes	yes	yes	yes
\n	yes	yes	yes	yes	yes	yes
\{m\}	yes	no	yes	yes	yes	yes
\{m,\}	yes	no	yes	yes	yes	yes
\{m,n\}	yes	no	yes	yes	yes	yes
\<RE\>	yes	yes	yes	yes	yes	no
RE+	no	no	no	yes	yes	yes
RE?	no	no	no	yes	yes	yes
RE¦RE	no	no	no	yes	yes	yes

2

Summary

Throughout this book, you will use regular expressions as you continue to learn about other UNIX System V Release 4 commands.

The more structured the information in a file, the easier it is to construct regular expressions to manipulate the information. Recall the Social Security number, the telephone number, and the date examples discussed here. Remember to keep regular expressions in mind whenever you edit a file.

## Chapter 3

The Most Fundamental

Commands

To make this tutorial more meaningful and more useful as a reference, I will group System V Release 4 UNIX commands according to conventional categories and then present the commands to you in a more-or-less sensible order. I say "more-or-less sensible" because most of the examples require that I use two or more commands to illustrate the meaning of the command being discussed. I will use the auxiliary command in a simple way and explain them in detail when it's their turn. Some of the commands could be logically placed in two or more categories, but I have decided to isolate each command in just a single category. The categories and their corresponding commands are the following:

- File system commands that manipulate files and directory files: basename, cd, chmod, chown, cp, dircmp, dirname, file, ln, ls, mkdir, mv, pwd, rm, rmdir, sum, and touch.

- File commands that manipulate or access the contents of files: awk, cat, col, compress, crypt, csplit, cut, egrep, fgrep, fmt, fold, grep, head, join, makekey, more, nawk, newform, nl, od, paste, pg, pr, sed, sort, split, strings, tail, tr, uniq, pack, pcat, uncompress, uudecode, uuencode, unpack, and zcat.

- Archive commands, which either combine two or more files into an archive, remove the individual files from an archive, or display the contents of files in an archive: ar, cpio, and tar.

- Editors, which let you create or modify text files: bfs, ed, edit, ex, and vi.

- Calculator programs: bc, dc, expr, factor, and units.

- Information retrievers, which report on various aspects of your environment and that of the system: cal, calendar, date, df, du, env, find, finger, groups, id, last, listusers, logname, news, stty, time, timex, tty, uname, uustat, wc, and who.

- Commands that send programs into the background and report on their status: at, atq, atrm, and batch.

- Programs that compare the contents of two or more files: bdiff, cmp, comm, diff, diff3, and sdiff.

- Process control programs: kill, nice, nohup, ps, and sleep.

- Communications programs: ct, cu, mail, mailx mesg, notify, talk, uucp, uustat, uuto, and write.

- Group manipulation commands: chgrp, newgrp, and groups

- Printer commands: lp, lpstat, and cancel.

- Miscellaneous commands: banner, clear, echo, getopts, passwd, set, script, tee, test, tput, and xargs.

The rest of the tutorial part of this book will discuss the commands that are significant in tool building. In this chapter, I will review some of the commands that you are likely to know already, and perhaps extend your knowledge of some of them. After you have a firm grounding in these fundamentals, you will proceed to the first chapter on building tools.

You may have noticed that I did not list 200 commands. You haven't been cheated—many of the commands supplied with UNIX System V Release 4 are oriented toward system administration, networking, and programming. Those are the ones I omitted.

Commands You Already Know

Let's begin with a review of the commands you already know something about. But first, let's review what a UNIX command is.

A UNIX command begins with a "verb" as the first word on the command line. For example, find, ls, and echo are command verbs that you already know. A command may be followed by zero or more options. An option changes the way a command operates. For example, ls outputs a list of filenames, but ls -l outputs a list of filenames along with a lot of information about each file. The dash (-) is the usual lead-in character for an option in UNIX, although certain commands use the plus sign (+) and others do not require a lead-in character at all. Finally, the verb and its options may be followed by zero or more arguments (the actual number of required arguments depends on the command being used). Each argument is usually an absolute or relative pathname.

The ls Command

Probably the first command you used was ls, the one that lets you list the files in your current directory. You may not realize that ls has *23* different options. The general form of ls is

```
ls [-abcdfgilmnopqrstuxCFLR1] [name(s)]
```

Part III, the reference section of this book, covers all of these options. For now, let's look only at the options that are most useful in tool building.

The name(s) argument is optional (you can tell it is optional because it is enclosed in square brackets, the convention this book uses when describing UNIX commands):

- If you omit name(s), ls reports on files stored in the current directory.

- If you provide the name of a directory, ls displays information about files stored in that directory.

- If you provide a filename—regular or special—ls provides a display about that file or files.

You can use absolute or relative pathnames for files and directories, and can "mix and match" names of every type of file.

With no options and no names as arguments, ls lists alphabetically, in multiple columns, the names of all files—except those beginning with "dot" (.)—in the current directory. For example:

```
$ ls
```

```
Makefile      extend.c      macro.h        random.c       ttydef.h
README        file.c        main.c         re_search.c    ttyio.c
basic.c       fileio.c      match.c        regex.c        ttykbd.c
buffer.c      help.c        mg             regex.h        tutorial
chrdef.h      kbd.c         mg.tex         region.c       tutorial~
cinfo.c       kbd.h         mg2a-dos.tar   search.c       version.c
def.h         key.h         mg2a.change    spawn.c        window.c
dir.c         keymap.c      mgidx.tex      sys            word.c
dired.c       line.c        mgprog.doc     sysdef.h
display.c     ls            modes.c        termlib
echo.c        macro.c       paragraph.c    tty.c
```

Five columns of filenames are listed vertically in alphabetic order. Notice that the columns are separated by *spaces*. I'll use that information when I discuss column-oriented commands.

The -p option lets you see which names are directories by appending a / to their names. In the following example, sys and termlib are directories:

```
$ ls -p
```

```
Makefile      extend.c      macro.h        random.c       ttydef.h
README        file.c        main.c         re_search.c    ttyio.c
basic.c       fileio.c      match.c        regex.c        ttykbd.c
buffer.c      help.c        mg             regex.h        tutorial
chrdef.h      kbd.c         mg.tex         region.c       tutorial~
cinfo.c       kbd.h         mg2a-dos.tar   search.c       version.c
def.h         key.h         mg2a.change    spawn.c        window.c
dir.c         keymap.c      mgidx.tex      sys/           word.c
dired.c       line.c        mgprog.doc     sysdef.h
display.c     ls            modes.c        termlib/
echo.c        macro.c       paragraph.c    tty.c
```

To see what is in the subdirectories, tell ls to "walk the directory tree" and visit each subdirectory (the R stands for "recursive"):

```
$ ls -R
```

```
Makefile      extend.c      macro.h        random.c       ttydef.h
README        file.c        main.c         re_search.c    ttyio.c
basic.c       fileio.c      match.c        regex.c        ttykbd.c
buffer.c      help.c        mg             regex.h        tutorial
chrdef.h      kbd.c         mg.tex         region.c       tutorial~
cinfo.c       kbd.h         mg2a-dos.tar   search.c       version.c
```

```
def.h           key.h        mg2a.change    spawn.c      window.c
dir.c           keymap.c     mgidx.tex      sys          word.c
dired.c         line.c       mgprog.doc     sysdef.h
display.c       ls           modes.c        termlib
echo.c          macro.c      paragraph.c    tty.c
```

```
./sys:
amiga    atari    bsd     default  osk     prime    sysv    vms
```

```
./sys/amiga:
Amiga.Doc       console.c    menustack.c    sysinit.c    ttykbd.c
Makefile.LATTI  dirio.c      offset.c       tty.c        ttymenu.c
Makefile.MANX   fileio.c     sleep.c        ttydef.h     ttymouse.c
alloca.asm      iconify      spawn.c        ttyicon.c    varargs.h
amiga_maps.c    malloc.c     sysdef.h       ttyio.c
```

```
./sys/amiga/iconify:
iconify.c   iconify.h
```

```
./sys/atari:
alloc.c      diredsup.c   makesys.mwc  misc.c       ttydef.h
build.g      fileio.c     maketop.mwc  readme.1st   ttyio.c
chrdef.h     gemstart.s   mg.ini       sysdef.h     varargs.h
cinfo.c      getn.s       mglink.inp   term.c
```

```
./sys/bsd:
Makefile  README   fileio.c  spawn.c  sysdef.h  ttyio.c
```

```
./sys/default:
README    chrdef.h   tty.c      ttykbd.c
alloca.c  cinfo.c    ttydef.h   varargs.h
```

```
./sys/osk:
fileio.c   readme.osk  sysdef.h   varargs.h
makefile   spawn.c     ttyio.c
```

```
./sys/prime:
cinfo.c     mg.64v.options  spawn.c       ttyio.c
fileio.c    mg.options.c    stackptr$.pma varargs.h.ins.
make.cpl    readme          sysdef.h
```

```
./sys/sysv:
Makefile  fileio.c  spawn.c   sysdef.h  ttyio.c
```

```
./sys/vms:
aaareadme.1st  fparse.c   mg.opt         sysdef.h   unixfns.mar
ccom.com       make.com   mgmailedit.com trnlnm.c
fileio.c       mg.com     spawn.c        ttyio.c
```

```
./termlib:
fgetlr.c   testtcp.c   tgetflag.c  tgetstr.c  tputs.c
isdigit.c  tgetent.c   tgetnum.c   tgoto.c    ttest.c
```

3

You also can have ls list the files as a comma-separated list across the screen:

```
$ ls -m
```

Makefile, README, basic.c, buffer.c, chrdef.h, cinfo.c, def.h, dir.c,
dired.c, display.c, echo.c, extend.c, file.c, fileio.c, help.c, kbd.c,
kbd.h, key.h, keymap.c, line.c, ls, macro.c, macro.h, main.c, match.c,
mg, mg.tex, mg2a-dos.tar, mg2a.change, mgidx.tex, mgprog.doc, modes.c,
paragraph.c, random.c, re_search.c, regex.c, regex.h, region.c, search.c,
spawn.c, sys, sysdef.h, termlib, tty.c, ttydef.h, ttyio.c, ttykbd.c,
tutorial, tutorial~, version.c, window.c, word.c

As you might expect, you can combine two or more options, or even reverse the order of the display:

```
$ ls -r
```

```
word.c        sys           mgidx.tex     keymap.c      dir.c
window.c      spawn.c       mg2a.change   key.h         def.h
version.c     search.c      mg2a-dos.tar  kbd.h         cinfo.c
tutorial~     region.c      mg.tex        kbd.c         chrdef.h
tutorial      regex.h       mg            help.c        buffer.c
ttykbd.c      regex.c       match.c       fileio.c      basic.c
ttyio.c       re_search.c   main.c        file.c        README
ttydef.h      random.c      macro.h       extend.c      Makefile
tty.c         paragraph.c   macro.c       echo.c
termlib       modes.c       ls            display.c
sysdef.h      mgprog.doc    line.c        dired.c
```

Here's a variation of columnar output. The -x option shows an alphabetized list of names running across the page:

```
$ ls -x
```

```
Makefile      README        basic.c       buffer.c      chrdef.h
cinfo.c       def.h         dir.c         dired.c       display.c
echo.c        extend.c      file.c        fileio.c      help.c
kbd.c         kbd.h         key.h         keymap.c      line.c
ls            macro.c       macro.h       main.c        match.c
mg            mg.tex        mg2a-dos.tar  mg2a.change   mgidx.tex
mgprog.doc    modes.c       paragraph.c   random.c      re_search.c
regex.c       regex.h       region.c      search.c      spawn.c
sys           sysdef.h      termlib       tty.c         ttydef.h
ttyio.c       ttykbd.c      tutorial      tutorial~     version.c
window.c      word.c
```

And here I've reversed the display so that it appears in reverse alphabetic order:

```
$ ls -xr
```

```
word.c        window.c      version.c     tutorial~     tutorial
ttykbd.c      ttyio.c       ttydef.h      tty.c         termlib
sysdef.h      sys           spawn.c       search.c      region.c
```

```
regex.h       regex.c       re_search.c   random.c      paragraph.c
modes.c       mgprog.doc    mgidx.tex     mg2a.change   mg2a-dos.tar
mg.tex        mg            match.c       main.c        macro.h
macro.c       ls            line.c        keymap.c      key.h
kbd.h         kbd.c         help.c        fileio.c      file.c
extend.c      echo.c        display.c     dired.c       dir.c
def.h         cinfo.c       chrdef.h      buffer.c      basic.c
README        Makefile
```

A potentially useful option causes ls to sort the display by one of the three file access or modification times, the time and date the contents of the file was last modified, the time and date the file was last accessed, and the time and date any of the information in the file's i-node was changed. In the following example, the -tc option causes ls to sort by i-node modification time (that is, *c-time*):

```
$ ls -tc
```

```
ls            sysdef.h      help.c        modes.c       display.c
mg            fileio.c      echo.c        main.c        dired.c
tutorial      Makefile      def.h         basic.c       mgidx.tex
tutorial~     mg2a-dos.tar  word.c        macro.h       mg.tex
ttykbd.c      termlib       mgprog.doc    line.c        random.c
tty.c         dir.c         buffer.c      key.h         regex.h
ttyio.c       match.c       window.c      keymap.c      mg2a.change
cinfo.c       re_search.c   version.c     kbd.h         README
ttydef.h      macro.c       search.c      file.c
chrdef.h      regex.c       paragraph.c   kbd.c
spawn.c       sys           region.c      extend.c
```

You probably noticed that that command didn't display the times. For that you need to specify the -l option:

```
$ ls -l
```

```
total 1745
-rw-r--r--  1 pjh      root          2909 Jul 11 13:49 Makefile
-rw-r--r--  1 pjh      root          8005 Jul  3  1988 README
-rw-r--r--  1 pjh      root          9439 Jul  3  1988 basic.c
-rw-r--r--  1 pjh      root         14526 Jul  3  1988 buffer.c
-rw-r--r--  2 pjh      root          1816 Jul  3  1988 chrdef.h
-rw-r--r--  2 pjh      root          3479 Jul  3  1988 cinfo.c
-rw-r--r--  1 pjh      root         10041 Jul  3  1988 def.h
-rw-r--r--  1 pjh      root          1047 Jul  3  1988 dir.c
-rw-r--r--  1 pjh      root          4112 Jul  3  1988 dired.c
-rw-r--r--  1 pjh      root         23355 Jul  3  1988 display.c
-rw-r--r--  1 pjh      root         11834 Jul  3  1988 echo.c
-rw-r--r--  1 pjh      root         19715 Jul  3  1988 extend.c
-rw-r--r--  1 pjh      root         11767 Jul  3  1988 file.c
-rw-r--r--  1 pjh      root          8831 Jul 11 13:49 fileio.c
-rw-r--r--  1 pjh      root          6804 Jul  3  1988 help.c
-rw-r--r--  1 pjh      root          8582 Jul  3  1988 kbd.c
-rw-r--r--  1 pjh      root          1448 Jul  3  1988 kbd.h
-rw-r--r--  1 pjh      root           333 Jul  3  1988 key.h
```

```
-rw-r--r--   1 pjh      root       28610 Jul  3  1988 keymap.c
-rw-r--r--   1 pjh      root       16438 Jul  3  1988 line.c
----------   1 pjh      root        8020 Oct 10 11:38 ls
-rw-r--r--   1 pjh      root        1573 Jul  3  1988 macro.c
-rw-r--r--   1 pjh      root         420 Jul  3  1988 macro.h
-rw-r--r--   1 pjh      root        3154 Jul  3  1988 main.c
-rw-r--r--   1 pjh      root        4412 Jul  3  1988 match.c
-rwxr-xr-x   2 pjh      root      317828 Jul 11 14:52 mg
-rw-r--r--   1 pjh      root       51044 Jul  3  1988 mg.tex
-rw-rw-rw-   1 pjh      root       65536 Jul 11 13:44 mg2a-dos.tar
-rw-r--r--   1 pjh      root        5409 Jul  3  1988 mg2a.change
-rw-r--r--   1 pjh      root        4292 Jul  3  1988 mgidx.tex
-rw-r--r--   1 pjh      root       10905 Jul  3  1988 mgprog.doc
-rw-r--r--   1 pjh      root        3114 Jul  3  1988 modes.c
-rw-r--r--   1 pjh      root        7375 Jul  3  1988 paragraph.c
-rw-r--r--   1 pjh      root       10803 Jul  3  1988 random.c
-rw-r--r--   1 pjh      root       17906 Jul  3  1988 re_search.c
-rw-r--r--   1 pjh      root       43105 Jul  3  1988 regex.c
-rw-r--r--   1 pjh      root        4430 Jul  3  1988 regex.h
-rw-r--r--   1 pjh      root        7226 Jul  3  1988 region.c
-rw-r--r--   1 pjh      root       13958 Jul  3  1988 search.c
-rw-r--r--   1 pjh      root        1564 Jul 11 13:49 spawn.c
drwxr-xr-x  10 pjh      root         160 Jul 11 13:40 sys
-rw-r--r--   1 pjh      root        1041 Jul 11 13:49 sysdef.h
drwxr-xr-x   2 pjh      root         192 Jul 11 13:40 termlib
-rw-r--r--   2 pjh      root       11296 Jul  3  1988 tty.c
-rw-r--r--   2 pjh      root         647 Jul  3  1988 ttydef.h
-rw-r--r--   1 pjh      root        5703 Jul 11 14:51 ttyio.c
-rw-r--r--   2 pjh      root        1128 Jul  3  1988 ttykbd.c
-rw-r--r--   1 pjh      root       24722 Jul 11 14:57 tutorial
-rw-r--r--   1 pjh      root       24697 Jul  3  1988 tutorial~
-rw-r--r--   1 pjh      root         392 Jul  3  1988 version.c
-rw-r--r--   1 pjh      root        9502 Jul  3  1988 window.c
-rw-r--r--   1 pjh      root        5399 Jul  3  1988 word.c
```

The times shown are the times of last modification, the so-called *m-time*. Here's a display of the same information sorted in reverse order by m-time:

```
$ ls -ltr

total 1752
-rw-r--r--   1 pjh      root        8005 Jul  3  1988 README
-rw-r--r--   1 pjh      root       24697 Jul  3  1988 tutorial~
-rw-r--r--   1 pjh      root        5409 Jul  3  1988 mg2a.change
-rw-r--r--   1 pjh      root       10803 Jul  3  1988 random.c
-rw-r--r--   1 pjh      root        4430 Jul  3  1988 regex.h
-rw-r--r--   1 pjh      root       51044 Jul  3  1988 mg.tex
-rw-r--r--   1 pjh      root        4292 Jul  3  1988 mgidx.tex
-rw-r--r--   1 pjh      root        4112 Jul  3  1988 dired.c
-rw-r--r--   1 pjh      root       23355 Jul  3  1988 display.c
-rw-r--r--   1 pjh      root       19715 Jul  3  1988 extend.c
```

```
-rw-r--r--    1 pjh      root         11767 Jul  3  1988 file.c
-rw-r--r--    1 pjh      root          8582 Jul  3  1988 kbd.c
-rw-r--r--    1 pjh      root          1448 Jul  3  1988 kbd.h
-rw-r--r--    1 pjh      root           333 Jul  3  1988 key.h
-rw-r--r--    1 pjh      root         28610 Jul  3  1988 keymap.c
-rw-r--r--    1 pjh      root         16438 Jul  3  1988 line.c
-rw-r--r--    1 pjh      root           420 Jul  3  1988 macro.h
-rw-r--r--    1 pjh      root          3154 Jul  3  1988 main.c
-rw-r--r--    1 pjh      root          9439 Jul  3  1988 basic.c
-rw-r--r--    1 pjh      root          3114 Jul  3  1988 modes.c
-rw-r--r--    1 pjh      root          7375 Jul  3  1988 paragraph.c
-rw-r--r--    1 pjh      root          7226 Jul  3  1988 region.c
-rw-r--r--    1 pjh      root         13958 Jul  3  1988 search.c
-rw-r--r--    1 pjh      root           392 Jul  3  1988 version.c
-rw-r--r--    1 pjh      root          9502 Jul  3  1988 window.c
-rw-r--r--    1 pjh      root          5399 Jul  3  1988 word.c
-rw-r--r--    1 pjh      root         10905 Jul  3  1988 mgprog.doc
-rw-r--r--    1 pjh      root         14526 Jul  3  1988 buffer.c
-rw-r--r--    1 pjh      root         10041 Jul  3  1988 def.h
-rw-r--r--    1 pjh      root         11834 Jul  3  1988 echo.c
-rw-r--r--    1 pjh      root          6804 Jul  3  1988 help.c
-rw-r--r--    1 pjh      root         43105 Jul  3  1988 regex.c
-rw-r--r--    1 pjh      root          1573 Jul  3  1988 macro.c
-rw-r--r--    2 pjh      root          1816 Jul  3  1988 chrdef.h
-rw-r--r--    2 pjh      root          3479 Jul  3  1988 cinfo.c
-rw-r--r--    2 pjh      root           647 Jul  3  1988 ttydef.h
-rw-r--r--    2 pjh      root         11296 Jul  3  1988 tty.c
-rw-r--r--    2 pjh      root          1128 Jul  3  1988 ttykbd.c
-rw-r--r--    1 pjh      root          4412 Jul  3  1988 match.c
-rw-r--r--    1 pjh      root          1047 Jul  3  1988 dir.c
-rw-r--r--    1 pjh      root         17906 Jul  3  1988 re_search.c
drwxr-xr-x   10 pjh      root           160 Jul 11 13:40 sys
drwxr-xr-x    2 pjh      root           192 Jul 11 13:40 termlib
-rw-rw-rw-    1 pjh      root         65536 Jul 11 13:44 mg2a-dos.tar
-rw-r--r--    1 pjh      root          2909 Jul 11 13:49 Makefile
-rw-r--r--    1 pjh      root          1564 Jul 11 13:49 spawn.c
-rw-r--r--    1 pjh      root          1041 Jul 11 13:49 sysdef.h
-rw-r--r--    1 pjh      root          8831 Jul 11 13:49 fileio.c
-rw-r--r--    1 pjh      root          5703 Jul 11 14:51 ttyio.c
-rwxr-xr-x    2 pjh      root        317828 Jul 11 14:52 mg
-rw-r--r--    1 pjh      root         24722 Jul 11 14:57 tutorial
----------    1 pjh      root         11297 Oct 10 11:38 ls
```

If you want to know the i-number of one or more files, use the -i option:

```
$ ls -i
 8308 Makefile      8307 fileio.c      7610 mg.tex         8306 spawn.c
 8181 README        8343 help.c        8342 mg2a-dos.tar   8345 sys
 7895 basic.c       8333 kbd.c         8207 mg2a.change    8310 sysdef.h
 7882 buffer.c      8341 kbd.h         8239 mgidx.tex       8279 termlib
 8363 chrdef.h      8332 key.h         8335 mgprog.doc      8370 tty.c
```

```
8369 cinfo.c       7894 keymap.c      8329 modes.c        8371 ttydef.h
8328 def.h         8309 line.c        8330 paragraph.c    8311 ttyio.c
8276 dir.c         7565 ls            7873 random.c       8372 ttykbd.c
8339 dired.c       8269 macro.c       8278 re_search.c    8129 tutorial
5574 display.c     7878 macro.h       8267 regex.c        7794 tutorial~
8227 echo.c        7257 main.c        7847 regex.h        8072 version.c
7497 extend.c      8270 match.c       8327 region.c       7637 window.c
8126 file.c        7422 mg            4081 search.c       7413 word.c
```

The -s option causes a display of file sizes in blocks (usually 512 bytes):

```
$ ls -s
```

```
total 1760         19 fileio.c      129 mg2a-dos.tar     3 sysdef.h
    6 Makefile      15 help.c         12 mg2a.change      1 termlib
   17 README        18 kbd.c           9 mgidx.tex       24 tty.c
   20 basic.c        3 kbd.h          23 mgprog.doc       2 ttydef.h
   30 buffer.c       1 key.h           7 modes.c         13 ttyio.c
    4 chrdef.h      57 keymap.c       16 paragraph.c      3 ttykbd.c
    7 cinfo.c       34 line.c         23 random.c        50 tutorial
   21 def.h         32 ls             36 re_search.c     50 tutorial~
    3 dir.c          4 macro.c        86 regex.c          1 version.c
    9 dired.c        1 macro.h         9 regex.h         20 window.c
   47 display.c      7 main.c         16 region.c        12 word.c
   25 echo.c         9 match.c        29 search.c
   40 extend.c     627 mg             4 spawn.c
   24 file.c       101 mg.tex          1 sys
```

The -a option adds the "hidden files"—those having names that begin
with a dot (.)—to the display.

```
$ ls -a
```

```
.                display.c      ls             modes.c        termlib
..               echo.c         macro.c        paragraph.c    tty.c
Makefile         extend.c       macro.h        random.c       ttydef.h
README           file.c         main.c         re_search.c    ttyio.c
basic.c          fileio.c       match.c        regex.c        ttykbd.c
buffer.c         help.c         mg             regex.h        tutorial
chrdef.h         kbd.c          mg.tex         region.c       tutorial~
cinfo.c          kbd.h          mg2a-dos.tar   search.c       version.c
def.h            key.h          mg2a.change    spawn.c        window.c
dir.c            keymap.c       mgidx.tex      sys            word.c
dired.c          line.c         mgprog.doc     sysdef.h
```

Finally, if you want a one-column display—the old System V Release 3
standard for ls—use the -1 (that's a *one*, not an *ell*) option.

The echo Command

The echo command simply displays its arguments on the screen (stdout) and then outputs a new line. It's useful for sending messages from within a shell script and for displaying the values of shell variables. For example:

```
$ echo $LOGNAME

pjh
```

or

```
$ echo This                    is     fun!

This is fun
```

The pwd Command

They don't come any simpler than pwd. It has no options and takes no arguments. It prints the full pathname of the current ("working") directory:

```
$ pwd

/usr/pjh/tools
```

The cd Command

The cd command can take a directory name, as either a full or relative pathname, as an argument. It then makes the directory you specify the new working directory. If the argument you supply is not a complete pathname, cd attempts to find a suitable directory relative to one of the paths specified by the CDPATH environmental variable. For example, suppose you are logged into your home directory (/usr/pjh) and the computer has other directories, named /u2/uP and /u1/notes (Note: /usr/pjh/uP and /u2/uP/unix do not exist):

```
$ echo $CDPATH

:/u2:/u1/notes
```

3

Now give a `cd` command that does not include an absolute or relative pathname but does include the name of a directory that's a subdirectory of one of the paths in your CDPATH variable:

$ cd uP

/u2/uP

$ pwd

/u2/uP

Here's another `cd` command of the same type:

$ cd unix

/u1/notes/unix

$ pwd

/u1/notes/unix

If you type `cd` with no argument, your home directory will be the new working directory.

If you're using the Korn shell and enter `cd -`, you'll be moved into the previous working directory. For example:

$ pwd

/usr/pjh

$ cd /usr/spool/uucppublic/pjh/from/princeton

$ pwd

/usr/spool/uucppublic/pjh/from/princeton

$ cd

$ pwd

/usr/pjh

$ cd -

$ pwd

/usr/spool/uucppublic/pjh/from/princeton

That can save a lot of typing!

The cp Command

This command copies a file to another file or to a directory. For example:

```
$ cp myfile newfile
```

makes a duplicate copy of myfile in the same directory and gives it the name newfile. On the other hand

```
$ cp myfile ..
```

makes a duplicate of myfile in the parent of the current directory; the new file also is named myfile. And, if that's not enough

```
$ cp myfile ../newname
```

copies myfile to the parent of the current directory and calls it newname.

If the last argument is a directory name, you can supply several filenames as arguments to cp. For example

```
$ cp file1 file2 file3 file4 ..
```

makes duplicates of the files *file[1-4]* in the parent of the current directory.

The cp command has several options that are discussed in Part III.

The mv Command

The mv command is related to cp. In fact, they do much the same thing, although mv has an additional step: after it makes the copy, it removes the original. That is, mv is functionally equivalent to executing cp followed by rm.

The following command has the effect of changing the name of the file from myfile to newfile:

```
$ mv myfile newfile
```

The next example moves myfile from the current directory to the parent:

```
$ mv myfile ..
```

The rm Command

The rm command is related to both cp and mv. It simply removes the file from the given directory. If no directory is specified, rm uses the current directory.

The syntax is

```
$ rm file
```

With the -r option specified, rm can also be used to remove directories:

```
$ rm -r
```

The who Command

The who command reports certain information about logged-in users, and, with some of its more esoteric options, about processes initiated by init. It also reports on reboots, changes to the system clock, and logoffs. Invoking who with no options or arguments yields the following:

```
$ who

juucp      tty00        Sep 28 11:13
pjh        slan05       Sep 28 12:08
```

The output shows that juucp, who logged in at 11:13, and pjh, who logged in at 12:08, are currently logged in. Notice that juucp is logged in on a *tty* line (actually, juucp is a neighboring site that called in over a modem) and that pjh logged in over a network (STARLAN, to be precise, shortened to slan in who's output).

The -u option adds the "time since last activity" (also called the *idle time*) and the process ID number for each logged-in user.

Note: If the user has been active in the last minute, who displays a dot (.) for the idle time.

```
$ who -u

juucp      tty00        Sep 28 11:13    .     5890
pjh        slan05       Sep 28 12:08    .     7354
```

The -T option reports a plus sign (+) if the terminal is writable by you, or a minus sign (-) if it is not. You can send a message to a user at a writable terminal (see mesg in Part III, the reference section).

```
$ who -T

juucp      + tty00      Sep 28 11:13
pjh        + slan05     Sep 28 12:08
```

The -H option causes who to put a heading on its output:

```
$ who -H

NAME       LINE       TIME
juucp      tty00      Sep 28 11:13
pjh        slan05     Sep 28 12:08
```

and the -q (or "quick") option simply shows login IDs and a count of the logged in users:

```
$ who -q

juucp    pjh
# users=2
```

If you want to know when the system was last booted, use -b:

```
$ who -b

    .          system boot   Sep 24 11:33
```

The other options are discussed in Part III.

The ps Command

The ps command displays information about active processes. Invoked without options, ps reports on the processes associated with your terminal.

```
$ ps

   PID TTY       TIME COMMAND
  3084 slan04    0:00 ttysrv
  3085 slan04    0:02 ksh
  3125 slan04    0:00 ps
```

Notice that ps, unlike the usual UNIX command, outputs a heading line by default. This indicates that the output of ps really is not intended to be piped to some other command. You can do this, but you would need to strip off the heading to get at the information. PID is the process ID of the COMMAND that is running. TTY is the process's *controlling terminal*. TIME is the cumulative execution time for the process. This number is far less than the clock time that has expired since the process began executing, because other processes need access to the central processor—and they get it.

Invoked with the -e options, ps reports on all processes currently running:

```
$ ps -e

   PID TTY       TIME COMMAND
     0 ?         0:07 sched
     1 ?        15:31 init
     2 ?         0:01 vhand
     3 ?         2:28 bdflush
  2360 console   0:00 getty
  1034 tty00     3:44 uucico
  3075 ?         0:00 uugetty
   107 ?         0:00 cat
    85 ?         0:27 cron
    89 ?         0:28 lpsched
  3058 ttyaa     0:00 uugetty
   112 ?         0:00 msgdmn
   113 ?         0:01 srvacct
  1067 ?         0:25 msnetfs
  3084 slan04    0:00 ttysrv
  3085 slan04    0:02 ksh
  3127 slan04    0:00 ps
 26094 ttyah     0:00 uugetty
 26101 ?         0:01 admdaemo
 26162 ?         0:00 listen
```

A question mark (?) means that the process does not have a controlling terminal.

The date Command

The date command does only one thing when used by an ordinary user: it tells you the date and the time. The system administrator can use date to set the date and the time.

```
$ date
```

```
Sat Sep 28 1:45:58 EDT 1991
```

This is the simplest form of executing the date command, but not the most useful. This command has many options that let you extract any part of the usual output and display that part alone or in combination with other parts. First, let's look at the individual options. The option string begins with a plus sign (+) and each option present is preceded with a percent sign (%). Ordinary text can be included in the option string, as you will see in the next example. This is not the usual case for UNIX commands; the most common beginning for an option string is the dash (-)! Also, it is good practice to enclose the option string in quotes—either single or double—so that the shell won't interpret any characters in the ordinary text portion that it believes are metacharacters.

The a option outputs the abbreviated name of the day, and the A option provides the unabbreviated name:

```
$ date +%a
```

```
Sat
```

```
$ date +%A
```

```
Saturday
```

The b option outputs the abbreviated name of the month, and the B options provides the unabbreviated name:

```
$ date +%b
```

```
Sep
```

```
$ date +%B
```

```
September
```

The d option provides the day of the month in two-digit numeric form, and the e option outputs the day of the month with a space preceding the day for days 1 to 9:

```
$ date +%d
```

```
28
```

```
$ date +%e
```

```
28
```

If you executed these two commands again early the next month—on the fourth, for example—you would see the following:

```
$ date +%d
```

```
4
```

```
$ date +%e
```

```
 4
```

The D outputs the common numerical date format used in the United States: month/day/year. There are other options that output the date in the format for whatever country was specified when SVR4 was installed: c, x, or X. If you designated a country other than the United States during installation, please try these options on your own: their output is different for different countries.

```
$ date +%D
```

```
09/28/91
```

Options H and I output the hour in numeric form: H in 24 hour or military form, and I in 12 hour form:

```
$ date +%H
```

```
13
```

```
$ date +%I
```

```
1
```

The j option is rather interesting. It outputs the so-called "Julian" date—the day as one of the 365 (or 366 in a leap year) days of the year. This is useful in a calculation of elapsed time between two dates:

```
$ date +%j
```

```
271
```

The U and W options both output the week as one of the 52 (53 in a leap year) weeks of the year. They differ in that U begins the week with Sunday, and W begins the week with Monday.

```
$ date +%U
```

```
39
```

```
$ date +%W
```

```
39
```

The m option outputs the month as one of the 12 months of the year:

```
$ date +%m
```

```
09
```

The M option gives the minutes value in the range 00 to 59, and the S option shows the seconds value in the range 00 to 61 (to allow for a "leap second" or two):

```
$ date +%M
```

```
48
```

```
$ date +%S
```

```
41
```

The R option combines the H and M options, and T combines H, M, and S:

```
$ date +%R
```

```
13:48
```

```
$ date +%T
```

```
13:48:51
```

The p option outputs either AM or PM, and r combines I, M, S, and p:

```
$ date +%p
```

```
AM
```

```
$ date +%r
```

```
1:48:25 AM
```

The w option shows the day of the week as a number between 0 and 6, with 0 representing Sunday:

```
$ date +%w
```

```
6
```

The y option shows the year as a number between 00 and 99, and the Y option shows the year as a four-digit value:

```
$ date +%y
```

```
91
```

```
$ date +%Y
```

```
1991
```

The Z option outputs the abbreviated time zone name for your computer.

```
$ date +%Z
```

```
EDT
```

You can combine two or more options along with text strings to produce more descriptive outputs, such as the following:

```
$ date "+Today is %A, the %e of %B, %Y"
```

```
Today is Saturday, the 28 of September, 1991
```

The set Command

The shell built-in command `set` has two major functions of interest to users who are building tools. One involves the shell special variables 1, 2, and so on. If you invoke `set` with arguments, it assigns each argument, in order, to one of the shell special variables. Retrieve the values of these variables by prefixing the name of the variable with the character $, as usual. The other use is to invoke `set` with no arguments. This results in a display of all of the environment variables and their values.

For example, here's a partial list of the output of the `set` command I executed on my system:

```
$ set

CDPATH=:/usr/local/bin:/usr/spool/uucppublic/pjh
EDITOR=/usr/local/bin/emacs
ENV=/usr/pjh/.env
ERRNO=25
HISTFILE=/usr/pjh/.sh_history
HOME=/usr/pjh
HOSTNAME=mccc
HZ=100
IFS=

KSH=/bin/ksh
LINENO=1
LOCAL=/usr/local/bin
LOGNAME=pjh
MAIL=/usr/mail/pjh
MAILCHECK=180
MAILER=/usr/bin/mailx
OPTIND=0
ORGANIZATION=The College on the Other Side of U. S. ONE
PAGER=/usr/local/bin/less
PATH=:/bin:/usr/bin:/usr/vmsys/bin:/usr/ccs/bin:/usr/local/bin
PWD=/usr/pjh/tools
RANDOM=26818
SECONDS=2
SHELL=/bin/ksh
TEMP=/usr/tmp
TERM=vt100
TERMCAP=/etc/termcap
TMOUT=900
TMP=/usr/tmp
TZ=EST5EDT
VISUAL=/usr/local/bin/emacs
```

Some of these system variables were explained in Chapter 1; other variables are "personal" and have no significance to anyone but this system's owner.

Here's an example of assigning values to the special shell variables that have numbers as their names. Notice that no assignment statement is used, nor is one permitted.

```
$ set a b c

$ echo $1

a

$ echo $3 $2 $1

c b a
```

A very useful tool results from the ability to combine set with the output of a back-quoted command (see Chapter 1). Each word of the output is assigned to one of the special shell variables, in order. For example, the output of the date command looks like this:

```
Sat Sep 28 10:45:58 EDT 1991
```

If you combined this output with set by entering

```
$ set `date`
```

you would assign Sat to the first special variable, Sep to the second special variable, 28 to the third, and so on. As the following example shows, you then could retrieve any of their values in any order:

```
$ echo $1 $6 $3

Sat 1991 28
```

In some respects, this is easier to use than calling up date with the appropriate options, because no one remembers all of date's options.

You will use set fairly often in your tools.

The cat Command

The cat command gets its name from the word *catenate*, an obsolete word that is related to the more modern word, *concatenate*. The dictionary defines *concatenate* as "link together in a series or chain." Thus

```
$ cat file1 file2 file3
```

sends the contents of the three files, one after the other as if they were chained together, to stdout. cat frequently has its output redirected to a file. If you were writing a book consisting of four parts and you wanted to send your publisher one file that contained all four parts, the following command would do it:

```
$ cat part1 part2 part3 part4 > mybook
```

You can force `cat` to take its input from stdin either by using redirection, by using the minus sign (-) as one of the filename arguments, or by omitting all arguments. For example, here's `cat` with no arguments:

```
$ cat
```

this is cat

```
this is cat
```

taking input from stdin and

```
taking input from stdin and
```

echoing it as soon as I hit <Enter>!

```
echoing it as soon as I hit <Enter>!
```

If you issue the command

```
$ echo foo ¦ cat file1 - file2
```

`cat` sends the contents of `file1` to the screen, then gets the output of the `echo` command (the string `foo`) and prints `foo`. Finally, `cat` sends the contents of `file2` to the screen. For another example, suppose you have a file called `begin` that contains

```
The following are the contents of my home directory:
```

followed by a blank line, and another file, called end, that contains

```
as of October 1, 1991.
```

followed by a blank line. The following command

```
$ ls ¦ cat begin - end > myfiles
```

creates a file called myfiles that contains the following:

```
The following are the contents of my home directory:
total 60
-rw-r--r--   1 pjh      root         1605 Sep  9 16:17 awk
drwxr-xr-x   4 pjh      root           64 Sep 14 15:16 book
-rw-r--r--   1 pjh      root         1989 Sep  9 16:17 cmd.line
-rw-r--r--   1 pjh      root          430 Sep  9 11:39 diff
-rw-r--r--   1 pjh      root         4814 Sep  9 16:17 ksh.prompt
-rw-r--r--   1 pjh      root        11044 Sep  9 16:17 ksh.prompts
-rw-------   1 pjh      root         1879 Sep 11 08:24 priv.user
-rw-r--r--   1 pjh      root         1174 Sep  9 16:17 pwd
-rw-r--r--   1 pjh      root         4471 Sep 12 10:27 raw-cooked
-rw-r--r--   1 pjh      root          493 Sep  9 16:17 sed
as of October 1, 1991.
```

If the file you want to cat includes some nonprinting characters, cat -v displays them in a special form.

Note: Tabs, newline characters, and form feed characters continue to be ignored. The special form depends on the ASCII code of the particular nonprinting character. If the code is in the range octal 000 to octal 037, cat's display is ^*n*, where *n* is the corresponding ASCII character in the range octal 100 to octal 137, that is, one on the following characters:

@ A B C... X Y Z [\ ] ^)

(See the ASCII code table in Appendix A.) The Del character displays as ^?. Other nonprintables display as M-*n*, where *n* is the character from the range octal 000 to octal 037 and 100 to 137.

If you want to display each tab as ^I and each form feed character as ^L, the correct option to cat is -vt. To get new line characters to display as dollar signs ($), use -ve. If you want to see everything, use -vte.

If cat can't find a file that's one of its arguments, it outputs an error message unless you use the -s (for "silent") option. To see the error message on your machine, enter the following command:

```
$ cat ´doors: paws too slippery´
```

The pg Command

The pg command sends the contents of a text file to the screen, a screenful at a time. This is an improvement over cat, which sends the contents to stdout without regard to screen size—or anything else, for that matter. (Some would call pg a "user-friendly feature.") You can scan forward or backward through a file and search for a pattern represented by a regular expression. Chapter 4 examines pg in detail. For now, simply understand that you can use pg to scan a file like this:

```
$ pg filename
```

The mkdir Command

The mkdir command enables you to create one or more new directories (provided you have permission to write in their parents). For example, suppose you were logged into your home directory—where you surely would have write permission—and entered

```
$ mkdir my-c-progs my-datafiles
```

This would create two new subdirectories under your home directory.

Information Retrievers

3

Many UNIX commands retrieve information—data or status—about a great many aspects of your system and its environment. You can combine these commands with others that process information to create reports.

The wc Command

The wc command is an innocent-looking command that counts the number of lines, words, and characters in a file. If you enter

```
$ wc REfile
```

(REfile is a file that Chapter 2 mentioned in its discussion of regular expressions), you get

```
$ wc REfile

    15     120     740 REfile
```

Here wc reports the number of lines, the number of words, the number of characters in REfile, and the name REfile. You can, of course, instruct wc to report on just one of these attributes by selecting the appropriate option:

```
$ wc -w REfile

    120 REfile
```

```
$ wc -l REfile

    15 REfile
```

```
$ wc -c REfile

    740 REfile
```

wc, however, is a *filter*. A filter is a program that can take its input from stdin and sends it to stdout. So wc is a little special: if you specify a filename on the command line, wc opens that file and reads its contents. If you don't specify a filename on the command line, wc expects input from stdin. For example:

```
$ wc -l < REfile
      15
```

In this case, I redirected stdin so that wc got its input from a file. But because wc didn't know that the input was coming from a file, it didn't echo the name of the file! The following example pipes the output of a command into wc:

```
$ cat REfile ¦ wc -l
      15
```

In both cases, wc merely reported the number of lines without further comment.

The importance of this is that wc can be used to count anything that is word- or line-oriented, such as the output of a good number of UNIX commands. For example, on my system I tried this while logged into the home directory:

```
$ ls ¦ wc -l
     139
```

Looks like the home directory needs some housekeeping!

wc can also count the number of users currently logged in:

```
$ who ¦ wc -l
7
```

The id Command

The id command reports four things: user ID number, login name, group ID number, and group name. If the real and effective IDs (see Chapter 1) are not the same, id prints both sets of values:

```
$ id
uid=102(pjh) gid=0(root)
```

Here the user ID is 102, the login name is pjh, and the user belongs to the root group, ID number 0.

The find Command

The find command probably is new to you, but it's one of the most useful commands in the toolmaker's kit. It lets you locate a file by any one or more criteria you supply. The most commonly used criteria include the following:

- A pattern to match the filename ("find all files whose names end in .c")

- The owner's login name or number ("find all files owned by pjh")

- The file's size ("find all files larger than 512000 characters")

- The time it was last accessed ("find all files that have not been accessed in the last 30 days")

The find command takes two arguments: a directory name (or possibly a list of directory names) and an expression. The directory list tells find where to begin; the expression tells find what to do.

For example, suppose you want to locate all files on your computer that have names ending in .c. Your starting place would therefore be the root directory. find searches the root directory, then visits each subdirectory under root, then each subdirectory under each of those, and so on. In this way, find visits every directory on the computer *if* you have access and read permissions for all of them. If you don't, find outputs an error message and continues visiting those you do have permission for.

You can use over 20 different expressions with find and can also combine expressions. The simplest expression is -print. For example

```
$ find /usr/home/ajh -print
```

causes the following list to be output:

```
find: cannot chdir to /usr/home/ajh/Mail
find: cannot chdir to /usr/home/ajh/.elm
/usr/home/ajh
/usr/home/ajh/.profile
/usr/home/ajh/.sh_history
/usr/home/ajh/LAST
/usr/home/ajh/.lastlogin
/usr/home/ajh/Mail
/usr/home/ajh/News
/usr/home/ajh/News/review
/usr/home/ajh/News/Misc.forsale
/usr/home/ajh/News/bbs
/usr/home/ajh/News/historylist
/usr/home/ajh/News/jrrt
/usr/home/ajh/News/rec
/usr/home/ajh/News/rec/arts
```

```
/usr/home/ajh/News/rec/arts/sf-lovers
/usr/home/ajh/.env
/usr/home/ajh/.signature
/usr/home/ajh/.oldnewsrc
/usr/home/ajh/.article
/usr/home/ajh/.newsrc
/usr/home/ajh/.pnewsexpert
/usr/home/ajh/.letter
/usr/home/ajh/.elm
/usr/home/ajh/.rnlast
/usr/home/ajh/.rnsoft
/usr/home/ajh/SCHED
```

Notice that `find` was prevented from entering /usr/home/ajh/.elm and /usr/home/ajh/Mail because whoever executed `find` didn't have read and access permissions for those directories. Here are all of user `ajh`'s directories:

```
$ ls -al /usr/home/ajh

total 148
drwxrwxr-x    5 ajh      other         448 Sep  8 23:35 .
drwxrwxr-x    8 root     root          128 Sep 24 15:14 ..
drwx------    2 ajh      other         128 Sep  8 23:34 .elm
drwx------    2 ajh      others       1328 Aug  4 05:17 Mail
drwxr-xr-x    3 ajh      others       1600 Jul 17 12:27 News
```

Notice that `find` had no trouble entering /usr/home/ajh/News.

The `-print` expression takes no arguments and is always true, so that whenever you use it, `find` prints what it finds. Conversely, if you omit `-print`, `find` is silent.

A slightly more restrictive search occurs if, in addition to `-print`, you specify the `-name` expression and an argument that is a pathname. You can use shell metacharacters in the pathname so that `find` looks for multiple files. For example

```
$ find /usr/pjh -name '*.c' -print
```

caused the following to be printed to my screen:

```
/usr/pjh/myfind.c
/usr/pjh/c/p4a.c
/usr/pjh/c/168q2p5.c
/usr/pjh/c/p333.c
/usr/pjh/c/side.c
/usr/pjh/c/gwyn.c
/usr/pjh/c/friedel.c
/usr/pjh/c/trans.c
/usr/pjh/c/10.10.c
/usr/pjh/c/last.c
/usr/pjh/c/fp4.c
```

3

```
/usr/pjh/c/tire1.c
/usr/pjh/c/ep4.c
/usr/pjh/mg2a/echo.c
/usr/pjh/mg2a/help.c
/usr/pjh/mg2a/sys/bsd/fileio.c
/usr/pjh/mg2a/sys/bsd/spawn.c
/usr/pjh/mg2a/sys/bsd/ttyio.c
/usr/pjh/mg2a/termlib/tgoto.c
/usr/pjh/mg2a/termlib/tputs.c
/usr/pjh/mg2a/termlib/ttest.c
/usr/pjh/mg2a/fileio.c
/usr/pjh/mg2a/spawn.c
/usr/pjh/mg2a/ttyio.c
/usr/pjh/mg2a/cinfo.c
/usr/pjh/mg2a/tty.c
/usr/pjh/mg2a/ttykbd.c
/usr/pjh/hello.c
```

Notice that I quoted the pathname to protect it from the shell.

To make things even more interesting, find permits you to combine expressions using the logical operators NOT (!), AND (-a), and OR (-o). Such expressions must be enclosed in *escaped* parentheses. (See Chapter 2 for a discussion on escaping.) I use the OR operator in the example for -prune, which follows.

In addition to the -print expression, a few other expressions are always true:

- -depth causes find to operate on the files in the directory specified before operating on the directory itself.

- -mount restricts find's search to the physical file system containing the directory that you specified as the starting point. This is useful if another file system is mounted on a directory lower in the hierarchy of directories than the starting point for the search and you do not want to search the other file system.

- -follow permits find to include symbolic links in its search path.

> **Caution:** Do not use this expression if you need to use the -type l expression. (More on -type follows.)

- -prune is used with the -name expression to designate that find should not examine any directories below the one designated as the argument to -name. For example, here's a list of all files ending with .c, beginning with the parent of my current directory:

```
$ find .. -name '*.c' -print
```

```
../vsdiff/regcmp.c
../vsdiff/vsdiff.c
../vsdiff/regex.c
../vsdiff/vsdiff3.c
../vsdiff/vsdiff2.c
../vsdiff/ORIG/vsdiff.c
../vsdiff/ORIG/vsdiff2.c
../asdiff/asdiff.c
../lib/filename.c
../lib/diffcmp.c
../lib/get_help_idx.c
../lib/maphint.c
../lib/get_hint.c
../lib/getdiff.c
../lib/diffmrg.c
../lib/ORIG/maphint.c
../mdiff/mdiff.c
../mdiff/hdiff.c
```

Now let's find all the files with names ending in `.c` *except* those in lib and its subdirectory, lib/ORIG:

```
$ find .. -name lib -prune -o -name '*.c' -print
```

```
../vsdiff/regcmp.c
../vsdiff/vsdiff.c
../vsdiff/regex.c
../vsdiff/vsdiff3.c
../vsdiff/vsdiff2.c
../vsdiff/ORIG/vsdiff.c
../vsdiff/ORIG/vsdiff2.c
../asdiff/asdiff.c
../mdiff/mdiff.c
../mdiff/hdiff.c
```

Notice that I had to supply two criteria: "not down the lib hierarchy" and "name ending in `.c`". If you omitted the latter, and made it

```
$ find .. -name lib -prune -print
```

find would still not have visited the lib hierarchy, and would have printed the names of *all* files in all the other hierarchies!

Other expressions specifying search criteria include the following:

- `-atime [+-]`*number* asks find to look at the time the file was last accessed (see Chapter 1). *number*, without a plus or minus sign, means "accessed exactly *number* days ago."

> **Note:** If you prepend a + to *number*, find identifies files that were accessed more than *number* days ago; if you prepend a - to *number*, find identifies files that were accessed less than *number* days ago.

For example:

```
find . -atime +7 -print
```

lists all the files in the current directory that were last accessed more than a week ago.

* -ctime [+-]*number* refers to the myfile of days since the last time the file's i-node was modified (see Chapter 1).

> **Note:** If you prepend a + to number, find identifies files whose i-nodes were modified more than *number* days ago; if you prepend a - to *number*, find identifies files whose i-nodes were modified less than *number* days ago.

* -mtime [+-]*number* refers to the number of days since the contents of the file were changed (see Chapter 1). (See -atime.) If the file is a directory, this refers to the number of days since a file was created in or removed from the directory.

> **Note:** If you prepend a + to *number*, find identifies files whose contents were changed more than *number* days ago; if you prepend a - to *number*, find identifies files whose contents were changed less than *number* days ago.

* -newer *filename* identifies files that have been modified more recently than the file *filename*.

* -perm [-]*number* asks find to search for a file that has the specified permissions. *number* must be given in octal. Recall that rwxrwxrwx is octal 777, r-xr-xr-x is octal 555, and so on. If the optional minus sign is omitted, find looks for an exact match between *number* and the file's permissions. If the minus is included, find does not check for unspecified permissions. For example:

```
find . -perm 777 -print
```

and

```
find . -perm -777 -print
```

both tell `find` to look for files with rwxrwxrwx permissions. However, although

```
find . -perm 755 -print
```

tells `find` to match files with rwxr-xr-x permissions

```
find . -perm -755 -print
```

instructs `find` to ignore whether either group or others have write permission. Thus the last command would match files having any of the following permissions:

```
rwxr-xr-x
rwxrwxr-x
rwxr-xrwx
rwxrwxrwx
```

- `-type [bcdlpf]` tells `find` to look for a file of the specified type:

  b for "block special file"

  c for "character special file"

  d for "directory file"

  l for "symbolic link"

  p for "named pipe"

  f for "regular file"

  For example:

  ```
  find . -type d -print
  ```

  prints the names of all directories and subdirectories in the hierarchy of the current directory.

- `-user` *name* and `-group` *name* identify a file by its owner's login name or user ID number, or by the name or number of the group associated with the file.

- `-nouser` and `-nogroup` identify a file whose owner is not found in /etc/passwd or whose group is not found in /etc/group.

- `-links [+-]`number finds files that have exactly number links.

> **Note:** If you prepend a + to *number*, find identifies files with more than *number* links; if you prepend a - to *numberr*, find identifies files with fewer than *number* links.

- `-inum [+-]number` finds the file(s) that have the specified i-node number. (I say *file(s)* because there may be more than one file with a given i-number if find visits more than one file system in its search.)

> **Note:** If you prepend a + to *number*, then find identifies files whose i-number is greater than *number*; if you prepend a - to number, then find identifies files whose i-number is smaller than *number*.

- `-size [+-]numberr[c]` identifies files that are exactly *number* blocks long (where a block is taken as 512 bytes). For example, a file that is five blocks long has anywhere from 2049 to 2600 bytes—that is, from four blocks plus one byte to exactly five bytes long. If you append the letter c to *number*, find identifies files that are exactly *number* bytes long.

> **Note:** If you prepend a + to *number*, then find identifies files whose size is more than *number* blocks (or bytes, if c is used), and if you prepend a - to *number*, then find identifies files whose size is less than *number* blocks (or bytes, if c is used).

One of the neatest things you can do with find (other than printing the names of files it finds or piping the list to another command) is to cause a command to be executed on the files in the list. find has two methods of specifying this: an unconditional one and an interactive one. For example, the expression -exec *command* executes *command* unconditionally on every file it finds, and the expression -ok *command* prompts you with a question mark before it executes *command* on each file it finds. To execute *command*, you must enter y.

Here is a command a professor could use (running as *root*) to visit the directory of each of the students taking his course and copy all their project files into his current directory:

```
find /u1/fall91/dp168 -name "[Pp][Rr][1-4]*c" -exec cp {} . \;
```

The project filename is assumed to begin with the letters PR or pr and ends in c. The -exec portion refers to each file in the list of files found by the strange notation {}. Also, find requires that you add \; to the end of *command*. If you run the following conditional version

```
find /u1/fall91/dp168 -name "[Pp][Rr][1-4]*c" -ok cp {} . \;
```

the result looks like this:

```
< cp ... /u1/fall91/dp168/allen/PR1A-allen.c >?     y
< cp ... /u1/fall91/dp168/dintron/PR1A-dintron.c >?    y
< cp ... /u1/fall91/dp168/norcros/test/PR1A_norcros.c >?    y
< cp ... /u1/fall91/dp168/wight/PR1A-wight.c >?    n
< cp ... /u1/fall91/dp168/delucia/PR1A-delucia.c >?    n
< cp ... /u1/fall91/dp168/dimemmo/PR1A-dimemmo.c >?    n
< cp ... /u1/fall91/dp168/fuchs/PR1A-fuchs.c >?    y
< cp ... /u1/fall91/dp168/lane/PR1A-lane.c >?    y
< cp ... /u1/fall91/dp168/nadaraj/PR1A-nadaraj.c >?    y
< cp ... /u1/fall91/dp168/small/PR1A-small.c >?    y
```

Earlier I used the OR logical operator with -prune. Here's another example of using logical operators with find. Suppose you want to remove old backup files created by your word processor and editors. Further, suppose that these programs use bak and ~ to signify backup files. Your command might be

```
find $HOME \( -name "*bak" -o -name "*~" \) -exec rm {} \;
```

The spaces after \(and before \) are absolutely mandatory. The logic here says "find every file that has a name that ends either in bak or in ~." That means that every file that meets either criterion is found. Also, don't forget that this command removes files named *bak and *~ not only from your home directory but also from every directory below your home!

In the last section, I used wc to count the number of files in a home directory. Because find is a more versatile command than ls, let's write some commands that count files in all directories in and under the home directory, and count just directories in the home hierarchy. You might think that

```
$ find $HOME -print -exec wc -l {} \;
```

would be just what you want, but it isn't. This command finds each file in the home directory and passes its name to -exec, one at a time.Then wc reports the number of lines in that file, and does that for every file in the home hierarchy. Instead, let's pipe the list of names to a wc command:

```
$ find $HOME -print | wc -l
```

830

Let's see how many of those files are directories:

```
$ find $HOME -print -type d | wc -l
```

> 830

That's not right! The find command examines the expressions from left to right, so first it printed and then it looked for files of type d. Here's the correct command:

```
$ find $HOME -type d -print | wc -l
```

> 53

Now let's use the logical NOT operator to find how many files in my home hierarchy are not directory files:

```
$ find $HOME ! -type d -print | wc -l
```

> 777

The expression -type d refers to files of type d, but the expression ! -type d refers to files that are not of type d. This might lead you to believe that ! means "NOT."

Chapter 1 mentioned the setuid and setgid bits in its discussion of permissions. Recall that a program with setuid permission executes with the permissions of the file's owner rather than those of the user causing the command to be executed. By using a find command with the appropriate expression, you can identify which files have these bits set, so you can then determine whether any of the files pose security problems. Here's the command:

```
find / \( -perm -4000 -o -perm -2000 \) -print
```

The tee Command

The tee command is one of those simple little programs that defy classification but are handy to have around. You put tee in a pipeline and it "siphons off" a copy of what's being piped in and writes it to a file. For that reason, tee often is called a "pipe fitting."

The syntax of tee is

```
tee [-i] [-a] file(s)
```

and a simple example is

```
$ who | tee users | wc -l
```

> 3

The presence of tee has not affected the operation of the original pipeline who | wc -1—the new command still reports the correct number of users currently logged in. However, this command creates the file users and dumps the output of who into it. In other words, tee takes the output of who and sends the output to two places: the users file and stdout (for piping to wc -1). Chapter 11 lists the options for the tee command.

Summary

This chapter reviewed some commands that you have had previous experience with, and introduced two new ones, find and tee.

I subtly emphasize the ways you use your old friends in tool building—perhaps you noticed that a number of examples used pipes with several commands and some added redirection as well. A number of examples used filters in the pipelines. These are the building blocks for creating tools.

3

Examining Text Files

C hapter 3 reviewed several System V Release 4 commands that you knew about and introduced a few that might have been new to you. One of them, find, is a wonderful command because it lets you locate files by specifying one or more things you know about the file: any part of its name, its size, and so on. After you find a file you're looking for, you can view its contents, modify them, and perhaps extract a portion for use elsewhere. The simplest thing to do is to just look, so in this chapter you will see how to find out what's inside files. The files that we are most interested in working with are text files—it's dangerous to manipulate binary files!—and the following commands are designed to work with text files.

"Look But Don't Touch" Commands

UNIX provides several commands that let you look at a portion or all of one or more text files. Use one of these commands when you want only to read the contents.

The `tail` Command

Use the `tail` command to look at the last few lines of a file. This is helpful when you have a large file and want to look only at the end. For example, suppose you want to see the last few entries in the log file that records the transactions that occur when files are transferred between your machine and a neighboring machine. That log file may be large, and you surely don't want to have to read all of the beginning and middle just to get to the end.

By default, `tail` prints the last 10 lines of a file to stdout (by default, the screen). For example:

```
$ cat names
```

results in

```
allen christopher
babinchak david
best betty
bloom dennis
boelhower joseph
bose anita
cacossa ray
chang liang
crawford patricia
crowley charles
cuddy michael
czyzewski sharon
delucia joseph
```

but

```
$ tail names
```

shows you

```
bloom dennis
boelhower joseph
bose anita
cacossa ray
chang liang
crawford patricia
crowley charles
cuddy michael
czyzewski sharon
delucia joseph
```

However, you can change this by specifying the number of lines to print. For example:

```
$ tail -5 names
```

prints the last five lines of names:

```
crawford patricia
crowley charles
cuddy michael
czyzewski sharon
delucia joseph
```

`tail` also can follow a file; that is, it can continue looking at a file as a program continues to add text to its end. The syntax is

```
tail -f logfile
```

where `logfile` is the name of the file being written to. If you're logged in on a busy system, try one of these:

$ **tail -f /var/uucp/.Log/uucico/***neighbor*

or

$ **tail -f /var/uucp/.Log/uuxqt/***neighbor*

The first is the log file that logs file transfer activity between your computer and *neighbor*, and the second is the log of commands that your computer has executed as requested by *neighbor*.

`tail` has a number of other useful options:

- Use +*n* instead of - to make `tail` begin printing at line *n* of the file.

- Use b to make `tail` count by *blocks* rather than lines (blocks are either 512 or 1024 characters long).

- Use c to make `tail` count by *characters* rather than lines.

- Use r to make `tail` print from the designated starting point in the reverse direction. For example, `tail -5r` *file* prints the next-to-last five lines of the file. Option r cannot be used with option f.

The head Command

The head command, new to System V in Release 4, by default prints the first 10 lines of a file. For example:

$ **head names**

results in

```
allen christopher
babinchak david
best betty
```

```
bloom dennis
boelhower joseph
bose anita
cacossa ray
chang liang
crawford patricia
crowley charles
```

As with `tail`, `head` lets you specify the number of lines:

$ head -4 names

```
allen christopher
babinchak david
best betty
bloom dennis
```

The cat Command

cat can be used to print the contents of a file, but you must either be a speed reader or be very good with the `^S` key! (`^S`—sometimes called *scroll lock*—stops the screen from scrolling; `^Q` restarts the scroll.) Instead you can pipe the output of cat into either of the following two commands or, better yet, ignore cat entirely and use one of the following two commands for interactive viewing. cat becomes much more important when you write shell scripts; scripts run without human intervention, so *paging* (displaying the contents of a file one *page*, or screenful of lines, at a time) is unimportant.

The more Command

The `more` command helps you view the contents of a file one page (a screenful of lines) at a time. Because it is meant to be used interactively, it will not usually be part of any tool you build. However, it may become important if you want to look at a tool one page at a time.

By default, `more` displays 23 lines of text at a time; pressing the space bar brings up the next 23 lines, with a two-line overlap between screens so that it's a bit easier to recall what was on the last line of the previous screen. Pressing the carriage return key displays one additional line. At the end of each display, the `--More--` prompt prints.

`more` has a number of options, illustrated with `REfile`:

```
$ cat REfile
```

A regular expression is a sequence of characters taken
from the set of uppercase and lowercase letters, digits,
punctuation marks, etc., plus a set of special regular
expression operators. Some of these operators may remind
you of file name matching, but be forewarned: in general,
regular expression operators are different from the
shell metacharacters we discussed in Chapter 1.

The simplest form of a regular expression is one that
includes only letters. For example, the would match only
the three-letter sequence t, h, e. This pattern is found
in the following words: the, therefore, bother. In other
words, wherever the regular expression pattern is found
-- even if it is surrounded by other characters --, it will
be matched.

- To start with a particular line instead of the first one, use *+number*:

  ```
  $ more +3 REfile
  ```

  punctuation marks, etc., plus a set of special regular
  expression operators. Some of these operators may remind
  you of file name matching, but be forewarned: in general,
  regular expression operators are different from the
  shell metacharacters we discussed in Chapter 1.

  The simplest form of a regular expression is one that
  includes only letters. For example, the would match only
  the three-letter sequence t, h, e. This pattern is found
  in the following words: the, therefore, bother. In other
  words, wherever the regular expression pattern is found
  --even if it is surrounded by other characters--, it is
  matched.

- Start at the line that matches a specific regular expression—*RE*.

Note: more uses the following metacharacters: the period (.), the
asterisk (*), the left square bracket ([), the right square bracket (]),
the backslash (\), the circumflex (^), and the dollar sign ($).

```
$ more +/example REfile
```

includes only letters. For example, the would match only
the three-letter sequence t, h, e. This pattern is found
in the following words: the, therefore, bother. In other
words, wherever the regular expression pattern is found
-- even if it is surrounded by other characters --, it will
be matched.

- -c clears the screen before beginning the display.

- -d displays error messages instead of ringing the terminal bell when you make an error. This can be useful if you work in a crowded office.

- -f prevents long lines (more than 80 columns wide) from being *folded*. You won't be able to see more than the first 80 characters, but such lines usually are the result of text processing programs and may contain things that are not decipherable by a human.

- -l ignores form feeds characters. Some people put form feed characters (^L) in their text to make more pause at the point of that character, but you don't have to put up with that. Just specify -l when you invoke more with such a file.

- -r causes certain control characters to be displayed as ^C, where C is the character.

- -s squeezes out multiple blank lines and replaces each group of multiple blank lines with one blank line.

- -u suppresses underlining.

- -w causes more to wait when it reaches the end of its input until you tap a key.

The general syntax for more is

```
$ more [-options] [-lines] [+num] [+/RE] [file(s)]
```

In addition to the command-line options, more has a number of internal commands, many of which can be preceded by a number. The notation used below for a single letter command, say x, preceded by a number is *numx*. The number defaults to 1.

- d scrolls forward by about half a screen.

- b scrolls backward by about half a screen.

- *num*s skips *num* lines and then displays a screenful.

- *num*f skips *num* screens and then prints a screenful.

- q or Q terminates more.

- = displays the current line number.

- f displays the current filename and line number.

- v calls up the editor that is the value of EDITOR, an environment variable, or calls up the ed editor if EDITOR has no value.

- h describes all of more's commands.

- *num/RE* searches forward for the *num*th occurrence of *RE*.

- *num*n searches for the *num*th occurrence of the last *RE*.

- ´ (single quotation mark) causes more to jump to the place in the file that the last search started from, or to the beginning of the file if no search was requested.

- . (dot) repeats the previous command.

- !*cmd* invokes a new copy of the shell to run the command *cmd*.

- *num*:n skips to the *num*th next file in the list of files you specified on the command line.

- *num*:p skips to the *num*th previous file.

The pg Command

The pg command, like more, prints 23 lines on your terminal and waits until you press Return to print the next 23 lines. It also lets you back up and review previously displayed text, search for text, begin printing at specified line numbers, and otherwise control the output. The syntax for pg is

pg [*-scrnlines*] [*-p promptstr*] [*-options*] [*+num*] [*+/RE/*] [*file(s)*]

The major difference between pg and more is that pg lets you search backward for a regular expression. For example, let's use the following file:

$ **cat REfile**

```
A regular expression is a sequence of characters taken
from the set of uppercase and lowercase letters, digits,
punctuation marks, etc., plus a set of special regular
expression operators. Some of these operators may remind
you of file name matching, but be forewarned: in general,
regular expression operators are different from the
shell metacharacters we discussed in Chapter 1.

The simplest form of a regular expression is one that
includes only letters. For example, the would match only
the three-letter sequence t, h, e. This pattern is found
in the following words: the, therefore, bother. In other
words, wherever the regular expression pattern is found
-- even if it is surrounded by other characters --, it will
be matched.
```

- To start with a particular line instead of the first one, use *+num*:

```
$ pg +3 REfile
```

```
punctuation marks, etc., plus a set of special regular
expression operators. Some of these operators may remind
you of file name matching, but be forewarned: in general,
regular expression operators are different from the
shell metacharacters we discussed in Chapter 1.

The simplest form of a regular expression is one that
includes only letters. For example, the would match only
the three-letter sequence t, h, e. This pattern is found
in the following words: the, therefore, bother. In other
words, wherever the regular expression pattern is found
-- even if it is surrounded by other characters --, it will
be matched.
```

- Start at the line that matches a specific regular expression.

> **Note:** pg uses the following metacharacters: the period(.), the
> asterisk (*), the left square bracket ([), the right square bracket (]),
> the backslash (\), the circumflex (^), and the dollar sign ($).

```
$ pg +/example REfile
```

```
includes only letters. For example, the would match only
the three-letter sequence t, h, e. This pattern is found
in the following words: the, therefore, bother. In other
words, wherever the regular expression pattern is found
-- even if it is surrounded by other characters --, it will
be matched.
```

- *-scrnlines* specifies the size of the window that pg uses instead of
  the default (23 on a 24-line screen). This is useful if you have more
  or fewer lines on your screen.

- *-c* causes the cursor to *home* (that is, sends the cursor to the top left-
  hand corner of the screen) and clears the screen before beginning
  the display.

- *-s* displays error messages in *standout* (usually reverse video)
  instead of ringing the terminal bell when you make an error. This
  can be useful if you work in a crowded office.

- *-f* prevents long lines (more than 80 columns wide) from being
  folded. You won't be able to see more than the first 80 characters,
  but such lines are usually the result of text processing programs and
  may contain things that are not decipherable by a human.

- -e keeps pg from waiting when it reaches the end of its input.

- -r prevents you from escaping to the shell to execute a command.

In addition to the command-line options, pg has a number of internal commands, many of which can be preceded by a *signed* or *unsigned* number. (This number defaults to +1.) An unsigned number refers to the number of lines (or pages—this depends on the particular command you're using) counted from the beginning of the file. A signed number refers to a line (or page) *relative* to the current line (or page).

- d scrolls forward by about one-half a screen. *num*d is OK.

- *num*l specifies the number of lines to scroll forward (or backward). If *num* is unsigned, pg prints a screenful beginning at line *num*.

- *num*f skips *num* screens and then prints a screenful.

- *num*/RE searches forward for the *num*th occurrence of RE.

- *num*?RE searches backward for the *num*th occurrence of RE.

- *num*n skips to the *num*th next file in the list of files you specified on the command line.

- *num*p skips to the *num*th previous file.

- s *filename* saves the current file to *filename*.

- !*cmd* invokes a new copy of the shell to run the command *cmd*.

- q or Q terminates pg.

- h provides a summary of pg's commands.

Retrieving Information from Files—The grep Family

Sometimes you have an idea of what you're looking for in a file and simply want to know whether it's there without having to browse through the file. For example, as a test, I executed a command that looked for the string pjh in an 800,000+ character file and printed out every line that had the string on it. The average time to do that was about two seconds—clearly, much faster than browsing.

The "search a file for a string and print every line that has it" action is performed by the grep family of commands.

grep means *global/regular expression/print*. That is, search through an entire file (do a "global" search) for a specified regular expression and display the line (or lines) that contain(s) the pattern. Use grep to search text files for specific patterns and to print the lines that contain those patterns—"matching" lines.

There are three members of the grep family:

grep	Uses a limited set of regular expressions, as defined with the ed editor.
fgrep	"Fast" grep. fgrep searches for a string, not a pattern. That is, fgrep does not use regular expressions. Therefore, fgrep interprets the characters $, *, [,], (,), and \ as ordinary characters.
egrep	Extended grep. egrep uses *full* regular expressions (expressions that have string values and use the full set of alphanumeric and special characters) to match patterns. Full regular expressions include all of the limited regular expressions of ed (with the exception of \(and \)), plus the following ones (where *RE* is any regular expression):
RE+	Matches one or more occurrence(s) of *RE*. (Contrast that with *RE**, which matches zero or more occurrences of *RE*.)
RE?	Matches no or one occurrence(s) of *RE*.
RE1 ¦ *RE2*	Matches *either RE1* or *RE2*. The ¦ acts as a logical OR operator.
(*RE*)	Used for grouping.

Examples of these expressions are found in the section on egrep.

Note: The $, *, [,], (,), and \ regular expression metacharacters also have special meaning to the shell, so you must enclose them in single quotation marks to prevent the shell from interpreting them.

The grep Command

The most frequently used command in the family is grep. Its syntax is

```
$ grep [options] RE [file(s)]
```

where *RE* is a "limited" regular expression. Table 2.1 lists the regular expressions that grep recognizes.

grep reads from the specified file on the command line or, if no files are specified, grep reads from standard input. grep takes the command-line options listed in Table 4.1.

Table 4.1. Command-line options for grep.

Option	Result
-b	Display, at the beginning of the line, the number of the block where the RE was found. This can be helpful in locating block numbers by context. (The first block is block zero.)
-c	Print the number of lines that contain the pattern; that is, the number of matching lines.
-i	Ignore uppercase/lowercase distinctions during comparisons.
-h	Prevent the name of the file containing the matching line from being displayed at the beginning of that line. When searching multiple files, grep normally reports not only the matching line but also the name of the file containing it.
-l	Print the names of files that contain lines that match the pattern just once (regardless of the actual number of matching lines in each file), on separate lines of the screen.
-n	Precede each matching line by its line number in the file.
-s	Suppress error messages about nonexistent or unreadable files.
-v	Print all lines except those that contain the pattern. This reverses the logic of the search.

4

Here are two sample files on which to exercise grep:

```
$ cat cron
```

In SCO Xenix 2.3, or SCO UNIX, you can edit a
crontab file to your heart's content, but it will
not be re-read, and your changes will not take
effect, until you come out of multi-user run
level (thus killing cron), and then re-enter
multi-user run level, when a new cron is started;
or until you do a reboot.

The proper way to install a new version of a
crontab (for root, or for any other user) is to
issue the command "crontab new.jobs", or "cat
new.jobs ¦ crontab", or if in ´vi´ with a new
version of the commands, "w ! crontab". I find it
easy to type "vi /tmp/tbl", then ":0 r !crontab
-l" to read the existing crontab into the vi
buffer, then edit, then type ":w !crontab", or
"!crontab %" to replace the existing crontab with
what I see on vi´s screen.

```
$ cat pax
```

This is an announcement for the MS-DOS version of
PAX version 2. See the README file and the man
pages for more information on how to run PAX,
TAR, and CPIO.

For those of you who don´t know, pax is a 3 in 1
program that gives the functionality of pax, tar,
and cpio.   It supports both the DOS filesystem
and the raw "tape on a disk" system used by most
micro UNIX systems. This will allow for easy
transfer of files to and from UNIX systems. It
also supports multiple volumes. Floppy density
for raw UNIX type read/writes can be specified on
the command line.

The source will eventually be posted to one of
the source groups.

Be sure to use a blocking factor of 20 with
pax-as-tar and B with pax-as-cpio for best
performance.

The following examples show how to find a string in a file:

```
$ grep ´you´ pax
```

For those of you who don't know, pax is a 3 in 1

```
$ grep 'you' cron
```

```
In SCO Xenix 2.3, or SCO UNIX, you can edit a
crontab file to your heart's content, but it will
not be re-read, and your changes will not take
effect, until you come out of multi-user run
or until you do a reboot.
```

Note that you appears in your in the second line.

You can find the same string in two (or more) files by using a variety of options. In this first example, case is ignored:

```
$ grep -i 'you' pax cron
```

```
pax:For those of you who don't know, pax is a 3 in 1
cron:In SCO Xenix 2.3, or SCO UNIX, you can edit a
cron:crontab file to your heart's content, but it will
cron:not be re-read, and your changes will not take
cron:effect, until you come out of multi-user run
cron:or until you do a reboot.
```

Notice that each line of output begins with the name of the file that contained a match. In the following example, output includes the name of the file and the number of the line of that file on which the match was found:

```
$ grep -in 'you' pax cron
```

```
pax:6:For those of you who don't know, pax is a 3 in 1
cron:1:In SCO Xenix 2.3, or SCO UNIX, you can edit a
cron:2:crontab file to your heart's content, but it will
cron:3:not be re-read, and your changes will not take
cron:4:effect, until you come out of multi-user run
cron:7:or until you do a reboot.
```

The following example inhibits printing the lines themselves:

```
$ grep -ci 'you' pax cron
```

```
pax:1
cron:5
```

The following output shows the matching lines without specifying which files they came from:

```
$ grep -hi 'you' pax cron
```

```
For those of you who don't know, pax is a 3 in 1
In SCO Xenix 2.3, or SCO UNIX, you can edit a
crontab file to your heart's content, but it will
not be re-read, and your changes will not take
effect, until you come out of multi-user run
or until you do a reboot.
```

The following specifies output of "every line in pax and cron that does not have [Yy][Oo][Uu] in it":

```
$ grep -vi ´you´ pax cron
```

```
pax:This is an announcement for the MS-DOS version of
pax:PAX version 2. See the README file and the man
pax:pages for more information on how to run PAX,
pax:TAR, and CPIO.
pax:
pax:program that gives the functionality of pax, tar,
pax:and cpio.  It supports both the DOS filesystem
pax:and the raw "tape on a disk" system used by most
pax:micro UNIX systems.  This will allow for easy
pax:transfer of files to and from UNIX systems.  It
pax:also support multiple volumes.  Floppy density
pax:for raw UNIX type read/writes can be specified on
pax:the command line.
pax:
pax:The source will eventually be posted to one of
pax:the source groups.
pax:
pax:Be sure to use a blocking factor of 20 with
pax:pax-as-tar and B with pax-as-cpio for best
pax:performance.
cron:level (thus killing cron), and then re-enter
cron:multi-user run level, when a new cron is started;
cron:
cron:The proper way to install a new version of a
cron:crontab (for root, or for any other user) is to
cron:issue the command "crontab new.jobs", or "cat
cron:new.jobs ¦ crontab", or if in ´vi´ with a new
cron:version of the commands, "w ! crontab". I find it
cron:easy to type "vi /tmp/tbl", then ":0 r !crontab
cron:-l" to read the existing crontab into the vi
cron:buffer, then edit, then type ":w !crontab", or
cron:"!crontab %" to replace the existing crontab with
cron:what I see on vi´s screen.
```

The following example is quite interesting. It lists every line that has r.*t in it but, unbeknownst to us, it matches the longest possible string in each line. First, let's see exactly how the strings are matched. For clarification, the matching strings in the listing are set in boldface type so that you can see how grep uses the longest matching string:

```
$ grep ´r.*t´ pax cron
```

```
pax:This is an announcement for the MS-DOS version of
pax:PAX version 2. See the README file and the man
pax:pages for more information on how to run PAX,
pax:For those of you who don´t know, pax is a 3 in 1
pax:program that gives the functionality of pax, tar,
```

```
pax:and cpio.  It supports both the DOS filesystem
pax:and the raw "tape on a disk" system used by most
pax:micro UNIX systems.  This will allow for easy
pax:transfer of files to and from UNIX systems.  It
pax:also supports multiple volumes.  Floppy density
pax:for raw UNIX type read/writes can be specified on
pax:The source will eventually be posted to one of
pax:Be sure to use a blocking factor of 20 with
pax:pax-as-tar and B with pax-as-cpio for best
cron:In SCO Xenix 2.3, or SCO UNIX, you can edit a
cron:crontab file to your heart's content, but it will
cron:not be re-read, and your changes will not take
cron:level (thus killing cron), and then re-enter
cron:multi-user run level, when a new cron is started;
cron:or until you do a reboot.
cron:The proper way to install a new version of a
cron:crontab (for root, or for any other user) is to
cron:issue the command "crontab new.jobs", or "cat
cron:new.jobs ¦ crontab", or if in ´vi´ with a new
cron:version of the commands, "w ! crontab". I find it
cron:easy to type "vi /tmp/tbl", then ":0 r !crontab
cron:-l" to read the existing crontab into the vi
cron:buffer, then edit, then type ":w !crontab", or
cron:"!crontab %" to replace the existing crontab with
```

Now look for two or more 1s:

```
$ grep ´111*´ pax cron
```

```
pax:micro UNIX systems.  This will allow for easy
pax:The source will eventually be posted to one of
cron:crontab file to your heart's content, but it will
cron:not be re-read, and your changes will not take
cron:level (thus killing cron), and then re-enter
cron:The proper way to install a new version of a
```

How about finding lines that begin with The?

```
$ grep ´^The´ pax cron
```

```
pax:The source will eventually be posted to one of
cron:The proper way to install a new version of a
```

Or lines that end with n?

```
$ grep ´n$´ pax cron
```

```
pax:PAX version 2. See the README file and the man
pax:for raw UNIX type read/writes can be specified on
cron:effect, until you come out of multi-user run
```

grep can search for "at least two consecutive uppercase letters" very easily:

```
$ grep ´[A-Z]\{2,\}´ pax cron
```

```
pax:This is an announcement for the MS-DOS version of
pax:PAX version 2. See the README file and the man
pax:pages for more information on how to run PAX,
pax:TAR, and CPIO.
pax:and cpio.   It supports both the DOS filesystem
pax:micro UNIX systems.  This will allow for easy
pax:transfer of files to and from UNIX systems.  It
pax:for raw UNIX type read/writes can be specified on
cron:In SCO Xenix 2.3, or SCO UNIX, you can edit a
```

The egrep Command

As mentioned earlier, egrep uses full regular expressions in the pattern string. The syntax of egrep is the same as the syntax for grep:

```
$ egrep [options] RE [files]
```

where *RE* means "regular expression."

The egrep command uses the same regular expressions as the ed editor, except for \(and \), and includes the following additional patterns:

RE+	Matches one or more occurrence(s) of *RE*. (Contrast that with *RE**, which matches zero or more occurrence(s) of *RE*.)
RE?	Matches zero or one occurrence(s) of *RE*.
RE1 ¦ RE2	Matches *either* *RE1* or *RE2*. The ¦ acts as a logical OR operator.
(RE)	Used for grouping.

egrep accepts the same command-line options as grep and adds the command-line options listed in Table 4.2.

Table 4.2. Additional command-line options for egrep.

Option	Result
-e special_expression	Search for a regular expression that begins with a -
-f file	The regular expressions have been put into file

Here are a few examples of egrep's extended regular expressions. The first finds one or more consecutive uppercase letters:

```
$ egrep '[A-Z]+' pax cron
```

```
pax:This is an announcement for the MS-DOS version of
pax:PAX version 2. See the README file and the man
pax:pages for more information on how to run PAX,
pax:TAR, and CPIO.
pax:For those of you who don't know, PAX is a 3-in-1
pax:and cpio. It supports both the DOS filesystem
pax:micro UNIX systems. This allows for easy
pax:transfer of files to and from UNIX systems. It
pax:also support multiple volumes. Floppy density
pax:for raw UNIX type read/writes can be specified on
pax:The source eventually is posted to one of
pax:Be sure to use a blocking factor of 20 with
pax:pax-as-tar and B with pax-as-cpio for best
cron:In SCO Xenix 2.3, or SCO UNIX, you can edit a
cron:The proper way to install a new version of a
cron:version of the commands, "w ! crontab". I find it
cron:what I see on vi's screen.
```

The following finds all lines containing either DOS or SCO:

```
$ egrep 'DOS¦SCO' pax cron
```

```
pax:This is an announcement for the MS-DOS version of
pax:and cpio. It supports both the DOS filesystem
cron:In SCO Xenix 2.3, or SCO UNIX, you can edit a
```

This example finds all lines that contain either new or now:

```
$ egrep 'n(e¦o)w' cron
```

```
multi-user run level, when a new cron is started;
The proper way to install a new version of a
issue the command "crontab new.jobs", or "cat
new.jobs ¦ crontab", or if in 'vi' with a new
```

The fgrep Command

fgrep searches a file for a *character string* and prints all lines that contain the string. Unlike grep and egrep, fgrep interprets all characters in the search string as literal characters; there are no metacharacters in fgrep. Although the manuals say that fgrep's searching algorithm is fast as well as compact, it does not run efficiently on some systems. Therefore, you should use the time command to test which of the grep family of searches is most efficient on your system.

The syntax of `fgrep` is

fgrep *[options]* **string** *[files]*

The options you use with the `fgrep` command are exactly the same ones you use for `egrep`, with the addition of `-x`, which prints only lines that are matched in their entirety.

Summary

This chapter investigated the contents of text files in two modes. The first was the file browser mode—you used commands that let you read as much of a file as you wanted. To find anything in a file that you opened with a browser, you must look for it among all the characters, words, and sentences in the file. The second was a faster approach that responded to the command "show me the line on which this pattern is matched." That is, you produced output that is exactly what you want—with nothing extra to clutter your screen or to distract you—and can be piped into another command.

4

## Chapter 5

Formatting and Working with Fields

You've met System V Release 4 commands for showing us the insides of a file: the beginning, the end, the whole thing, or one or more lines. Now you want to do something with what you found in that file. In truth, you aren't going to change the original files at all but instead create new files that are modified versions of the old ones. This approach preserves the original files and may save you much grief some day.

Note: Never, *never* use the same filename as both input file and output file! If you do, the shell opens it for writing and "zaps" its contents before it processes the file. You'll always end up with a "0 byte" file.

In this chapter, you'll see how to format files, how to extract information from formatted files, and how to build new files containing that information.

Formatting Commands

UNIX has a number of tools for changing the format of a file. Of course, these commands don't actually change the original file. Instead, they write their output to stdout, from which you can redirect it to a new file.

The nl Command

The nl command formats a file in the sense that it adds numbers to its lines. Later in this section, I'll show you how nl can be used to number lines within pages in a file by using special delimiters.

Because it's unusual to find a UNIX text file having these peculiar delimiters, I'll use an example of a plain text file to show nl's many options:

```
$ cat text
```

```
NIC Mail Services                                        June 1990

    This is an automated service provided by the DDN Network Information
Center.  It allows access to NIC documents and information via ordinary
electronic mail.  This is especially useful for people who do not have
access to the NIC via a direct Internet link, such as BITNET, CSNET
and UUCP sites.

    To use the mail service, send a mail message to SERVICE@NIC.DDN.MIL.
In the SUBJECT field, request the type of service you wish followed by
any needed arguments.  The message body is normally ignored; however, if the
SUBJECT field is empty, the first line of the message body will be used
as the request.  Large files will be broken into smaller separate messages.
However, a few files are too large to be sent through the mail system.
Requests are processed automatically once a day.

The following services are currently available:

HELP            This message; a list of current services.
HOST xxx        Returns information about host xxx.  WHOIS xxx can
                also be used to get more details about a host.
IEN nnn         nnn is the IEN number or the word INDEX.
INDEX           Returns the master list of available index files.
NETINFO xxx     xxx is a file name or the word INDEX.
RFC nnn         nnn is the RFC number or the word INDEX.
RFC nnn.PS      to retrieve an available Postscript RFC. Check RFC INDEX for
                form of RFC.
FYI nnn         nnn is the FYI number or the word INDEX.
FYI nnn.PS      to retrieve postscript versions of FYI files.
SEND xxx        xxx is a fully specified file name.
WHOIS xxx       Returns information about xxx from the WHOIS service.
                Use "WHOIS HELP" for information on how to use WHOIS.
```

```
        Example SUBJECT lines:

            HELP
            RFC 822
            RFC INDEX
            RFC 1119.PS
            FYI 1
            NETINFO DOMAIN-TEMPLATE.TXT
            SEND RFC:ASSIGNED-NUMBERS.TXT
            SEND IETF:1WG-SUMMARY
            SEND INTERNET-DRAFTS:DRAFT-IETF-IWG-BGP-OO.TXT
            HOST NIC.DDN.MIL
            WHOIS LOTTOR, MARK

        Send comments or suggestions to SUGGESTIONS@NIC.DDN.MIL.  Send questions
        and bug reports to BUG-SERVICE@NIC.DDN.MIL.
```

First, let's see what nl with no options does to the file:

$ nl text

```
    1   NIC Mail Services                                         June 1990

    2       This is an automated service provided by the DDN Network Information
    3   Center.  It allows access to NIC documents and information via ordinary
    4   electronic mail.  This is especially useful for people who do not have
    5   access to the NIC via a direct Internet link, such as BITNET, CSNET
    6   and UUCP sites.

    7       To use the mail service, send a mail message to SERVICE@NIC.DDN.MIL.
    8   In the SUBJECT field, request the type of service you wish followed by
    9   any needed arguments.  The message body is normally ignored; however, if the
   10   SUBJECT field is empty, the first line of the message body will be used
   11   as the request.  Large files will be broken into smaller separate messages.
   12   However, a few files are too large to be sent through the mail system.
   13   Requests are processed automatically once a day.

   14   The following services are currently available:

   15   HELP            This message; a list of current services.
   16   HOST xxx        Returns information about host xxx.  WHOIS xxx can
   17                   also be used to get more details about a host.
   18   IEN nnn         nnn is the IEN number or the word INDEX.
   19   INDEX           Returns the master list of available index files.
   20   NETINFO xxx     xxx is a file name or the word INDEX.
   21   RFC nnn         nnn is the RFC number or the word INDEX.
   22   RFC nnn.PS      to retrieve an available Postscript RFC. Check RFC INDEX for
   23                   form of RFC.
   24   FYI nnn         nnn is the FYI number or the word INDEX.
   25   FYI nnn.PS      to retrieve postscript versions of FYI files.
   26   SEND xxx        xxx is a fully specified file name.
```

5

```
27    WHOIS xxx         Returns information about xxx from the WHOIS service.
28                      Use "WHOIS HELP" for information on how to use WHOIS.

29    Example SUBJECT lines:

30       HELP
31       RFC 822
32       RFC INDEX
33       RFC 1119.PS
34       FYI 1
35       NETINFO DOMAIN-TEMPLATE.TXT
36       SEND RFC:ASSIGNED-NUMBERS.TXT
37       SEND IETF:1WG-SUMMARY
38       SEND INTERNET-DRAFTS:DRAFT-IETF-IWG-BGP-OO.TXT
39       HOST NIC.DDN.MIL
40       WHOIS LOTTOR, MARK

41    Send comments or suggestions to SUGGESTIONS@NIC.DDN.MIL.  Send questions
42    and bug reports to BUG-SERVICE@NIC.DDN.MIL.
```

That's pretty straightforward. nl numbers every line that has text on it and then inserts a tab character between the number and the text. Note that the blank lines are not numbered.

You can specify the starting number to be other than 1 by using the -v option:

$ nl -v4 text

```
4    NIC Mail Services                                      June 1990

5       This is an automated service provided by the DDN Network Information
6    Center.  It allows access to NIC documents and information via ordinary
7    electronic mail.  This is especially useful for people who do not have
8    access to the NIC via a direct Internet link, such as BITNET, CSNET
9    and UUCP sites.

10      To use the mail service, send a mail message to SERVICE@NIC.DDN.MIL.
11   In the SUBJECT field, request the type of service you wish followed by
12   any needed arguments.  The message body is normally ignored; however, if the
13   SUBJECT field is empty, the first line of the message body will be used
14   as the request.  Large files will be broken into smaller separate messages.
15   However, a few files are too large to be sent through the mail system.
16   Requests are processed automatically once a day.

17   The following services are currently available:

18   HELP              This message; a list of current services.
19   HOST xxx          Returns information about host xxx.  WHOIS xxx can
20                     also be used to get more details about a host.
21   IEN nnn           nnn is the IEN number or the word INDEX.
22   INDEX             Returns the master list of available index files.
```

```
23   NETINFO xxx      xxx is a file name or the word INDEX.
24   RFC nnn          nnn is the RFC number or the word INDEX.
25   RFC nnn.PS       to retrieve an available Postscript RFC. Check RFC INDEX for
26                    form of RFC.
27   FYI nnn          nnn is the FYI number or the word INDEX.
28   FYI nnn.PS       to retrieve postscript versions of FYI files.
29   SEND xxx         xxx is a fully specified file name.
30   WHOIS xxx        Returns information about xxx from the WHOIS service.
31                    Use "WHOIS HELP" for information on how to use WHOIS.

32   Example SUBJECT lines:

33      HELP
34      RFC 822
35      RFC INDEX
36      RFC 1119.PS
37      FYI 1
38      NETINFO DOMAIN-TEMPLATE.TXT
39      SEND RFC:ASSIGNED-NUMBERS.TXT
40      SEND IETF:1WG-SUMMARY
41      SEND INTERNET-DRAFTS:DRAFT-IETF-IWG-BGP-OO.TXT
42      HOST NIC.DDN.MIL
43      WHOIS LOTTOR, MARK

44   Send comments or suggestions to SUGGESTIONS@NIC.DDN.MIL.  Send questions
45   and bug reports to BUG-SERVICE@NIC.DDN.MIL.
```

You can make nl number all the lines—even blank ones—by specifying -ba:

```
$ nl -ba -v4 text

4    NIC Mail Services                                       June 1990
5
6       This is an automated service provided by the DDN Network Information
7    Center.  It allows access to NIC documents and information via ordinary
8    electronic mail.  This is especially useful for people who do not have
9    access to the NIC via a direct Internet link, such as BITNET, CSNET
10   and UUCP sites.
11
12      To use the mail service, send a mail message to SERVICE@NIC.DDN.MIL.
13   In the SUBJECT field, request the type of service you wish followed by
14   any needed arguments.  The message body is normally ignored; however, if the
15   SUBJECT field is empty, the first line of the message body will be used
16   as the request.  Large files will be broken into smaller separate messages.
17   However, a few files are too large to be sent through the mail system.
18   Requests are processed automatically once a day.
19
20   The following services are currently available:
21
22   HELP             This message; a list of current services.
23   HOST xxx         Returns information about host xxx.  WHOIS xxx can
```

```
24                    also be used to get more details about a host.
25   IEN nnn          nnn is the IEN number or the word INDEX.
26   INDEX            Returns the master list of available index files.
27   NETINFO xxx      xxx is a file name or the word INDEX.
28   RFC nnn          nnn is the RFC number or the word INDEX.
29   RFC nnn.PS       to retrieve an available Postscript RFC. Check RFC INDEX for
30                    form of RFC.
31   FYI nnn          nnn is the FYI number or the word INDEX.
32   FYI nnn.PS       to retrieve postscript versions of FYI files.
33   SEND xxx         xxx is a fully specified file name.
34   WHOIS xxx        Returns information about xxx from the WHOIS service.
35                    Use "WHOIS HELP" for information on how to use WHOIS.
36
37   Example SUBJECT lines:
38
39      HELP
40      RFC 822
41      RFC INDEX
42      RFC 1119.PS
43      FYI 1
44      NETINFO DOMAIN-TEMPLATE.TXT
45      SEND RFC:ASSIGNED-NUMBERS.TXT
46      SEND IETF:1WG-SUMMARY
47      SEND INTERNET-DRAFTS:DRAFT-IETF-IWG-BGP-OO.TXT
48      HOST NIC.DDN.MIL
49      WHOIS LOTTOR, MARK
50
51   Send comments or suggestions to SUGGESTIONS@NIC.DDN.MIL.  Send questions
52   and bug reports to BUG-SERVICE@NIC.DDN.MIL.
53
```

Line numbers need not increment by 1, either. Specify -i and an increment value to change the default:

```
$ nl -ba -i5 text
```

```
 1   NIC Mail Services                                          June 1990
 6
11      This is an automated service provided by the DDN Network Information
16   Center.  It allows access to NIC documents and information via ordinary
21   electronic mail.  This is especially useful for people who do not have
26   access to the NIC via a direct Internet link, such as BITNET, CSNET
31   and UUCP sites.
36
41      To use the mail service, send a mail message to SERVICE@NIC.DDN.MIL.
46   In the SUBJECT field, request the type of service you wish followed by
51   any needed arguments.  The message body is normally ignored; however, if the
56   SUBJECT field is empty, the first line of the message body will be used
61   as the request.  Large files will be broken into smaller separate messages.
66   However, a few files are too large to be sent through the mail system.
71   Requests are processed automatically once a day.
76
```

```
 81    The following services are currently available:
 86
 91    HELP              This message; a list of current services.
 96    HOST xxx          Returns information about host xxx.  WHOIS xxx can
101                      also be used to get more details about a host.
106    IEN nnn           nnn is the IEN number or the word INDEX.
111    INDEX             Returns the master list of available index files.
116    NETINFO xxx       xxx is a file name or the word INDEX.
121    RFC nnn           nnn is the RFC number or the word INDEX.
126    RFC nnn.PS        to retrieve an available Postscript RFC. Check RFC INDEX for
131                      form of RFC.
136    FYI nnn           nnn is the FYI number or the word INDEX.
141    FYI nnn.PS        to retrieve postscript versions of FYI files.
146    SEND xxx          xxx is a fully specified file name.
151    WHOIS xxx         Returns information about xxx from the WHOIS service.
156                      Use "WHOIS HELP" for information on how to use WHOIS.
161
166    Example SUBJECT lines:
171
176       HELP
181       RFC 822
186       RFC INDEX
191       RFC 1119.PS
196       FYI 1
201       NETINFO DOMAIN-TEMPLATE.TXT
206       SEND RFC:ASSIGNED-NUMBERS.TXT
211       SEND IETF:1WG-SUMMARY
216       SEND INTERNET-DRAFTS:DRAFT-IETF-IWG-BGP-OO.TXT
221       HOST NIC.DDN.MIL
226       WHOIS LOTTOR, MARK
231
236    Send comments or suggestions to SUGGESTIONS@NIC.DDN.MIL.  Send questions
241    and bug reports to BUG-SERVICE@NIC.DDN.MIL.
246
```

Normally, nl prints a tab after each number. You can change that by using the -s option along with any character you want:

```
$ nl -ba -s´:´ text
```

```
 1:NIC Mail Services                                    June 1990
 2:
 3:   This is an automated service provided by the DDN Network Information
 4:Center.  It allows access to NIC documents and information via ordinary
 5:electronic mail.  This is especially useful for people who do not have
 6:access to the NIC via a direct Internet link, such as BITNET, CSNET
 7:and UUCP sites.
 8:
 9:   To use the mail service, send a mail message to SERVICE@NIC.DDN.MIL.
10:In the SUBJECT field, request the type of service you wish followed by
11:any needed arguments.  The message body is normally ignored; however, if the
12:SUBJECT field is empty, the first line of the message body will be used
13:as the request.  Large files will be broken into smaller separate messages.
```

```
14:However, a few files are too large to be sent through the mail system.
15:Requests are processed automatically once a day.
16:
17:The following services are currently available:
18:
19:HELP              This message; a list of current services.
20:HOST xxx          Returns information about host xxx.  WHOIS xxx can
21:                  also be used to get more details about a host.
22:IEN nnn           nnn is the IEN number or the word INDEX.
23:INDEX             Returns the master list of available index files.
24:NETINFO xxx       xxx is a file name or the word INDEX.
25:RFC nnn           nnn is the RFC number or the word INDEX.
26:RFC nnn.PS        to retrieve an available Postscript RFC. Check RFC INDEX for
27:                  form of RFC.
28:FYI nnn           nnn is the FYI number or the word INDEX.
29:FYI nnn.PS        to retrieve postscript versions of FYI files.
30:SEND xxx          xxx is a fully specified file name.
31:WHOIS xxx         Returns information about xxx from the WHOIS service.
32:                  Use "WHOIS HELP" for information on how to use WHOIS.
33:
34:Example SUBJECT lines:
35:
36:    HELP
37:    RFC 822
38:    RFC INDEX
39:    RFC 1119.PS
40:    FYI 1
41:    NETINFO DOMAIN-TEMPLATE.TXT
42:    SEND RFC:ASSIGNED-NUMBERS.TXT
43:    SEND IETF:1WG-SUMMARY
44:    SEND INTERNET-DRAFTS:DRAFT-IETF-IWG-BGP-OO.TXT
45:    HOST NIC.DDN.MIL
46:    WHOIS LOTTOR, MARK
47:
48:Send comments or suggestions to SUGGESTIONS@NIC.DDN.MIL.  Send questions
49:and bug reports to BUG-SERVICE@NIC.DDN.MIL.
50:
```

You can select different formats for the numbers other than the default, which is right-justified with any leading zeros suppressed. Here, for example, is the previous example with the addition of the `-nrz` option. The line numbers are right-justified with leading zeros displayed.

```
$ nl -ba -s´:´ -nrz text
```

```
000001:NIC Mail Services                                    June 1990
000002:
000003:   This is an automated service provided by the DDN Network Information
000004:Center.  It allows access to NIC documents and information via ordinary
000005:electronic mail.  This is especially useful for people who do not have
```

```
000006:access to the NIC via a direct Internet link, such as BITNET, CSNET
000007:and UUCP sites.
000008:
000009:   To use the mail service, send a mail message to SERVICE@NIC.DDN.MIL.
000010:In the SUBJECT field, request the type of service you wish followed by
000011:any needed arguments.  The message body is normally ignored; however, if the
000012:SUBJECT field is empty, the first line of the message body will be used
000013:as the request.  Large files will be broken into smaller separate messages.
000014:However, a few files are too large to be sent through the mail system.
000015:Requests are processed automatically once a day.
000016:
000017:The following services are currently available:
000018:
000019:HELP             This message; a list of current services.
000020:HOST xxx         Returns information about host xxx.  WHOIS xxx can
000021:                 also be used to get more details about a host.
000022:IEN nnn          nnn is the IEN number or the word INDEX.
000023:INDEX            Returns the master list of available index files.
000024:NETINFO xxx      xxx is a file name or the word INDEX.
000025:RFC nnn          nnn is the RFC number or the word INDEX.
000026:RFC nnn.PS       to retrieve an available Postscript RFC. Check RFC INDEX for
000027:                 form of RFC.
000028:FYI nnn          nnn is the FYI number or the word INDEX.
000029:FYI nnn.PS       to retrieve postscript versions of FYI files.
000030:SEND xxx         xxx is a fully specified file name.
000031:WHOIS xxx        Returns information about xxx from the WHOIS service.
000032:                 Use "WHOIS HELP" for information on how to use WHOIS.
000033:
000034:Example SUBJECT lines:
000035:
000036:    HELP
000037:    RFC 822
000038:    RFC INDEX
000039:    RFC 1119.PS
000040:    FYI 1
000041:    NETINFO DOMAIN-TEMPLATE.TXT
000042:    SEND RFC:ASSIGNED-NUMBERS.TXT
000043:    SEND IETF:1WG-SUMMARY
000044:    SEND INTERNET-DRAFTS:DRAFT-IETF-IWG-BGP-OO.TXT
000045:    HOST NIC.DDN.MIL
000046:    WHOIS LOTTOR, MARK
000047:
000048:Send comments or suggestions to SUGGESTIONS@NIC.DDN.MIL.  Send questions
000049:and bug reports to BUG-SERVICE@NIC.DDN.MIL.
000050:
```

One of nl's more interesting options lets you select a subset of all lines and number just those lines by specifying a regular expression as the argument to the -bp option. The following asks nl to number just the lines that have the regular expression RFC on them:

$ nl -bpRFC text

NIC Mail Services   June 1990

This is an automated service provided by the DDN Network Information
Center. It allows access to NIC documents and information via ordinary
electronic mail. This is especially useful for people who do not have
access to the NIC via a direct Internet link, such as BITNET, CSNET
and UUCP sites.

To use the mail service, send a mail message to SERVICE@NIC.DDN.MIL.
In the SUBJECT field, request the type of service you wish followed by
any needed arguments. The message body is normally ignored; however, if the
SUBJECT field is empty, the first line of the message body will be used
as the request. Large files will be broken into smaller separate messages.
However, a few files are too large to be sent through the mail system.
Requests are processed automatically once a day.

The following services are currently available:

```
    HELP            This message; a list of current services.
    HOST xxx        Returns information about host xxx.  WHOIS xxx can
                    also be used to get more details about a host.
    IEN nnn         nnn is the IEN number or the word INDEX.
    INDEX           Returns the master list of available index files.
    NETINFO xxx     xxx is a file name or the word INDEX.
1   RFC nnn             nnn is the RFC number or the word INDEX.
2   RFC nnn.PS         to retrieve an available Postscript RFC. Check RFC INDEX for
3                      form of RFC.
    FYI nnn         nnn is the FYI number or the word INDEX.
    FYI nnn.PS      to retrieve postscript versions of FYI files.
    SEND xxx        xxx is a fully specified file name.
    WHOIS xxx       Returns information about xxx from the WHOIS service.
                    Use "WHOIS HELP" for information on how to use WHOIS.
```

Example SUBJECT lines:

```
    HELP
4       RFC 822
5       RFC INDEX
6       RFC 1119.PS
    FYI 1
    NETINFO DOMAIN-TEMPLATE.TXT
7       SEND RFC:ASSIGNED-NUMBERS.TXT
    SEND IETF:1WG-SUMMARY
    SEND INTERNET-DRAFTS:DRAFT-IETF-IWG-BGP-OO.TXT
    HOST NIC.DDN.MIL
    WHOIS LOTTOR, MARK
```

Send comments or suggestions to SUGGESTIONS@NIC.DDN.MIL. Send questions
and bug reports to BUG-SERVICE@NIC.DDN.MIL.

Any full regular expression may be used with nl. nl can also recognize *logical pages* if the file contains the appropriate delimiters. nl resets the line numbers at the beginning of each logical page. If a file doesn't have the appropriate delimiters, nl treats the entire file as a single page. To create logical pages, you must insert lines that contain special strings. That is, if a file contains the following string on a line by itself

```
\:\:\:
```

the nl command treats the material that follows (up to the next delimiter) as if it were the header section of that logical page. Therefore, line number 1 starts with the first line after the header. A logical page is one that begins with such a header.

The end of the header is marked with the delimiter

```
\:\:
```

on a line by itself, indicating that the next line is the beginning of the body of the page. Finally, a line that contains only

```
\:
```

indicates that the next line begins the footer of the same logical page. The next delimiter in the file must be

```
\:\:\:
```

on a line by itself. This line marks the end of the current logical page and the start of the next one. If there are no delimiters, nl treats the entire file as one logical page.

nl resets its line numbers for each logical page.

You'll find all of the options in Part III, the reference section.

The fold Command

fold is a "brute force" program that breaks each line of text at the specified column and spills the rest of the text onto the next line, pushing everything after that down one line. With no column specified, fold breaks at column 80. If your file includes tabs, you should choose a column that is a multiple of 8, unless you prefer to expand the tabs into spaces with tr or another suitable tool before using fold. (See Chapter 6 for more information on tr.)

The syntax is

```
fold [-width] [file(s)]
```

Here's the sample file:

```
$ cat x
                        General Information

        Tickets are sold ONLY at the door, on Saturday, April 20 and
Sunday, April 21.  Each ticket has a stub that can be entered into the
door prize drawing.  Usually, a prize is awarded each hour the
festival is open.

        A ticket purchased on Saturday costs $7.00 and entitles the
purchaser to admission on both Saturday and Sunday.  A ticket
purchased on Sunday is available at a reduced price.  Also, senior
citizens and students are entitled to purchase reduced price tickets
on Saturday.

        There is no advanced ticket sale.

        If you would like to rent an indoor booth or a flea market
spot, please call the number below for more information.

        If you would like to reserve a table for your computer club,
please call the number below.

        If you would like to speak at TCF´91, download the speaker
form, fill it out and mail it TODAY!

        Any other questions, please call the number below or send
email to
                        "pjh@mccc.edu"


General information:
        The Concordia Group
        (609) 655-4999
        (609) 655-4989
```

Now let's fold the file at column 50:

```
$ fold -50 x
                        General Information

        Tickets are sold ONLY at the door, on Satu
rday, April 20 and
Sunday, April 21.  Each ticket has a stub that can
 be entered into the
door prize drawing.  Usually, a prize is awarded e
ach hour the
festival is open.
```

```
        A ticket purchased on Saturday costs $7.00
 and entitles the
purchaser to admission on both Saturday and Sunday
. A ticket
purchased on Sunday is available at a reduced pric
e.  Also, senior
citizens and students are entitled to purchase red
uced price tickets
on Saturday.

        There is no advanced ticket sale.

        If you would like to rent an indoor booth
or a flea market
spot, please call the number below for more inform
ation.

        If you would like to reserve a table for y
our computer club,
please call the number below.

        If you would like to speak at TCF´91, down
load the speaker
form, fill it out and mail it TODAY!

        Any other questions, please call the numbe
r below or send
email to
                "pjh@mccc.edu"



General information:
        The Concordia Group
        (609) 655-4999
        (609) 655-4989
```

That's it! Nothing very sophisticated here. You might want a more sophisticated tool that folds line on word boundaries.

The `fmt` Command

`fmt` formats files by combining short lines into longer ones and wrapping lines that are too long, much as a word processor would do.

The syntax is

```
fmt [-cs] [-w width] [file(s)]
```

The default width is 72 characters per line, but you can change it with the -w option. The -s option prevents combining short lines and only splits long lines. Thus, if the file is already partially formatted—perhaps it's a source code file or a shell script—the short lines of code are not combined.

Let's use the same file used for fold so that you can compare what the two commands do:

```
$ fmt x

                    General Information

        Tickets are sold ONLY at the door, on Saturday, April 20 and
Sunday, April 21.  Each ticket has a stub that can be entered into the
door prize drawing.  Usually, a prize is awarded each hour the festival
is open.

        A ticket purchased on Saturday costs $7.00 and entitles the
purchaser to admission on both Saturday and Sunday.  A ticket purchased
on Sunday is available at a reduced price.  Also, senior citizens and
students are entitled to purchase reduced price tickets on Saturday.

        There is no advanced ticket sale.

        If you would like to rent an indoor booth or a flea market
spot, please call the number below for more information.

        If you would like to reserve a table for your computer club,
please call the number below.

        If you would like to speak at TCF´91, download the speaker
form, fill it out and mail it TODAY!

        Any other questions, please call the number below or send email
to:
                "pjh@mccc.edu"



General information:
        The Concordia Group (609) 655-4999 (609) 655-4989
```

fmt doesn't do much to a file whose lines are all less than 72 characters long. However, it did "join" the last three lines into one.

Let's choose a new width:

```
$ fmt -50 x
```

                    General Information

        Tickets are sold ONLY at the door, on
Saturday, April 20 and Sunday, April 21. Each
ticket has a stub that can be entered into the
door prize drawing. Usually, a prize is awarded
each hour the festival is open.

        A ticket purchased on Saturday costs
$7.00 and entitles the purchaser to admission on
both Saturday and Sunday. A ticket purchased on
Sunday is available at a reduced price. Also,
senior citizens and students are entitled to
purchase reduced price tickets on Saturday.

        There is no advanced ticket sale.

        If you would like to rent an indoor booth
or a flea market spot, please call the number
below for more information.

        If you would like to reserve a table for
your computer club, please call the number
below.

        If you would like to speak at TCF´91,
download the speaker form, fill it out and mail
it TODAY!

        Any other questions, please call the
number below or send email to: "pjh@mccc.edu"

General information: The Concordia Group (609)
        655-4999 (609) 655-4989

Notice how nicely fmt did its job, preserving words rather than chopping them into two pieces.

Here's a more highly formatted file to feed to fmt:

```
$ cat list
```

NOTE: This list was created on Mon, 16 Sep 91 03:18:14 MDT.
Some files may have been added or deleted since that date.
See file PD1:<MSDOS.FILEDOCS>AAAREAD.ME for additional information.

NOTE: Type B is Binary; Type A is ASCII

```
Directory PD1:<MSDOS.BATUTL>
 Filename  Type Length   Date   Description
=================================================
ASK.ASM      A   14015  860422  Query from within .BAT file
ASK.DOC      A    7893  860422  Doc for ASK.ASM
ASK11.ZIP    B   13714  910810  Asks questions in BATch files, with timeout
ASK3.ARC     B   22077  880615  Timed Ask from BAT w/config. errorlevels
ASK_BAT.ARC  B   18625  890217  Timed response to Y/N prompts in .BAT files
ATSIGN.ARC   B    5765  880801  Command line batch utility
AUTOEXEC.ARC B   45799  890806  Select different AUTOEXEC boot-up batch files
AUTOSTOP.ARC B    7324  881115  Batch file utility. Good for BBS's
BAT-TIME.ARC B   12955  881005  A batch-time type utility. For system use
BATBRNCH.ARC B     896  870613  Add Yes/No branching to .BAT files with errlvl
BATCD.ASM    A    3711  840403  Change dir within .BAT file
BATCD.DOC    A    1853  840103  Doc for BATCD.ASM
BATCH.ARC    B   10437  890524  Useful BAT files, color prompts prn commands
```

First let's split long lines that are more than 50 characters long. Notice that blank lines are preserved:

$ fmt -50 -s list

```
NOTE: This list was created on Mon, 16 Sep 91
03:18:14 MDT.
Some files may have been added or deleted since
that date.
See file PD1:<MSDOS.FILEDOCS>AAAREAD.ME for
additional information.


NOTE: Type B is Binary; Type A is ASCII

Directory PD1:<MSDOS.BATUTL>
 Filename    Type Length   Date   Description
=================================================
ASK.ASM        A   14015  860422  Query from
within .BAT file
ASK.DOC        A    7893  860422  Doc for ASK.ASM
ASK11.ZIP      B   13714  910810  Asks questions
in BATch files, with timeout
ASK3.ARC       B   22077  880615  Timed Ask from
BAT w/config. errorlevels
ASK_BAT.ARC    B   18625  890217  Timed response
to Y/N prompts in .BAT files
ATSIGN.ARC     B    5765  880801  Command line
batch utility
AUTOEXEC.ARC   B   45799  890806  Select different
AUTOEXEC boot-up batch files
AUTOSTOP.ARC   B    7324  881115  Batch file
utility. Good for BBS's
BAT-TIME.ARC   B   12955  881005  A batch-time
```

```
type utility. For system use
BATBRNCH.ARC  B     896  870613  Add Yes/No
branching to .BAT files with errlvl
BATCD.ASM     A    3711  840403  Change dir
within .BAT file
BATCD.DOC     A    1853  840103  Doc for
BATCD.ASM
BATCH.ARC     B   10437  890524  Useful BAT
files, color prompts prn commands
```

Here's what happens if you simply define the width to be 50 characters: long lines are split and short lines are joined together to try to create a file in which each line is 50 characters long. Notice that fmt is smart enough to know the boundaries of each word and does all its wrapping at word boundaries:

$ fmt -50 list

```
NOTE: This list was created on Mon, 16 Sep 91
03:18:14 MDT.  Some files may have been added or
deleted since that date.  See file
PD1:<MSDOS.FILEDOCS>AAAREAD.ME for additional
information.

NOTE: Type B is Binary; Type A is ASCII

Directory PD1:<MSDOS.BATUTL>
 Filename   Type Length   Date    Description
==================================================
ASK.ASM       A   14015  860422  Query from
within .BAT file ASK.DOC      A    7893  860422
Doc for ASK.ASM ASK11.ZIP    B   13714  910810
Asks questions in BATch files, with timeout
ASK3.ARC      B   22077  880615  Timed Ask from
BAT w/config. errorlevels ASK_BAT.ARC    B
18625  890217  Timed response to Y/N prompts in
.BAT files ATSIGN.ARC     B    5765  880801
Command line batch utility AUTOEXEC.ARC   B
45799  890806  Select different AUTOEXEC boot-up
batch files AUTOSTOP.ARC     B    7324  881115
Batch file utility. Good for BBS's BAT-TIME.ARC
B    12955  881005  A batch-time type utility. For
system use BATBRNCH.ARC   B     896  870613  Add
Yes/No branching to .BAT files with errlvl
BATCD.ASM     A    3711  840403  Change dir
within .BAT file BATCD.DOC      A    1853  840103
Doc for BATCD.ASM BATCH.ARC      B   10437
890524  Useful BAT files, color prompts prn
commands
```

Clearly fmt is at its best when you feed it unformatted files!

The newform Command

Because of its array of options, newform is a more powerful command than any I've already discussed. However, newform acts on its options from left to right, so the order you specify is the order it follows. newform works well with files that contain tabs, and easily removes line numbers or strips comments off the ends of lines.

I use the same text file to illustrate newform as I used to illustrate nl.

First let's see how newform can strip 10 characters from the beginning of each line. Notice that you have to change the line length from the default value of 72 characters to 50 so that -b10 has an effect. The -b option affects only the lines that are longer than the line length value.

```
$ newform -l50 -b10 text
```

```
ervices                                        June 1990

 an automated service provided by the DDN Network Information
t allows access to NIC documents and information via ordinary
 mail.  This is especially useful for people who do not have
the NIC via a direct Internet link, such as BITNET, CSNET
and UUCP sites.

the mail service, send a mail message to SERVICE@NIC.DDN.MIL.
JECT field, request the type of service you wish followed by
 arguments.  The message body is normally ignored; however, if the
eld is empty, the first line of the message body will be used
uest.  Large files will be broken into smaller separate messages.
 few files are too large to be sent through the mail system.
Requests are processed automatically once a day.

The following services are currently available:

        This message; a list of current services.
        Returns information about host xxx.  WHOIS xxx can
        also be used to get more details about a host.
        nnn is the IEN number or the word INDEX.
urns the master list of available index files.
x       xxx is a file name or the word INDEX.
        nnn is the RFC number or the word INDEX.
        to retrieve an available Postscript RFC. Check RFC INDEX for
                form of RFC.
        nnn is the FYI number or the word INDEX.
        to retrieve postscript versions of FYI files.
        xxx is a fully specified file name.
        Returns information about xxx from the WHOIS service.
        Use "WHOIS HELP" for information on how to use WHOIS.
```

Example SUBJECT lines:

```
    HELP
    RFC 822
    RFC INDEX
    RFC 1119.PS
    FYI 1
    NETINFO DOMAIN-TEMPLATE.TXT
    SEND RFC:ASSIGNED-NUMBERS.TXT
    SEND IETF:1WG-SUMMARY
    SEND INTERNET-DRAFTS:DRAFT-IETF-IWG-BGP-OO.TXT
    HOST NIC.DDN.MIL
    WHOIS LOTTOR, MARK
```

nts or suggestions to SUGGESTIONS@NIC.DDN.MIL. Send questions and
bug reports to BUG-SERVICE@NIC.DDN.MIL.

Now let's strip 20 characters from the end of every line longer than 40 characters:

$ newform -l40 -e20 text

```
NIC Mail Services

    This is an automated service provided by the DDN
Center.  It allows access to NIC documents and info
electronic mail.  This is especially useful for pe
access to the NIC via a direct Internet link, s
and UUCP sites.

    To use the mail service, send a mail message to
In the SUBJECT field, request the type of service
any needed arguments.  The message body is normally igno
SUBJECT field is empty, the first line of the messa
as the request.  Large files will be broken into smalle
However, a few files are too large to be sent thro
Requests are processed autom

The following services are

HELP            This message; a list
HOST xxx        Returns information about host
                also be used to get more d
IEN nnn         nnn is the IEN numbe
INDEX           Returns the master list of av
NETINFO xxx     xxx is a file nam
RFC nnn         nnn is the RFC numbe
RFC nnn.PS      to retrieve an available Postscript RFC.
                form of RFC.
FYI nnn         nnn is the FYI numbe
```

```
FYI nnn.PS      to retrieve postscript ve
SEND xxx        xxx is a fully
WHOIS xxx       Returns information about xxx fro
                Use "WHOIS HELP" for information
```

Example SUBJECT lines:

```
HELP
RFC 822
RFC INDEX
RFC 1119.PS
FYI 1
NETINFO DOMAIN-TEMPLATE.TXT
SEND RFC:ASSIGNED-NUMBERS.TXT
SEND IETF:1WG-SUMMARY
SEND INTERNET-DRAFTS:DRAFT
HOST NIC.DDN.MIL
WHOIS LOTTOR, MARK
```

```
Send comments or suggestions to SUGGESTIONS@NIC.DDN.
and bug reports to BUG-
```

The names file provides data for the rest of the examples of newform:

$ cat names

```
allen christopher
babinchak david
best betty
bloom dennis
boelhower joseph
bose anita
cacossa ray
chang liang
crawford patricia
crowley charles
cuddy michael
czyzewski sharon
delucia joseph
```

Let's see how newform makes every line the same length (50) by pre-fixing (-p) a + sign (-c+):

$ newform -150 -p -c+ names

```
                          allen christopher
                            babinchak david
                                 best betty
                               bloom dennis
                          boelhower joseph
                                 bose anita
                                cacossa ray
```

```
                      chang liang
                 crawford patricia
                  crowley charles
                   cuddy michael
               czyzewski sharon
                 delucia joseph
```

Oops! It prefixed each line with the default character, a space. Looks like I didn't put the options in the correct order. Let's put the character option (-c+) before the prefix option (-p) and see what happens:

$ newform -150 -c+ -p names

```
+++++++++++++++++++++++++++++++++++allen christopher
++++++++++++++++++++++++++++++++++++babinchak david
+++++++++++++++++++++++++++++++++++++++best betty
+++++++++++++++++++++++++++++++++++++++bloom dennis
+++++++++++++++++++++++++++++++++++++boelhower joseph
+++++++++++++++++++++++++++++++++++++++++bose anita
++++++++++++++++++++++++++++++++++++++++++cacossa ray
+++++++++++++++++++++++++++++++++++++++++++chang liang
++++++++++++++++++++++++++++++++++++++crawford patricia
++++++++++++++++++++++++++++++++++++++crowley charles
++++++++++++++++++++++++++++++++++++++++cuddy michael
++++++++++++++++++++++++++++++++++++++czyzewski sharon
+++++++++++++++++++++++++++++++++++++++delucia joseph
```

Aha! Next, let's append some + signs:

$ newform -150 -c+ -a names

```
allen christopher++++++++++++++++++++++++++++++++++
babinchak david++++++++++++++++++++++++++++++++++++
best betty++++++++++++++++++++++++++++++++++++++++++
bloom dennis++++++++++++++++++++++++++++++++++++++++
boelhower joseph+++++++++++++++++++++++++++++++++++
bose anita++++++++++++++++++++++++++++++++++++++++++
cacossa ray+++++++++++++++++++++++++++++++++++++++++
chang liang++++++++++++++++++++++++++++++++++++++++
crawford patricia+++++++++++++++++++++++++++++++++
crowley charles+++++++++++++++++++++++++++++++++++
cuddy michael+++++++++++++++++++++++++++++++++++++
czyzewski sharon+++++++++++++++++++++++++++++++++++
delucia joseph+++++++++++++++++++++++++++++++++++++
```

Notice that `newform`, unlike `fmt`, makes each line the same length without filling in a short line with one or more lines that occur beneath it.

Source code files are somewhat formatted in that the programmer frequently uses the tab for indentation. Let's take a C language source code file, copy.c, number its lines, and then manipulate the result with `newform`:

```
$ cat copy.c

#include <stdio.h>
int main(int argc, char * argv[])
{
    FILE * in, * out;
    int ch;
    char fname[40];

    if (argc < 2)
    {
        fprintf(stderr, "Usage: %s filename\n", argv[0]);
        exit(1);
    }

    if ((in = fopen(argv[1], "r")) == NULL)
    {
        fprintf(stderr, "Couldn't open %s\n", argv[1]);
        exit(2);
    }

    strcpy(fname, argv[1]);
    strcat(fname, ".new");

    if ((out = fopen(fname, "wb")) == NULL)
    {
        fprintf(stderr, "Can't create %s\n", fname);
        exit(3);
    }

    while ((ch = getc(in)) != EOF)
        putc(ch, out);

    fclose(in);
    fclose(out);

    fprintf(stdout, "All done!\n");
}

$ nl -ba < copy.c > copy-1.c

$ cat copy-1.c

     1    #include <stdio.h>
     2    int main(int argc, char * argv[])
     3    {
     4        FILE * in, * out;
     5        int ch;
     6        char fname[40];
     7
     8        if (argc < 2)
     9        {
```

```
10                    fprintf(stderr, "Usage: %s filename\n", argv[0]);
11                    exit(1);
12            }
13
14            if ((in = fopen(argv[1], "r")) == NULL)
15            {
16                    fprintf(stderr, "Couldn't open %s\n", argv[1]);
17                    exit(2);
18            }
19
20            strcpy(fname, argv[1]);
21            strcat(fname, ".new");
22
23            if ((out = fopen(fname, "wb")) == NULL)
24            {
25                    fprintf(stderr, "Can't create %s\n", fname);
26                    exit(3);
27            }
28
29            while ((ch = getc(in)) != EOF)
30                    putc(ch, out);
31
32            fclose(in);
33            fclose(out);
34
35            fprintf(stdout, "All done!\n");
36    }
37
```

copy-1.c is the numbered file. newform can remove the characters at the beginning of a line—up to a tab—and move them to the end (-s). I'll have newform "pad" each line with blanks (-a) so that all lines are the same length (65) before I append the numbers. I'll also tell newform to replace all tabs after the first one with an appropriate number of spaces (-i), and then truncate all lines (-e) so that all lines are the same length after the number is appended.

```
$ newform -s -i -165 -a -e copy-1.c
```

```
#include <stdio.h>                                                      1
int main(int argc, char * argv[])                                       2
{                                                                       3
        FILE * in, * out;                                               4
        int ch;                                                         5
        char fname[40];                                                 6
                                                                        7
        if (argc < 2)                                                   8
        {                                                               9
                fprintf(stderr, "Usage: %s filename\n", argv[0]);       10
                exit(1);                                                11
        }                                                               12
                                                                        13
        if ((in = fopen(argv[1], "r")) == NULL)                         14
```

```
        {                                                      15
                fprintf(stderr, "Couldn't open %s\n", argv[1]);   16
                exit(2);                                       17
        }                                                      18
                                                               19
        strcpy(fname, argv[1]);                                20
        strcat(fname, ".new");                                 21
                                                               22
        if ((out = fopen(fname, "wb")) == NULL)                23
        {                                                      24
                fprintf(stderr, "Can't create %s\n", fname);   25
                exit(3);                                       26
        }                                                      27
                                                               28
        while ((ch = getc(in)) != EOF)                         29
                putc(ch, out);                                 30
                                                               31
        fclose(in);                                            32
        fclose(out);                                           33
                                                               34
        fprintf(stdout, "All done!\n");                        35
}                                                              36
                                                               37
```

Finally, let's use newform to remove the first seven characters (-b7)—the line numbers and the first tab—from each line. Notice that I set the effective line length to one (-l1) so that -b7 would work on lines that did not contain any C language code.

$ newform -l1 -b7 < copy-1.c

```
#include <stdio.h>
int main(int argc, char * argv[])
{
    FILE * in, * out;
    int ch;
    char fname[40];

    if (argc < 2)
    {
        fprintf(stderr, "Usage: %s filename\n", argv[0]);
        exit(1);
    }

    if ((in = fopen(argv[1], "r")) == NULL)
    {
        fprintf(stderr, "Couldn't open %s\n", argv[1]);
        exit(2);
    }

    strcpy(fname, argv[1]);
    strcat(fname, ".new");
```

```
    if ((out = fopen(fname, "wb")) == NULL)
    {
        fprintf(stderr, "Can't create %s\n", fname);
        exit(3);
    }

    while ((ch = getc(in)) != EOF)
        putc(ch, out);

    fclose(in);
    fclose(out);

    fprintf(stdout, "All done!\n");
}
```

newform also has options to convert tabs to spaces and vice versa, and these are detailed in Part III, "Reference."

The pr Command

The pr command is the granddaddy of the formatters. It can separate a file into pages of a specified number of lines, number the pages, put a header on each page, and so on. This section looks at some of the more useful options.

First I'll work with the same names file I used to demonstrate newform:

```
$ cat names

allen christopher
babinchak david
best betty
bloom dennis
boelhower joseph
bose anita
cacossa ray
chang liang
crawford patricia
crowley charles
cuddy michael
czyzewski sharon
delucia joseph
```

pr prints a file with a five-line header and a five-line footer. The header, by default, consists of two blank lines, a date/time/page number line, and two more blank lines. The footer consists of five blank lines. The blank lines afford proper top and bottom margins so that, if you want, you can pipe the output of the pr command to the printer. pr normally uses 66-line pages, but to save space I'll change that to 17: ten lines of header and footer and seven lines of text:

```
$ pr -l17 names
```

```
Sep 19 15:05 1991   names Page 1
```

```
allen christopher
babinchak david
best betty
bloom dennis
boelhower joseph
bose anita
cacossa ray
```

(Seven blank lines follow.)

```
Sep 19 15:05 1991   names Page 2
```

```
chang liang
crawford patricia
crowley charles
cuddy michael
czyzewski sharon
delucia joseph
```

Notice that pr put the name for the file in the header, just before the page number. You can specify your own header with -h.

```
$ pr -l17 -h "This is the NAMES file" names
```

```
Sep 19 15:05 1991   This is the NAMES file Page 1
```

```
allen christopher
babinchak david
best betty
bloom dennis
boelhower joseph
bose anita
cacossa ray
```

(Seven blank lines follow.)

```
Sep 19 15:05 1991   This is the NAMES file Page 2
```

```
chang liang
crawford patricia
crowley charles
cuddy michael
czyzewski sharon
delucia joseph
```

The header you specify replaces the filename.

Multicolumn output is a pr option. Here I requested two-column output (-2):

```
$ pr -l17 -2 names

Sep 19 15:05 1991   names Page 1


allen christopher        chang liang
babinchak david          crawford patricia
best betty               crowley charles
bloom dennis             cuddy michael
boelhower joseph         czyzewski sharon
bose anita               delucia joseph
cacossa ray
```

You can number the lines but, unlike with n1, numbering always begins with *1*:

```
$ pr -l17 -n names

Sep 19 15:05 1991   names Page 1


    1      allen christopher
    2      babinchak david
    3      best betty
    4      bloom dennis
    5      boelhower joseph
    6      bose anita
    7      cacossa ray

(Seven blank lines follow.)

Sep 19 15:05 1991   names Page 2


    8      chang liang
    9      crawford patricia
   10      crowley charles
   11      cuddy michael
   12      czyzewski sharon
   13      delucia joseph
```

Combining numbering and multicolumns results in the following:

```
$ pr -l17 -n -2 names

Sep 19 15:05 1991   names Page 1
```

1	allen christopher	8	chang liang
2	babinchak david	9	crawford patricia
3	best betty	10	crowley charles
4	bloom dennis	11	cuddy michael
5	boelhower joseph	12	czyzewski sharon
6	bose anita	13	delucia joseph
7	cacossa ray		

Now let's use the same file as before, text, to demonstrate more things about using pr.

I'll use a 35-line page for this file:

```
$ pr -135 text
```

```
Oct  8 13:06 1991  text Page 1



NIC Mail Services                                          June 1990

   This is an automated service provided by the DDN Network Information
Center.  It allows access to NIC documents and information via ordinary
electronic mail.  This is especially useful for people who do not have
access to the NIC via a direct Internet link, such as BITNET, CSNET
and UUCP sites.

   To use the mail service, send a mail message to SERVICE@NIC.DDN.MIL.
In the SUBJECT field, request the type of service you wish followed by
any needed arguments.  The message body is normally ignored; however, if the
SUBJECT field is empty, the first line of the message body will be used
as the request.  Large files will be broken into smaller separate messages.
However, a few files are too large to be sent through the mail system.
Requests are processed automatically once a day.

The following services are currently available:

HELP           This message; a list of current services.
HOST xxx       Returns information about host xxx.  WHOIS xxx can
               also be used to get more details about a host.
IEN nnn        nnn is the IEN number or the word INDEX.
INDEX          Returns the master list of available index files.
NETINFO xxx    xxx is a file name or the word INDEX.
RFC nnn        nnn is the RFC number or the word INDEX.

(Seven blank lines follow.)

Oct  8 13:06 1991  text Page 2



RFC nnn.PS     to retrieve an available Postscript RFC. Check RFC INDEX for
               form of RFC.
FYI nnn        nnn is the FYI number or the word INDEX.
FYI nnn.PS     to retrieve postscript versions of FYI files.
```

```
SEND xxx          xxx is a fully specified file name.
WHOIS xxx         Returns information about xxx from the WHOIS service.
                  Use "WHOIS HELP" for information on how to use WHOIS.
```

```
Example SUBJECT lines:

    HELP
    RFC 822
    RFC INDEX
    RFC 1119.PS
    FYI 1
    NETINFO DOMAIN-TEMPLATE.TXT
    SEND RFC:ASSIGNED-NUMBERS.TXT
    SEND IETF:1WG-SUMMARY
    SEND INTERNET-DRAFTS:DRAFT-IETF-IWG-BGP-OO.TXT
    HOST NIC.DDN.MIL
    WHOIS LOTTOR, MARK
```

```
Send comments or suggestions to SUGGESTIONS@NIC.DDN.MIL.  Send questions
and bug reports to BUG-SERVICE@NIC.DDN.MIL.
```

Let's see what happens if you try to format this into two columns:

$ pr -135 -2 text

```
Oct  8 13:06 1991  text Page 1


NIC Mail Services          RFC   nnn.PS        to retrieve     an avai
                                 form of RFC.
   This  is an automated     service  pro FYI   nnn      nnn   is the FYI numb
Center.   It allows access to NIC do FYI    nnn.PS         to retrieve      postscr
electronic mail. This is especiall SEND xxx     xxx  is a fully spec
access to the NIC via a  direct Inte WHOIS xxx        Returns information
and UUCP sites.                      Use   "WHOIS HELP" fo


   To use the mail service, send a  Example SUBJECT lines:
In the SUBJECT field, request the t
any needed arguments.  The message HELP
SUBJECT   field is empty,     the first l    RFC 822
as the request.      Large files will b RFC INDEX
However, a few files are too large RFC 1119.PS
Requests are processed automaticall    FYI 1
                    NETINFO  DOMAIN-TEMPLATE.TXT
The following services are currentl    SEND RFC:ASSIGNED-NUMBERS.TXT
                    SEND IETF:1WG-SUMMARY
HELP     This message; a    lis SEND INTERNET-DRAFTS:DRAFT-IETF
HOST xxx Returns   information   HOST NIC.DDN.MIL
         also be   used to  get WHOIS LOTTOR, MARK
IEN nnn      nnn is the IEN numb
INDEX        Returns  the master Send comments or suggestions to SUG
NETINFO  xxx xxx is a file name  and  bug reports to BUG-SERVICE@NIC.
RFC nnn      nnn is the RFC numb
```

So pr isn't too smart about taking ordinary, document-type text and formatting it into columns.

pr is, however, good about combining two or more files. Here are three files created from fields in /etc/passwd:

```
$ cat p-login

allen
babinch
best
bloom
boelhow
bose
cacossa
chang
crawfor
crowley
cuddy
czyzews
delucia
diesso
dimemmo
dintron

$ cat p-home

/u1/fall91/dp168/allen
/u1/fall91/dp270/babinch
/u1/fall91/dp163/best
/u1/fall91/dp168/bloom
/u1/fall91/dp163/boelhow
/u1/fall91/dp168/bose
/u1/fall91/dp270/cacossa
/u1/fall91/dp168/chang
/u1/fall91/dp163/crawfor
/u1/fall91/dp163/crowley
/u1/fall91/dp270/cuddy
/u1/fall91/dp168/czyzews
/u1/fall91/dp168/delucia
/u1/fall91/dp270/diesso
/u1/fall91/dp168/dimemmo
/u1/fall91/dp168/dintron

$ cat p-uid

278
271
312
279
314
298
```

```
259
280
317
318
260
299
300
261
301
281
```

The -m option tells pr to merge the files:

```
$ pr -m -120 p-home p-uid p-login

Oct 12 14:15 1991    Page 1


/u1/fall91/dp168/allen   278                allen
/u1/fall91/dp270/babinc  271                babinch
/u1/fall91/dp163/best    312                best
/u1/fall91/dp168/bloom   279                bloom
/u1/fall91/dp163/boelho  314                boelhow
/u1/fall91/dp168/bose    298                bose
/u1/fall91/dp270/cacoss  259                cacossa
/u1/fall91/dp168/chang   280                chang
/u1/fall91/dp163/crawfo  317                crawfor
/u1/fall91/dp163/crowle  318                crowley

(Seven blank lines follow.)

Oct 12 14:15 1991    Page 2


/u1/fall91/dp270/cuddy   260                cuddy
/u1/fall91/dp168/czyzew  299                czyzews
/u1/fall91/dp168/deluci  300                delucia
/u1/fall91/dp270/diesso  261                diesso
/u1/fall91/dp168/dimemm  301                dimemmo
/u1/fall91/dp168/dintro  281                dintron
```

You can tell pr what to put between fields by using -s and a character. If you omit the character, pr uses a tab character.

```
$ pr -m -120 -s p-home p-uid p-login

Oct 12 14:16 1991    Page 1


/u1/fall91/dp168/allen   278 allen
/u1/fall91/dp270/babinch     271 babinch
/u1/fall91/dp163/best    312 best
/u1/fall91/dp168/bloom   279 bloom
```

```
/u1/fall91/dp163/boelhow        314   boelhow
/u1/fall91/dp168/bose     298   bose
/u1/fall91/dp270/cacossa        259   cacossa
/u1/fall91/dp168/chang    280   chang
/u1/fall91/dp163/crawfor        317   crawfor
/u1/fall91/dp163/crowley        318   crowley

(Seven blank lines follow.)

Oct 12 14:16 1991    Page 2


/u1/fall91/dp270/cuddy    260   cuddy
/u1/fall91/dp168/czyzews        299   czyzews
/u1/fall91/dp168/delucia        300   delucia
/u1/fall91/dp270/diesso   261   diesso
/u1/fall91/dp168/dimemmo        301   dimemmo
/u1/fall91/dp168/dintron        281   dintron
```

You can specify the order of merging and even tell pr not to print (or even leave room for) the header and footer by including the -t option. This option makes pr act somewhat like cat.

```
$ pr -m -t -s p-uid p-login p-home
   278   allen     /u1/fall91/dp168/allen
   271   babinch   /u1/fall91/dp270/babinch
   312   best      /u1/fall91/dp163/best
   279   bloom     /u1/fall91/dp168/bloom
   314   boelhow   /u1/fall91/dp163/boelhow
   298   bose      /u1/fall91/dp168/bose
   259   cacossa   /u1/fall91/dp270/cacossa
   280   chang     /u1/fall91/dp168/chang
   317   crawfor   /u1/fall91/dp163/crawfor
   318   crowley   /u1/fall91/dp163/crowley
   260   cuddy     /u1/fall91/dp270/cuddy
   299   czyzews   /u1/fall91/dp168/czyzews
   300   delucia   /u1/fall91/dp168/delucia
   261   diesso    /u1/fall91/dp270/diesso
   301   dimemmo   /u1/fall91/dp168/dimemmo
   281   dintron   /u1/fall91/dp168/dintron
```

Finally, pr has the ability to fold lines, just like the fold command.

Field-Oriented Commands

In the last example, I mentioned that I created three individual files from the *fields* of /etc/passwd. To do so, you need a command that recognizes fields.

Field is a word from the world of data management, where information is stored according to a predefined format. One such format, common among database programs, divides a file of information into *records*, usually one record per line, and then divides each record into fields. There are a number of line-oriented commands supplied with System V Release 4 UNIX and you have already met many of them. However, you need to learn about the field-oriented ones. Typically, a UNIX *database file* has one of two common *field separators*: either a tab or a colon. For example, here's a file called Passwd (a section of /etc/passwd), which is a colon-separated database:

$ cat Passwd

```
root:x:0:0:System Administrator:/usr/root:/bin/ksh
slan:x:57:57:StarGROUP Software NPP Administration:/usr/slan:
nuucp:x:10:10:0000-uucp(0000):/usr/spool/uucppublic:/usr/lib/uucp/uucico
labuucp:x:21:100:shevett's UPC:/usr/spool/uucppublic:/usr/lib/uucp/uucico
puucp:x:22:100:princeton:/usr/spool/uucppublic:/usr/lib/uucp/uucico
juucp:x:24:100:Jon LaBadie:/usr/spool/uucppublic:/usr/lib/uucp/uucico
couucp:x:25:100:Bill Michaelson:/usr/spool/uucppublic:/usr/lib/uucp/uucico
fanuucp:x:32:100:Jo Poplawski:/usr/spool/uucppublic:/usr/lib/uucp/uucico
pjh:x:102:0:Peter J. Holsberg:/usr/pjh:/bin/ksh
pete:x:200:1:PJH:/usr/home/pete:/bin/ksh
lkh:x:250:1:lkh:/usr/lkh:/bin/ksh
shevett:x:251:1:dave shevett:/usr/shevett:/bin/ksh
moser:x:252:1:sue moser:/usr/moser:/bin/ksh
```

You see the following fields:

- A login ID

- An x—this is a pointer to /etc/shadow, a file that contains encrypted passwords for all users listed in /etc/passwd

- A user ID number

- A group ID number

- The GECOS (or comment) field; in this example, it is used for the user's actual name

- The home directory pathname

- The login shell pathname

Fields in /etc/passwd are separated with colons. On the other hand, here's an excerpt from a database file, named /etc/magic, that uses a variable number of spaces as separators to achieve *fixed-length* fields:

```
$ cat magic.1

0       short       070707          cpio archive
0       string      070707          ASCII cpio archive
0       long        0177555         obsolete ar archive
0       long        0100554         apl workspace
0       short       017037          packed data
0       short       0407            pdp11/pre System V vax executable
0       short       0401            unix-rt ldp
0       short       0405            pdp11 overlay
0       short       0410            pdp11/pre System V vax pure executable
0       short       0411            pdp11 separate I&D
0       short       0432            Compiled Terminfo Entry
0       short       0433            Curses screen image
0       short       0434            Curses screen image
```

This file, by the way, is what the file command uses to determine what type a file is. Somewhere in the first 512 bytes of every UNIX file is one of the numbers listed in the third field, the so-called *magic number* that tells file what to say about the file.

Use the cut command, described in the next section, to extract selected fields from each line in any file.

5

The cut Command

pr's ability to do merges is secondary to its formatting ability. paste and join follow the discussion of cut.

The syntax for cut is one of the following:

```
cut -clist [file(s)]
```

```
cut -flist [-dchar] [-s] [file(s)]
```

The fact that you may specify zero or more filenames on the command line as arguments to cut indicates that cut is indeed a filter, and therefore can be used in a pipe or with redirection.

The first form indicates that cut can be column-oriented, so you can cut things from data files that don't use a well-defined field separator. Such files are said to have fixed-length fields; that is, the length is referred to as a certain number of columns. For example, the magic file's files are, respectively, 8, 16, 16, and 40 columns long. This is typical of files that use one or more spaces to pad each data value out to fixed number of characters. The *list* in -c*list* is a comma-separated list of column numbers, such as 1,3,7..., where the first column is number 1. You can specify a range of columns, such as 4 to 7 inclusive, like this: -c4-7. If you omit the first number in a range, cut starts at column 1; if you omit the last, cut continues through to the end of the line.

Here's the *list* that specifies columns 1 through 6, 8, 10, 13, and 20 to the end:

`-c-6,8,10,13,20-`

The columns must be specified in increasing order.

The second form is for data files with distinct field separators, files that have *variable-length* fields. The default field separator for cut is the tab. You can change it with the -d option. The -f option specifies the fields to be extracted, and uses the same rules for numbering as does the -c option.

The following examples show some uses of cut:

Cut the login names and actual names from the previously listed /etc/ passwd excerpt:

```
$ cut -d: -f1,5 Passwd
```

```
root:System Administrator
slan:StarGROUP Software NPP Administration
nuucp:0000-uucp(0000)
labuucp:shevett's UPC
puucp:princeton
juucp:Jon LaBadie
couucp:Bill Michaelson
fanuucp:Jo Poplawski
pjh:Peter J. Holsberg
pete:PJH
lkh:lkh
shevett:dave shevett
moser:sue moser
```

Notice that a delimiter has been inserted between fields in the output—the same delimiter that was in the data file.

Extract just the first field from Passwd and save it in the file f1:

```
$ cut -d: -f1 Passwd > f1
```

```
$ cat f1
```

```
root
slan
nuucp
labuucp
puucp
juucp
couucp
fanuucp
pjh
pete
lkh
```

5

```
shevett
moser
irv
ajh
mccollo
rechter
reeve
regh
sicigna
small
solarsk
steill
temple
varvar
vaas
washing
weiner
wiedenh
wight
william
```

Extract just the fifth field from Passwd and save it in the file f5:

```
$ cut -d: -f5 Passwd > f5
```

```
$ cat f5
```

```
System Administrator
StarGROUP Software NPP Administration
0000-uucp(0000)
shevett´s UPC
princeton
Jon LaBadie
Bill Michaelson
Jo Poplawski
Peter J. Holsberg
PJH
lkh
dave shevett
sue moser
Irv Ashkenazy
Alan Holsberg
Carol McCollough
rechter jay
reeve michael j
regh jeff l
sicignano joseph p
small thomas j
solarski linda m
steill keith r
temple linda c
varvar anthony j
vaas eric
```

```
washington reginald
weiner sibylle u
wiedenhofer allen e
wight charles n
williams tony j
```

Extract the characters from positions 9 through 14 and 41 through the end of each line from magic.1:

$ cut -c9-14,41- magic.1

```
short cpio archive
stringASCII cpio archive
long   obsolete ar archive
long   apl workspace
short packed data
short pdp11/pre System V vax executable
short unix-rt ldp
short pdp11 overlay
short pdp11/pre System V vax pure executable
short pdp11 separate I&D
short Compiled Terminfo Entry
short Curses screen image
short Curses screen image
```

Column 9 is the beginning of the second fixed-length field, the one that contains the names of the data types that `file` searches for, and is eight characters long. I extracted only six columns from that field, just enough to pick up "string."

The paste Command

paste is cut's partner: it merges two or more files, line by line, by treating each file as a column of a table.

Note: The word *column* as used in describing the action of paste is different from the column used in cut. cut's columns are each one character wide, but paste's columns can each contain one or more characters.

---

paste then pastes the columns next to one another—separated from each other by a tab—and prints the result on stdout.

paste has the following syntax:

```
paste [-dlist] file1 file(s)

paste -s [-dlist] file1 file(s)
```

Any filename can be replaced by a `-`. This tells `paste` to take a line from stdin.

The `-dlist` option lets you replace the default "tab between columns" with another character. For example, `-d:` replaces each tab with a colon. You can specify more than one delimiter, so that `-d:=#` replaces the first tab on each line with a colon, the second with an equal sign, and the third with a pound sign (#).

The `-s` option tells `paste` to create a multicolumn file from a single-column one.

Here are some examples of the use of `paste`, which usually but not necessarily follows the application of one or more `cut` commands. I'll use the files f1 and f5 as previously defined, plus this file:

```
$ cat f3

0
57
10
21
22
24
25
32
102
200
250
251
252
257
258
329
293
308
331
327
309
294
269
295
270
325
310
276
311
296
297
```

5

To paste three files together, use the following expression:

```
$ paste f1 f3 f5
```

```
root       0     System Administrator
slan       57    StarGROUP Software NPP Administration
nuucp      10    0000-uucp(0000)
labuucp    21    shevett's UPC
puucp      22    princeton
juucp      24    Jon LaBadie
couucp     25    Bill Michaelson
fanuucp    32    Jo Poplawski
pjh        102   Peter J. Holsberg
pete       200   PJH
lkh        250   lkh
shevett    251   dave shevett
moser      252   sue moser
irv        257   Irv Ashkenazy
ajh        258   Alan Holsberg
mccollo    329   Carol McCollough
rechter    293   rechter jay
reeve      308   reeve michael j
regh       331   regh jeff l
sicigna    327   sicignano joseph p
small      309   small thomas j
solarsk    294   solarski linda m
steill     269   steill keith r
temple     295   temple linda c
varvar     270   varvar anthony j
vaas       325   vaas eric
washing    310   washington reginald
weiner     276   weiner sibylle u
wiedenh    311   wiedenhofer allen e
wight      296   wight charles n
william    297   williams tony j
```

Paste two files together with an equal sign as the separator rather than the default tab:

```
$ paste -d= f1 f3
```

```
root=0
slan=57
nuucp=10
labuucp=21
puucp=22
juucp=24
couucp=25
fanuucp=32
pjh=102
pete=200
lkh=250
```

```
shevett=251
moser=252
irv=257
ajh=258
mccollo=329
rechter=293
reeve=308
regh=331
sicigna=327
small=309
solarsk=294
steill=269
temple=295
varvar=270
vaas=325
washing=310
weiner=276
wiedenh=311
wight=296
william=297
```

You can paste a file onto itself (making a multicolumn file from a single-column one) as follows (**Note:** If you try this on your own computer, you may get slightly different formatting):

```
$ paste -s f1

root     slan     nuucp    labuucp  puucp    juucp    couucp
fanuucp  pjh      pete     lkh      shevett  moser    irv
ajh      mccollo  rechter  reeve    regh     sicigna  small
solarsk  steill   temple   varvar   vaas     washing  weiner
wiedenh  wight    william
```

You can repeat the paste but do it with two files. Notice that paste does not mix the two files, but simply has the output of the first followed by the output of the second.

```
$ paste -s f1 f3

root     slan     nuucp    labuucp  puucp    juucp    couucp
fanuucp  pjh      pete     lkh      shevett  moser    irv
ajh      mccollo  rechter  reeve    regh     sicigna  small
solarsk  steill   temple   varvar   vaas     washing  weiner
wiedenh  wight    william

         0        57       10       21       22       24
25       32       102      200      250      251      252
257      258      329      293      308      331      327
309      294      269      295      270      325      310
276      311      296      297
```

You can use the -s option on a single file. If you do, change the delimiters to tab and the newline character. Notice that the delimiter string is quoted to protect it from the shell, like this:

```
$ paste -s -d"\t\n" f1
```

```
root      slan
nuucp     labuucp
puucp     juucp
couucp    fanuucp
pjh       pete
lkh       shevett
moser     irv
ajh       mccollo
rechter   reeve
regh      sicigna
small     solarsk
steill    temple
varvar    vaas
washing   weiner
wiedenh   wight
william
```

That was interesting! By selecting the appropriate delimiters, I turned each successive pair of lines into one line. Let's try that with two files:

```
$ paste -s -d"\t\n" f1 f3
```

```
root      slan
nuucp     labuucp
puucp     juucp
couucp    fanuucp
pjh       pete
lkh       shevett
moser     irv
ajh       mccollo
rechter   reeve
regh      sicigna
small     solarsk
steill    temple
varvar    vaas
washing   weiner
wiedenh   wight
william
          0
57        10
21        22
24        25
32        102
200       250
251       252
257       258
329       293
308       331
327       309
294       269
295       270
```

```
325   310
276   311
296   297
```

Not very interesting. It looks like the -s option is best applied to a single file.

Because paste can take input from stdin, you can pipe things to it. In this example, I send it the output of ls -1, the one-column output of ls, and paste outputs it four names to the line:

```
$ ls -1 | paste -d"\t" - - - -
```

644	644-	666	EOL
Magic	Passwd	RE	REs
UNIX.times	all.caps	and	and.1
awk	blanks-at-EOL	book	cal
cat	cat-u	cat-u.1	cmd.line
convert.a.char	copy-1.c	copy.c	copy.c.1
count.c	cron	cut	cut.1
df	diff	dir.stuff	dos
dos.1	du	env	f1
f2	f3	f5	file.times
find.1	find.2	find.ok	find.prune
find.wc	grep	id	idiom-1
idiom-2	ksh.prompt	ksh.prompts	ksh.strings
logname	ls	ls-1	ls-lc
ls-lu	magic	magic.1	names
newform	newform.a	newform.b	newform.tab
nl	nl.1	no.blanks	no.caps
no.no-caps	no.no-caps.1	nonprint	nxx
nxx$	nxx.1	p	p-home
p-login	p-uid	p4.c	pass1
pass2	pass3	pass4	passwd
paste	pax	pr	pr.1
pr.2	priv.user	ps	pwd
raw-cooked	refile	refile.1	refile.11
sed	set	some.caps	sp
sp.1	sp.2	space	space.1
space.2	space.3	squeezed	stty
text	text.tab	time	tty
ugt-pjh.txt	uname	unix	uustat
wc	who	who.dat	xx
xx.1	xxx		

Remember that each - is an argument to paste that tells paste to read a line from stdin. ls -1 supplies one filename per line and pipes it to paste, but paste waits until it receives four names before it prints a newline.

The sort Command

The sort command, like cut, is useful with database files because it can sort or merge one or more text files into a sequence you select. sort sees a blank or a tab as a delimiter. If you have multiple blanks, multiple tabs, or both between two fields, only the first is considered a delimiter and all the others belong to the next field. The -b option tells sort to ignore the blanks and tabs that are not delimiters, throwing them away instead of adding them to the beginning of the next field.

The normal ordering for sort follows the ASCII code sequence.

The syntax for sort is

```
sort [-cmu] [-ooutfile] [-ymemsize] [-zrecsize] [-dfiMnr]
     [-btchar] [+pos1 [-pos2]] [file(s)]
```

Table 5.1 describes the options of sort.

Table 5.1. The options of the sort command.

Option	Meaning
-c	Tells sort only to check whether the file is in the order specified.
-u	Tells sort to ignore any repeated lines.
-m	Tells sort to merge (and sort) the already-sorted files. (This section features an example.)
-zrecsize	Used only when merging files. Specifies the length of the longest line to be merged and prevents sort from terminating abnormally when it sees a longer-than-usual line.
-ooutfile	Specifies the name of the output file. This option is an alternative to and an improvement on redirection in that outfile can have the same name as the file being sorted.
-ymemsize	Specifies the amount of memory that sort uses. This option exists to keep sort from eating all the available memory. -y0 causes sort to begin with the minimum possible memory your system permits, and -y initially gives sort the most it can get. memsize is specified in kilobytes.
-d	Causes a *dictionary order* sort, in which sort ignores everything except letters, digits, blanks, and tabs.
-f	Causes sort to ignore upper- and lowercase distinctions in sorting.
-i	Causes sort to ignore nonprinting characters (decimal ASCII codes 0 to 31 and 127).

continues

Table 5.1. Continued.

Option	Meaning
-M	Compares the contents of specified fields as if they contained the name of month by examining the first three letters or digits in each field, converting the letters to uppercase, and sorting them in *calendar order*.
-n	Causes sort to ignore blanks and sort in numerical order: digits and associated characters—the plus sign, the minus sign, the decimal point, and so on—have their usual mathematical meanings.
-r	Added to any option causes sort to sort in reverse.
-t*char*	Selects the delimiter used in the file (unnecessary if the file uses a blank or a tab as its delimiter).
+pos1 [-pos2]	Restricts the key on which the sort is based to one that begins at field pos1 and ends at field pos2. For example, to sort on field 2, you must say +1 -2—begin just after field 1 and continue through field 2.

In addition, you can use - as an argument to force sort to take its input from stdin.

Let's run some examples that demonstrate some common options. The file auto is a tab-delimited list of the results of an automobile race. The fields are: class, driver's name, car year, car make, car model, and time.

```
$ cat auto

ES    Arther    85    Honda      Prelude    49.412
BS    Barker    90    Nissan     300ZX      48.209
AS    Saint     88    BMW        M-3        46.629
ES    Straw     86    Honda      Civic      49.543
DS    Swazy     87    Honda      CRX-Si     49.693
ES    Downs     83    VW         GTI        47.133
ES    Smith     86    VW         GTI        47.154
AS    Neuman    84    Porsche    911        47.201
CS    Miller    84    Mazda      RX-7       47.291
CS    Carlson   88    Pontiac    Fiero      47.398
DS    Kegler    84    Honda      Civic      47.429
ES    Sherman   83    VW         GTI        48.489
DS    Arbiter   86    Honda      CRX-Si     48.628
DS    Karle     74    Porsche    914        48.826
```

```
ES    Shorn     87    VW        GTI       49.357
CS    Chunk     85    Toyota    MR2       49.558
CS    Cohen     91    Mazda     Miata     50.046
DS    Lisanti   73    Porsche   914       50.609
CS    McGill    83    Porsche   944       50.642
AS    Lisle     72    Porsche   911       51.030
ES    Peerson   86    VW        Golf      54.493
```

If you invoke sort with no options, it sorts on the entire line:

```
$ sort auto
```

```
AS    Lisle     72    Porsche   911       51.030
AS    Neuman    84    Porsche   911       47.201
AS    Saint     88    BMW       M-3       46.629
BS    Barker    90    Nissan    300ZX     48.209
CS    Carlson   88    Pontiac   Fiero     47.398
CS    Chunk     85    Toyota    MR2       49.558
CS    Cohen     91    Mazda     Miata     50.046
CS    McGill    83    Porsche   944       50.642
CS    Miller    84    Mazda     RX-7      47.291
DS    Arbiter   86    Honda     CRX-Si    48.628
DS    Karle     74    Porsche   914       48.826
DS    Kegler    84    Honda     Civic     47.429
DS    Lisanti   73    Porsche   914       50.609
DS    Swazy     87    Honda     CRX-Si    49.693
ES    Arther    85    Honda     Prelude   49.412
ES    Downs     83    VW        GTI       47.133
ES    Peerson   86    VW        Golf      54.493
ES    Sherman   83    VW        GTI       48.489
ES    Shorn     87    VW        GTI       49.357
ES    Smith     86    VW        GTI       47.154
ES    Straw     86    Honda     Civic     49.543
```

If you want a list alphabetized by driver's name, you want sort to begin with the second field (+1 can be thought of as meaning "skip the first field"):

```
$ sort +1 auto
```

```
DS    Arbiter   86    Honda     CRX-Si    48.628
ES    Arther    85    Honda     Prelude   49.412
BS    Barker    90    Nissan    300ZX     48.209
CS    Carlson   88    Pontiac   Fiero     47.398
CS    Chunk     85    Toyota    MR2       49.558
CS    Cohen     91    Mazda     Miata     50.046
ES    Downs     83    VW        GTI       47.133
DS    Karle     74    Porsche   914       48.826
DS    Kegler    84    Honda     Civic     47.429
DS    Lisanti   73    Porsche   914       50.609
AS    Lisle     72    Porsche   911       51.030
CS    McGill    83    Porsche   944       50.642
CS    Miller    84    Mazda     RX-7      47.291
AS    Neuman    84    Porsche   911       47.201
```

5

```
ES    Peerson    86    VW        Golf      54.493
AS    Saint      88    BMW       M-3       46.629
ES    Sherman    83    VW        GTI       48.489
ES    Shorn      87    VW        GTI       49.357
ES    Smith      86    VW        GTI       47.154
ES    Straw      86    Honda     Civic     49.543
DS    Swazy      87    Honda     CRX-Si    49.693
```

Note that the "key" to this sort is only the driver's name. However, had there been two drivers with the same name, they would have been sorted by the car year. In other words, +1 means "skip the first field and sort on the rest of the line."

Here's a list sorted by time:

```
$ sort +5 auto
```

```
AS    Saint      88    BMW       M-3       46.629
ES    Downs      83    VW        GTI       47.133
ES    Smith      86    VW        GTI       47.154
AS    Neuman     84    Porsche   911       47.201
CS    Miller     84    Mazda     RX-7      47.291
CS    Carlson    88    Pontiac   Fiero     47.398
DS    Kegler     84    Honda     Civic     47.429
BS    Barker     90    Nissan    300ZX     48.209
ES    Sherman    83    VW        GTI       48.489
DS    Arbiter    86    Honda     CRX-Si    48.628
DS    Karle      74    Porsche   914       48.826
ES    Shorn      87    VW        GTI       49.357
ES    Arther     85    Honda     Prelude   49.412
ES    Straw      86    Honda     Civic     49.543
CS    Chunk      85    Toyota    MR2       49.558
DS    Swazy      87    Honda     CRX-Si    49.693
CS    Cohen      91    Mazda     Miata     50.046
DS    Lisanti    73    Porsche   914       50.609
CS    McGill     83    Porsche   944       50.642
AS    Lisle      72    Porsche   911       51.030
ES    Peerson    86    VW        Golf      54.493
```

Suppose you want a list of times by class. You try the following and see that it fails:

```
$ sort +0 +5 auto
```

```
AS    Lisle      72    Porsche   911       51.030
AS    Neuman     84    Porsche   911       47.201
AS    Saint      88    BMW       M-3       46.629
BS    Barker     90    Nissan    300ZX     48.209
CS    Carlson    88    Pontiac   Fiero     47.398
CS    Chunk      85    Toyota    MR2       49.558
CS    Cohen      91    Mazda     Miata     50.046
CS    McGill     83    Porsche   944       50.642
CS    Miller     84    Mazda     RX-7      47.291
```

```
DS    Arbiter    86    Honda      CRX-Si    48.628
DS    Karle      74    Porsche    914       48.826
DS    Kegler     84    Honda      Civic     47.429
DS    Lisanti    73    Porsche    914       50.609
DS    Swazy      87    Honda      CRX-Si    49.693
ES    Arther     85    Honda      Prelude   49.412
ES    Downs      83    VW         GTI       47.133
ES    Peerson    86    VW         Golf      54.493
ES    Sherman    83    VW         GTI       48.489
ES    Shorn      87    VW         GTI       49.357
ES    Smith      86    VW         GTI       47.154
ES    Straw      86    Honda      Civic     49.543
```

Why did it fail? Because I told sort to skip nothing and sort on the rest of the line, then sort on the sixth field. To restrict the first sort to just the class, and then sort on time as the secondary sort, use the following expression:

```
$ sort +0 -1 +5 auto
```

```
AS    Saint      88    BMW        M-3       46.629
AS    Neuman     84    Porsche    911       47.201
AS    Lisle      72    Porsche    911       51.030
BS    Barker     90    Nissan     300ZX     48.209
CS    Miller     84    Mazda      RX-7      47.291
CS    Carlson    88    Pontiac    Fiero     47.398
CS    Chunk      85    Toyota     MR2       49.558
CS    Cohen      91    Mazda      Miata     50.046
CS    McGill     83    Porsche    944       50.642
DS    Kegler     84    Honda      Civic     47.429
DS    Arbiter    86    Honda      CRX-Si    48.628
DS    Karle      74    Porsche    914       48.826
DS    Swazy      87    Honda      CRX-Si    49.693
DS    Lisanti    73    Porsche    914       50.609
ES    Downs      83    VW         GTI       47.133
ES    Smith      86    VW         GTI       47.154
ES    Sherman    83    VW         GTI       48.489
ES    Shorn      87    VW         GTI       49.357
ES    Arther     85    Honda      Prelude   49.412
ES    Straw      86    Honda      Civic     49.543
ES    Peerson    86    VW         Golf      54.493
```

That is, skip nothing and stop after sorting on the first field, then skip to the end of the fifth field and sort on the rest of the line—in this case, the rest of the line is just the sixth field.

Here's a simple merge example. Notice that both files are already sorted by class and name.

```
$ cat auto.1
```

```
AS    Neuman     84    Porsche    911       47.201
AS    Saint      88    BMW        M-3       46.629
BS    Barker     90    Nissan     300ZX     48.209
```

```
CS   Carlson    88   Pontiac   Fiero     47.398
CS   Miller     84   Mazda     RX-7      47.291
DS   Swazy      87   Honda     CRX-Si    49.693
ES   Arther     85   Honda     Prelude   49.412
ES   Downs      83   VW        GTI       47.133
ES   Smith      86   VW        GTI       47.154
ES   Straw      86   Honda     Civic     49.543
```

$ cat auto.2

```
AS   Lisle      72   Porsche   911       51.030
CS   Chunk      85   Toyota    MR2       49.558
CS   Cohen      91   Mazda     Miata     50.046
CS   McGill     83   Porsche   944       50.642
DS   Arbiter    86   Honda     CRX-Si    48.628
DS   Karle      74   Porsche   914       48.826
DS   Kegler     84   Honda     Civic     47.429
DS   Lisanti    73   Porsche   914       50.609
ES   Peerson    86   VW        Golf      54.493
ES   Sherman    83   VW        GTI       48.489
ES   Shorn      87   VW        GTI       49.357
```

$ sort -m auto.1 auto.2

```
AS   Lisle      72   Porsche   911       51.030
AS   Neuman     84   Porsche   911       47.201
AS   Saint      88   BMW       M-3       46.629
BS   Barker     90   Nissan    300ZX     48.209
CS   Carlson    88   Pontiac   Fiero     47.398
CS   Chunk      85   Toyota    MR2       49.558
CS   Cohen      91   Mazda     Miata     50.046
CS   McGill     83   Porsche   944       50.642
CS   Miller     84   Mazda     RX-7      47.291
DS   Arbiter    86   Honda     CRX-Si    48.628
DS   Karle      74   Porsche   914       48.826
DS   Kegler     84   Honda     Civic     47.429
DS   Lisanti    73   Porsche   914       50.609
DS   Swazy      87   Honda     CRX-Si    49.693
ES   Arther     85   Honda     Prelude   49.412
ES   Downs      83   VW        GTI       47.133
ES   Peerson    86   VW        Golf      54.493
ES   Sherman    83   VW        GTI       48.489
ES   Shorn      87   VW        GTI       49.357
ES   Smith      86   VW        GTI       47.154
ES   Straw      86   Honda     Civic     49.543
```

5

For a final example, let's take an excerpt from /etc/passwd and sort it on the user ID field. I'll also use the -t option so that the field separator used by sort will be the colon, as used by /etc/passwd.

```
$ cat pass1

root:x:0:0:System Administrator:/usr/root:/bin/ksh
slan:x:57:57:StarGROUP Software NPP Administration:/usr/slan:
labuucp:x:21:100:shevett's UPC:/usr/spool/uucppublic:/usr/lib/uucp/uucico
pcuucp:x:35:100:PCLAB:/usr/spool/uucppublic:/usr/lib/uucp/uucico
techuucp:x:36:100:The 6386:/usr/spool/uucppublic:/usr/lib/uucp/uucico
pjh:x:102:0:Peter J. Holsberg:/usr/pjh:/bin/ksh
lkh:x:250:1:lkh:/usr/lkh:/bin/ksh
shevett:x:251:1:dave shevett:/usr/shevett:/bin/ksh
mccollo:x:329:1:Carol McCollough:/usr/home/mccollo:/bin/ksh
gordon:x:304:20:gordon gary g:/u1/fall91/dp168/gordon:/bin/csh
grice:x:273:20:grice steven a:/u1/fall91/dp270/grice:/bin/ksh
gross:x:305:20:gross james l:/u1/fall91/dp168/gross:/bin/ksh
hagerho:x:326:20:hagerhorst paul j:/u1/fall91/dp168/hagerho:/bin/ksh
hendric:x:274:20:hendrickson robbin:/u1/fall91/dp270/hendric:/bin/ksh
hinnega:x:320:20:hinnegan dianna:/u1/fall91/dp163/hinnega:/bin/ksh
innis:x:262:20:innis rafael f:/u1/fall91/dp270/innis:/bin/ksh
intorel:x:286:20:intorelli anthony:/u1/fall91/dp168/intorel:/bin/ksh
```

Now I'll set the delimiter and sort:

```
$ sort -t: +2 -3 pass1

root:x:0:0:System Administrator:/usr/root:/bin/ksh
pjh:x:102:0:Peter J. Holsberg:/usr/pjh:/bin/ksh
labuucp:x:21:100:shevett's UPC:/usr/spool/uucppublic:/usr/lib/uucp/uucico
lkh:x:250:1:lkh:/usr/lkh:/bin/ksh
shevett:x:251:1:dave shevett:/usr/shevett:/bin/ksh
innis:x:262:20:innis rafael f:/u1/fall91/dp270/innis:/bin/ksh
grice:x:273:20:grice steven a:/u1/fall91/dp270/grice:/bin/ksh
hendric:x:274:20:hendrickson robbin:/u1/fall91/dp270/hendric:/bin/ksh
intorel:x:286:20:intorelli anthony:/u1/fall91/dp168/intorel:/bin/ksh
gordon:x:304:20:gordon gary g:/u1/fall91/dp168/gordon:/bin/csh
gross:x:305:20:gross james l:/u1/fall91/dp168/gross:/bin/ksh
hinnega:x:320:20:hinnegan dianna:/u1/fall91/dp163/hinnega:/bin/ksh
hagerho:x:326:20:hagerhorst paul j:/u1/fall91/dp168/hagerho:/bin/ksh
mccollo:x:329:1:Carol McCollough:/usr/home/mccollo:/bin/ksh
pcuucp:x:35:100:PCLAB:/usr/spool/uucppublic:/usr/lib/uucp/uucico
techuucp:x:36:100:The 6386:/usr/spool/uucppublic:/usr/lib/uucp/uucico
slan:x:57:57:StarGROUP Software NPP Administration:/usr/slan:
```

That's not right: why does *35* come after *329*? For the same reason that *liver* comes after *live* in the dictionary! We want the user ID field to be sorted by numerical value, so we correct the command to the following one:

```
$ sort -t: -n +2 -3 pass1
```

```
root:x:0:0:System Administrator:/usr/root:/bin/ksh
labuucp:x:21:100:shevett's UPC:/usr/spool/uucppublic:/usr/lib/uucp/uucico
pcuucp:x:35:100:PCLAB:/usr/spool/uucppublic:/usr/lib/uucp/uucico
techuucp:x:36:100:The 6386:/usr/spool/uucppublic:/usr/lib/uucp/uucico
slan:x:57:57:StarGROUP Software NPP Administration:/usr/slan:
pjh:x:102:0:Peter J. Holsberg:/usr/pjh:/bin/ksh
lkh:x:250:1:lkh:/usr/lkh:/bin/ksh
shevett:x:251:1:dave shevett:/usr/shevett:/bin/ksh
innis:x:262:20:innis rafael f:/u1/fall91/dp270/innis:/bin/ksh
grice:x:273:20:grice steven a:/u1/fall91/dp270/grice:/bin/ksh
hendric:x:274:20:hendrickson robbin:/u1/fall91/dp270/hendric:/bin/ksh
intorel:x:286:20:intorelli anthony:/u1/fall91/dp168/intorel:/bin/ksh
gordon:x:304:20:gordon gary g:/u1/fall91/dp168/gordon:/bin/csh
gross:x:305:20:gross james l:/u1/fall91/dp168/gross:/bin/ksh
hinnega:x:320:20:hinnegan dianna:/u1/fall91/dp163/hinnega:/bin/ksh
hagerho:x:326:20:hagerhorst paul j:/u1/fall91/dp168/hagerho:/bin/ksh
mccollo:x:329:1:Carol McCollough:/usr/home/mccollo:/bin/ksh
```

Got it!

The uniq Command

uniq compares adjacent lines of a file. If it finds duplicates, it does not pass them on to stdout. Duplicate adjacent lines imply that the file has been sorted before being given to uniq for processing. Here is uniq's syntax:

```
uniq [-udc [+n] [-m]] [input.file [output.file]]
```

The following examples demonstrate the options. Recently I asked users on my computer what newsgroups they read. (Newsgroups are a part of the structure of USENET News, an international electronic bulletin board.) *I catted their responses into a single file and sorted it. ngs is a piece of that* file.

```
$ cat ngs
```

```
alt.dcom.telecom
alt.sources
comp.archives
comp.bugs.sys5
comp.databases
comp.databases.informix
comp.dcom.telecom
comp.lang.c
comp.lang.c
comp.lang.c
comp.lang.c
comp.lang.c++
comp.lang.c++
```

```
comp.lang.postscript
comp.laserprinters
comp.mail.maps
comp.sources
comp.sources.3b
comp.sources.3b
comp.sources.3b
comp.sources.bugs
comp.sources.d
comp.sources.misc
comp.sources.reviewed
comp.sources.unix
comp.sources.unix
comp.sources.wanted
comp.std.c
comp.std.c
comp.std.c++
comp.std.c++
comp.std.unix
comp.std.unix
comp.sys.3b
comp.sys.att
comp.sys.att
comp.unix.questions
comp.unix.shell
comp.unix.sysv386
comp.unix.wizards
u3b.sources
```

5

I compiled the list in response to a request by the manager of the site that feeds USENET News to the computer. I wanted to give him a list that contained no duplicates, and that was easy:

```
$ uniq ngs

alt.dcom.telecom
alt.sources
comp.archives
comp.bugs.sys5
comp.databases
comp.databases.informix
comp.dcom.telecom
comp.lang.c
comp.lang.c++
comp.lang.postscript
comp.laserprinters
comp.mail.maps
comp.sources
comp.sources.3b
comp.sources.bugs
comp.sources.d
comp.sources.misc
comp.sources.reviewed
```

```
comp.sources.unix
comp.sources.wanted
comp.std.c
comp.std.c++
comp.std.unix
comp.sys.3b
comp.sys.att
comp.unix.questions
comp.unix.shell
comp.unix.sysv386
comp.unix.wizards
u3b.sources
```

This is the desired list. I could have gotten the same result by using the
-u option to sort while sorting the original file.

The -c option displays the so-called *repetition count*—the number of
times each line appears in the original file:

$ uniq -c ngs

```
1 alt.dcom.telecom
1 alt.sources
1 comp.archives
1 comp.bugs.sys5
1 comp.dcom.telecom
1 comp.databases
1 comp.databases.informix
4 comp.lang.c
2 comp.lang.c++
1 comp.lang.postscript
1 comp.laserprinters
1 comp.mail.maps
1 comp.sources
3 comp.sources.3b
1 comp.sources.bugs
1 comp.sources.d
1 comp.sources.misc
1 comp.sources.reviewed
2 comp.sources.unix
1 comp.sources.wanted
2 comp.std.c
2 comp.std.c++
2 comp.std.unix
1 comp.sys.3b
2 comp.sys.att
1 comp.unix.questions
1 comp.unix.shell
1 comp.unix.sysv386
1 comp.unix.wizards
1 u3b.sources
```

The -u command tells uniq to output only the truly unique lines; that is, the lines that have a repetition count of 1:

```
$ uniq -u ngs

alt.dcom.telecom
alt.sources
comp.archives
comp.bugs.sys5
comp.databases
comp.databases.informix
comp.dcom.telecom
comp.lang.postscript
comp.laserprinters
comp.mail.maps
comp.sources
comp.sources.bugs
comp.sources.d
comp.sources.misc
comp.sources.reviewed
comp.sources.wanted
comp.sys.3b
comp.unix.questions
comp.unix.shell
comp.unix.sysv386
comp.unix.wizards
u3b.sources
```

The -d option tells uniq to output only those lines that have a repetition count of 2 or more:

```
$ uniq -d ngs

comp.lang.c
comp.lang.c++
comp.sources.3b
comp.sources.unix
comp.std.c
comp.std.c++
comp.std.unix
comp.sys.att
```

uniq also can handle lines that are divided into fields if the separator is one or more spaces or tabs. The -n option tells uniq to skip the first n fields. The file mccc.ngs contains an abbreviated and modified newgroup list; I changed every dot (.) to a tab:

```
$ cat mccc.ngs

alt     dcom    telecom
alt     sources
```

```
comp    dcom    telecom
comp    sources
u3b     sources
```

Notice that there are some duplicates if you ignore the first field:

```
$ uniq -1 mccc.ngs
```

```
alt     dcom    telecom
alt     sources
comp    dcom    telecom
comp    sources
```

Here I forgot to resort mccc.ngs on the second field, so let's do that now:

```
$ sort +1 mccc.ngs > mccc.ngs-1
```

```
$ cat mccc.ngs-1
```

```
alt     dcom    telecom
comp    dcom    telecom
alt     sources
comp    sources
u3b     sources
```

Now I'm ready to try uniq again:

```
$  uniq -1 mccc.ngs-1
```

```
alt     dcom    telecom
alt     sources
```

This works. uniq also can ignore the first *m* columns of a sorted file. The +*m* option tells uniq to skip the first *m* columns. I adjusted the file mccc.ngs-2 so that the first "field" has four characters in it for every line:

```
$ cat mccc.ngs-2
```

```
alt .dcom.telecom
comp.dcom.telecom
alt .sources
comp.sources
u3b .sources
```

```
$ uniq +4 mccc.ngs-2
```

```
alt .dcom.telecom
alt .sources
```

The join Command

The `join` command is another database manipulator. It combines corresponding lines from two files. Each line must have a *join field*, usually the first string on each line. The syntax is

```
join [-afilenum] [-e string] [-jfilenum fieldnum] [-o list]
    [-tchar] file1 file2
```

file1 and *file2* must already be sorted on the join field. Each output line normally has the join field first, followed by the rest of the line from *file1*, followed by the rest of the line from *file2*.

Here's a very simple example. auto.1.1 and auto.2.1 were built from the auto files used for earlier examples. They contain only classes and driver's names. (As a test of your tool building prowess, determine what command line applied to auto will produce these two files.)

> **Note:** Each file has been sorted on the class field.

```
$ cat auto.1.1

AS    Neuman Saint
BS    Barker
CS    Carlson Miller
DS    Swazy
ES    Arther Downs Smith Straw

$ cat auto.2.1

AS    Lisle
CS    Chunk Cohen McGill
DS    Arbiter Karle Kegler Lisanti
ES    Peerson Sherman Shorn
```

If you join these two on the class field (remember, the first field is the default join field), you get the following:

```
$ join auto.1.1 auto.2.1

AS Neuman Saint Lisle
CS Carlson Miller Chunk Cohen McGill
DS Swazy Arbiter Karle Kegler Lisanti
ES Arther Downs Smith Straw Peerson Sherman Shorn
```

Lisle from *AS* in the second file has been joined with *Newman* and *Saint* from *AS* in the first file. *Barker* from *BS* in the first file is not in the output merely because there is no *BS* line in file 2. The other classes, however, have members in both files and the output contains the appropriate combinations.

You can specify which fields should appear in the output by using the -o option. It takes a space-separated list of what appear to be decimal numbers (1.1, 1.2, 3.2, and so on). These numbers are interpreted as `filenumber.fieldnumber`. For example, 1.2 represents the second field of the first file.

```
$ cat auto.1.3
```

```
AS    Neuman    84    Porsche    911      47.201
BS    Barker    90    Nissan     300ZX    48.209
CS    Miller    84    Mazda      RX-7     47.291
DS    Swazy     87    Honda      CRX-Si   49.693
ES    Straw     86    Honda      Civic    49.543
```

```
$ cat auto.2.3
```

```
AS    Lisle      72    Porsche    911      51.030
CS    Chunk      85    Toyota     MR2      49.558
DS    Arbiter    86    Honda      CRX-Si   48.628
ES    Peerson    86    VW         Golf     54.493
```

Now join just the name fields of these two files:

```
$ join -o 1.2 2.2 auto.1.3 auto.2.3
```

```
Neuman Lisle
Miller Chunk
Swazy Arbiter
Straw Peerson
```

The join field is missing from the output because the -o option outputs only the fields you specify. In other words, if you want the join field in the output, you must add either 1.1 or 2.1 to the list:

```
$ join -o 1.1 1.2 2.2 auto.1.3 auto.2.3
```

```
AS Neuman Lisle
CS Miller Chunk
DS Swazy Arbiter
ES Straw Peerson
```

From either file, you can include lines that have no corresponding lines in the other file by using the -a option. Notice that I've specified both -a1 and -a2 so that unpaired lines from both files, if any exist, appear in the output. The *BS Barker* line from auto.1.3 is the only unmatched line in either file in this example.

```
$ join -o 1.1 1.2 2.2 -a1 -a2 auto.1.3 auto.2.3
```

```
AS Neuman Lisle
BS Barker
CS Miller Chunk
DS Swazy Arbiter
ES Straw Peerson
```

If it's not obvious that a line in the output was an "orphan" (a line of output that contains information from just one of the input files is an orphan), you can make it obvious by using the -e option. This lets you specify any string to replace empty fields in the output.

```
$ join -o 1.1 1.2 2.2 -a1 -a2 -e BLANK auto.1.3 auto.2.3
```

```
AS Neuman Lisle
BS Barker BLANK
CS Miller Chunk
DS Swazy Arbiter
ES Straw Peerson
```

Another example works with office management files. Suppose you have two databases, the first containing employees' personnel information and the second containing employees' work information:

```
$ cat personnel
```

```
John Smith¦22 First Street¦Denver¦CO¦65432
Mary Jones¦876 Rosey Road¦Bolder¦CO¦65498
```

```
$ cat professional
```

```
John Smith¦Sales Manager¦404-546-1227
Mary Jones¦Technical Manager¦302-455-1289
```

Notice that the two files have employees' names as the common field, and that the fields are separated with a pipe symbol (¦). (Of course, the character is not a pipe symbol as far as the database file is concerned.) You make join recognize the separator with the -t option:

```
$ join -t"¦" personnel professional
```

```
John Smith¦22 First Street¦Denver¦CO¦65432¦Sales Manager¦404-546-1227
Mary Jones¦876 Rosey Road¦Bolder¦CO¦65498¦Technical Manager¦302-455-1289
```

In each of the preceding examples, I use the default field—the first one—as the join field. You can change this with the -j option. The -j option takes two space-separated arguments: a *file number*—a 1 for the first file or a 2 for the second file—and a *field number*. If the desired join field is in the same position (that is, has the same field number) in both files, you can omit the file number, in which case join uses the field number following the -j in both files. If the join field is in different positions in the two files, you must include *two* -j options, one specifying the field for the first file and the second specifying the field for the second file. For example, -j1 4 specifies the fourth field of the first file.

For the last example, let's again play with the excerpt from /etc/passwd and add an excerpt from /etc/group so that you can see sort and join working together:

$ **cat pass.1**

```
root:x:0:0:System Administrator:/usr/root:/bin/ksh
slan:x:57:57:StarGROUP Software NPP Administration:/usr/slan:
labuucp:x:21:100:shevett's UPC:/usr/spool/uucppublic:/usr/lib/uucp/uucico
pcuucp:x:35:100:PCLAB:/usr/spool/uucppublic:/usr/lib/uucp/uucico
techuucp:x:36:100:The 6386:/usr/spool/uucppublic:/usr/lib/uucp/uucico
pjh:x:102:0:Peter J. Holsberg:/usr/pjh:/bin/ksh
lkh:x:250:1:lkh:/usr/lkh:/bin/ksh
shevett:x:251:1:dave shevett:/usr/shevett:/bin/ksh
mccollo:x:329:1:Carol McCollough:/usr/home/mccollo:/bin/ksh
gordon:x:304:20:gordon gary g:/u1/fall91/dp168/gordon:/bin/csh
grice:x:273:20:grice steven a:/u1/fall91/dp270/grice:/bin/ksh
gross:x:305:20:gross james l:/u1/fall91/dp168/gross:/bin/ksh
hagerho:x:326:20:hagerhorst paul j:/u1/fall91/dp168/hagerho:/bin/ksh
hendric:x:274:20:hendrickson robbin:/u1/fall91/dp270/hendric:/bin/ksh
hinnega:x:320:20:hinnegan dianna:/u1/fall91/dp163/hinnega:/bin/ksh
innis:x:262:20:innis rafael f:/u1/fall91/dp270/innis:/bin/ksh
intorel:x:286:20:intorelli anthony:/u1/fall91/dp168/intorel:/bin/ksh
```

Now sort it in ASCII sequence on the fourth field, the one that contains the group ID number:

$ **sort -t":" +3 -4 pass.1 > out-p**

$ **cat out-p**

```
pjh:x:102:0:Peter J. Holsberg:/usr/pjh:/bin/ksh
root:x:0:0:System Administrator:/usr/root:/bin/ksh
lkh:x:250:1:lkh:/usr/lkh:/bin/ksh
mccollo:x:329:1:Carol McCollough:/usr/home/mccollo:/bin/ksh
shevett:x:251:1:dave shevett:/usr/shevett:/bin/ksh
labuucp:x:21:100:shevett's UPC:/usr/spool/uucppublic:/usr/lib/uucp/uucico
pcuucp:x:35:100:PCLAB:/usr/spool/uucppublic:/usr/lib/uucp/uucico
techuucp:x:36:100:The 6386:/usr/spool/uucppublic:/usr/lib/uucp/uucico
gordon:x:304:20:gordon gary g:/u1/fall91/dp168/gordon:/bin/csh
grice:x:273:20:grice steven a:/u1/fall91/dp270/grice:/bin/ksh
gross:x:305:20:gross james l:/u1/fall91/dp168/gross:/bin/ksh
hagerho:x:326:20:hagerhorst paul j:/u1/fall91/dp168/hagerho:/bin/ksh
hendric:x:274:20:hendrickson robbin:/u1/fall91/dp270/hendric:/bin/ksh
```

```
hinnega:x:320:20:hinnegan dianna:/u1/fall91/dp163/hinnega:/bin/ksh
innis:x:262:20:innis rafael f:/u1/fall91/dp270/innis:/bin/ksh
intorel:x:286:20:intorelli anthony:/u1/fall91/dp168/intorel:/bin/ksh
slan:x:57:57:StarGROUP Software NPP Administration:/usr/slan:
```

Notice that, in the ASCII sequence, 100 follows 1 and precedes 20. Now, to the excerpt from /etc/group. This is the data file that keeps track of the groups that users belong to. Its first field is the group name; the second, an optional group password; the third, the group ID number; and the fourth, an optional list of the logins of the members of that group.

```
$ cat grp.1
```

```
root::0:root
other::1:
bin::2:root,bin,daemon
sys::3:root,bin,sys,adm
adm::4:root,adm,daemon
uucp::5:uucp
mail::6:root
news::7:news
daemon::12:root,daemon
slan::57:slan,root
stu::20:
others::100:
dp::200:
talk::9999:
```

Now sort it on the group ID number:

```
$ sort -t":" +2 -3 grp.1 > out-g
```

```
$ cat out-g
```

```
root::0:root
other::1:
others::100:
daemon::12:root,daemon
bin::2:root,bin,daemon
stu::20:
dp::200:
sys::3:root,bin,sys,adm
adm::4:root,adm,daemon
uucp::5:uucp
slan::57:slan,root
mail::6:root
news::7:news
talk::9999:
```

And now let's join the two, using the group ID number—field 4 in file 1 and field 3 in file 2—as the join field. The output contains the join field, the group name, and the home directory for each user.

```
$ join -j1 4 -j2 3 -t: -o 1.1 2.1 1.6 out-p out-g

pjh:root:/usr/pjh
root:root:/usr/root
lkh:other:/usr/lkh
mccollo:other:/usr/home/mccollo
shevett:other:/usr/shevett
labuucp:others:/usr/spool/uucppublic
pcuucp:others:/usr/spool/uucppublic
techuucp:others:/usr/spool/uucppublic
gordon:stu:/u1/fall91/dp168/gordon
grice:stu:/u1/fall91/dp270/grice
gross:stu:/u1/fall91/dp168/gross
hagerho:stu:/u1/fall91/dp168/hagerho
hendric:stu:/u1/fall91/dp270/hendric
hinnega:stu:/u1/fall91/dp163/hinnega
innis:stu:/u1/fall91/dp270/innis
intorel:stu:/u1/fall91/dp168/intorel
slan:slan:/usr/slan
```

Summary

This chapter examined commands for manipulating the contents of files. One set deals with the format of the body of the file, and another set lets you extract information from some files and build new files with the extracted information.

## Chapter 6

Changing Characters
and Strings in Files

You've met System V Release 4 commands that show you the contents of a file, that reformat those contents in a variety of ways, and that extract parts of files and build new ones from those parts. It's time to look at a command that can *change* sets of characters in a file into other sets, and at a command that can change one or more lines in a file. As usual, you do not actually change the original file at all, but instead can create a new file that is the modified version of the old one.

Changing Characters with tr

The tr command translates or changes any character or set of characters to any other character or set of characters. tr also can delete characters.

tr is a *character filter*. It can look at each character coming in via stdin and delete the character or change it to some other character before passing the result along to stdout. You can change all uppercase letters to lowercase, all periods to commas, all digits to letters, and so on. The syntax is

```
tr [ -cds] [search [substitute]]
```

where

    -c complements the set of *search* characters

-d deletes all the *search* characters

-s squeezes all strings of repeated characters specified in the *substitution* string to single characters

The *search* and *substitute* strings are lists of printable ASCII characters, and can include nonprintable ones if you write each as a \ followed by its octal ASCII code number. For example, the octal code of the carriage return (CR) character must be written as "\15" or "\015", and should be quoted just as shown. In fact, it doesn't hurt to quote both strings, just to be sure that the shell doesn't interpret any potentially special characters.

The remainder of this section shows examples of the use of the tr command.

First, you can convert an MS-DOS text file to a UNIX text file. People who use both UNIX and MS-DOS realize that the two operating systems differ in, among other things, the way they treat the end of a line in a text file. UNIX uses the single character, line feed (also known as *newline*), ASCII code \013; but MS-DOS uses the carriage return/line feed pair, codes \015 and \013 respectively. This is the result of MS-DOS's heritage from an earlier operating system called CP/M. Use the following tr command to change an MS-DOS file to a UNIX file:

```
tr -d '\015' < msdos-file > unix-file
```

Although it would be interesting to contemplate an inverse command, tr isn't smart enough to substitute two characters for one.

You can change one character to another. Chapter 5 showed examples in which I changed every period (.) in a certain file to a tab. Here's how:

```
$ cat mccc.ngs-1

alt.dcom.telecom
comp.dcom.telecom
alt.sources
comp.sources
u3b.sources

$ tr '.' '    ' < mccc.ngs-1

alt       dcom      telecom
comp      dcom      telecom
alt       sources
comp      sources
u3b       sources
```

The second quoted character in the preceding tr command is just the tab key. If it bothers you to see an "empty" pair of single quotation marks that supposedly enclose a tab, write the second quoted character as `'\009'` instead.

You can change a class of characters to another class. Remember the names file? I use it here to demonstrate some `tr` commands:

```
$ cat names

allen christopher
babinchak david
best betty
bloom dennis
boelhower joseph
bose anita
cacossa ray
chang liang
crawford patricia
crowley charles
cuddy michael
czyzewski sharon
delucia joseph

$ tr '[a-z]' 'nopqrstuvwxyzabcdefghijklm' < names > who.dat

$ cat who.dat

nyyra puevfgbcure
onovapunx qnivq
orfg orggl
oybbz qraavf
obryubjre wbfrcu
obfr navgn
pnpbffn enl
punat yvnat
penjsbeq cngevpvn
pebjyrl puneyrf
phqql zvpunry
pmlmrjfxv funeba
qryhpvn wbfrcu
```

The *search* string was actually a regular expression, the one that means "all lowercase characters from a to z." When that is expanded, `tr` recognizes a one-to-one relationship between the 26 characters in each of the strings. Thus, each a was replaced by an n, each b by an o, each c by a p, and so on. Notice that you can use the left-right bracket pair metacharacter for *search* but, because the characters in *substitute* were not in ASCII code order, you could not use `'[n-za-m]'` in the *substitute* string.

You can change all lowercase characters to uppercase:

```
$ tr '[a-z]' '[A-Z]' < names > all.caps
```

```
$ cat all.caps
```

```
ALLEN CHRISTOPHER
BABINCHAK DAVID
BEST BETTY
BLOOM DENNIS
BOELHOWER JOSEPH
BOSE ANITA
CACOSSA RAY
CHANG LIANG
CRAWFORD PATRICIA
CROWLEY CHARLES
CUDDY MICHAEL
CZYZEWSKI SHARON
DELUCIA JOSEPH
```

Just as we expected. But what happens if *substitute* is shorter than *search*?

```
$ tr '[a-z]' '[A-E]' < names > some.caps
```

```
$ cat some.caps
```

```
AllEn ChristophEr
BABinChAk DAviD
BEst BEtty
Bloom DEnnis
BoElhowEr josEph
BosE AnitA
CACossA rAy
ChAng liAng
CrAwforD pAtriCiA
CrowlEy ChArlEs
CuDDy miChAEl
CzyzEwski shAron
DEluCiA josEph
```

Only the first five characters in *search* were changed, because there were only five characters in *substitute*.

As you have seen, you can delete a character by using tr. Let's try to eliminate all the uppercase letters from some.caps:

```
$ tr -d '[A-Z]' < some.caps > no.caps
```

```
$ cat no.caps
```

```
lln hristophr
inhk vi
st tty
loom nnis
olhowr josph
os nit
oss ry
```

```
hng ling
rwfor ptrii
rowly hrls
uy mihl
zyzwski shron
lui josph
```

Now try the -c option, the one that complements the set of search characters. The following command deletes all characters *except* uppercase letters from some.caps:

```
$ tr -dc '[A-Z]' < some.caps > not.caps
```

```
$ cat not.caps
```

AECEBABCADADBEBEBDEBEEEBEAACACAACAACADACACECAECDDCAECEADECAE

Aha! It even deleted the newlines! If you want to preserve the line orientation of some.caps, you must tell tr to delete everything but uppercase *and* newlines:

```
$ tr -dc '\012[A-Z]' < some.caps > not.caps.2
```

```
$ cat not.caps.1
```

```
AECE
BABCADAD
BEBE
BDE
BEEE
BEAA
CACAA
CAA
CADACA
CECAE
CDDCAE
CEA
DECAE
```

Much better!

You can squeeze out multiple characters. Consider the use of the "squeeze" option, -s, with the following file:

```
$ cat spaces
```

```
A regular      expression  is a sequence  of  characters taken
from  the set     of uppercase and lowercase letters and digits.
```

```
$ tr -s ' ' < spaces > no.spaces
```

```
A regular expression is a sequence of characters taken
from the set of uppercase and lowercase letters and digits.
```

As advertised, all multiple spaces have been removed.

6

tr has one other format for *substitute*: the repetition specification. If you'd like *substitute* to be *n* of the same character, say x, you would write

```
$ tr search ´[X*n]´ < infile > outfile
```

If you omit *n*, tr understands that you want as many xs as there are characters in *search*.

The sed Command

sed is a *streaming editor*. Unlike ed and vi, which are interactive editors, sed takes a command (or a series of commands, or even a file full of commands) and applies it to lines of a file *without* any further human intervention. That is, when you use an editor like vi, it reads the file you specify and displays a screenful of it to you. You then enter commands that either add to the contents of the file, modify what's already there, or both. Then you command the editor to write the result back to the disk.

sed, on the other hand, reads in commands and then the file to be edited is passed through those commands. The commands are applied to the data as it "flies by" sed, changing lines or portions of lines as instructed. Because sed reads data from stdin and writes its output to stdout, it is a filter. But because the output depends on the set of commands sed receives, it can be described as a *programmable filter*.

There are many situations in which using sed is more advantageous than using an interactive editor, including the following:

- When the file to be edited is very large

- When the same editing commands have to be invoked in numerous files

- When editing actions for a line (or multiple lines) must be taken from a shell script

- When writing conversion programs

sed Actions and Syntax

Here's the simplest syntax for the sed command line:

```
sed [-n] [action] [file(s)]
```

sed executes the *action* on the lines in the *file(s)* specified, or on whatever appears at stdin if no files are specified. An *action* consists of an *address* and one or more *command*s. The address tells sed which lines of the file to apply the command(s) to. The -n option prevents sed from writing any output to stdout; however, you will soon see that part of *command* can tell sed to write all changes to stdout.

The following is a more general way of writing the sed command line:

```
sed [-n] [-e action] [-f script] [file(s)]
```

You can repeat the -e *action* to give sed more than one command. In addition to one or more commands specified with -e, you also can write a *script file*, or *script* for short, containing sed commands and use the -f option to tell sed where to find it.

sed commands are similar to those used by ed and by the *colon-command* (ex) *mode* of vi. The general form of an action is one of the following:

```
command [argument(s)]
```

or

```
address command [argument(s)]
```

or

```
address,address command [argument(s)]
```

command can be replaced by two or more commands that you want performed at the same address, like this:

```
{
command-1
command-2
...
command-n
}
```

sed usually follows these steps:

1. sed reads the first line from the first file in the list of input files into what is called the *pattern space*. All editing occurs on the contents of the pattern space.

2. sed then reads the first action from either the command line or from the script. If the *address* of the command indicates that this line should be edited, sed takes action on the contents of the pattern space, changing what is contained in it.

3. sed then reads the next action and determines whether or not this command should operate on this line. If so, sed takes the specified command action on the contents of the pattern space.

4. sed repeats step 3 until all commands that pertain to this line have had a crack at the contents of the pattern space. sed then writes the contents of the pattern space to stdout and empties ("flushes") the pattern space.

5. sed then reads the next line from the current input file into the pattern space, and repeats steps 2 through 4 until all lines in the current input file have been examined.

6. If there's another file in the list of input files, sed reads the first line from it (making it the current file) into the pattern space.

7. sed repeats steps 2 through 6 until it has processed all lines of all files.

It's important that you understand that sed applies each command in a script to each line from the input file before reading the next line. sed, therefore, always is working with the latest version of a line, not with the original line. For example, if your commands include these two search-and-substitute commands

```
s/305/407/
s/407/618/
```

all instances of the string 305 and the string 407 are replaced by the string 618.

Addresses

Addresses can take three different forms: numerical, pattern matching (as in regular expressions), and the special address $, the last line of the last file.

- A numerical address represents a line number. This form is useful if you're working with a highly structured file, such as the output of a pr command. If there are multiple files on the command line, sed consecutively numbers the lines in the files. For example, if you have a 32-line file followed by a 40-line file, the first line of the second file is number 33.

- If you surround a regular expression with slashes (/), sed identifies lines containing strings that match that regular expression. (See Chapter 2 for a refresher on regular expressions.) For example, if you say

```
/uucp/
```

sed copies each line that has uucp in it into the pattern space, one at a time. If you say

```
/^[Tt]his/
```

then every line that begins with This or this gets its turn in the pattern space.

This last form is undoubtedly the most useful and most frequently used.

A sed command may have 0, 1, or 2 addresses:

- If there is no address, the action pertains to every line.

- If there is one address, the action pertains to every line that matches that address (remember that the address can be a pattern and that several lines in a file may match a pattern).

- If there are two addresses, they refer to a *range* of lines and must be separated by a comma (,). sed operates on the group of lines which include the first line that matches the first address *and* all succeeding lines up to and including the first line that matches the second address.

- When any address has an exclamation mark (!) appended to it, sed looks for lines that do *not* match that address.

The following are a few examples using the delete action (d). I've taken our old regular expression practice file REfile and used nl to number its lines:

```
$ cat refile.1

     1    A regular expression is a sequence of characters taken
     2    from the set of uppercase and lowercase letters, digits,
     3    punctuation marks, etc., plus a set of special regular
     4    expression operators. Some of these operators may remind
     5    you of file name matching, but be forewarned: in general,
     6    regular expression operators are different from the
     7    shell metacharacters we discussed in Chapter 1.
     8
     9    The simplest form of a regular expression is one that
    10    includes only letters. For example, the would match only
    11    the three-letter sequence t, h, e. This pattern is found
    12    in the following words: the, therefore, bother. In other
    13    words, wherever the regular expression pattern is found
    14    -- even if it is surrounded by other characters --, it will
    15    be matched.
```

You tell sed to delete the first line by giving it the command 1d, putting the command in quotation marks to protect it from the shell. Using quotation marks isn't necessary for this command, but it's a good habit to learn.

```
$ sed '1d' refile.1

     2    from the set of uppercase and lowercase letters, digits,
     3    punctuation marks, etc., plus a set of special regular
     4    expression operators. Some of these operators may remind
     5    you of file name matching, but be forewarned: in general,
     6    regular expression operators are different from the
     7    shell metacharacters we discussed in Chapter 1.
     8
     9    The simplest form of a regular expression is one that
    10    includes only letters. For example, the would match only
    11    the three-letter sequence t, h, e. This pattern is found
    12    in the following words: the, therefore, bother. In other
    13    words, wherever the regular expression pattern is found
    14    -- even if it is surrounded by other characters --, it will
    15    be matched.
```

Now remove the last line, using the special address for the last line, $:

```
$ sed '$d' refile.1

     1    A regular expression is a sequence of characters taken
     2    from the set of uppercase and lowercase letters, digits,
     3    punctuation marks, etc., plus a set of special regular
     4    expression operators. Some of these operators may remind
     5    you of file name matching, but be forewarned: in general,
     6    regular expression operators are different from the
     7    shell metacharacters we discussed in Chapter 1.
     8
     9    The simplest form of a regular expression is one that
    10    includes only letters. For example, the would match only
    11    the three-letter sequence t, h, e. This pattern is found
    12    in the following words: the, therefore, bother. In other
    13    words, wherever the regular expression pattern is found
    14    -- even if it is surrounded by other characters --, it will
```

To demonstrate numerical addresses, the following command deletes lines 3, 4, 5 and 6:

```
$ sed '3,6d' refile.1

     1    A regular expression is a sequence of characters taken
     2    from the set of uppercase and lowercase letters, digits,
     7    shell metacharacters we discussed in Chapter 1.
     8
     9    The simplest form of a regular expression is one that
    10    includes only letters. For example, the would match only
    11    the three-letter sequence t, h, e. This pattern is found
    12    in the following words: the, therefore, bother. In other
    13    words, wherever the regular expression pattern is found
    14    -- even if it is surrounded by other characters --, it will
    15    be matched.
```

To demonstrate the use of a regular expression as an address, remove all lines that have `regu` in them:

```
$ sed '/regu/d' refile.1
```

```
2    from the set of uppercase and lowercase letters, digits,
4    expression operators. Some of these operators may remind
5    you of file name matching, but be forewarned: in general,
7    shell metacharacters we discussed in Chapter 1.
8
10   includes only letters. For example, the would match only
11   the three-letter sequence t, h, e. This pattern is found
12   in the following words: the, therefore, bother. In other
14   -- even if it is surrounded by other characters --, it will
15   be matched.
```

Notice that the regular expression is surrounded by slashes (/). Now remove all lines that do *not* have `regu` in them. You can do this by appending an exclamation mark (!) to the address:

```
$ sed '/regu/!d' refile.1
```

```
1    A regular expression is a sequence of characters taken
3    punctuation marks, etc., plus a set of special regular
6    regular expression operators are different from the
9    The simplest form of a regular expression is one that
13   words, wherever the regular expression pattern is found
```

To illustrate using regular expressions in a range of addresses, let's delete all lines between the line that has `char` in it and the line that has `letter` in it. Let's take another look at the original file first:

```
$ cat refile.1
```

```
1    A regular expression is a sequence of characters taken
2    from the set of uppercase and lowercase letters, digits,
3    punctuation marks, etc., plus a set of special regular
4    expression operators. Some of these operators may remind
5    you of file name matching, but be forewarned: in general,
6    regular expression operators are different from the
7    shell metacharacters we discussed in Chapter 1.
8
9    The simplest form of a regular expression is one that
10   includes only letters. For example, the would match only
11   the three-letter sequence t, h, e. This pattern is found
12   in the following words: the, therefore, bother. In other
13   words, wherever the regular expression pattern is found
14   -- even if it is surrounded by other characters --, it will
15   be matched.
```

char is found in line 1, and letter on line 2. However, char also is found on line 7 and letter also is found on line 10. Although char is also found on line 14, there is no corresponding occurrence of `letter`. Thus only two groups of lines match the address we're using, and two groups of lines are deleted. Here's the command line and the result:

```
$ sed '/char/,/letter/d' refile.1
```

```
    3     punctuation marks, etc., plus a set of special regular
    4     expression operators. Some of these operators may remind
    5     you of file name matching, but be forewarned: in general,
    6     regular expression operators are different from the
   11     the three-letter sequence t, h, e. This pattern is found
   12     in the following words: the, therefore, bother. In other
   13     words, wherever the regular expression pattern is found
```

Even though `letter` also appears on line 10, sed doesn't see line 10 as the end of a single range. Unlike the grep family, which looks for the longest string of characters that matches a pattern, sed does not look for the longest sequence of lines that matches an address. Instead, sed bails out as soon as it finds a line that matches the second address. Of course, when sed is looking for regular expressions, it matches the longest string just as grep does.

sed's Commands

The following is an overview of sed's fundamental commands. Details of each command follow later in the chapter.

- *Append*, *insert*, and *change* are like their interactive counterparts in vi. The *append* command adds the accompanying text to the end of the pattern space, the *insert* command adds the accompanying text to the beginning of the pattern space, and the *change* command empties the pattern space and fills it with the accompanying text.

- *Comments* can be placed in sed scripts to document the script. Comments aren't really commands because they don't cause any changes to the pattern space. A comment is any line in the script that begins with a pound sign (#). For example:

  ```
  # this is a comment
  ```

- *Delete* removes a line by emptying the pattern space and causing sed to begin a new command cycle (see step 5 in the preceding description of how sed processes lines with commands).

- *List* displays the contents of the pattern space on stdout, showing nonprinting characters as their octal ASCII code numbers, and folding long lines.

- *Print* displays the contents of the pattern space on stdout.

- *Quit* stops sed from reading any additional input lines and then stops execution of sed.

- *Read* causes sed to read the contents of the file given as its argument and append it to the pattern space.

- *Search-and-substitute* causes sed to look for a pattern that matches a specified regular expression and then replace it with the substitute string. The syntax is

```
[address]s/regular expression/substitute string/[flags]
```

I discuss the details later in this chapter, but you should review Chapter 2's discussion of the regular expression characters \(and \) and the concept of a *hold space*.

- *Transform* acts like tr in that one set of characters replaces another.

- *Write* appends the contents of the pattern space to the file given as its argument. Now look at the more advanced commands:

- *Add to hold space* appends the contents of the pattern space to the hold space.

- *Add to pattern space* appends the contents of the hold space to the pattern space.

- *Append next* appends a newline character and the next line (from the input file) to the pattern space

- *Branch to* label alters the sequence of commands by jumping to a specified place in the script.

- *Copy through newline* displays the beginning of the pattern space up to and including a newline (see the print command).

- *Delete through newline* deletes the beginning of the pattern space up to and including a newline (see the *append next* command), and starts the next command cycle.

- *Exchange hold and pattern* exchanges the contents of the pattern and hold spaces.

- *Next* copies the pattern space to stdout and reads the next line as its replacement. Continue with the command that follows in the command script or from the command line.

- *Replace hold space* replaces the hold space with the contents of the pattern space.

- *Replace pattern space* replaces the pattern space with the contents of the hold space.

These advanced commands are beyond the scope of this book.

6

Some Actual sed Scripts

Having had an overview of sed's commands and some exposure to the s and d commands, earlier in this chapter and in Chapter 2, you're ready to see some details of what sed can do. The following examples introduce some details of sed's syntax and use both command-line and sed script forms to demonstrate both ways of feeding one or more commands to sed.

Grouping Two or More Commands Together

Sometimes you might want to apply more than one set of edits to a line found through the use of an address. Use curly braces ({ }) to group edit commands.

For an example, I'll operate on the rolodex file:

```
$ cat rolodex

George Seer:Hightstown:NJ:08520:609-448-1860
Mark Tondayo:Levittown:PA:19054:215-946-5771
Clifford Dice:Manalapan:NJ:07726:201-446-2164
Marc Arturo:Trenton:NJ:08601:609-396-8765
James Lizzaro:Wrightstown:NJ:08520:609-758-7057
William Jefferson:Trenton:NJ:08638:609-883-7799
Sidney Hoffman:Trenton:NJ:08638:609-298-1952
Jeremy Dukakis:Mercerville:08619:609-587-7041
Leon Franks:Trenton:NJ:08610:609-888-1352
Ramesh Patel:Lawrenceville:NJ:08648:609-584-2100
Anne Sheridan:Trenton:NJ:08619:609-586-6705
Kevin Nasnek:Trenton:NJ:08690:609-587-9617
Barbara Fire:Hamilton Square:NJ:08690:201-287-9015
Tom Kowski:Bayonne:NJ:07002:201-823-6683
Thomas Large:Trenton:NJ:08629:215-596-0123
Richard Street:Mercerville:NJ:08619:609-587-1238
```

Let's change all instances of NJ to New Jersey and, on the same lines, change 08 to 99. The command script is called sed-1.scr. The name is purely arbitrary.

```
$ cat sed-1.scr

/NJ/{
s//New Jersey/
s/08/99/
}
```

6

This command script says to match all lines that contain NJ, and on those lines, change NJ to New Jersey and 08 to 99. The two commands are search-and-substitute commands, which I'll explain after showing you how the command script affects the rolodex file:

```
$ sed -f sed-1.scr rolodex

George Seer:Hightstown:New Jersey:99520:609-448-1860
Mark Tondayo:Levittown:PA:19054:215-946-5771
Clifford Dice:Manalapan:New Jersey:07726:201-446-2164
Marc Arturo:Trenton:New Jersey:99601:609-396-8765
James Lizzaro:Wrightstown:New Jersey:99520:609-758-7057
William Jefferson:Trenton:New Jersey:99638:609-883-7799
Sidney Hoffman:Trenton:New Jersey:99638:609-298-1952
Jeremy Dukakis:Mercerville:08619:609-587-7041
Leon Franks:Trenton:New Jersey:99610:609-888-1352
Ramesh Patel:Lawrenceville:New Jersey:99648:609-584-2100
Anne Sheridan:Trenton:New Jersey:99619:609-586-6705
Kevin Nasnek:Trenton:New Jersey:99690:609-587-9617
Barbara Fire:Hamilton Square:New Jersey:99690:201-287-9015
Tom Kowski:Bayonne:New Jersey:07002:201-823-6683
Thomas Large:Trenton:New Jersey:99629:215-596-0123
Richard Street:Mercerville:New Jersey:99619:609-587-1238
```

Let's find out what that command means. You know that search-and-substitute commands have the following syntax:

```
[address]s/regular expression/string/[flags]
```

I've already discussed what an `address` is and what a `regular expression` is. You know what a `string` is, too, so let's look at the lines in sed-1.scr:

```
$ cat sed-1.scr

/NJ/{
s//New Jersey/
s/08/99/
}
```

The /NJ/ is the address and it is followed by a pair of search-and-substitute commands, each written on its own line, and the pair enclosed in braces. Thus, /NJ/ is the address for both commands. The first command, s//New Jersey/, is special in that it does not specify a regular expression but uses an empty search pattern. In that case, sed uses the address as the search pattern. The second command, s/08/99/, is more straightforward: substitute 99 for 08.

Now let's discuss the four *flags*. They control actions taken after a substitution. First, the g (*global*) option causes sed to replace all occurrences of the search pattern on a line. In the refile.1 file, you saw the following line:

```
in the following words: the, therefore, bother. In other
```

If you wanted to replace every occurrence of the with XYZ, you might try

```
s/the/XYZ/
```

which would result in

```
in XYZ following words: the, therefore, bother. In other
```

The problem is that sed is easily satisfied, considering its job done when it completes the first possible substitution. To tell sed not to quit until every possible substitution on a line is done, you need to append g to the previous command:

```
s/the/XYZ/g
```

This results in

```
in XYZ following words: XYZ, XYZrefore, boXYZr. In oXYZr
```

The n flag (where n is a number between 1 and 512) changes only the specified occurrence of a pattern on a line. For example, to change the third the on the refile.1 line just used, you would say

```
s/the/XYZ/3
```

This results in

```
in the following words: the, XYZrefore, bother. In other
```

Use the p or w flags when the default output is suppressed (by specifying the -n option on the command line). These flags cause sed to output all lines on which changes have been made. Using p sends the output to stdout, but using w *outfile* causes the output to be written to *outfile*. Remember, the default of sed is to print all lines, regardless of changes made, so using -n is quite common.

6

Caution: If you use the p or w flag without suppressing the default output, you may end up with some duplicated lines. For example, suppose you wanted to change Trenton to TTN for all people in the rolodex file who have an area code of 609, and you wanted to see only those lines that changed:

```
$ sed -n ´/609/s/Trenton/TTN/p´ rolodex
```

```
Marc Arturo:TTN:NJ:08601:609-396-8765
William Jefferson:TTN:NJ:08638:609-883-7799
Sidney Hoffman:TTN:NJ:08638:609-298-1952
Leon Franks:TTN:NJ:08610:609-888-1352
Anne Sheridan:TTN:NJ:08619:609-586-6705
Kevin Nasnek:TTN:NJ:08690:609-587-9617
```

Displaying the entire file with changes is perhaps a better way to see that only certain lines were indeed changed:

```
$ sed ´/609/s/Trenton/TTN/p´ rolodex
```

```
George Seer:Hightstown:NJ:08520:609-448-1860
Mark Tondayo:Levittown:PA:19054:215-946-5771
Clifford Dice:Manalapan:NJ:07726:201-446-2164
Marc Arturo:TTN:NJ:08601:609-396-8765
James Lizzaro:Wrightstown:NJ:08520:609-758-7057
William Jefferson:TTN:NJ:08638:609-883-7799
Sidney Hoffman:TTN:NJ:08638:609-298-1952
Jeremy Dukakis:Mercerville:08619:609-587-7041
Leon Franks:TTN:NJ:08610:609-888-1352
Ramesh Patel:Lawrenceville:NJ:08648:609-584-2100
Anne Sheridan:TTN:NJ:08619:609-586-6705
Kevin Nasnek:TTN:NJ:08690:609-587-9617
Barbara Fire:Hamilton Square:NJ:08690:201-287-9015
Tom Kowski:Bayonne:NJ:07002:201-823-6683
Thomas Large:Trenton:NJ:08629:215-596-0123
Richard Street:Mercerville:NJ:08619:609-587-1238
```

You then could use the w flag like this:

```
$ sed -n ´/Trenton/s/:/-/w TTN´ rolodex
```

This sends the seven changed lines to a file called TTN.

```
$ cat TTN
```

```
Marc Arturo:TTN:NJ:08601:609-396-8765
William Jefferson:TTN:NJ:08638:609-883-7799
Sidney Hoffman:TTN:NJ:08638:609-298-1952
Leon Franks:TTN:NJ:08610:609-888-1352
Anne Sheridan:TTN:NJ:08619:609-586-6705
Kevin Nasnek:TTN:NJ:08690:609-587-9617
```

6

Append, Insert, and Change Commands

You can append (a), insert (i), and change (c) lines in the same way as you can with the vi editor.

The syntax for the append command is

```
/pattern/a\
new text
```

This places *new text* on the line after each one that matches *pattern*.

The syntax for the insert command is

```
/pattern/i\
new text
```

This places *new text* on the line before each line that matches *pattern*.

The syntax for the change command is

```
/pattern/c\
new text
```

This replaces each line that matches *pattern* with the line *new text*.

For example, let's play with the rolodex file and some of the ZIP codes:

```
$ cat rolodex
```

```
George Seer:Hightstown:NJ:08520:609-448-1860
Mark Tondayo:Levittown:PA:19054:215-946-5771
Clifford Dice:Manalapan:NJ:07726:201-446-2164
Marc Arturo:Trenton:NJ:08601:609-396-8765.
James Lizzaro:Wrightstown:NJ:08520:609-758-7057
William Jefferson:Trenton:NJ:08638:609-883-7799
Sidney Hoffman:Trenton:NJ:08638:609-298-1952
Jeremy Dukakis:Mercerville:08619:609-587-7041
Leon Franks:Trenton:NJ:08610:609-888-1352
Ramesh Patel:Lawrenceville:NJ:08648:609-584-2100
Anne Sheridan:Trenton:NJ:08619:609-586-6705
Kevin Nasnek:Trenton:NJ:08690:609-587-9617
Barbara Fire:Hamilton Square:NJ:08690:201-287-9015
Tom Kowski:Bayonne:NJ:07002:201-823-6683
Thomas Large:Trenton:NJ:08629:215-596-0123
Richard Street:Mercerville:NJ:08619:609-587-1238
```

In the following command, the > on the second line is the shell's *secondary prompt*; it signals that the shell is expecting additional input. The output includes the line MY ZIP after each line that has 638.

```
$ sed ´/638/a\
> MY ZIP´ rolodex
```

```
George Seer:Hightstown:NJ:08520:609-448-1860
Mark Tondayo:Levittown:PA:19054:215-946-5771
Clifford Dice:Manalapan:NJ:07726:201-446-2164
Marc Arturo:Trenton:NJ:08601:609-396-8765
James Lizzaro:Wrightstown:NJ:08520:609-758-7057
William Jefferson:Trenton:NJ:08638:609-883-7799
MY ZIP
Sidney Hoffman:Trenton:NJ:08638:609-298-1952
MY ZIP.
Jeremy Dukakis:Mercerville:08619:609-587-7041
Leon Franks:Trenton:NJ:08610:609-888-1352
Ramesh Patel:Lawrenceville:NJ:08648:609-584-2100
Anne Sheridan:Trenton:NJ:08619:609-586-6705
Kevin Nasnek:Trenton:NJ:08690:609-587-9617
Barbara Fire:Hamilton Square:NJ:08690:201-287-9015
Tom Kowski:Bayonne:NJ:07002:201-823-6683
Thomas Large:Trenton:NJ:08629:215-596-0123
Richard Street:Mercerville:NJ:08619:609-587-1238
```

In the following, each line with 619 on it is preceded by a line having a tab followed by YOUR ZIP on it:

```
$ sed ´/619/i\
>       YOUR ZIP´ rolodex.
```

```
George Seer:Hightstown:NJ:08520:609-448-1860
Mark Tondayo:Levittown:PA:19054:215-946-5771
Clifford Dice:Manalapan:NJ:07726:201-446-2164
Marc Arturo:Trenton:NJ:08601:609-396-8765
James Lizzaro:Wrightstown:NJ:08520:609-758-7057
William Jefferson:Trenton:NJ:08638:609-883-7799
Sidney Hoffman:Trenton:NJ:08638:609-298-1952
    YOUR ZIP
Jeremy Dukakis:Mercerville:08619:609-587-7041
Leon Franks:Trenton:NJ:08610:609-888-1352
Ramesh Patel:Lawrenceville:NJ:08648:609-584-2100
    YOUR ZIP
Anne Sheridan:Trenton:NJ:08619:609-586-6705
Kevin Nasnek:Trenton:NJ:08690:609-587-9617
Barbara Fire:Hamilton Square:NJ:08690:201-287-9015.
Tom Kowski:Bayonne:NJ:07002:201-823-6683
Thomas Large:Trenton:NJ:08629:215-596-0123
    YOUR ZIP
Richard Street:Mercerville:NJ:08619:609-587-1238
```

The following command outputs a line saying

```
------ ZIPZIP ------
```

to replace each line with 520:

```
$ sed ´/520/c\
>       ------ ZIPZIP ------´ rolodex
```

```
      ······ ZIPZIP ······
Mark Tondayo:Levittown:PA:19054:215-946-5771
Clifford Dice:Manalapan:NJ:07726:201-446-2164
Marc Arturo:Trenton:NJ:08601:609-396-8765
      ······ ZIPZIP ······
William Jefferson:Trenton:NJ:08638:609-883-7799
Sidney Hoffman:Trenton:NJ:08638:609-298-1952
Jeremy Dukakis:Mercerville:08619:609-587-7041
Leon Franks:Trenton:NJ:08610:609-888-1352
Ramesh Patel:Lawrenceville:NJ:08648:609-584-2100
Anne Sheridan:Trenton:NJ:08619:609-586-6705
Kevin Nasnek:Trenton:NJ:08690:609-587-9617
Barbara Fire:Hamilton Square:NJ:08690:201-287-9015.
Tom Kowski:Bayonne:NJ:07002:201-823-6683
Thomas Large:Trenton:NJ:08629:215-596-0123
Richard Street:Mercerville:NJ:08619:609-587-1238
```

Notice the use of the backslash (\) after each command. This informs sed that new text follows. If *new text* is made up of several lines, place a backslash at the end of each line except for the last line.

The append and insert commands cannot be applied to a range of addresses. However, the change command can be applied to a range of addresses. The change command replaces *all* addressed lines with a single copy of the changed text. For example:

```
/pattern1/,/pattern2/c\.
new text
```

or

```
/line_number1/,/line_number2/c\
new text
```

Suppose you want to delete everyone between Marc Arturo and Anne Sheridan from the rolodex file:

$ cat rolodex

```
George Seer:Hightstown:NJ:08520:609-448-1860
Mark Tondayo:Levittown:PA:19054:215-946-5771
Clifford Dice:Manalapan:NJ:07726:201-446-2164
Marc Arturo:Trenton:NJ:08601:609-396-8765
James Lizzaro:Wrightstown:NJ:08520:609-758-7057
William Jefferson:Trenton:NJ:08638:609-883-7799
Sidney Hoffman:Trenton:NJ:08638:609-298-1952
Jeremy Dukakis:Mercerville:08619:609-587-7041
Leon Franks:Trenton:NJ:08610:609-888-1352
Ramesh Patel:Lawrenceville:NJ:08648:609-584-2100
Anne Sheridan:Trenton:NJ:08619:609-586-6705
Kevin Nasnek:Trenton:NJ:08690:609-587-9617
Barbara Fire:Hamilton Square:NJ:08690:201-287-9015.
Tom Kowski:Bayonne:NJ:07002:201-823-6683
Thomas Large:Trenton:NJ:08629:215-596-0123
Richard Street:Mercerville:NJ:08619:609-587-1238
```

```
$ sed '/Marc/,/Anne/c\
> -- deleted --' rolodex

George Seer:Hightstown:NJ:08520:609-448-1860
Mark Tondayo:Levittown:PA:19054:215-946-5771
Clifford Dice:Manalapan:NJ:07726:201-446-2164
-- deleted --
Kevin Nasnek:Trenton:NJ:08690:609-587-9617
Barbara Fire:Hamilton Square:NJ:08690:201-287-9015
Tom Kowski:Bayonne:NJ:07002:201-823-6683
Thomas Large:Trenton:NJ:08629:215-596-0123
Richard Street:Mercerville:NJ:08619:609-587-1238
```

sed deleted them and replaced all of the lines in the range with the a single -- deleted -- line. If you want -- deleted -- in place of each line that's deleted, you must insert a command that references each line:.

```
$ sed '/Marc/,/Anne/{
> s//x/
> c\
> -- deleted --
> }' rolodex

George Seer:Hightstown:NJ:08520:609-448-1860
Mark Tondayo:Levittown:PA:19054:215-946-5771
Clifford Dice:Manalapan:NJ:07726:201-446-2164
-- deleted --
-- deleted --
-- deleted --
-- deleted --
-- deleted --
-- deleted --
-- deleted --
-- deleted --
Kevin Nasnek:Trenton:NJ:08690:609-587-9617
Barbara Fire:Hamilton Square:NJ:08690:201-287-9015
Tom Kowski:Bayonne:NJ:07002:201-823-6683
Thomas Large:Trenton:NJ:08629:215-596-0123
Richard Street:Mercerville:NJ:08619:609-587-1238
```

The command says "for every line in the range *line that contains Marc* to *line that contains Anne*, inclusive, substitute an x for the address of the line, and then change that line to -- deleted --.

Here's a semigraphical application for sed and some of its options. You want to make a table, complete with lines, from the auto file.

```
$ cat auto

ES    Arther    85    Honda    Prelude 49.412
BS    Barker    90    Nissan   300ZX   48.209
AS    Saint     88    BMW      M-3     46.629
ES    Straw     86    Honda    Civic   49.543
DS    Swazy     87    Honda    CRX-Si  49.693
ES    Downs     83    VW       GTI     47.133
```

```
ES    Smith      86    VW         GTI      47.154
AS    Neuman     84    Porsche    911      47.201
CS    Miller     84    Mazda      RX-7     47.291
CS    Carlson    88    Pontiac    Fiero    47.398.
DS    Kegler     84    Honda      Civic    47.429
ES    Sherman    83    VW         GTI      48.489
DS    Arbiter    86    Honda      CRX-Si   48.628
DS    Karle      74    Porsche    914      48.826
ES    Shorn      87    VW         GTI      49.357
CS    Chunk      85    Toyota     MR2      49.558
CS    Cohen      91    Mazda      Miata    50.046
DS    Lisanti    73    Porsche    914      50.609
CS    McGill     83    Porsche    944      50.642
AS    Lisle      72    Porsche    911      51.030
ES    Peerson    86    VW         Golf     54.493
```

You need to draw a line consisting of a pipe symbol (¦), some dashes, another ¦, some more dashes, and another ¦ after each line of text and before the first line. You also want to put a ¦ in three places on each line: at the beginning, at the end, and before the model year column. Here's the sed script that does it:.

$ **cat draw.lines**

```
s/^/¦ /
s/[7-9][0-9]  /¦ &/
s/$/ ¦/
1i\
¦---------------¦-----------------------------¦
a\
¦---------------¦-----------------------------¦
```

Not terribly readable, is it? Let's dissect it.

The first line is a search-and-substitute command that replaces the beginning of each line (/^/) with a ¦ and a space. The next command replaces any string of two digits followed by two spaces, with a ¦, a space, and the matched string (&). The third command replaces the end of the line with a space followed by a ¦. All three of these commands draw vertical lines in the final figure.

The fourth command is an insert command that inserts, before the first line (1i), a ¦ followed by a number of dashes, followed by another ¦, followed by another ¦, followed by more dashes and a terminating ¦.

The last command appends after each line—because there's no address, the command is applied to each line—the same string of pipe symbols and dashes that was just inserted before the first line of the original file. Here's the result:

$ **sed -f draw.lines auto**

```
+----------------+------------------------------------+
| ES   Arther    | 85   Honda     Prelude 49.412      |
+----------------+------------------------------------+
| BS   Barker    | 90   Nissan    300ZX   48.209      |
+----------------+------------------------------------+
| AS   Saint     | 88   BMW       M-3     46.629      |
+----------------+------------------------------------+
| ES   Straw     | 86   Honda     Civic   49.543      |
+----------------+------------------------------------+
| DS   Swazy     | 87   Honda     CRX-Si  49.693      |
+----------------+------------------------------------+
| ES   Downs     | 83   VW        GTI     47.133      |
+----------------+------------------------------------+
| ES   Smith     | 86   VW        GTI     47.154      |
+----------------+------------------------------------+
| AS   Neuman    | 84   Porsche   911     47.201      |
+----------------+------------------------------------+
| CS   Miller    | 84   Mazda     RX-7    47.291      |
+----------------+------------------------------------+
| CS   Carlson   | 88   Pontiac   Fiero   47.398      |
+----------------+------------------------------------+
| DS   Kegler    | 84   Honda     Civic   47.429      |
+----------------+------------------------------------+
| ES   Sherman   | 83   VW        GTI     48.489      |
+----------------+------------------------------------+
| DS   Arbiter   | 86   Honda     CRX-Si  48.628      |
+----------------+------------------------------------+
| DS   Karle     | 74   Porsche   914     48.826      |
+----------------+------------------------------------+
| ES   Shorn     | 87   VW        GTI     49.357      |
+----------------+------------------------------------+
| CS   Chunk     | 85   Toyota    MR2     49.558      |
+----------------+------------------------------------+
| CS   Cohen     | 91   Mazda     Miata   50.046      |
+----------------+------------------------------------+
| DS   Lisanti   | 73   Porsche   914     50.609      |
+----------------+------------------------------------+
| CS   McGill    | 83   Porsche   944     50.642      |
+----------------+------------------------------------+
| AS   Lisle     | 72   Porsche   911     51.030      |
+----------------+------------------------------------+
| ES   Peerson   | 86   VW        Golf    54.493      |
+----------------+------------------------------------+
```

Isn't *that* impressive?

The List Command

The list (1) command displays the contents of the pattern space and prints nonprinting characters (those represented by octal ASCII codes \000 through \040 and \177 though \377) as their numeric octal ASCII code counterparts. This command is helpful when locating control characters in a file.

For example, suppose you have a file that has some control or other nonprinting characters and you want to see what they are. cat -v shows them as control characters, but sed ´l´ shows you their ASCII codes.

```
$ cat -v nonprint

These are ^Z some ^A nonprinting ^E characters.
^E^T^M^?abcde.
This line has no nonprinting characters on it.
```

```
$ sed ´l´ nonprint

These are \32 some \01 nonprinting \05 characters.

\05\24\15\177abcde.

    abcde.
This line has no nonprinting characters on it.
This line has no nonprinting characters on it.
```

Oops. Forgot that default behavior!

```
$ sed -n ´l´ nonprint

These are \32 some \01 nonprinting \05 characters.
\05\24\15\177abcde.
This line has no nonprinting characters on it.
```

The Transform Command

The transform command (y) transforms each character in string *s1* to its equivalent character in string *s2* by position, just as *tr* does. For example:

```
$ sed ´y/ABC/abc/´ file
```

replaces each instance of A on each line of the file with a, each instance of B with b, and each instance of C with c. This command does not use pattern matching at all. The command shown replaces all instances of A on the line, not just those preceding B.

```
$ cat names

allen christopher
babinchak david
best betty
bloom dennis
boelhower joseph
bose anita
cacossa ray
chang liang
crawford patricia
```

```
crowley charles
cuddy michael
czyzewski sharon
delucia joseph
```

$ **sed 'y/abcdef/ABCDEF/' names**

```
AllEn ChristophEr
BABinChAk DAviD
BEst BEtty
Bloom DEnnis
BoElhowEr josEph
BosE AnitA
CACossA rAy
ChAng liAng
CrAwForD pAtriCiA
CrowlEy ChArlEs
CuDDy miChAEl
CzyzEwski shAron
DEluCiA josEph
```

sed insists that the two strings be exactly the same length.

Line Numbering

An address followed by an equals sign (=) prints the line number of that line. For example:

$ **cat TTN**

```
Marc Arturo:Trenton:NJ:08601:609-396-8765
William Jefferson:Trenton:NJ:08638:609-883-7799
Sidney Hoffman:Trenton:NJ:08638:609-298-1952
Leon Franks:Trenton:NJ:08610:609-888-1352
Anne Sheridan:Trenton:NJ:08619:609-586-6705
Kevin Nasnek:Trenton:NJ:08690:609-587-9617
Thomas Large:Trenton:NJ:08629:215-596-0123
```

The following command displays the line number of the line that contains Leon:

$ **sed '/Leon/=' TTN**

```
Marc Arturo:Trenton:NJ:08601:609-396-8765
William Jefferson:Trenton:NJ:08638:609-883-7799
Sidney Hoffman:Trenton:NJ:08638:609-298-1952
4
Leon Franks:Trenton:NJ:08610:609-888-1352
Anne Sheridan:Trenton:NJ:08619:609-586-6705
Kevin Nasnek:Trenton:NJ:08690:609-587-9617
Thomas Large:Trenton:NJ:08629:215-596-0123
```

If you want only the line number, you can kill the default output:

```
$ sed -n ´/Leon/=´ TTN

4
```

If you want to number each line, you need to specify a pattern that can be found on each line, because = does not accept a range of addresses. One such pattern is ^, the beginning of the line:

```
$ sed ´/^/=´ TTN

1
Marc Arturo:Trenton:NJ:08601:609-396-8765
2
William Jefferson:Trenton:NJ:08638:609-883-7799
3
Sidney Hoffman:Trenton:NJ:08638:609-298-1952
4
Leon Franks:Trenton:NJ:08610:609-888-1352
5
Anne Sheridan:Trenton:NJ:08619:609-586-6705
6
Kevin Nasnek:Trenton:NJ:08690:609-587-9617
7
Thomas Large:Trenton:NJ:08629:215-596-0123
```

The Print Command

The print command (p) simply copies the pattern space to stdout. Unlike the print option to s, no changes are required. Of course, you must remember to inhibit default behavior.

```
$ sed -n ´/Trenton/p´ rolodex

Marc Arturo:Trenton:NJ:08601:609-396-8765
William Jefferson:Trenton:NJ:08638:609-883-7799
Sidney Hoffman:Trenton:NJ:08638:609-298-1952
Leon Franks:Trenton:NJ:08610:609-888-1352
Anne Sheridan:Trenton:NJ:08619:609-586-6705
Kevin Nasnek:Trenton:NJ:08690:609-587-9617
Thomas Large:Trenton:NJ:08629:215-596-0123
```

Read and Write Commands

The read (r) and write (w) commands provide a method of direct input and output with files. Each takes a single argument: the name of a file. The read command reads the named file into the pattern space after the addressed line. The write command outputs the pattern space to the named file.

> **Note:** You must include a single space between the r or w command and the filename.

When the named file does not exist, the write command creates it. When it exists, the new information replaces the old. However, if read's named file does not exist, the read command fails to print an error message.

The write command is helpful when *context-splitting* a file, and the read command is helpful when joining files together. (Context-splitting involves identifying where to split a file by patterns rather than by a number of lines or characters.) You can accomplish the same effect with other UNIX commands, such as cat, but sed provides more flexibility. For example, from the auto file, you want to create a new file that contains information about all model year 1986 cars. You could context-split the file by writing all lines that contain the pattern 1986 into a new file.

Of course, there are more practical applications for the r command in the world of databases.

Summary

This chapter discussed only two commands: tr and sed. You've seen that the tr is quite useful for small jobs that involve changing or deleting specific characters or classes of characters. sed, on the other hand, is a power tool. Despite its fairly large number of options, sed is used mostly to either delete lines or to make substitutions.

6

## Chapter 7

The awk Language

U p to this point you've seen a number of very useful but small tools based on System V Release 4 commands. You have met the ideas behind pipelines and redirection, and have some ideas of combining some of the small tools into a larger, special purpose tool. You are about to meet the "Swiss Army Knife" of tools, awk.

Many have said that the name derives from the anguished cry of those who attempt to use awk, but nothing could be further from the truth. awk is more complicated than most simple tools, to be sure, but it has a syntax and rules that are not difficult to learn. The name comes from the authors of awk— Aho, Weinberger, and Kernighan—who supplied their initials to form the name.

Using awk

Like sed, awk can apply a set of commands contained in a script file to one or more data files. However, awk has a much wider range of commands, including many that make it look like a programming language. If you're not a programmer, do not be concerned: the awk language you'll see isn't difficult to use. If you're a programmer, you'll immediately recognize some common elements between awk and other languages: variables, decisions, loops, arrays, and so on.

The awk command has a syntax that is not unlike that of other commands you've already seen:

```
awk [ -Fc ] [commands ¦ -f file] [parameter assignments] [file(s)]
```

awk sees data files as being divided into records and fields. Each record is separated from the next by the default record separator, the newline. Each field is separated from the next by the default record separator, one or more tabs or spaces (also known as *whitespace*). You can change the default record separator on the command line by specifying a different character for c in -Fc. For example, -F: would be a good choice if you're processing the /etc/passwd file, because it uses a colon (:) as the separator between fields.

If you have a very simple thing to do with awk, you can simply write the commands on the command line. In general, you'll want to tell awk to take its commands from the script designated as file in -f file.

Parameter assignments are of the form var=15 x=2 and so on, and define variables and their initial values to be used in the processing of the files designated as file(s). (A *variable* is simply a name that has a value. The thing that makes it variable is that you can change the value whenever you want.)

To use awk as a tool requires that you have a good overview of what awk can do and awk script structure.

Overview of awk

awk is a programming language designed to scan files for patterns and act on any matches, a little like sed does. Its primary application is report genera-tion—that is, producing the results of a number of calculations on one or more data files. awk also is an excellent tool for solving many data transforma-tion problems. awk has extended regular expression capabilities (the same as found in egrep), most of the flow control and arithmetic operations found in the C language, built-in string and math functions, user variables, and arrays.

There are two versions of awk. The original version was first released in 1977. In 1985, an enhanced version of awk was released, including major new features such as user-defined functions, regular expressions with text substi-tution and pattern-matching functions, new built-in functions and variables, new operators and statements, input from multiple files, better error mes-sages, and access to command-line arguments. On older versions of UNIX, the original version is awk and the newer, enhanced version is nawk (if available). With UNIX System V, after Release 3.1, the enhanced version is awk and the older version oawk. Older awk scripts should work with the new version of awk without modification. The chapter discusses the newest version of awk, as supplied with System V Release 4.

The Format of an awk Script

An awk script may have as many as three sections:

- A BEGIN section that initializes the script. This section is executed only at the start of the script, before any records are read from the input file(s).

- A *pattern statement* or *main body* section containing lines that have the syntax

  ```
  pattern { action }
  ```

  The pattern statement section of the program is data-driven—that is, awk reads a record from the input file. If the specified pattern is matched anywhere in the record, the specified action is taken.

- An END section that executes after reading the entire data file. Usually the END section is used for final computations that cannot occur until after processing the input data.

  Any two sections can be omitted from any awk script.

  The BEGIN section of an awk program starts with the word BEGIN in all capital letters, followed on the same line by an opening brace ({). Use a space or tab to separate the BEGIN keyword and opening curly brace.

  After the opening brace, BEGIN contains either a single statement or a list of statements, each separated by semicolons or newlines. The BEGIN section terminates with a closing brace (}).

  The BEGIN section usually is typed in one of these forms:

```
BEGIN {
    statement
    statement
    statement
}
```

or

```
BEGIN { statement }
```

or

```
BEGIN { statement; statement; statement }
```

The *pattern section* starts with an opening brace, followed by one or more *pattern {action}* statements. The statement list executes whenever the pattern expression is matched by a record from the input file.

If no action is specified for a given pattern, awk simply prints the records that match the pattern statement. If no pattern is supplied for a given action, the action is applied to every record of the input file.

Examples of the contents of the pattern section are

```
/regular expression/ { statement }
```

and

```
/regular expression/ {
        statement
        statement
}
```

or

```
/regular expression/ { statement; statement; statement }
```

The `regular expression` also may be a *pattern range*, just as in sed:

```
/RE1/,/RE2/ { statement }
```

or it may even be omitted.

The END section has a syntax similar to that of the BEGIN section. It starts with the word END in all capital letters, followed by an opening brace on the same line, followed by one or more statements, then a closing brace.

Examples of the END statement are

```
END {
    statement
    statement
    statement
}
```

and

```
END { statement }
```

and

```
END { statement; statement; statement }
```

Because the shell tries to interpret certain characters as if they were shell metacharacters, you'll find it less aggravating to write an awk script than to try to supply awk commands on the command line.

This first example is a script that simply prints a message:

```
$ cat 1.awk

BEGIN { print "hello world!" }
```

```
$ awk -f 1.awk
```

hello world!

This script works despite the absence of a data filename on the command line because the action is placed in the BEGIN section. Here's a slight variation of the first script, just to show that the typing format is meant only to make the script more readable by us humans:

```
$ cat 2.awk

BEGIN {
    print "hello world!"
}

$ awk -f 2.awk
```

hello world!

The next script has an action in the main body (i.e., the pattern statement section):

```
$ cat 3.awk

{
    print "hello world!"
}

$ awk -f 3.awk
```

When you try to execute the preceding command without a data filename on the command line, nothing happens until you press either Enter or ^d. Then the command would execute but not return us to the prompt. You must press the interrupt key (either Del or ^C) to get the prompt back. The reason for this strange behavior lies in awk's need for a file to which awk will apply the commands in the main body of the awk script.

The next example is a two-for-one. First, it uses awk to print the contents of the data file. In other words, the command makes awk behave like cat.

```
$ awk '{ print }' names

allen christopher
babinchak david
best betty
bloom dennis
boelhower joseph
bose anita
cacossa ray
chang liang
crawford patricia
```

7

```
crowley charles
cuddy michael
czyzewski sharon
delucia joseph
```

Second, use wc -l to find out how many lines there are in the names file:

```
$ wc -l names
```

```
   13 names
```

And now execute the third script using names as the data file:

```
$ awk -f 3.awk names
```

```
hello world!
hello world!
hello world!
hello world!
hello world!
hello world!
hello world!
hello world!
hello world!
hello world!
hello world!
hello world!
hello world!
```

You could count the hello world! lines by hand, but why not build a tool for that?

```
$ awk -f 3.awk names ¦ wc -l
```

```
   13
```

What can you conclude from this? awk read the names file and, because the action in 3.awk had no pattern to be matched, applied the action (print "hello, world!") to each line in names. Thus, the awk command can be interpreted as meaning "for each line in names, display hello, world! on stdout."

To include comments in awk scripts, use the pound sign (#). awk ignores everything to the right of it.

```
$ cat 1a.cat
```

```
# my first AWK script!!
#
BEGIN { print "hello world!" }
```

Records and Fields

Each line of an input file is a record. In each record are fields delimited by a separator character (by default, a space or tab). The following file (auto, as used in previous chapters) is a typical input file:

```
ES   Arther    85   Honda     Prelude  49.412
BS   Barker    90   Nissan    300ZX    48.209
AS   Saint     88   BMW       M-3      46.629
ES   Straw     86   Honda     Civic    49.543
DS   Swazy     87   Honda     CRX-Si   49.693
ES   Downs     83   VW        GTI      47.133
ES   Smith     86   VW        GTI      47.154
AS   Neuman    84   Porsche   911      47.201
CS   Miller    84   Mazda     RX-7     47.291
CS   Carlson   88   Pontiac   Fiero    47.398
DS   Kegler    84   Honda     Civic    47.429
ES   Sherman   83   VW        GTI      48.489
DS   Arbiter   86   Honda     CRX-Si   48.628
DS   Karle     74   Porsche   914      48.826
ES   Shorn     87   VW        GTI      49.357
CS   Chunk     85   Toyota    MR2      49.558
CS   Cohen     91   Mazda     Miata    50.046
DS   Lisanti   73   Porsche   914      50.609
CS   McGill    83   Porsche   944      50.642
AS   Lisle     72   Porsche   911      51.030
ES   Peerson   86   VW        Golf     54.493
```

You may recall that the columns represent class, driver name, car model year, car make, car model, and best time. This file contains 21 records. Each record has six fields; it may not be obvious from the preceding listing, but I've used multiple spaces to separate fields and format the table. You can use awk with this file to calculate the average time for all drivers, for all cars in a certain class, for all VWs, for all cars from the 86 model year, and so on.

Each field in a record becomes the value of an awk internal variable (of course, you can define additional variables in your awk scripts). You can retrieve the values by referring to the appropriate variables, like this:

$0	The value of the entire record
$1	The value in the first field
$2	The value in the second field
$n	A general variable, representing the value in the *n*th field

Here are some examples of printing selected fields:

```
$ cat 4.awk

# 4.awk - print driver names and car makes
#
    { print $2 $4 }

$ awk -f 4.awk auto

ArtherHonda
BarkerNissan
SaintBMW
StrawHonda
SwazyHonda
DownsVW
SmithVW
NeumanPorsche
MillerMazda
CarlsonPontiac
KeglerHonda
ShermanVW
ArbiterHonda
KarlePorsche
ShornVW
ChunkToyota
CohenMazda
LisantiPorsche
McGillPorsche
LislePorsche
PeersonVW
```

To get a space printed between field values, you need to separate the field variables in the print statement with commas:

```
$ cat 5.awk

# 5.awk - print driver names and car makes with a space between fields
#
    { print $2, $4 }

$ awk -f 5.awk auto

Arther Honda
Barker Nissan
Saint BMW
Straw Honda
Swazy Honda
Downs VW
Smith VW
Neuman Porsche
Miller Mazda
```

```
Carlson Pontiac
Kegler Honda
Sherman VW
Arbiter Honda
Karle Porsche
Shorn VW
Chunk Toyota
Cohen Mazda
Lisanti Porsche
McGill Porsche
Lisle Porsche
Peerson VW
```

A list with a comma after each driver name would be nice. To obtain that, you need to add a third argument to print—", "— to cause awk to print a comma and then a space after it prints the value in field 2 and before it prints the value of field 4:

$ **cat 6.awk**

```
# 6.awk - print driver names and car makes with ", " between fields
#
    { print $2", "$4 }
```

```
$ awk -f 6.awk auto
Arther, Honda
Barker, Nissan
Saint, BMW
Straw, Honda
Swazy, Honda
Downs, VW
Smith, VW
Neuman, Porsche
Miller, Mazda
Carlson, Pontiac
Kegler, Honda
Sherman, VW
Arbiter, Honda
Karle, Porsche
Shorn, VW
Chunk, Toyota
Cohen, Mazda
Lisanti, Porsche
McGill, Porsche
Lisle, Porsche
Peerson, VW
```

Here's a sample script that uses all three sections and one of the built-in variables, NR (the number of records read so far):

```
$ cat roster.awk

BEGIN {
    print
    print "Class Roster"
    print
}

# main body of 'awk' script...
    { print $2, $1 }

END {
    print
    print "Number of students: " NR
}
```

When used in the END section, NR is the total number of records read:

```
$ awk -f roster.awk names

Class Roster

christopher allen
david babinchak
betty best
dennis bloom
joseph boelhower
anita bose
ray cacossa
liang chang
patricia crawford
charles crowley
michael cuddy
sharon czyzewski
joseph delucia

Number of students: 13
```

The BEGIN section of the script printed a blank line, the string Class Roster, and another blank line. The main body read each line of the names file, assigned field values to the field variables, and printed their values with the second field first. The END section printed a blank line, the string Number of students:, and then supplied the value of the number of records that awk had read from the names file. awk got this value from the built-in variable NR.

awk Programming Variables

awk contains some built-in variables that provide information about the size and composition of the input records, as well as format control. Table 7.1 lists these variables.

Table 7.6. Format conversion specifications.

Specification	Meaning
%d	Print output as a decimal (that is, a base 10) integer value.
%f	Print output as a floating point value.
%o	Print output as an octal integer value.
%x	Print output as a hexadecimal integer value.
%s	Print output as a string.
%e	Print output as floating point with scientific notation.
%g	Use %f or %e format, whichever is shorter. Trailing zeros are omitted and the decimal point does not print if there is no fractional part.

You can include options fields in the conversion specification string. For example, %7.2f specifies a field of seven characters with two characters to the right of the decimal point (the decimal point counts as one of the seven characters). %-10s specifies a field 10 characters wide, left-justified.

For an example, let's print the class, driver name, and time from the auto file. To illustrate conversion specifications, I'll print the values of the time field (field 6) right-justified in a field that's 12 columns wide, and insist that each number have two digits to the right of the decimal point.

Note: I inserted a left and right bracket ([and]) around the %12.2f conversion to make it easier for you to see in the output that there are indeed 12 columns.

Incidentally, the \n at the end of the string is a newline character; it makes the output that results from processing each record appear on the next line (that is, on a new line) of the output.

```
$ cat printf.awk

{ printf "%s  %s\t[%12.2f]\n", $1, $2, $6 }

$ awk -f printf.awk auto
```

```
ES   Arther     [        49.41]
BS   Barker     [        48.21]
AS   Saint      [        46.63]
ES   Straw      [        49.54]
DS   Swazy      [        49.69]
ES   Downs      [        47.13]
ES   Smith      [        47.15]
AS   Neuman     [        47.20]
CS   Miller     [        47.29]
CS   Carlson    [        47.40]
DS   Kegler     [        47.43]
ES   Sherman    [        48.49]
DS   Arbiter    [        48.63]
DS   Karle      [        48.83]
ES   Shorn      [        49.36]
CS   Chunk      [        49.56]
CS   Cohen      [        50.05]
DS   Lisanti    [        50.61]
CS   McGill     [        50.64]
AS   Lisle      [        51.03]
ES   Peerson    [        54.49]
```

The output of either print statement can be redirected into a file or piped into another command. Be sure to enclose the output filename or command in double quotation marks. Look at the following examples:

$ cat printf1.awk

```
{ printf "%s  %s\t[%12.2f]\n", $1, $2, $6 > "results" }
```

$ awk -f printf1.awk auto

$ cat results

```
ES   Arther     [        49.41]
BS   Barker     [        48.21]
AS   Saint      [        46.63]
ES   Straw      [        49.54]
DS   Swazy      [        49.69]
ES   Downs      [        47.13]
ES   Smith      [        47.15]
AS   Neuman     [        47.20]
CS   Miller     [        47.29]
CS   Carlson    [        47.40]
DS   Kegler     [        47.43]
ES   Sherman    [        48.49]
DS   Arbiter    [        48.63]
DS   Karle      [        48.83]
ES   Shorn      [        49.36]
CS   Chunk      [        49.56]
CS   Cohen      [        50.05]
DS   Lisanti    [        50.61]
CS   McGill     [        50.64]
AS   Lisle      [        51.03]
ES   Peerson    [        54.49]
```

Here's an example of piping:

```
$ cat printf.awk

{ printf "%s  %s\t[%12.2f]\n", $1, $2, $6 ¦ "sort" }

$ awk -f printf.awk auto
```

```
AS   Lisle     [        51.03]
AS   Neuman    [        47.20]
AS   Saint     [        46.63]
BS   Barker    [        48.21]
CS   Carlson   [        47.40]
CS   Chunk     [        49.56]
CS   Cohen     [        50.04]
CS   McGill    [        50.64]
CS   Miller    [        47.29]
DS   Arbiter   [        48.63]
DS   Karle     [        48.83]
DS   Kegler    [        47.43]
DS   Lisanti   [        50.61]
DS   Swazy     [        49.69]
ES   Arther    [        49.41]
ES   Downs     [        47.13]
ES   Peerson   [        54.49]
ES   Sherman   [        48.49]
ES   Shorn     [        49.36]
ES   Smith     [        47.15]
ES   Straw     [        49.54]
```

In addition to the \n character, printf has a number of other special characters, as shown in Table 7.7.

Table 7.7. printf special characters.

Character	Meaning
\a	Alert—usually causes the terminal's beeper to beep
\b	Backspace—move the cursor one column to the left
\f	Form feed
\r	Carriage return—move the cursor to the left hand edge of the screen, on the same line
\t	Tab
\ddd	ASCII code for any ASCII character
\c	Any literal character—lets you use a special character such as ¦ as if it were just a ¦ and not the symbol for piping (\¦)

7

Conditional Statements

awk supports two forms of conditional statements—implied and explicit. The if and if-else conditional statements are explicit. They have the following syntax:

```
if (expression)
    action
```

If *expression* is true, *action* is performed. Otherwise, *action* is skipped. "True" is either an obvious truth (for example, 7 > 3) or a numerical value other than zero; zero means "false."

```
if (expression)
    action-1
else
    action-2
```

If *expression* evaluates as true, *action-1* is performed and *action-2* is skipped. On the other hand, if *expression* is false, *action-1* is skipped and *action-2* is performed. For example:

```
if ($3 > 1000)
    print $3;
```

or

```
if ($3 > 1000)
    print $3
else
    print "Invalid value"
```

In the preceding, print $3 is *action-1*, and print "Invalid value" is *action-2*. *expression* is $3 > 1000.

When an *action* involves more than one statement, enclose all of them in a pair of braces. For example:

```
if ($3 > 1000)
{
    print $3
    total += 1000;
}
```

says "if the value in the third field is greater than 1000, do both of the following steps: print that value, and add 1000 to total."

The syntax of the implied conditional statement is

```
pattern containing a relational expression { action }
```

For example:

```
$3 > 1000 { print $3 }
```

The "if" is implied: "if the value in the third field is greater than 1000, print it."

Here's an example that combines a number of the concepts I've discussed. Suppose you want to know the name of the driver; the year, make, and model of the car; and the winning time from the data in the auto file. Let's also calculate the average time for everyone. The following awk script does the job:

```
$ cat awk.4

# awk.4 -- find the fastest driver and the average time

BEGIN {
    lowest = 999.99
    total = 0
}

# main body
{
    if ($6 < lowest)
    {
        lowest = $6
        driver = $2
        year = $3
        make = $4
        model = $5
    }
    total += $6
}

END {
    printf "Today's winner was %s, driving a 19%s %s %s,\n",
        driver, year, make, model
    printf "with a time of %.2f.  Average time was %.2f.\n",
        lowest, total/NR
}
```

The BEGIN section initializes two variables, lowest and total (although if you omitted the initialization of total, awk would have set it to 0 for you). Here I've assumed that no driver had a time greater than 999.99. The technique used, as shown in the body of the script, is to compare the value of lowest with a driver's actual time (field 6). If that time is lower than the value of lowest, I'll use it as the new value of lowest. At the same time, I'll save the values of several other fields—driver's name, car year, car make, and car model. And I'll accumulate the times. In the END section, I have two printf statements. The first uses %s four times, as a place holder for four strings. They are, in order, the driver's name, the car year, the car make, and the car model. The second printf outputs the value of lowest and the calculated average

time, both using `%.2f`. I could have combined these into one `printf`, but that
would have been hard to read.

```
$ awk -f awk.4 auto
```

```
Today's winner was Saint, driving a 1988 BMW M-3,
with a time of 46.63.  Average time was 48.99.
```

Loops

One of the statements that controls repetition in `awk` is the `while` statement.
The syntax is

```
while ( expression )
    action
```

If `action` consists of two or more statements, surround them with
braces. As long as `expression` evaluates to true, `action` is performed. For
example:

```
num = 1
time = 0        # explicit initialization again
while ( num <= 7}
{
    time += $6
    num++
}
```

adds the first seven values of `$6` to `time`. `num` controls the loop because it starts
with a value of 1, is tested as part of `expression`, and is incremented inside the
loop (`num++`). The `while` loop performs the following actions: "as long as the
value of `num` is less than or equal to 7, add the value of field 6 to `time` and add
one to num."

The `do-while` statement provides a slightly different kind of loop. Its
form is

```
do {
    action
} while ( expression )
```

For example:

```
num = 5
time = 0
do {
    time += $3
    num--
} while (num > 0)
```

Notice that num controls the loop, starting with a value of 5 and decreasing by one each time the loop is executed. When num has been decreased to 0, the loop terminates. The action in the loop is "add the current value in the third field to the variable time and subtract 1 from num." The difference between a while loop and a do-while loop lies in where the test takes place. *expression* is tested before entering a while loop. If *expression* is false, none of the statements in the loop are executed. Thus, the theoretical minimum number of times the statements in the body of a while loop are executed is 0. On the other hand, the test in a do-while occurs *after* the statements in the loop body have been executed. So the theoretical minimum number of times the statements in the body of a do-while loop are executed is 1. Because this is such a slight difference, many programmers ignore do-while and do all their looping with while or for.

The for statement is another form of loop in awk. It's frequently used when you know the number of times you want the statements in the loop to be executed (as I did in the while and do-while examples).

for takes three expressions as arguments: an initialization, a test expression, and one that is executed after action is executed. The syntax is

```
for ( expr-1; expr-2; expr-3 )
    action
```

As usual, if *action* is two or more statements, surround them with braces. *expr-1* is evaluated one time only—on entry to the for loop. Next, *expr-2* is evaluated. If *expr-2* is true, action is executed; if false, the loop terminates. After action is executed, *expr-3* is executed and then *expr-2* is once again evaluated. If true, the looping action is repeated; otherwise, the loop terminates. Here's a simple example that prints the fields of each record, each on a separate line:

```
for (i = 1; i <= NF; i++)
    print $i
```

On entry to the for loop, the variable i is given a value of 1. For the purpose of this example, suppose that the number of fields (NF) is 3. The test i <= NF is then 1 <= 3, which certainly is true, so the action print $i is executed. Because i has a value of 1, the action is equivalent to print $1: print the first field.

Next, the expression i++ is executed, which causes i to increment to 2. The test i <= NF becomes 2 <= 3, still true, so print $i, now equal to print $2, is executed. i++ causes i to increment to 3, and because 3 <= 3 is true, the value of the third field is printed. Incrementing i now makes it 4, and because 4 <= 3 is false, the loop terminates.

7

Here's the equivalent of the earlier `while` loop, written as a `for` loop:

```
time = 0
for ( num = 1; num <= 7; num++ }
{
    time += $6
}
```

Note that the `for` loop is tested "at the top," just like the `while` loop.

The `break` and `continue` statements provide additional control in a loop. A `break` statement inside a loop causes an immediate exit from the loop. Try to arrange your scripts so as to avoid using `break`, because it disturbs the orderly flow of a program. The test expression in the `while` or `for` can almost always be modified easily to include a test for the condition that would have caused you to break out of the loop. A `continue` statement, on the other hand, causes an immediate return to the top of the loop, and need not be avoided.

The following is a fragment of the main body of a script and illustrates the use of `break`. Suppose the loop contains statements that process some of the fields in the current record as long as the value in field 3 is not negative. Then

```
while ( expression )
{
    ...
    ...
    if ($3 < 0)
    {
        break
    }
    # process the values because we know
    # that $3 >= 0
    ...
    ...
}
# this is the first statement after the loop
```

If the value in field 3 is negative, the statements that follow the comment `process the values because we know that $3 >= 0` is not executed. In fact, the next statement to be executed is the one following the comment `this is the first statement after the loop`. On the other hand, suppose you want to skip over the processing steps if the value in the third field is negative:

```
while ( expression )
{
    ...
    ...
    if ($3 < 0)
    {
        continue
    }
```

```
      # process the values because we know
      # that $3 >= 0
      ...
      ...
}
```

If the value in the third field is negative, the statements that follow the comment process the values because we know that $3 >= 0 are skipped, but the loop does not end. *expression* is tested and, if true, the loop is executed again.

Actually, you can avoid most uses of break and continue by rewriting the logical part of the script. For example, you could rewrite the script with break as follows:

```
while ( expression )
{
      ...
      ...
      if ($3 > 0)
      {
            # process the values because we know
            # that $3 >= 0
      }
      ...
      ...
}
# this is the first statement after the loop
```

and rewrite the one that used continue as follows:

```
while ( expression )
{
      ...
      ...
      if ($3 >= 0)
      {
            # process the values because we know
            # that $3 >= 0
      }
      ...
      ...
}
```

The next and exit statements control flow in the main body, a little like break and continue do in loops. When encountering the next statement, awk reads in the next input line and returns to the beginning of the pattern section of the program. For example, if you want to skip all records with fewer than four fields, you could use

```
{
      NF < 4 { next }
}
```

The `exit` statement causes immediate termination of the program. `exit` is used with a number (0 through 255) that is passed back to the invoking program. Use this as a return code to the shell to examine the success or failure of the awk script. You might use a fragment like this in a script

```
print "Invalid number"
exit 10
```

to terminate a program if an incorrect value is read from a data file. The number 10 is passed back to the shell, where it can be examined. (Chapter 8, "Introduction to Writing Shell Scripts," explains how this is done.)

String Manipulation

awk is an excellent tool for manipulating strings. There are five built-in string-manipulation functions. Table 7.8 lists the functions.

Table 7.8. String-manipulation functions.

Function	Use
length	Returns the length of a string
substr	Returns a substring of a string, given a character as a starting point
index	Returns the position of a character in a string
sprintf	Returns a string compiled with expressions similar to those used in the `printf` statement
getline	Inserts the next input record

Each of these is discussed in this section.

The `length` function returns the number of characters in the current record (`$0`), or, if given an argument, returns the number of characters in the argument. The value can be assigned to a variable, printed, used in an expression, and so on. For example, to display the length of the value in the fourth field, use the following:

```
{
    print length($4)
}
```

Later examples will combine `length` with some of the other awk constructs.

The substr function returns the *n*-character substring in string *s*, beginning at position *m*. Here is the syntax for the substr function:

```
substr(s,m,n)
```

If string *s* appears to be a number, it's treated as a string of digit characters rather than as a numeric value. When *n* is omitted, all characters from position *m* to the end of the string are returned.

Examples of the uses of the substr function follow.

Example 1: Print the abbreviated day.

The script

```
{
    print substr("Monday", 1, 3);
}
```

displays

```
Mon
```

The function says "extract a three-character substring from the string Monday beginning with the first character of the string." Notice that the string was enclosed in double quotation marks because it was a constant, or *literal*, string.

You could do something similar for the string in, say, field 2 by writing

```
{
    print substr($2, 1, 3);
}
```

Example 2: Print the "cents."

The script

```
{
    print substr(1298.76, 6);
}
```

displays

```
76
```

The request was to extract all the characters from character number 6—the 7—to the end of the string.

The index function returns the position of the first occurrence of string *t* in string *s*, in numeric form. The syntax for the index function is

```
index(s,t)
```

If *t* is not a substring of *s*, index returns a zero.

index often is combined with substr to locate a place to split a string. In the example that printed the "cents," the substr function worked properly because I counted off where the decimal point was and added 1. To make the program more flexible than that, you can use index to determine where the decimal point is and then have the script add it.

```
$ cat nums

123.45
1987.34
19.87

$ cat dp.awk

# dp.awk
{
    dp = index($1, ".")
    print substr($1, dp + 1)
}

$ awk -f dp.awk nums

45
34
87
```

This, of course, is much more flexible than the original approach.

The sprintf function builds a complex string from other strings and numbers, and returns that string. sprintf does not display anything. The syntax is

```
x = sprintf("format", exp1, exp2, ...);
```

where *format* is the same as the formatting string used in printf. The following example demonstrates a typical use of sprintf:

```
{
    message = sprintf("John is %d years old and makes %7.2f\n", age, sal);
}
```

If you were to add the line

```
print message
```

to the preceding body, you would see a display. That is, the combination

```
{
    message = sprintf("John is %d years old and makes %7.2f\n", age, sal);
    print message
}
```

is the same as

```
{
    printf("John is %d years old and makes %7.2f\n", age, sal);
}
```

One major application of sprintf is to perform character conversions. For example, the next fragment converts each number between 65 and 90 to an ASCII character:

```
for (num = 65; num <= 90; num++)
{
    char = sprintf("%c", num)
}
```

This technique will be more useful when you meet the *array*.

The getline function immediately reads the next input record. getline differs from next in that getline does not cause program execution to return to the beginning of the program. getline returns 1 when it's successful in reading a line, or 0 if it's not successful.

The following program demonstrates the use of getline to join lines that end in a backslash. First, here's the data file:

```
$ cat cal.bksl
```

```
The cal command in UNIX is \
very useful. It prints a
calendar of the month you \
specify.
ES   Arther    85   Honda      Prelude 49.412
BS   Barker    90   Nissan     300ZX   48.209
AS   Saint     88   BMW        M-3     46.629
```

Note that lines 1 and 3 end with backslashes. If you recreate this file, be sure to let nothing be inserted between the backslash and the Enter key! I included some completely unrelated data in the file so you could see that this script will leave it alone. The script is

```
$ cat awk.bksl
```

```
# join a line that ends with a \ and the following one.
{
    if (substr($0, length, 1) == "\\")
    {
        printf("%s", substr($0, 1, length($0) - 1))
        getline
    }
    printf("%s\n", $0)
}
```

Let's examine the script before feeding it to awk.

The if test says to look at the last character on the line—substr($0, length, 1. Notice that if length doesn't have an argument, it counts the number of characters in the current record. Then, if compares that last character to a backslash ("\\").

Recall that the backslash character is special; its usual job is either to give new meaning to an ordinary character or to take the special meaning away from a special character. Double quotation marks are special (they start and end a string), so if you had written "\" as the pattern, awk would have complained that you had not terminated the string. Why? Because "\" is interpreted as "special double quotation marks (that is, the start of a string) followed by ordinary double quotation marks, period"! Therefore, you must use a backslash to remove the special meaning of the second backslash. This enables if to check whether the last character in the record is an ordinary backslash.

"\\" means "special double quotation marks followed by a special backslash followed by a special character"—oops, the first backslash removes the special meaning of the second one, so I should start again. "\\" means "special double quotation marks followed by an ordinary backslash followed by special double quotation marks."

Back to the if statement and its actions: "If the last character in the current record is a backslash, print all of the current record except the backslash, make the next line the current record, and print it followed by a newline; otherwise, just print the current record followed by a newline."

Here's the output:

```
$ awk -f awk.bksl cal.bksl

The cal command in UNIX is very useful. It prints a
calendar of the month you specify.
ES   Arther    85   Honda    Prelude 49.412
BS   Barker    90   Nissan   300ZX   48.209
AS   Saint     88   BMW      M-3     46.629
```

Unfortunately, this particular script does not work on files that contain consecutive lines that end in backslashes, but the following one does:

```
{
    while (substr($0, length, 1) == "\\")
    {
        printf("%s", substr($0, 1, length($0) - 1))
        getline
    }

    printf("%s\n", $0)
}
```

I've used a while loop so that you can examine the ends of consecutive lines. If a line ends with a backslash, the script prints the line (with neither a backslash nor a newline at the end) and gets the next line with getline. Then the end of this line is examined; if it's a backslash, the script prints it on the same line as the previous line; if the line ends with some other character, the script leaves the while loop and prints the line and a newline. Then the script goes back and processes the next line in the data file.

Mathematical Functions

awk has several built-in mathematical functions, which are listed in Table 7.9.

Table 7.9. awk mathematical functions.

Function	Result
sqrt	Returns the square root of an argument
exp	Returns the exponential value of an argument
log	Returns the base *e* (natural) logarithm of an argument
sin	Returns the sine of an argument in radians
cos	Returns the cosine of an argument in radians
int	Returns the integer value of an argument
rand	Returns a random number in the range (0,1)
srand	"Seeds" rand()

This section discusses each of these functions.

The first five functions in the table—sqrt(x), exp(x), log(x), sin(x) and cos(x)—work exactly the same way the similarly named keys on your scientific calculator do.

7

> **Note:** If you don't use a scientific calculator, you probably won't need these functions in your awk scripts, either.

Notice that log(x) and exp(x) are mathematical inverses of one another.

int simply truncates a number so that any digits to the right of the decimal point—and the decimal point itself—are discarded. For example:

int(25.4567) returns the value 25

int(-345) returns the value -345

and so on.

rand() and srand(x) deal with *pseudo-random numbers*, numbers that appear to be random but, if enough of them are displayed, you'll see eventually that they begin to repeat. The range of values produced is

0 <= rand() < 1

Normally, you get the same sequence of values each time you use rand(). This is handy for testing programs, but not so nice when the application demands a more truly random set of numbers. To change the numbers that rand() produces, simply change rand()'s *seed* by calling srand(x).

Note: If you omit a value for x, awk will use the computer's time-of-day clock.

Here's a simple demonstration:

```
$ cat rand.awk

BEGIN {
     print rand()
     print rand()
     print rand()
     print "----"
     srand()
     print rand()
     print rand()
     print rand()
}

$ awk -f rand.awk

0.487477
0.0715607
0.00395315
----
0.0512361
0.645071
0.922862
```

```
$ awk -f rand.awk

0.487477
0.0715607
0.00395315
----
0.394808
0.926987
0.48203
```

The script simply prints three random numbers and a row of dashes, reseeds rand(), and prints three more numbers. Notice that in the two runs, the first three numbers in each run are the same. This demonstrates that rand() has a default seed that it uses if srand() is not invoked. However, notice what numbers occur after srand() is used in each case—the call to srand() changes what rand() produces.

Arrays

An *array* is a variable that can contain a set of values. Each value is stored in a *member* or *element* of the array and can be accessed by using the name of the array and an *index*. The index is either a number or a string. If the index is a string, the array is called an *associative array*; that is, there's a relationship between each index and the value of the corresponding element of the array. You'll get a better feel for what this means when you see some of the following examples.

You create an array by assigning a value to an element. Specify an element by writing the name of the array, an opening square bracket ([), the index (a value or a variable name), and a closing square bracket (]). For example, the following are legal assignments to elements:

```
time[1] = 49.438
driver[3] = "Arther"
```

And here's a script that shows them in context:

```
$ cat array.awk

BEGIN {
    time[1] = 49.438
    driver[3] = "Arther"

    print time[1], driver[1], driver[2], driver[3], driver[4]
}
```

7

```
$ awk -f array.awk
```

```
49.438    Arther
```

Note that awk simply ignored the "empty" elements—the ones having index values 1, 2 and 4—of the driver array when it was time to print their values. In more technical terms, the value of each was *null*, so awk printed nothing.

Arrays and loops go hand in hand. If you had an array time of the times from the file auto and wanted to display the first five, you could write

```
for (i = 1; i <= 5; i++)
{
    print time[i]
}
```

When i is 1, time[i] is time[1]; when i is 2, time[i] is time[2]: and so on.

To build the time array, you need just a simple statement in the main body of your script:

```
time[NR] = $6
```

That seems too simple! But recall that the main body of an awk script is in fact a loop, because each command in it is executed on all of the appropriate lines of the file. In this case, because there is no pattern, every line will be processed. NR is the number of records read so far; it's incremented automatically when a new record is read. Check out this script:

```
$ cat array1.awk
```

```
# array1.awk -- build an array from values in field 6
{
    time[NR] = $6
}
END {
    for (i = 1; i <= 5; i++)
        print time[i]
}
```

```
$ awk -f array1.awk auto
```

```
49.412
48.209
46.629
49.543
49.693
```

Of course, you can build several arrays simultaneously if you want:

```
$ cat ra2.awk

# ra2.awk -- build two arrays simultaneously
{
    time[NR] = $6
    driver[NR] = $2
}
END {
    for (i = 1; i <= 5; i++)
    {
        printf("%-10s%.3f\n", driver[i], time[i])
    }
}

$ awk -f ra2.awk auto

Arther     49.412
Barker     48.209
Saint      46.629
Straw      49.543
Swazy      49.693
```

Look at the printf format string. I used %-10s to cause the driver's name to be printed, left-justified, in a field that's 10 characters wide, and %.3f to cause the time to be printed to three decimal places.

As a final example, let's use arrays to calculate the average time for all drivers:

```
$ cat ra3.awk

# ra3.awk -- average time for all drivers
{
    time[NR] = $6
}
END {
# calculate average time by first adding all times
    for (i = 1; i <= NR; i++)
    {
        time += time[i]
    }
    aver = time / NR
#
# Count the number who had faster and slower times
    for (i = 1; i <= NR; i++)
    {
        if (time[i] >= aver)
        {
            ++slower
        }
```

7

```
          else
          {
              ++faster
          }
      }
      print "Average time = ", aver
      print "Number of faster drivers: ", faster
      print "Number of slower drivers: ", slower
}
```

$ **awk -f ra3.awk auto**

```
Average time =  48.989
Number of faster drivers:  11
Number of slower drivers:  10
```

In the script, the main body was used merely to fill the array with the times of all the drivers. After the file auto was processed—the processing here was merely reading it and saving the values for field 6—the script calculated the average time by summing all time[i] in the first loop and then dividing by NR. Next, the script went through the array a second time so it can count how many drivers were faster than average, and how many were slower. This second loop shows a major reason for having arrays—you can keep the data from the data file and use it as many times as you need, even though the file had already been dispensed with.

So far, I've demonstrated arrays with numeric indices. Arrays that use strings as indices are called *associative arrays*. One of the most useful string indices is the value of a field, an example of which you see shortly as an alternative solution for this problem: suppose you want to calculate the average time for the drivers in each class. Using only numeric arrays, you would have to modify the previous script by adding an array for class, and then a number of tests, as the following example shows:

$ **cat ra4.awk === calculate average times in each class**

```
{
    time[NR] = $6
    class[NR] = $1
}

END {
    for (i = 1; i <= NR; i++)
    {
        if (class[i] == "AS")
        {
            timeAS += time[i]
            countAS++
        }
        else if (class[i] == "BS")
```

```
        {
                timeBS += time[i]
                countBS++
        }
        else if (class[i] == "CS")
        {
                timeCS += time[i]
                countCS++
        }
        else if (class[i] == "DS")
        {
                timeDS += time[i]
                countDS++
        }
        else
        {
                timeES += time[i]
                countES++
        }
    }
    printf "AS: %8.3f %3d %8.2f\n", timeAS, countAS, timeAS/countAS
    printf "BS: %8.3f %3d %8.2f\n", timeBS, countBS, timeBS/countBS
    printf "CS: %8.3f %3d %8.2f\n", timeCS, countCS, timeCS/countCS
    printf "DS: %8.3f %3d %8.2f\n", timeDS, countDS, timeDS/countDS
    printf "ES: %8.3f %3d %8.2f\n", timeES, countES, timeES/countES
}

$ awk -f ra4.awk auto

AS:  144.860   3    48.29
BS:   48.209   1    48.21
CS:  244.935   5    48.99
DS:  245.185   5    49.04
ES:  345.581   7    49.37
```

This works, but is fairly involved, and includes a lot of nearly identical lines of code: they differ only in the class letters—AS, BS, CS, DS and ES.

However, what if you could make the index value be the class letters? That is, instead of having time[1], time[2], and so on, suppose you could have time["AS"], time["BS"], and so on. You would need no extra tests. Look at this:

```
$ cat ra5.awk

# ra5.awk === calculate average times in each class
# using associative arrays.
{
    time[$1] += $6
    ct[$1]++
}
#
```

```
# In the above main body, we create an array time having 5
# elements: time["AS"], time["BS"], and so on, and accumulate
# total time per class in each element.
# We also create an associative array for the ct of
# drivers in each class.
#
END {
    printf "AS: %8.3f %3d %8.2f\n", time["AS"], ct["AS"],
        time["AS"]/ct["AS"]
    printf "BS: %8.3f %3d %8.2f\n", time["BS"], ct["BS"],
        time["BS"]/ct["BS"]
    printf "CS: %8.3f %3d %8.2f\n", time["CS"], ct["CS"],
        time["CS"]/ct["CS"]
    printf "DS: %8.3f %3d %8.2f\n", time["DS"], ct["DS"],
        time["DS"]/ct["DS"]
    printf "ES: %8.3f %3d %8.2f\n", time["ES"], ct["ES"],
        time["ES"]/ct["ES"]
}
```

$ awk -f ra5.awk auto

```
AS:  144.860   3    48.29
BS:   48.209   1    48.21
CS:  244.935   5    48.99
DS:  245.185   5    49.04
ES:  345.581   7    49.37
```

See how much simpler the new script is? There's no need to test whether a time belongs to a given class; it's placed there automatically. However, you still must write a printf line for each class—or do you?

awk has a rather nice way of letting us refer to the indices of an associative array—(i in *array*). Here's a new version of the script:

```
{
    time[$1] += $6
    ct[$1]++
}
#
# In the above main body, we create an array time having 5
# elements: time["AS"], time["BS"], and so on, and accumulate
# total time per class in each element.
# We also create an associative array for the ct of
# drivers in each class.
#
END {
    for (i in time)
    {
        printf "%s: %8.3f %3d %8.2f\n", i, time[i], ct[i], time[i]/ct[i] | "sort"
    }
}
```

The `for` loop causes `i` to take on each of the indices of the `time` array, but in random order. (That's why the output of `printf` is piped to `sort`.) Thus the first `printf` uses an `i` value that is either AS, BS, CS, DS, or ES. Each time through the loop, `i` will have a different value, until each index has been accounted for. The following is the output of this command:

```
$ awk -f ra6.awk auto

AS:   144.860   3     48.29
BS:    48.209   1     48.21
CS:   244.935   5     48.99
DS:   245.185   5     49.04
ES:   345.581   7     49.37
```

awk has some rather nifty functions that deal with arrays. The `split` function assigns substrings of string *x* to corresponding array elements in array *y*. The syntax of the `split` function is

```
split(x,y[,c])
```

where

- *x* is the string to be split

- *y* is the array that will receive the substring

- *c* is the character that the split will be based on (default value of *c* is FS)

`split` returns the number of elements in the array. For example, suppose you want to split a date field, such as `03/05/91`, into the month, day, and year. The following program accomplishes this:

```
$ cat dates

10/17/34
12/31/99
3/4/56

$ cat split.awk

# split.awk -- divide a MM/DD/YY date
{
    split($1, date, "/")
    printf("%2s %2s %2s\n", date[1], date[2], date[3])
}

$ awk -f split.awk dates

10 17 34
12 31 99
 3  4 56
```

7

You could write the script a little differently to utilize the value that split returns and a loop:

$ cat split1.awk

```
# split1.awk -- divide a MM/DD/YY date
{
    num = split($1, date, "/")
    for (i = 1; i <= num; i++)
    {
        printf("%2s ", date[i])
    }
    printf("\n")
}
```

$ awk -f split1.awk dates

```
10 17 34
12 31 99
 3  4 56
```

That would be nice if num were a larger number. But read on.

A variation of the for statement helps to manipulate arrays. for recognizes the number of elements in an array and can be used to access them. The following is an alteration of the previous program using the for loop to print each element:

$ cat split2.awk

```
# split2.awk -- divide a MM/DD/YY date
{
    split($1, date, "/")
    for (i in date)
    {
        printf("%2s ", date[i])
    }
    printf("\n")
}
```

$ awk -f split2.awk dates

```
10 17 34
12 31 99
 3  4 56
```

Note that the i used in i in date must be the index of the array and not the value of an element. That is, i will be either 1, 2, or 3, as used in the preceding example. In general, i in date is a conditional expression that can be used in any conditional statement. For example, refer back to the array time in the ra5.awk script. There the indices were the classes, so you could legitimately write

```
if ("AS" in time)
{
    print "There is at least one car in the AS class."
}
```

Summary

This chapter discussed the awk command and its programming language. You saw how to use awk both with simple commands and with scripts to process files of data and produce reports.

7

## Chapter 8

Introduction to Writing
Shell Scripts

I n previous chapters, you learned of a number of UNIX System V Release 4 commands called *tools*, and I also introduced you to the ideas behind piping and running commands in the background. To make these commands truly useful as tools, you must combine them—usually in *shell scripts*, which are nothing more than lists of UNIX commands and arguments in files. Shell scripts are similar to awk scripts, and like awk, the shell has such features as variables, loops, decisions, and so on. An awk script is limited to awk commands, but a shell script can use shell commands—that is, any command that can be written at a UNIX shell prompt can be placed in a shell script. Thus you will be able to use awk and sed and any other commands available on the UNIX system.

Running a Shell Script

As Chapter 1 stated, you have three ways to get a shell script to *execute*, that is, to cause it to execute the commands it contains.

- Use chmod +x *scriptfilename* to make the script file executable. This is truly a "magical" part of UNIX because you don't have to feed a program to a translator, as you must if you were to write a program in C, Pascal, or any other language. By making a shell script executable with chmod +x, you cause the shell to execute each command in the script as if it had been typed on a command line.

  To execute the shell script, you simply type its name at a shell prompt. In this way, you have created a new command.

- Use sh *scriptfilename*. If the script is not executable, you simply hand it to the shell as a parameter. You do a similar thing in awk when you type awk -f awkscript.

- Use . *scriptfilename*. This is a variation of the previous method. It differs in two aspects. First, the commands in the script are executed in the current shell, not in a new shell. This means that the script can change the values of shell environment variables that exist in the current shell. By contrast, the above two ways cause a subshell to be created (see Chapter 1, "Overview of UNIX"), so that the script can then change the variable values in the subshell but not in the original shell. (I'll do more with this later.) Second, this form does not enable you to put any arguments on the command line. That is, the shell will not accept a command of the following form:

  . *scriptfilename argument*

Constitution of a Shell Script

Now, let's investigate the things you might use in a shell script besides the commands you already know about. Throughout this discussion I will use autologoff, a fairly complex script, as an example. This script is meant to be run by root (for example, by the system administrator) on a regular basis. It checks whether there are any logged-in users who have not typed anything, or who have been "idle" for an arbitrarily determined period of time. If so, this usually indicates that the user forgot to log out, so this script logs the user out automatically.

I'll go through the script, section by section, and often line by line, and introduce shell programming ideas as we encounter them in the script.

```
$ cat autologoff
```

```
1    # autologoff shell script
2    # Set the maximum idle time allowed
3    maxtime=10
4    who -u ¦ \
5    while read line
6    do
7    set -- `echo $line ¦ awk ´{

9    # pick up the minutes from the sixth field
10   idletime = substr($6, index($6, ":") + 1, 2);

12   # if idletime is greater than the maximum allowed time
13   if(idletime != "." && idletime > '$maxtime')

15       # print the user name, process id, and tty line
16   printf("%s %s %s", $1, $7, $2);
17   }´`

19   # The shell positional parameters will contain:
20   #    $1 - login name
21   #    $2 - process id of login shell
22   #    $3 - tty line (in case user is logged
23   #                   in more than once).
24   #
25   # Only process lines that are not null
26   if [ "$1" ]
27   then

29       # Send a message to the user
30       echo "You were automatically logged off due to inactivity"
¦ \
31        mail $1

33       # Kill off their login shell
34       kill -9 $2
35   fi
36 done
```

Comments

You see that the first two lines

```
# autologoff shell script
# Set the maximum idle time allowed
```

begin with the pound sign. Just as in awk, the pound sign introduces a comment. The shell ignores all characters on a line beginning with the pound sign and continuing through the end of the line.

8

Variables

The next line in the script is

```
maxtime=10
```

This is an assignment statement, similar to the assignment statement in awk. maxtime is also a variable. This statement gives it a value of 10. You met shell variables briefly in Chapter 1. A unique feature of the shell is that it has no variables that have numbers as their values, so that maxtime contains the string consisting of the character 1 followed by the character 0. This attribute of the Bourne shell makes doing arithmetic quite awkward, and it is one of the reasons why UNIX System V Release 4 includes both the Bourne and the Korn shells.

The Korn shell, however, does have numeric variables (like awk), and you will learn how to use Korn shell numeric variables later in this chapter. But nearly all of the 20 years' worth of existing UNIX scripts were written using the Bourne shell, so it is also important that you learn how to understand scripts which have no numeric variables. On the other hand, when you develop your own tools, you'll certainly want to take advantage of everything the Korn shell has to offer. In this chapter, you'll see how to program in the Bourne shell, and I'll point out Korn shell differences where appropriate as we go along.

The name of a variable can be anything you want, provided that the first character is a letter or an underscore (_).

Note: The shell does not allow an assignment statement that contains embedded spaces.

This is written correctly:

```
maxtime=10
```

However, all of the following are not:

```
maxtime =10
```

```
maxtime= 10
```

```
maxtime = 10
```

If you want to retrieve the value of a variable, you must preface its name with a dollar sign ($). For example:

8

```
$ maxtime=10
```

```
$ echo $maxtime
```

would cause

```
10
```

to be displayed.

This is quite different from awk, where the $ is used to refer to the fields in the records of the file being processed. awk variables do not require the $.

You also have learned that awk automatically initializes each variable to a null value. The shell does the same thing. For example:

```
$ echo $new_var
```

```
$
```

To help you see this better, let's surround the reference to the variable with some arbitrary characters—perhaps a pair of minus signs:

```
$ echo -$new_var-
```

```
--
$
```

There are no characters between the minus signs on the output; that is, the null value is displayed.

The shell has a special set of variables called *positional parameters* that refer to the arguments on the command line. These variables are numbered rather than named, similar to the way in which awk numbers fields. Like awk's field variables, these variables do not get their values through the use of assignment statements. Instead, the shell reads the command line and makes these assignments for you. The command name itself is the first parameter and is assigned to variable 0. The first argument is assigned to 1, and so on. Here's an example:

```
$ cat show.parms
```

```
echo $1 $2 $3 $0
```

```
$ chmod +x show.parms
```

```
$ show.parms apple peach pear
```

```
apple peach pear show.parms
```

Note that a reference to one of these variables also requires the dollar sign prefix.

Here's a more reasonable shell script that uses the wc command:

```
$ cat count.lines

# count.lines: counts the number of lines in the
# file whose name is supplied on the command line.
wc -l $1

$ chmod +x count.lines

$ count.lines auto

    21 auto
```

At this point, you might be wondering if you can indicate in a script that you want it to handle an unspecified number of command-line arguments. You could try the following to handle five files.

```
$ cat count.lines

# count.lines: counts the number of lines in the
# file whose name is supplied on the command line.
wc -l $1 $2 $3 $4 $5
```

But even this isn't very satisfactory because you had to specify five variables. The shell has an additional special variable, *, that refers to all command-line arguments. Thus, you could have

```
$ cat count.lines

# count.lines: counts the number of lines in the
# file whose name is supplied on the command line.
wc -l $*
```

Incidentally, the name of this special variable, *, is quite sensible when you think of the shell metacharacters discussed in Chapter 1. The shell metacharacter * matches all characters; the shell special variable * matches all arguments on the command line.

The shell has another special variable, #, called "number sign" or "pound sign." It tells how many arguments there were on the command line. For example:

```
$ cat count.lines

# count.lines: counts the number of lines in the
# file whose name is supplied on the command line.
echo "There were $# filenames on the command line."
wc -l $*

$ count.lines pjh*
```

```
There were 6 files on the command line.
     21 pjh-00
    628 pjh-01
    519 pjh-02
    843 pjh-03
    513 pjh-04
   2585 pjh-05
   5109 total
```

Here you see an interesting shell feature, *filename generation*. The command line apparently had only one argument, pjh*. However, when the shell sees one of its metacharacters in an argument, it expands that metacharacter before it calls on the command itself. In the directory in which we ran the pjh* command, there were six files that matched that filename pattern: pjh-00, pjh-01, pjh-02, pjh-03, pjh-04, and pjh-05. Consequently, the shell changed the command line to

```
$ count.line pjh-00 pjh-01 pjh-02 pjh-03 pjh-04 pjh-05
```

and then executed it.

Making Decisions

Referring again to the example shell script—autologoff—consider lines 26 through 35. They constitute an if statement, similar to the one in awk.

```
26   if [ "$1" ]
27   then

29       # Send a message to the user
30       echo "You were automatically logged off due to inactivity"
| \
31          mail $1

33       # Kill off their login shell
34       kill -9 $2
35 fi
```

The if statement has the form

```
if command1
then
     command2
     command3
     ...      commandN
fi
```

When the shell executes this statement, it does so by first executing *command1*, and then it tests the *exit status* of this command—that is, whether the command execution was successful or not. Success is signified by the numerical value 0. That is, if *command1* returns 0 when it completes execution, it was successful. Under that circumstance, the rest of the commands, 2...*N*, will be executed. If *command1* returns any nonzero value, these other commands are not executed. Note that the `if` command begins with the "keyword" `if`, includes `then`, and ends with the keyword `fi` (which is `if` written backwards). No braces are used in the shell to group commands as are required in `awk`.

You can examine the exit status of any command immediately after it was executed, because the shell has yet another special variable, `?`, whose value is the exit status of the last command executed. For example, you can check the exit status of the command count.lines by executing it and then printing the value of `?`:

```
$ count.lines pjh*

There were 6 files on the command line.
     21 pjh-00
    628 pjh-01
    519 pjh-02
    843 pjh-03
    513 pjh-04
   2585 pjh-05
   5109 total

$ echo $?

0
```

The following simple modification to count.lines illustrates the use of `if.`:

```
$ cat count.lines

# count.lines: counts the number of lines in the
# file whose name is supplied on the command line.
if [ $# -eq 0 ]
then
     echo "You must specify at least one filename."
     exit 1
fi
#
echo "There were $# filenames on the command line."
wc -l $*
```

command1 looks strange indeed: `[ $# -eq 0 ]`. You recognize `$#` and could probably guess that `$# -eq 0` means "the number of arguments equals 0," or, in other words, "there are no arguments." The brackets tell the shell to evaluate the expression within them, and return a value (usually either "true" or "false" as discussed previously). So if [$# -eq 0] means "if there were no arguments on the command line."

> **Note:** The spaces shown—after [, before and after -eq, and before]— are *absolutely mandatory*.

If you don't like to use brackets, you can alternatively write the first line as

```
if test $# -eq 0
```

but you must respect the shell's need to separate everything with spaces.

The shell actually has several numerical if tests, as shown in Table 8.1. In these tests, the shell expects that *var1* and *var2* will have digit strings as values, and it will treat those values as if they were numbers.

Table 8.1. The shell's numerical tests [*var1* op *var2*].

op	True If
-eq	*var1* is numerically equal to *var2*
-ne	*var1* is not equal to *var2*
-gt	*var1* is greater than *var2*
-ge	*var1* is greater than or equal to *var2*
-lt	*var1* is less than *var2*
-le	*var1* is less than or equal to *var2*

You use the exit command to assign an arbitrary exit status value to a script. The modification to count.lines says exit 1, which means that if there were no arguments on the command line, print a message to that effect and then terminate the script with an exit status of 1.

The shell also has some non-numeric tests that are intended to be applied to files and to character strings. Table 8.2 shows the tests for files, and Table 8.3 shows the tests for strings.

8

Table 8.2. The shell's file tests [test *file*].

Test	True If
-r	*file* exists and is readable
-w	*file* exists and is writable
-x	*file* exists and is executable
-f	*file* exists and is a regular (ordinary) file
-d	*file* exists and is a directory file
-h	*file* exists and is a symbolic link
-c	*file* exists and is a character special file
-b	*file* exists and is a block special file
-s	*file* exists and has a file size greater than 0

You may want to refer to Chapter 1 to review discussions of the terms in Table 8.2. For example, a file is only readable by you if you have permission to read it.

Table 8.3. The shell's string tests.

Test	True If
-z *string*	The string's length is 0
-n *string*	The string's length is not 0
str1 = *str2*	The strings are identical
str1 != *str2*	The strings are not identical
string	*string* is not null

Now suppose (as the following code demonstrates) you want a command that tells you what kind of file a given file is—regular, directory, special, or unknown.

```
$ cat tests.0

if [ -d "$1" ]
then
    echo "$1 is a directory"
fi

if [ -f "$1" ]
then
    echo "$1 is a regular file"
```

```
fi

if [ -c "$1" -o -b "$1" ]
then
     echo "$1 is a special file"
fi
```

Note that in each test the variable $1 is enclosed in double quotation marks. This is to protect against a null value for $1 (in case the user forgets to type a filename on the command line). Without these quotation marks, and with a null value for $1, the shell prints the error message test: argument expected and terminates the script.

$ sh tests.0 x

```
x is a regular file
```

$ sh tests.0 xx

$ sh tests.0 xxx

```
xxx is a directory
```

The tests.0 script included three tests: one for directory, one for regular, and one for special. (In the current directory, x is a regular file, xx doesn't exist, and xxx is a directory file.) The script had three if statements, the third of which is the most interesting:

```
if [ -c "$1" -o -b "$1" ]
then
     echo "$1 is a special file"
fi
```

The -o in the middle is the symbol for OR. This test says, "if the file is a character special file OR is a block special file, then say that it's a special file." Similarly, (-a) is a symbol for AND, and (!) is a symbol for NOT.

tests.0 was silent when it encountered the nonexistent file. You can improve this by using the if...then...else...fi form of the decision statement. Its syntax is

```
if command1
then
     command2
     command3
     ...
     commandN
else
     command0
     commandP
     ...
     commandZ
fi
```

8

This means that if *command1* exits with a true status, the commands listed between then and else will be executed and the commands between else and fi will be ignored. If *command1* exits with false, however, the commands between then and else will be ignored and the commands between else and fi will be executed.

```
$ cat tests.1

if [ -d "$1" ]
then
    echo "$1 is a directory"
else if [ -f "$1" ]
then
    echo "$1 is a regular file"
else if [ -c "$1" -o -b "$1" ]
then
    echo "$1 is a special file"
else
    echo "I don't know what $1 is!"
fi
fi
fi

$ sh tests.1 x

x is a regular file

$ sh tests.1 xx

I don't know what xx is!

$ sh tests.2 xxx

xxx is a directory
```

tests.1 does the job quite well, but it's a little unwieldy with all those fis at the end. This kind of structure—in which the else part contains another if statement—is so common that the shell has a special form for it: the elif. You can see that elif is a contraction for else if but, even better, it needs only a single fi at the end.

```
$ cat tests.2

if [ -d "$1" ]
then
    echo "$1 is a directory"
elif [ -f "$1" ]
then
    echo "$1 is a regular file"
elif [ -c "$1" -o -b "$1" ]
then
```

8

```
      echo "$1 is a special file"
else
      echo "I don't know what $1 is!"
fi
```

$ **sh tests.2** x

x is a regular file

$ **sh tests.2** xx

I don't know what xx is!

$ **sh tests.2** xxx

xxx is a directory

tests.2 is also successful and is a little simpler script than tests.1.

You now know enough to examine lines 26 through 35 of the original example:

```
26   if [ "$1" ]
27   then

29        # Send a message to the user
30        echo "You were automatically logged off due to inactivity"
¦ \
31            mail $1
33        # Kill off their login shell
34        kill -9 $2
35 fi
```

Line 26 tests the string that is the value of the first positional parameter. If the string is not null (see Table 8.3), then the commands following then and up to fi will be executed.

Line 29 is a comment and line 30 echoes a string that is piped to the mail command. (The \ at the end of line 30 escapes the following newline so that lines 30 and 31 form a single command line.) mail takes one argument, the login name of a user.

Line 34 executes the kill command, usually available only to the system administrator. kill -9 means "terminate with extreme prejudice" (in the words of the modern spy novel!) and takes as an argument a process ID number (presumably supplied as the value of the second positional parameter) that should be this particular user's login process. This logs off the user in a most abrupt manner.

To summarize, this section of the script says, "if there is a non-null login name, send that user mail and kill that user's login process."

Loops

Lines 5 through 36 constitute a while loop, again much like the while loop in awk.

```
5    while read line
6    do
7    # commands omitted for clarity
...
36 done
```

The syntax is

```
while command1
do
     command2
     command3
     ...
     commandN
done
```

As with if, the exit status of *command1* is tested and, if *command1* was successful, the commands between do and done are executed. Then *command1* is executed again, and its exit status is tested again. This continues until *command1* fails, at which point the shell continues with the rest of the program (if anything remains to be done).

Input from a User

In addition to getting parameter values from the command line, the shell has a mechanism for a script to accept strings typed by the user *after* the script has started. The command for this is called read and has the syntax:

```
read var
```

or

```
read var1 var2 var3 ...
```

In the first form—in which there is just one variable—read takes a line from stdin and stores the entire line in that variable. If there are two or more variables, read stores the first word the user types on the line in the first variable, the second word in the second variable, and so on. If there are more variables than words, the extra variables get null values. If there are more words than variables, the last variable gets its appropriate word plus the rest of the line. Here's an example:

```
$ cat read.1

echo "Enter the names of your pets."
```

```
read dog cat
echo "Your pets are named $dog and $cat."
```

> From now on, I'm not going to write the command that makes your
> script executable:
>
> $ **chmod +x script.name**
>
> Please remember to include this command.

In the previous script, read has two arguments; but the user (see the
following) has five pets!

$ **read.1**

Enter the names of your pets.

fido scratcher polly tony bill

Your pets are named fido and scratcher polly tony bill.

Having to handle five names doesn't faze read. It assigns fido to dog, and
scratcher polly tony bill to cat.

read will also take a line from a file if you employ input redirection. For
example:

read < datafile

In the autologoff script, you saw that lines 5 through 36 represented a
while loop, and now you know that *command1* is read line for this example.
But where does the information come from? For that, you must look to
line 4.

```
 4   who -u ¦ \
 5   while read line
 6   do
     ...
36 done
```

This script pipes the output of the who -u command into the while read
line so that each line of output from who -u is stored in the variable line, one
at a time. The who -u—you may recall from Chapter 1, "Overview of UNIX"—
provides output like this:

$ **who -u**

```
juucp      tty00       Sep 28 11:13    .    5890
pjh        slan05      Sep 28 12:08    .    7354
```

The first field is the login ID, the second is the device that the user is logged in on, the third/fourth/fifth are the date and time, the sixth is the "idle time" (the . means that the login has not been idle), and the seventh is the ID of each user's login process.

I've combined some elements in line 7 that you've never seen combined before:

- The set command. It takes each argument on its command line and assigns it to one of the shell's positional parameters.

- `--` as an argument to a shell command. This tells the command that any subsequent argument that just happens to have a minus sign as the first character in its name is really an argument and not an option (you'll recall that options to most UNIX commands begin with a minus sign).

- The back quote mechanism of the shell. When back quotes surround a command, the command is executed and its output replaces the backquoted command at the place—usually in a script—the backquoted command appears.

- The use of echo to pipe the value of a variable to another command.

On line 7, set has two arguments: `--` and the result of executing everything contained in back quotes—from line 7 to line 17.

```
7    set -- `echo $line ¦ awk '{

9    # pick up the minutes from the sixth field
10   idletime = substr($6, index($6, ":") + 1, 2)

12   # if idletime is greater than the maximum allowed time
13   if(idletime != "." && idletime > '$maxtime')

15       # print the user name, process id, and tty line
16       printf("%s %s %s", $1, $7, $2);
17   }'`
```

The following script illustrates the use of set with a backquoted command and positional parameters:

```
$ date

Fri Nov  1 17:13:28 EST 1991

$ set -- `date`

$ echo $2, $6. Today is $1.

Nov, 1991. Today is Fri.
```

The second command line executes the `date` command, tells `set` to ignore subsequent arguments that begin with `-`, and splits the "words" of the output of the `date` command into the positional parameters. As you can see, 1 got `Fri`, 2 got `Nov`, and so on. Notice that the `- -` itself is not assigned to any of the positional parameters. Now you need to look at the `awk` script that is embedded in this shell script.

```
 7    set -- `echo $line ¦ awk '{

 9    # pick up the minutes from the sixth field
10    idletime = substr($6, index($6, ":") + 1, 2)

12    # if idletime is greater than the maximum allowed time
13    if(idletime != "." && idletime > 'maxtime')

15        # print the user name, process id, and tty line
16        printf("%s %s %s", $1, $7, $2)
17    }'
```

For each logged in user, the `echo` command will print a string like this

```
juucp      tty00        Sep 28 11:13    1:23      5890
```

to the `awk` command. Note that the variable `idletime` is assigned a value created by `awk`'s `substr` function and uses the `index` function to locate a possible colon (`:`) as would appear in an idle time display such as `1:23` (one hour and 23 minutes). In this case, `idletime` would be assigned the value 23.

Next comes an `awk` `if` statement. Recall that `awk` variables do not need the `$` prefix when you retrieve their values. The `awk` `if` statement checks whether `idletime` is a dot (`.`)—indicating that the user is not idle—and whether idletime is greater than maxtime. (The "and" is provided by the `&&` characters.)

Remember that `maxtime` was set to a value of `10` on line 3 of the original script. You might be wondering why `$maxtime` is enclosed in single quotation marks. The reason is that it is a shell variable in an `awk` script. If you leave `maxtime` unprotected (that is, without any quotation marks), `awk` reports that it is an illegal field variable. If you enclose it in double quotation marks, `awk` will use the literal string `$maxtime` and not its value! Only when it is enclosed in single quotation marks will `awk` receive the value of `maxtime`.

If `idletime` is indeed a number greater than 10, then `awk` will print the values of the user ID, the user's login process ID, and the designation of the device on which the user has logged in. Recall that this section of code was enclosed in back quotes and was an argument to a `set  - -` command. Thus, the values that `awk` prints will be assigned to shell positional variables.

8

Because awk is a report generator, it does not have a mechanism to return a value to whatever called it. The scheme of backquoting the awk command and making it an argument to set enables the values that awk would ordinarily display to be assigned to shell positional parameters. The next section of the code in the original script shows what you do with those values:

```
26    if [ "$1" ]
27    then

29        # Send a message to the user
30        echo "You were automatically logged off due to inactivity"
¦ \
31            mail $1

33        # Kill off their login shell
34        kill -9 $2
35 fi
```

Now that you have created autologoff, you can install it on your system so that it will automatically log out users who have been idle for an arbitrarily determined period of time—particularly users who most likely have forgotten to log out.

As mentioned earlier, if the user ID is not blank, the script mails a message to the user and executes the kill command on his or her login process. This terminates the user's login.

Other Shell Constructs for Scripts

In addition to the constructs I have already discussed, a few more can be particularly useful when you are writing shell scripts.

The case Statement

In an earlier example, you learned how to use multiple ifs and elifs. However, there is a special case in which multiple decision-making can be written with a new construct—the case statement. This statement replaces a whole string of ifs, such as

```
if [ $x -eq 2 ] ...
if [ $x -eq 3 ] ...
if [ $x -eq 4 ] ...
```

and

```
if [ $s1 = $s2 ] ...
if [ $s1 = $s3 ] ...
if [ $s1 = $s3 ] ...
```

and so on. Note that in each case, only equality is tested. The `case` statement cannot test for "less than" or "greater than." The syntax for `case` is

```
case var in
    value1)    list_of_commands;;
    value2)    list_of_commands;;
    ...
esac
```

var is any shell variable, usually quoted for protection. *valueN* is any string that could be a value for *var*. Each command is usually written on a separate line, and the last one must be terminated with ;;. esac is just case spelled backwards. In addition to constant strings, *valueN* also can include shell metacharacters as used in filename generation.

Note: This does not mean *valueN* can be a regular expression. In fact, a regular expression will be misinterpreted if used as a *valueN*, because the rules for regular expression evaluation are different from those for filename generation.

The following is a sample script that uses a `case` statement to identify whether or not a character is a digit:

$ **cat case.1**

```
case "$1" in
    0) echo "$1 is a digit";;
    1) echo "$1 is a digit";;
    2) echo "$1 is a digit";;
    3) echo "$1 is a digit";;
    4) echo "$1 is a digit";;
    5) echo "$1 is a digit";;
    6) echo "$1 is a digit";;
    7) echo "$1 is a digit";;
    8) echo "$1 is a digit";;
    9) echo "$1 is a digit";;
    *) echo "$1 is NOT a digit";;
esac
```

You can see a lot of redundant typing here. Also notice the last line before the esac. The * is the shell metacharacter that matches 0 or more of any characters. The command to its right will be executed if the value of $1 is

8

anything except a digit. Think of this as the "none of the above" or "default" situation.

```
$ sh case.1 3
```

```
3 is a digit
```

```
$ sh case.1 e
```

```
e is NOT a digit
```

To avoid the redundant typing, you can use the shell metacharacter ¦ (which stands for OR).

```
$ cat case.2
```

```
case "$1" in
    0¦1¦2¦3¦4¦5¦6¦7¦8¦9) echo "$1 is a digit";;
    *) echo "$1 is NOT a digit";;
esac
```

This will execute in exactly the same way as case.1, but it is much easier to type. To make it easier to read, you can insert spaces around each "or" character:

```
$ cat case.2a
```

```
case "$1" in
    0 ¦ 1 ¦ 2 ¦ 3 ¦ 4 ¦ 5 ¦ 6 ¦ 7 ¦ 8 ¦ 9 ) echo "$1 is a digit";;
    *) echo "$1 is NOT a digit";;
esac
```

That can cause your line to extend off the page, however, which makes the script even harder to read. Better yet is the metacharacter that permits a choice of a range of values:

```
$ cat case.3
```

```
case "$1" in
    [0-9] )  echo "$1 is a digit";;
    *     )  echo "$1 is NOT a digit";;
esac
```

This example produces the same results as the other two scripts, but it is much easier to type than ten if...elif...fi statements.

More Loops

The shell has two additional looping constructs, until and for. until is much like while, and the syntax is

```
until command1
do
     command2
     command3
     ...
     commandN
done
```

As with `while`, the exit status of `command1` is tested. Unlike `while`, if `command1` is *unsuccessful*, the commands between `do` and `done` are executed. Then `command1` is executed again, and its exit status is tested again. This continues until `command1` is successful, at which point your script exits from the loop.

$ **cat until.sh**

```
until who ¦ grep joe > /dev/null
do
     echo "joe has not logged in"
     sleep 60
done
```

If `grep` fails to find `joe` in the output of the `who` command, the script will report that "joe has not logged in," pause for 60 seconds, and reexecute the `who ¦ grep joe` command. The `> /dev/null` at the end of the command redirects the output that `grep` would produce, so as not to clutter your screen. `/dev/null` is an "infinite sink" or "garbage pail," and anything sent there is lost forever.

The `for` command is like the one that `awk` uses with associative arrays. The syntax is

```
for var in list-of-values
do
     command1
     command2
     ...
     commandN
done
```

`list-of-values` can be an explicit list of values, the output of a command (using back quotes), a list of filenames generated from shell metacharacters, or a list of positional parameters. The first example shows an explicit list of values.

$ **cat for.1**

```
for x in a b c d
do
     echo $x is a value
done
```

8

```
$ sh for.1
```

```
a is a value
b is a value
c is a value
d is a value
```

The second example shows the use of shell metacharacters in generating filenames. It's interesting that the shell assumes you want it to look at the files in the current directory when you give it metacharacters as the list of values.

```
$ cat for.2
```

```
for file in ???
do
     echo $file has a 3 character name
done
```

```
$ sh for.2
```

```
REs has a 3 character name
awk has a 3 character name
cal has a 3 character name
for has a 3 character name
pax has a 3 character name
pwd has a 3 character name
tty has a 3 character name
xxx has a 3 character name
```

The third example generates the list of values by executing a command placed in back quotes.

```
$ cat for.3
```

```
for file in `ls *[0-9]`
do
     echo $file is in this directory
done
```

```
$ sh for.3
```

```
awk.1 is in this directory
case.1 is in this directory
case.2 is in this directory
case.3 is in this directory
for.1 is in this directory
for.2 is in this directory
for.3 is in this directory
for.4 is in this directory
for.5 is in this directory
pass.1 is in this directory
pjh-00 is in this directory
```

8

```
pjh-01 is in this directory
pjh-02 is in this directory
pjh-03 is in this directory
pjh-04 is in this directory
pjh-05 is in this directory
read.1 is in this directory
refile.1 is in this directory
tests.0 is in this directory
tests.1 is in this directory
tests.2 is in this directory
```

> **Note:** The `for` statement in this script could also have been
>
> ```
> for file in *[0-9]
> ```
>
> but then you would not have seen where and how a backquoted command is used.

The final example shows how the `for` loop can gain access to all the parameters on the command line.

```
$ cat for.4

for x in $*
do
      echo $x
done

$ sh for.4 1 2 3 4

1
2
3
4
```

Korn Shell Arithmetic

The Korn shell can perform integer arithmetic without resorting to the `expr` command (see following section). Because of this, and the Korn shell's features for interactive use—covered in *UNIX Desktop Guide to the Korn Shell* by John Valley—you should prefer the Korn shell over the Bourne shell. The Korn shell facilities for doing arithmetic include the `typeset` command, the `let` command, the `(( expression ))` command, and the assignment statement.

8

Integer Variables

The `integer` command enables you to *declare* an integer variable, like this:

```
$ integer num
```

For example, suppose you want to calculate the sum of two integer values, 7 and 32. Here's how to do it on the command line:

```
$ integer val

$ val=7+32

$ print $numval
```

```
39
```

Note that the assignment statement does not tolerate spaces. The Korn shell `print` command is an enhanced version of `echo`. As used here, it behaves identically to `echo` but has a number of options that `echo` doesn't have. These are explained in *UNIX Desktop Guide to the Korn Shell*.

You'll recall that the Bourne shell treats all variables as non-numeric. That is, the value of a variable is a string of characters. Even if that string includes only digits, the shell refuses to recognize it as a number. The Korn shell recognizes a variable that, as in the preceding example, is declared as a truly numeric variable. If you omit the `integer` command, the example would look like this:

```
$ val=7+32

$ print $numval
```

```
7+32
```

One advantage of declaring a variable with `integer` is that you do not have to have a dollar sign prefix when you want to retrieve its value for use in an arithmetic expression. However, you need the dollar sign when the variable is an argument to `echo` and `print`.

Arithmetic Expressions

You have already learned about shell logical expressions as used with `if` and the looping constructs. Both shells can do arithmetic, but you must first understand arithmetic expressions. You can create such an expression by combining variables, operators, and constants. The Korn shell has many arithmetic operators, as listed in Table 8.4. The *Result* column shows the value of X as a result of evaluating the expression shown in the *Example* column, assuming that I=5 and J=8.

Table 8.4. Korn shell arithmetic operators.

Operator	Operation	Example	Result
+	Add	X=I+J	13
-	Subtract	X=I-J	−3
*	Multiply	X=I*J	40
/	Divide	X=I/J	0
%	Remainder	X=I%J	5
&	And	X=I&J	0
¦	Or	X=I¦J	13
^	Exclusive OR	X=I^J	13
==	Equal	X=I==J	0
!=	Not equal	X=I!=J	1
>	Greater than	X=I>J	0
>=	Greater than or equal to	X=I>=J	0
<	Less than	X=I<J	1
<=	Less than OR equal to	X=I<=J	1

The Korn shell treats non-numeric variables that appear in arithmetic expressions in an interesting way: it temporarily "promotes" them to numeric. For example, consider this:

```
$ integer i j

$ i=5

$ num=i+3   # num is non-numeric!

$ print $num

i+3

$ j=num*3

$ print $j

24
```

The command that assigns the value of num*3 to j is where the Korn shell promotes num. It calculates num+3 to be 5 so that j is assigned the value 8.

Let's write a script that counts from 1 to 10 by using Korn shell arithmetic:

```
$ cat korn.1

integer n=0 # declares n and initializes it to 0
while [ n -lt 10 ]
do
     n=n+1
     print $n
done

$ chmod +x korn.1

$ korn.1

1
2
3
4
5
6
7
8
9
10
```

Note that you can omit the dollar sign when the variable is used in a logical expression such as [n -lt 10].

Using the let Command

There's an alternative to using the integer command for variables that appear on the left-hand side of assignments. The Korn shell let command evaluates non-numeric variables as if they were numeric variables, using this syntax:

let *var=expression* [*var1=expression1*] ...

where *var*, *var1*, and so on are not declared.

Here's a let command that evaluates three expressions:

```
$ let i=2 j=3 k=i*6

$ print $1 $j $k

2 3 12
```

The let command causes the shell to evaluate each of the non-numeric variables to be evaluated as if they had been declared integer. The variables are still non-numeric, but their values are the string versions of the numeric values they would have contained had they been declared numeric.

Because many Korn shell arithmetic operators are also shell metacharacters, you should make a habit of enclosing in quotation marks the string to the right of the `let` command.

Using the ((. . .)) Statement

The Korn shell has a shorthand notation for `let` *expression*. It is ((*expression*)). Not only is this a little simpler to type, but it also removes the need to quote *expression*.

More Commands for Scripts

A number of other commands are also quite helpful in writing Bourne shell scripts. The following section covers those that are most useful.

The expr Command

The `expr` command is used to evaluate and compare expressions. You must use it in Bourne shell scripts if you want to do any arithmetic because it converts strings of digits to numerical values. Any of the following expressions can be evaluated:

- Numeric operations (addition, subtraction, multiplication, and so on)

- Logical operations (equal to, not equal to, greater than, less than, and so on)

- Regular expressions

The results of an evaluation are written to stdout. If the result is null, a zero appears rather than a blank.

```
$ cat bourne.1

n=0
while [ $n -lt 10 ]
do
     n=`expr $n + 1`
     echo $n
done
```

8

```
$ chmod +x bourne.1

$ bourne.1

1
2
3
4
5
6
7
8
9
10
```

The fourth line is the one that uses expr to evaluate a string as if it were a number. For example, the first time through the loop, n is the string 0. The fourth line forms $n + 1, which is 0 + 1. Then expr performs the addition. The result of the expr is the number 1 and this is assigned—as a string—to n. Ugly.

If any argument to expr is a shell metacharacter, you must escape it with a backslash (\) (or enclose it in quotation marks). This means that if you are going to multiply, you must enter

```
n=`expr $n \* 2`
```

or

```
n=`expr $n '*' 2`
```

or

```
n=`expr $n "*" 2`
```

because the * is a shell metacharacter.

Another form of expr is

```
expr arg1 : arg2
```

In this situation, expr checks whether or not the characters in *arg1* match the characters in *arg2*. *arg2* may be a regular expression but *arg1* must be a constant string with no metacharacters in it. expr will return the number of characters in *arg1* matched by *arg2*, starting at the beginning of *arg1*. Consider the following:

```
$ expr expression : exp

3

$ expr expression : 'e.*e'
```

```
5

$ expr expression : ´.*´

10

$ expr expression : press

0
```

The first example used two strings. All three of the characters in *arg2* matched consecutive characters in *arg1*. The second example used a regular expression for *arg2*: "e, followed by zero or more characters, followed by another e." That matched the first five characters of the string expression. The third example used the "universal regular expression wildcard" as *arg2*: .*. Naturally, it matched all ten characters of *arg1*. The last example might be an eye-opener if you forgot that expr begins searching at the beginning of *arg1*. It is *not* like the substr function of awk. Thus, even though press can be found in expression, it cannot be found at the *beginning* of expression, so expr reports that press cannot be found!

Table 8.5 shows all of expr's expressions.

Table 8.5. The expressions of expr.

Expression	*Meaning*
arg1 : *arg2*	Compare *arg1* and *arg2* (see text)
arg1 + *arg2*	Add the numeric values of the two arguments
arg1 - *arg2*	Subtract *arg2* from *arg1*
arg1 * *arg2*	Multiply *arg1* and *arg2*
arg1 / *arg2*	Divide *arg1* by *arg2*
arg1 % *arg2*	Report the remainder of *arg1* divided by *arg2*
arg1 = *arg2*	1 if *arg1* and *arg2* are equal, 0 otherwise
arg1 \> *arg2*	1 if *arg1* is greater than *arg2*, 0 otherwise
arg1 \>= *arg2*	1 if *arg1* is greater than or equal to *arg2*, 0 otherwise
arg1 \< *arg2*	1 if *arg1* is less than *arg2*, 0 otherwise
arg1 \<= *arg2*	1 if *arg1* is less than or equal to *arg2*, 0 otherwise
arg1 != *arg2*	1 if *arg1* and *arg2* are not equal, 0 otherwise
arg1 \& *arg2*	*arg1* if neither is null, 0 otherwise
arg1 \! *arg2*	*arg1* if *arg1* is not null, *arg2* otherwise

8

The `printf` Command

The shell `printf` command is like `awk`'s `printf`: it enables you to specify the format of a string to print. The syntax is

```
printf format_specification [ arg(s) ]
```

`printf` requires at least one argument. The mandatory argument is a *format specification* string. Any other arguments represent what must be printed under the format specification string's control. The format specification may contain

- Literal characters that simply print "as is." For example:

```
printf "hello, world"
```

- A conversion specification made up of a percent sign (%), the conversion character s, and optional flags, for formatting each argument.

- Metacharacter constants (as used by `echo`) such as \n, \t, \b, for newline, tab, and backspace, respectively.

  The simplest form of `printf` is

```
$ printf ´hello world\n´
```

```
hello world
```

This conversion specification contains only literal characters plus a newline character, and there are no additional arguments.

You can use `printf` with shell variables. For example:

```
$ cat printf.1
```

```
var=xyzzy
printf "The value of var is %s\n" $var
```

```
$ sh printf.1
```

```
The value of var is xyzzy
```

The s in %s is the conversion character. It can be augmented by adding one or more flags—a *field width* numeric value and/or a *precision* numeric value. The field width value specifies the minimum number of columns in which the converted value will be displayed. If the field width value is negative, the value will be left-justified in the field; otherwise, it will be right-justified. The precision value is the actual number of characters to be printed. Here are some examples:

8

```
$ cat pf.2

echo $HOME
printf "00000000001111111111\n"
printf "01234567890123456789\n"
printf "%s\n" $HOME
printf "%20s\n" $HOME
printf "%-20s\n" $HOME
printf "%20.4s\n" $HOME
printf "%-20.4s\n" $HOME
printf "%.4s\n" $HOME
printf "%-.4s\n" $HOME

$ sh pf.2

/usr/pjh
00000000001111111111
01234567890123456789
/usr/pjh
            /usr/pjh
/usr/pjh
                 /usr
/usr
/usr
/usr
```

The first two `printf` commands display a "ruler" by numbering the first 20 columns. The next `printf` command displays the value of the shell environment variable HOME (/usr/pjh) in the default format, followed by a `printf` command that places it, right-justified, in a 20-column field. The next `printf` command left-justifies it, and the remaining four `printf`s use a precision of 4. Note that you can omit the field width if you like, but then no justification is possible.

A full explanation of the `printf` command and its arguments is contained in Chapter 11, "UNIX System V Release 4 Command Reference."

The xargs Command

The `xargs` command transforms the output of one command into a series of commands. This gives you a way to work around the operating system's limit on the number of arguments it enables you to put on a command line. It also lets you construct and execute commands from a list sent to its standard input. An advantage of `xargs` is that it repeats the command for any given number of arguments. Thus, instead of creating a shell script with a looping mechanism to repeat a command, you simply use `xargs`.

8

The syntax of xargs is

```
xargs [ options ] [ command [ initial arguments ] ]
```

The following options available with xargs:

-lnumber	command is executed for the number of lines of input from stdin. The default is 1.
-isubstitute	substitute is replaced by each input line and inserted into initial arguments.
-nnumber	number is the maximum number of arguments from stdin for each command.
-p	The user is asked to reply whether or not the command displayed is to be executed.
-t	The command and its argument list are echoed to stderr just prior to being executed ("trace" mode of operation).
-snumber	number is the maximum number of characters in each argument list, and must not exceed 470.
-x	Causes xargs to terminate if any argument list is bigger than 470, or the number given with the -s option.
-estring	string is the end-of-file marker. The default is the underscore character (_). This marker tells xargs when to stop reading from stdin.

xargs reads from the standard input and executes a specified command for each line of input. When a command is not given, xargs uses echo. A simple example using xargs is

```
$ date ¦ xargs

Tue May 28 08:35:04 EDT 1991
```

Although the output appears the same as the standard output of the date command, xargs has read the output of the date command from stdin and used echo to print it. The *trace* (-t) mode of xargs, as follows, illustrates this better:

```
$ date ¦ xargs -t

/bin/echo Tue May 28 08:37:06 EDT 1991
Tue May 28 08:37:06 EDT 1991
```

Note that xargs uses the UNIX command /bin/echo because it cannot access the echo that is built into the shell.

8

You can limit the number of arguments placed on each command line by using the -n option. You must provide an integer value to n. This value represents the number of words that xargs will accept from stdin for each invocation of the command. For example, to cause /bin/echo to print two words from the date command each time /bin/echo is called, you use -n2, as follows:

```
$ date ¦ xargs -n2
```

```
Tue May
28 08:44:19
EDT 1991
```

Using trace mode results in the following:

```
$ date ¦ xargs -t -n2
```

```
/bin/echo Tue May
Tue May
/bin/echo 28 08:44:19
28 08:44:19
/bin/echo EDT 1991
```

Note that xargs prints two words each time it executes date, until it runs out of arguments at stdin.

Here is another example. Suppose you want to move a large number of files from a given directory to a variety of destination directories (first file to first directory, second file to second directory, and so on). You create two data files, the first containing the names of the source files and the second containing the names of the destination directories in the proper order. For example, suppose you want to move book.part1 to directory chapt1, table_of_contents to directory toc, and database to directory dbase. You would create a file called, for example, sources to contain

```
book.part1
table_of_contents
database
```

and a file called destination to contain

```
chapt1
toc
dbase
```

Next, use the paste command to join the lines of the two files

```
$ paste sources destination
```

```
book.part1 chapt1
table_of_contents toc
database dbase
```

8

so that each line of paste's output will contain a filename and a destination directory name. Now pipe the output of the paste command to xargs -n2, and you'll see how xargs is going to handle it:

```
$ paste sources destination ¦ xargs -n2

book.part1 chapt1
table_of_contents toc
database dbase
```

This shows that xargs is reading stdin two words at a time.

The final step is to provide the command mv for xargs to execute for each input line. I included the -t option so that you can see there are actually three separate mv commands generated by xargs.

```
$ paste sources destination ¦ xargs -n2 -t mv

mv book.part1 chapt1
mv table_of_contents toc
mv database dbase
```

If you are not sure what xargs will generate, you can "fool" it into displaying the commands like this:

```
$ paste sources destination ¦ xargs -n2 echo mv

mv book.part1 chapt1
mv table_of_contents toc
mv database dbase
```

Placing echo as the first argument to xargs prints the resulting command lines from xargs—without actually executing the command.

You also can use the -p option, which makes xargs prompt you before executing each command.

```
$ paste sources destination ¦ xargs -n2 -p mv

mv book.part1 chapt1 ?...y<enter>
mv table_of_contents toc ?...y<enter>
mv database dbase ?...n<enter>
```

When you type a y and press Enter at the ? prompt, the command will be executed. Entering anything else, however, means the command will not be executed.

xargs is also helpful for building a list of options for another command. For example, suppose you want to edit only those files that contain a certain pattern, say, "Florida." First, you use grep with the -l option to list the names of the files that contain the pattern.

8

```
$ grep -l Florida *
```

```
database
states
personnel
```

You then pipe the output of the grep command to xargs, with vi as the command to execute on the arguments.

```
$ grep -l Florida * ¦ xargs vi
```

```
3 files to edit
```

Use the -t option to show the command line that xargs generates.

```
$ grep -l Florida * ¦ xargs -t vi
```

```
vi file1 file2 file3
```

Use the -l option for xargs to specify the number of lines xargs is to process from its input. For example, when a command produces four lines of output, xargs, by default, joins all four lines together as one command-line argument. If you supply a -l1 argument, xargs executes the command four times—once with each line of input. If you supply a -l2 argument, xargs executes the command two times—once with the first two lines of input, and again with the last two lines.

Suppose you want to write a shell script for backing up files that will prompt you with the names of the files to include in the backup list. Use xargs to build the filename list as shown in the following script:

```
# interactive backup script
$ ls ¦ xargs -p -l ¦ cpio -oc > /dev/rdsk/fd096
```

This command first lists the files in the current directory and sends the names to xargs. The name of each file prints and, when the user types a y, the name of the file goes to the cpio command. On my machine, /dev/rdsk/fd096 is the floppy disk drive.

xargs has an interesting flag that causes automatic substitution of what it reads from stdin for a special string in its argument list. The -i option inserts lines from the standard input into the command for xargs to execute. The following example shows how xargs prompts you for the names of files you want to copy from your *current* directory to the *old* directory.

```
$ ls ¦ xargs -i -p cp {} old
```

This command inserts each line of the standard input into the braces ({}) and this becomes the first argument to the cp command. Alternatively, you might have written the command like this, specifying the special string to -i:

8

```
$ ls ¦ xargs -iXXX -p cp XXX old
```

Let's see what the command does by eliminating `-p` and inserting `echo` just before `cp`:

```
$ ls
```

```
REs          ksh.prompts  no.blanks    xargs.2
UNIX.times   ksh.strings  x
```

```
$ ls ¦ xargs -iXXX echo cp XXX old
```

```
cp REs old
cp UNIX.times old
cp ksh.prompts old
cp ksh.strings old
cp no.blanks old
cp x old
cp xargs.2 old
```

`xargs` is a helpful utility for improving shell programs. It enables you to build and execute new commands from a list—typically, the output of another command. It is worthwhile to spend some additional time experimenting with `xargs`.

Summary

This chapter introduced you to the concepts and techniques of writing shell scripts. By no means did it cover everything there is to know about the topic. However, as you gain programming experience, you will be able to extend your knowledge of shell scripts by reading the reference manual for `sh` and `ksh`, and by reading other SAMS books on shell programming.

8

Miscellaneous File Commands

This chapter adds a number of utilities to your arsenal of UNIX tools. The utilities range from programs that compare the contents of files, to programs that copy a group of files into a so-called *archive file* for storage or transfer to another computer. Such activities occur quite frequently in the UNIX environment.

File Comparison

UNIX System V Release 4 provides a number of commands that enable you to compare two or more files. These commands are quite useful when you are trying to determine what has changed between two versions of the same text, script, or program source code files. These commands also are useful in keeping files up to date. If someone sends you a file that describes the differences between the version you have and the latest version, you can use the "difference" file and your old version to create the new one.

The cmp Command

The simplest command for comparing two files, cmp, simply tells you whether the files are different or not. If they are different, it tells you where in the file it spotted the first difference. Its syntax is

```
cmp [ -l ] [ -s ] file1 file2
```

where

-l   Prints the number of the character that is different (the first character in the file is number 1), and then prints the octal value of the ASCII code of each character that is different.

-s   Prints nothing but returns an appropriate result code (0 if no differences, 1 if one or more differences).

Here are some sample executions:

```
$ cat na.1

allen christopher
babinchak david
best betty
bloom dennis
boelhower joseph
bose anita
cacossa ray
delucia joseph

$ cat na.2

allen christopher
babinchak David
best betty
boelhower joseph
bose
cacossa ray
delucia joseph
```

You can see that the two files have their first difference on line 2. The "d" is the 29th character, counting the newline character at the end of the first line.

```
$ cmp na.1 na.2

na.1 na.2 differ: char 29, line 2
```

9

```
$ cmp -l na.1 na.2

cmp:
    29 144 104
    68 141  12
    69 156 143
    70 151 141
    71 164 143
    72 141 157
    73  12 163
    74 143 163
    76 143  40
    77 157 162
    78 163 141
    79 163 171
    80 141  12
    81  40 144
    82 162 145
    83 141 154
    84 171 165
    85  12 143
    86 144 151
    87 145 141
    88 154  40
    89 165 152
    90 143 157
    91 151 163
    92 141 145
    93  40 160
    94 152 150
    95 157  12
```

This is quite a list! The 29th character is octal 144 in the first file and octal 104 in the second. If you look them up in the ASCII table in the reference section of this book, you'll see that the former is a "d" while the latter is a "D"! Character 68 is the first "a" in "anita" in na.1 and the newline after the space after "bose" in na.2

Now let's try the -s option on the two files:

```
$ cmp -s na.1 na.2

$ echo $?

1
```

You'll recall from Chapter 8, "Introduction to Writing Shell Scripts," that ? is the shell variable that contains the result code of the last command. The 1 means that cmp found at least one difference between the two files.

9

Next, for contrast, let's compare a file with itself.

```
$ cmp -s na.1 na.1

$ echo $?

0
```

The 0 means that cmp found no differences.

The comm Command

The comm command requires that files being compared must be sorted. It selects or rejects the common lines in the two files, and produces three columns of output by default:

Column 1   Lines that are unique to *file1*

Column 2   Lines that are unique to *file2*

Column 3   Lines that are common to both

The syntax is simply

```
comm [ -123 ] file1 file2
```

where the 123 options indicate which of the columns should not be printed. For example, comm -12 prints only the lines that are common to both; comm -23 prints only the lines that appear in *file1* but do not appear in *file2*.

It is helpful to use comm when you try to determine information that is new or has been deleted. For example, if you have two files that contain the names of all the files in a directory—but that were created at different times—you can use comm to determine the added, deleted, and unchanged files.

Let's use na.1 and na.2 as our test files for comm, as we did for cmp. You don't specify any options, you get a three-column listing:

```
$ comm na.1 na.2

                                allen christopher
                babinchak David
babinchak david
                                best betty
bloom dennis
                                boelhower joseph
                bose
bose anita
                                cacossa ray
                                delucia joseph
```

Let's print only the lines that are not in the first file, as follows:

```
$ comm -1 na.1 na.2

                        allen christopher
babinchak David
                        best betty
                        boelhower joseph
bose
                        cacossa ray
                        delucia joseph
```

Note that, because the original first column is suppressed, the first column in this example is the second column from the previous example. Now let's display only the lines that are unique to na.1:

```
$ comm -23 na.1 na.2

babinchak david
bloom dennis
bose anita
```

And here are the lines that are common to both:

```
$ comm -12 na.1 na.2

allen christopher
best betty
boelhower joseph
cacossa ray
delucia joseph
```

And, finally, here are the lines that are unique to na.2:

```
$ comm -13 na.1 na.2

babinchak David
bose
```

The comm command shows the differences between files in a manner that's more suited to interactive use.

The diff Command

The diff command is a much more powerful command than the two I've discussed so far—it shows you the differences between two files by outputting the editing changes you would need to make in order to convert one file to the other. The syntax of diff is one of the following lines:

9

```
diff [-bitw] [-c ¦ -e ¦ -f ¦ -h ¦ -n] file1 file2
diff [-bitw] [-C number] file1 file2
diff [-bitw] [-D string] file1 file2
diff [-bitw] [-c ¦ -e ¦ -f ¦ -h ¦ -n] [-l] [-r] [-s] [-S name] dir1 dir2
```

The three sets of options—cefhn, -C *number*, and -D *string*—are mutually exclusive. The common options are

-b   Ignores trailing blanks; treats all other strings of blanks as equivalent to one another

-i   Ignores upper- or lowercase distinctions

-t   Preserves indentation level of the original file by expanding tabs in the output

-w   Ignores all blanks (spaces and tabs)

Each of these other options is explained by example later in the chapter. First, let's look at the two files I'm using to show off what diff does:

$ **cat p1**

```
root:x:0:0:System Administrator:/usr/root:/bin/ksh
slan:x:57:57:StarGROUP Software NPP Administration:/usr/slan:
juucp:x:24:100:Jon LaBadie:/usr/spool/uucppublic:/usr/lib/uucp/uucico
couucp:x:25:100:Bill Michaelson:/usr/spool/uucppublic:/usr/lib/uucp/uucico
fanuucp:x:32:100:Jo Poplawski:/usr/spool/uucppublic:/usr/lib/uucp/uucico
pjh:x:102:0:Peter J. Holsberg:/usr/pjh:/bin/ksh
pete:x:200:1:PJH:/usr/home/pete:/bin/ksh
irv:x:257:1:Irv Ashkenazy:/usr/home/irv:/bin/ksh
ajh:x:258:1:Alan Holsberg:/usr/home/ajh:/bin/ksh
mccollo:x:329:1:Carol McCollough:/usr/home/mccollo:/bin/ksh
rechter:x:293:20:rechter jay:/u1/fall91/dp168/rechter:/bin/ksh
reeve:x:308:20:reeve michael j:/u1/fall91/dp168/reeve:/bin/ksh
regh:x:331:20:regh jeff l:/u1/fall91/dp270/regh:/bin/ksh
sicigna:x:327:20:sicignano joseph p:/u1/fall91/dp168/sicigna:/bin/ksh
small:x:309:20:small thomas j:/u1/fall91/dp168/small:/bin/ksh
solarsk:x:294:20:solarski linda m:/u1/fall91/dp168/solarsk:/bin/ksh
steill:x:269:20:steill keith r:/u1/fall91/dp270/steill:/bin/ksh
temple:x:295:20:temple linda c:/u1/fall91/dp168/temple:/bin/ksh
varvar:x:270:20:varvar anthony j:/u1/fall91/dp270/varvar:/bin/ksh
vaas:x:325:20:vaas eric:/u1/fall91/dp270/vaas:/bin/ksh
washing:x:310:20:washington reginald:/u1/fall91/dp168/washing:/bin/ksh
weiner:x:276:20:weiner sibylle u:/u1/fall91/dp270/weiner:/bin/ksh
wiedenh:x:311:20:wiedenhofer allen e:/u1/fall91/dp168/wiedenh:/bin/ksh
wight:x:296:20:wight charles n:/u1/fall91/dp168/wight:/bin/ksh
william:x:297:20:williams tony j:/u1/fall91/dp168/william:/bin/ksh
```

9

```
$ cat p2

root:x:0:0:System Administrator:/usr/root:/bin/ksh
slan:x:57:57:StarGROUP Software NPP Administration:/usr/slan:
nuucp:x:10:10:0000-uucp(0000):/usr/spool/uucppublic:/usr/lib/uucp/uucico
labuucp:x:21:100:shevett's UPC:/usr/spool/uucppublic:/usr/lib/uucp/uucico
puucp:x:22:100:princeton:/usr/spool/uucppublic:/usr/lib/uucp/uucico
juucp:x:24:100:Jon LaBadie:/usr/spool/uucppublic:/usr/lib/uucp/uucico
couucp:x:25:100:Bill Michaelson:/usr/spool/uucppublic:/usr/lib/uucp/uucico
fanuucp:x:32:100:Jo Poplawski:/usr/spool/uucppublic:/usr/lib/uucp/uucico
pjh:x:102:0:Peter J. Holsberg:/usr/pjh:/bin/ksh
pete:x:200:1:PJH:/usr/home/pete:/bin/ksh
lkh:x:250:1:lkh:/usr/lkh:/bin/ksh
shevett:x:251:1:dave shevett:/usr/shevett:/bin/ksh
moser:x:252:1:sue moser:/usr/moser:/bin/ksh
irv:x:257:1:Irv Ashkenazy:/usr/home/irv:/bin/ksh
ajh:x:258:1:Alan Holsberg:/usr/home/ajh:/bin/ksh
mccollo:x:329:1:Carol McCollough:/usr/home/mccollo:/bin/ksh
rechter:x:293:20:rechter jay:/u1/fall91/dp168/rechter:/bin/ksh
reeve:x:308:20:reeve michael j:/u1/fall91/dp168/reeve:/bin/ksh
regh:x:331:20:regh jeff l:/u1/fall91/dp270/regh:/bin/ksh
sicigna:x:327:20:sicignano joseph p:/u1/fall91/dp168/sicigna:/bin/ksh
small:x:309:20:small thomas j:/u1/fall91/dp168/small:/bin/ksh
solarsk:x:294:20:solarski linda m:/u1/fall91/dp168/solarsk:/bin/ksh
steill:x:269:20:steill keith r:/u1/fall91/dp270/steill:/bin/ksh
```

I've deliberately chosen more complicated files for diff than I did for cmp and comm to show you just how powerful diff is. You may have some difficulty perceiving differences between p1 and p2, but be assured that diff has no such difficulty at all.

```
$ diff p1 p2

2a3,5
> nuucp:x:10:10:0000-uucp(0000):/usr/spool/uucppublic:/usr/lib/uucp/uucico
> labuucp:x:21:100:shevett's UPC:/usr/spool/uucppublic:/usr/lib/uucp/uucico
> puucp:x:22:100:princeton:/usr/spool/uucppublic:/usr/lib/uucp/uucico
7a11,13
> lkh:x:250:1:lkh:/usr/lkh:/bin/ksh
> shevett:x:251:1:dave shevett:/usr/shevett:/bin/ksh
> moser:x:252:1:sue moser:/usr/moser:/bin/ksh
18,25d23
< temple:x:295:20:temple linda c:/u1/fall91/dp168/temple:/bin/ksh
< varvar:x:270:20:varvar anthony j:/u1/fall91/dp270/varvar:/bin/ksh
< vaas:x:325:20:vaas eric:/u1/fall91/dp270/vaas:/bin/ksh
< washing:x:310:20:washington reginald:/u1/fall91/dp168/washing:/bin/ksh
< weiner:x:276:20:weiner sibylle u:/u1/fall91/dp270/weiner:/bin/ksh
< wiedenh:x:311:20:wiedenhofer allen e:/u1/fall91/dp168/wiedenh:/bin/ksh
< wight:x:296:20:wight charles n:/u1/fall91/dp168/wight:/bin/ksh
< william:x:297:20:williams tony j:/u1/fall91/dp168/william:/bin/ksh
```

9

Note that `diff` displayed a cryptic "alphanumeric" string on a line by itself, and then listed several lines with either > or < prepended. Those with the > are lines in *file2* that are not in *file1*. Those with the < are lines in *file1* that are not in *file2*. For example:

```
2a3,5
> nuucp:x:10:10:0000-uucp(0000):/usr/spool/uucppublic:/usr/lib/uucp/uucico
> labuucp:x:21:100:shevett's UPC:/usr/spool/uucppublic:/usr/lib/uucp/uucico
> puucp:x:22:100:princeton:/usr/spool/uucppublic:/usr/lib/uucp/uucico
```

The `2a3,5` is an `ed` editor command that says "append lines 3 through 5 of *file2* to *file1*, beginning just after what is now line 2 of *file1*."

The `diff` output in the example had another set of similar editor commands, as follows:

```
7a11,13
> lkh:x:250:1:lkh:/usr/lkh:/bin/ksh
> shevett:x:251:1:dave shevett:/usr/shevett:/bin/ksh
> moser:x:252:1:sue moser:/usr/moser:/bin/ksh
```

The editor command `7a11,13` says, "beginning with what is presently line 7 of *file1*, append lines 11 through 13 of *file2*."

The last part of `diff`'s output had the instructions `18,25d23`, followed by a group of lines that began with <. This means: "Delete lines 18 through 25 of the original *file1*, to make the two files match up to but not including line 23 of *file2*."

Now let's apply `diff` to the files na.1 and na.2:

```
$ diff na.1 na.2

2c2
< babinchak david
---
> babinchak David
4d3
< bloom dennis
6c5
< bose anita
---
> bose
```

These editor commands are quite different from what `diff` printed before. The first four lines show

```
 2c2
< babinchak david
---
> babinchak David
```

9

which means that the second line of *file1* can be changed to match the second line of *file2* by executing the command, which means "change line 2 of *file1* to line 2 of *file2*." Note that both the line from *file1*—- prefaced with <—and the line from *file2*—separated by three dashes—are shown.

The next command says to delete line 4 from *file1* to bring it into agreement with *file2* up to—but not including—line 3 of *file2*. Finally, notice there is another *change* command, 6c5, which says, "Change line 6 of *file1* by replacing it with line 5 of *file2*."

Note that in line 2, the difference that diff found was the "d" versus "D" letter in the second word.

You can tell diff to ignore the case of the characters by using the -i option, as follows:

```
$ diff -i na.1 na.2

4d3
< bloom dennis
6c5
< bose anita
- - -
> bose
```

The -c option causes the differences to be printed "in context"; that is, several surrounding lines of both files are shown and each difference is marked with either an exclamation point, ! (meaning that corresponding lines in the two files are similar but not the same); a minus sign, - (meaning this line was not in *file2*); or a plus sign, + (meaning this line was in *file2* but not in *file1*). Note that a header is printed; it shows the names of the two files and times and dates of their last changes, and it also shows either stars (***) or dashes (- - -) as the markers for each file.

```
$ diff -c na.1 na.2

*** na.1     Sat Nov  9 12:57:55 1991
--- na.2     Sat Nov  9 12:58:27 1991
***************
*** 1,8 ****
  allen christopher
! babinchak david
  best betty
- bloom dennis
  boelhower joseph
! bose anita
  cacossa ray
  delucia joseph
--- 1,7 ----
  allen christopher
! babinchak David
  best betty
```

```
  boelhower joseph
! bose
  cacossa ray
  delucia joseph
```

Next comes a star-filled header showing which lines of *file1* will be printed next (1,8), followed by the lines themselves. You see that the babinchak line is different in the two files, as is the bose line. Also, bloom dennis does not appear in *file2*. Next, you see a header of dashes and an indication of which lines of *file2* will follow (1,7). Note that for the *file2* list, the babinchak line and the bose line are "flagged" with exclamation points. The number of lines displayed depends on how close together the differences are (the default is 3 lines of context). You will see an example of how to change the number of context lines later in the chapter, when I discuss diff again with p1 and p2.

diff can create an ed script that you can use to change *file1* into *file2*. For example, let's take the command

```
$ diff -e na.1 na.2

6c
bose
.
4d
2c
babinchak David
.
```

and redirect its output to a file

```
$ diff -e na.1 na.2 > ed.scr
```

Edit the file by adding two lines, w and q, resulting in

```
$ cat ed.scr

6c
bose
.
4d
2c
babinchak David
.
w
q
```

and apply it as follows:

```
$ ed na.1 < ed.scr
```

9

This will change na.1 into na.2. For such a small example, this isn't very impressive, but here's one that is. Suppose you have a large program written in C that does something special for you. Perhaps it manages your investments or keeps track of sales leads. Further, suppose that the people who provided the program discover that it has bugs (and what program doesn't?). They could either ship out new disks containing the rewritten program, or they could run `diff` on the original and the corrected copy and send you an `ed` script so that you could make the changes yourself. If the script were small enough (less than 50,000 characters or so), they could even distribute it through electronic mail!

The `-f` option creates what appears to be an `ed` script that would change *file2* into *file1*. However, it is not an `ed` script at all. It's a rather puzzling "feature."

```
$ diff -f na.1 na.2

c2
babinchak David
.
d4
c6
bose
.
```

Also of limited value is the `-h` option, which causes `diff` to work in a "half-hearted" manner (according to the official AT&T UNIX System V Release 4 Users Reference Manual)! `diff` with the `-h` option is supposed to work best—and fast—on very large files having sections of change that encompass only a few lines at a time and that are widely separated in the files. Without `-h`, `diff` slows dramatically as the sizes of the files being `diff`ed increases.

```
$ diff -h na.1 na.2

2c2
< babinchak david
---
> babinchak David
4d3
< bloom dennis
6c5
< bose anita
---
> bose
```

As you can see, `diff` with the `-h` option also works pretty well with the original files that are too small to show a measurable difference in `diff`'s speed.

The `-n` and `-D` options will be covered in Part III of this book.

9

Now let's look at some context `diff`s on larger files. First, the following is one with the three-line default:

```
$ diff -c p1 p2

*** p1      Mon Nov  4 20:48:10 1991
--- p2      Mon Nov  4 20:48:21 1991
***************
*** 1,10 ****
--- 1,16 ----
  root:x:0:0:System Administrator:/usr/root:/bin/ksh
  slan:x:57:57:StarGROUP Software NPP Administration:/usr/slan:
+ nuucp:x:10:10:0000-uucp(0000):/usr/spool/uucppublic:/usr/lib/uucp/uucico
+ labuucp:x:21:100:shevett's UPC:/usr/spool/uucppublic:/usr/lib/uucp/uucico
+ puucp:x:22:100:princeton:/usr/spool/uucppublic:/usr/lib/uucp/uucico
  juucp:x:24:100:Jon LaBadie:/usr/spool/uucppublic:/usr/lib/uucp/uucico
  couucp:x:25:100:Bill Michaelson:/usr/spool/uucppublic:/usr/lib/uucp/uucico
  fanuucp:x:32:100:Jo Poplawski:/usr/spool/uucppublic:/usr/lib/uucp/uucico
  pjh:x:102:0:Peter J. Holsberg:/usr/pjh:/bin/ksh
  pete:x:200:1:PJH:/usr/home/pete:/bin/ksh
+ lkh:x:250:1:lkh:/usr/lkh:/bin/ksh
+ shevett:x:251:1:dave shevett:/usr/shevett:/bin/ksh
+ moser:x:252:1:sue moser:/usr/moser:/bin/ksh
  irv:x:257:1:Irv Ashkenazy:/usr/home/irv:/bin/ksh
  ajh:x:258:1:Alan Holsberg:/usr/home/ajh:/bin/ksh
  mccollo:x:329:1:Carol McCollough:/usr/home/mccollo:/bin/ksh
***************
*** 15,25 ****
  small:x:309:20:small thomas j:/u1/fall91/dp168/small:/bin/ksh
  solarsk:x:294:20:solarski linda m:/u1/fall91/dp168/solarsk:/bin/ksh
  steill:x:269:20:steill keith r:/u1/fall91/dp270/steill:/bin/ksh
- temple:x:295:20:temple linda c:/u1/fall91/dp168/temple:/bin/ksh
- varvar:x:270:20:varvar anthony j:/u1/fall91/dp270/varvar:/bin/ksh
- vaas:x:325:20:vaas eric:/u1/fall91/dp270/vaas:/bin/ksh
- washing:x:310:20:washington reginald:/u1/fall91/dp168/washing:/bin/ksh
- weiner:x:276:20:weiner sibylle u:/u1/fall91/dp270/weiner:/bin/ksh
- wiedenh:x:311:20:wiedenhofer allen e:/u1/fall91/dp168/wiedenh:/bin/ksh
- wight:x:296:20:wight charles n:/u1/fall91/dp168/wight:/bin/ksh
- william:x:297:20:williams tony j:/u1/fall91/dp168/william:/bin/ksh
--- 21,23 ----
```

You can see that none of the lines of *file1* are printed for the first set of differences. This happens because *file2* differs from *file1* by the addition of the six lines marked with plus signs. Also, no lines from *file2* are printed in the second group because the differences are the eight lines that are in *file1* but not in *file2*.

Now let's try a two-line context by using `-C 2`. This produces some differences in the display but not in the results.

```
$ diff -C 2 p1 p2

*** p1      Mon Nov  4 20:48:10 1991
--- p2      Mon Nov  4 20:48:21 1991
***************
*** 1,4 ****
--- 1,7 ----
  root:x:0:0:System Administrator:/usr/root:/bin/ksh
  slan:x:57:57:StarGROUP Software NPP Administration:/usr/slan:
+ nuucp:x:10:10:0000-uucp(0000):/usr/spool/uucppublic:/usr/lib/uucp/uucico
+ labuucp:x:21:100:shevett's UPC:/usr/spool/uucppublic:/usr/lib/uucp/uucico
+ puucp:x:22:100:princeton:/usr/spool/uucppublic:/usr/lib/uucp/uucico
  juucp:x:24:100:Jon LaBadie:/usr/spool/uucppublic:/usr/lib/uucp/uucico
  couucp:x:25:100:Bill Michaelson:/usr/spool/uucppublic:/usr/lib/uucp/uucico
***************
*** 6,9 ****
--- 9,15 ----
  pjh:x:102:0:Peter J. Holsberg:/usr/pjh:/bin/ksh
  pete:x:200:1:PJH:/usr/home/pete:/bin/ksh
+ lkh:x:250:1:lkh:/usr/lkh:/bin/ksh
+ shevett:x:251:1:dave shevett:/usr/shevett:/bin/ksh
+ moser:x:252:1:sue moser:/usr/moser:/bin/ksh
  irv:x:257:1:Irv Ashkenazy:/usr/home/irv:/bin/ksh
  ajh:x:258:1:Alan Holsberg:/usr/home/ajh:/bin/ksh
***************
*** 16,25 ****
  solarsk:x:294:20:solarski linda m:/u1/fall91/dp168/solarsk:/bin/ksh
  steill:x:269:20:steill keith r:/u1/fall91/dp270/steill:/bin/ksh
- temple:x:295:20:temple linda c:/u1/fall91/dp168/temple:/bin/ksh
- varvar:x:270:20:varvar anthony j:/u1/fall91/dp270/varvar:/bin/ksh
- vaas:x:325:20:vaas eric:/u1/fall91/dp270/vaas:/bin/ksh
- washing:x:310:20:washington reginald:/u1/fall91/dp168/washing:/bin/ksh
- weiner:x:276:20:weiner sibylle u:/u1/fall91/dp270/weiner:/bin/ksh
- wiedenh:x:311:20:wiedenhofer allen e:/u1/fall91/dp168/wiedenh:/bin/ksh
- wight:x:296:20:wight charles n:/u1/fall91/dp168/wight:/bin/ksh
- william:x:297:20:williams tony j:/u1/fall91/dp168/william:/bin/ksh
--- 22,23 ----
```

Now you can better understand what a "line of context" is. You see in the first group of differences that the first change (the line that has nuucp on it) is preceded by two unchanged lines, and the last change (the line with puucp on it) is followed by two unchanged lines. These unchanged lines provide the context.

If you use 10 lines of context, you get the following:

```
$ diff -C10 p1 p2

*** p1      Mon Nov  4 20:48:10 1991
--- p2      Mon Nov  4 20:48:21 1991
***************
*** 1,25 ****
```

```
  root:x:0:0:System Administrator:/usr/root:/bin/ksh
  slan:x:57:57:StarGROUP Software NPP Administration:/usr/slan:
  juucp:x:24:100:Jon LaBadie:/usr/spool/uucppublic:/usr/lib/uucp/uucico
  couucp:x:25:100:Bill Michaelson:/usr/spool/uucppublic:/usr/lib/uucp/uucico
  fanuucp:x:32:100:Jo Poplawski:/usr/spool/uucppublic:/usr/lib/uucp/uucico
  pjh:x:102:0:Peter J. Holsberg:/usr/pjh:/bin/ksh
  pete:x:200:1:PJH:/usr/home/pete:/bin/ksh
  irv:x:257:1:Irv Ashkenazy:/usr/home/irv:/bin/ksh
  ajh:x:258:1:Alan Holsberg:/usr/home/ajh:/bin/ksh
  mccollo:x:329:1:Carol McCollough:/usr/home/mccollo:/bin/ksh
  rechter:x:293:20:rechter jay:/u1/fall91/dp168/rechter:/bin/ksh
  reeve:x:308:20:reeve michael j:/u1/fall91/dp168/reeve:/bin/ksh
  regh:x:331:20:regh jeff l:/u1/fall91/dp270/regh:/bin/ksh
  sicigna:x:327:20:sicignano joseph p:/u1/fall91/dp168/sicigna:/bin/ksh
  small:x:309:20:small thomas j:/u1/fall91/dp168/small:/bin/ksh
  solarsk:x:294:20:solarski linda m:/u1/fall91/dp168/solarsk:/bin/ksh
  steill:x:269:20:steill keith r:/u1/fall91/dp270/steill:/bin/ksh
- temple:x:295:20:temple linda c:/u1/fall91/dp168/temple:/bin/ksh
- varvar:x:270:20:varvar anthony j:/u1/fall91/dp270/varvar:/bin/ksh
- vaas:x:325:20:vaas eric:/u1/fall91/dp270/vaas:/bin/ksh
- washing:x:310:20:washington reginald:/u1/fall91/dp168/washing:/bin/ksh
- weiner:x:276:20:weiner sibylle u:/u1/fall91/dp270/weiner:/bin/ksh
- wiedenh:x:311:20:wiedenhofer allen e:/u1/fall91/dp168/wiedenh:/bin/ksh
- wight:x:296:20:wight charles n:/u1/fall91/dp168/wight:/bin/ksh
- william:x:297:20:williams tony j:/u1/fall91/dp168/william:/bin/ksh
--- 1,23 ----
  root:x:0:0:System Administrator:/usr/root:/bin/ksh
  slan:x:57:57:StarGROUP Software NPP Administration:/usr/slan:
+ nuucp:x:10:10:0000-uucp(0000):/usr/spool/uucppublic:/usr/lib/uucp/uucico
+ labuucp:x:21:100:shevett's UPC:/usr/spool/uucppublic:/usr/lib/uucp/uucico
+ puucp:x:22:100:princeton:/usr/spool/uucppublic:/usr/lib/uucp/uucico
  juucp:x:24:100:Jon LaBadie:/usr/spool/uucppublic:/usr/lib/uucp/uucico
  couucp:x:25:100:Bill Michaelson:/usr/spool/uucppublic:/usr/lib/uucp/uucico
  fanuucp:x:32:100:Jo Poplawski:/usr/spool/uucppublic:/usr/lib/uucp/uucico
  pjh:x:102:0:Peter J. Holsberg:/usr/pjh:/bin/ksh
  pete:x:200:1:PJH:/usr/home/pete:/bin/ksh
+ lkh:x:250:1:lkh:/usr/lkh:/bin/ksh
+ shevett:x:251:1:dave shevett:/usr/shevett:/bin/ksh
+ moser:x:252:1:sue moser:/usr/moser:/bin/ksh
  irv:x:257:1:Irv Ashkenazy:/usr/home/irv:/bin/ksh
  ajh:x:258:1:Alan Holsberg:/usr/home/ajh:/bin/ksh
  mccollo:x:329:1:Carol McCollough:/usr/home/mccollo:/bin/ksh
  rechter:x:293:20:rechter jay:/u1/fall91/dp168/rechter:/bin/ksh
  reeve:x:308:20:reeve michael j:/u1/fall91/dp168/reeve:/bin/ksh
  regh:x:331:20:regh jeff l:/u1/fall91/dp270/regh:/bin/ksh
  sicigna:x:327:20:sicignano joseph p:/u1/fall91/dp168/sicigna:/bin/ksh
  small:x:309:20:small thomas j:/u1/fall91/dp168/small:/bin/ksh
  solarsk:x:294:20:solarski linda m:/u1/fall91/dp168/solarsk:/bin/ksh
  steill:x:269:20:steill keith r:/u1/fall91/dp270/steill:/bin/ksh
```

Wherever possible, changes here are surrounded by ten unchanged lines. What follows now is the attempt to generate an ed script for these two files.

```
$ diff -e p1 p2

18,25d
7a
lkh:x:250:1:lkh:/usr/lkh:/bin/ksh
shevett:x:251:1:dave shevett:/usr/shevett:/bin/ksh
moser:x:252:1:sue moser:/usr/moser:/bin/ksh
.
2a
nuucp:x:10:10:0000-uucp(0000):/usr/spool/uucppublic:/usr/lib/uucp/uucico
labuucp:x:21:100:shevette´s UPC:/usr/spool/uucppublic:/usr/lib/uucp/uucico
puucp:x:22:100:princeton:/usr/spool/uucppublic:/usr/lib/uucp/uucico
.
```

Therefore, you will probably want to use the default three-line context, unless some extraordinary files appear.

The sdiff Command

The sdiff command is really the diff command with a built-in formatter that produces a side-by-side listing of the two files. It shows the differences in a visually pleasing manner. The syntax is

```
sdiff [ -w number ] [ -l ] [ -s ] [ -o output ] file1 file2
```

The -w *number* option specifies the width of the output line. The default value is 130, but I'll use 80 in the examples. The next two options control what is displayed when sdiff encounters lines that are identical between files: -l prints only the left side of lines that are the same, while -s suppresses them. Here are some examples:

```
$ sdiff -w80 na.1 na.2

allen christopher                        allen christopher
babinchak david                     |    babinchak David
best betty                               best betty
boelhower joseph                         boelhower joseph
bose anita                          |    bose
cacossa ray                              cacossa ray
delucia joseph                           delucia joseph
```

This is kind of nice. Both files are displayed, side by side, with changed lines indicated by the ¦. Here's the same thing with the right side of identical lines suppressed:

```
$ sdiff -l -w80 na.1 na.2

allen christopher
babinchak david                     |    babinchak David
best betty
```

```
boelhower joseph
bose anita                                            |  bose
cacossa ray
delucia joseph
```

When I suppress all identical lines, `sdiff`'s output reverts to a `diff`-like ed command telling you how to change *file1* into *file2*.

$ sdiff -s -w80 na.1 na.2

```
2c2
babinchak david                               |  babinchak David
5c5
bose anita                                    |  bose
```

On a larger pair of files with other kinds of differences, you see some additional notations: specifically, each line that is unique to a file is printed with an "arrow" (either > or <) pointing to it. Note that each line is truncated so that the display will fit in *number* columns.

$ sdiff -w80 p1 p2

```
root:x:0:0:System Administrator:/usr/       root:x:0:0:System Administrator:/u
slan:x:57:57:StarGROUP Software NPP A       slan:x:57:57:StarGROUP Software NP
                                        >   nuucp:x:10:10:0000-uucp(0000):/usr
                                        >   labuucp:x:21:100:shevett´s UPC:/us
                                        >   puucp:x:22:100:princeton:/usr/spoo
juucp:x:24:100:Jon LaBadie:/usr/spool       juucp:x:24:100:Jon LaBadie:/usr/sp
couucp:x:25:100:Bill Michaelson:/usr/       couucp:x:25:100:Bill Michaelson:/u
fanuucp:x:32:100:Jo Poplawski:/usr/sp       fanuucp:x:32:100:Jo Poplawski:/usr
pjh:x:102:0:Peter J. Holsberg:/usr/pj       pjh:x:102:0:Peter J. Holsberg:/usr
pete:x:200:1:PJH:/usr/home/pete:/bin/       pete:x:200:1:PJH:/usr/home/pete:/b
                                        >   lkh:x:250:1:lkh:/usr/lkh:/bin/ksh
                                        >   shevett:x:251:1:dave shevett:/usr/
                                        >   moser:x:252:1:sue moser:/usr/moser
irv:x:257:1:Irv Ashkenazy:/usr/home/i       irv:x:257:1:Irv Ashkenazy:/usr/hom
ajh:x:258:1:Alan Holsberg:/usr/home/a       ajh:x:258:1:Alan Holsberg:/usr/hom
mccollo:x:329:1:Carol McCollough:/usr       mccollo:x:329:1:Carol McCollough:/
rechter:x:293:20:rechter jay:/u1/fall       rechter:x:293:20:rechter jay:/u1/f
reeve:x:308:20:reeve michael j:/u1/fa       reeve:x:308:20:reeve michael j:/u1
regh:x:331:20:regh jeff l:/u1/fall91/       regh:x:331:20:regh jeff l:/u1/fall
sicigna:x:327:20:sicignano joseph p:/       sicigna:x:327:20:sicignano joseph
small:x:309:20:small thomas j:/u1/fal       small:x:309:20:small thomas j:/u1/
solarsk:x:294:20:solarski linda m:/u1       solarsk:x:294:20:solarski linda m:
steill:x:269:20:steill keith r:/u1/fa       steill:x:269:20:steill keith r:/u1
temple:x:295:20:temple linda c:/u1/fa   <
varvar:x:270:20:varvar anthony j:/u1/   <
vaas:x:325:20:vaas eric:/u1/fall91/dp   <
washing:x:310:20:washington reginald:   <
weiner:x:276:20:weiner sibylle u:/u1/   <
wiedenh:x:311:20:wiedenhofer allen e:   <
wight:x:296:20:wight charles n:/u1/fa   <
william:x:297:20:williams tony j:/u1/   <
```

9

Now I'll suppress the right side of identical lines:

```
$ sdiff -w80 -l p1 p2
```

```
root:x:0:0:System Administrator:/usr/
slan:x:57:57:StarGROUP Software NPP A
                                        >   nuucp:x:10:10:0000-uucp(0000):/usr
                                        >   labuucp:x:21:100:shevett's UPC:/us
                                        >   puucp:x:22:100:princeton:/usr/spoo

juucp:x:24:100:Jon LaBadie:/usr/spool
couucp:x:25:100:Bill Michaelson:/usr/
fanuucp:x:32:100:Jo Poplawski:/usr/sp
pjh:x:102:0:Peter J. Holsberg:/usr/pj
pete:x:200:1:PJH:/usr/home/pete:/bin/
                                        >   lkh:x:250:1:lkh:/usr/lkh:/bin/ksh
                                        >   shevett:x:251:1:dave shevett:/usr/
                                        >   moser:x:252:1:sue moser:/usr/moser

irv:x:257:1:Irv Ashkenazy:/usr/home/i
ajh:x:258:1:Alan Holsberg:/usr/home/a
mccollo:x:329:1:Carol McCollough:/usr
rechter:x:293:20:rechter jay:/u1/fall
reeve:x:308:20:reeve michael j:/u1/fa
regh:x:331:20:regh jeff l:/u1/fall91/
sicigna:x:327:20:sicignano joseph p:/
small:x:309:20:small thomas j:/u1/fal
solarsk:x:294:20:solarski linda m:/u1
steill:x:269:20:steill keith r:/u1/fa
temple:x:295:20:temple linda c:/u1/fa   <
varvar:x:270:20:varvar anthony j:/u1/   <
vaas:x:325:20:vaas eric:/u1/fall91/dp   <
washing:x:310:20:washington reginald:   <
weiner:x:276:20:weiner sibylle u:/u1/   <
wiedenh:x:311:20:wiedenhofer allen e:   <
wight:x:296:20:wight charles n:/u1/fa   <
william:x:297:20:williams tony j:/u1/   <
```

Here's the case where I suppress all identical lines:

```
$ sdiff -w80 -s p1 p2
```

```
2a3,5
                                        >   nuucp:x:10:10:0000-uucp(0000):/usr
                                        >   labuucp:x:21:100:shevett's UPC:/us
                                        >   puucp:x:22:100:princeton:/usr/spoo

7a11,13
                                        >   lkh:x:250:1:lkh:/usr/lkh:/bin/ksh
                                        >   shevett:x:251:1:dave shevett:/usr/
                                        >   moser:x:252:1:sue moser:/usr/moser

18,25d23
temple:x:295:20:temple linda c:/u1/fa   <
varvar:x:270:20:varvar anthony j:/u1/   <
vaas:x:325:20:vaas eric:/u1/fall91/dp   <
washing:x:310:20:washington reginald:   <
```

9

```
weiner:x:276:20:weiner sibylle u:/u1/  <
wiedenh:x:311:20:wiedenhofer allen e:  <
wight:x:296:20:wight charles n:/u1/fa  <
william:x:297:20:williams tony j:/u1/  <
```

The `sdiff` utility also has a highly interactive mode of operation, using the `-o` *output* option. This option lets you specify the name of a file that will receive `sdiff`'s output, a controlled merge of *file1* and *file2*.

File Archives and Compression

For the purposes of doing backups or transferring files from one computer to another, users are often faced with the need to create a single large file from a group of small ones. To store or transfer the resulting *archive* more efficiently, computer users often try to compress the archive file into a smaller representation. If you have experience with MS-DOS, you might be familiar with programs that produce files having names that end with .ZIP or .ARC or .ZOO. These programs are designed to first compress each of the many small files and then archive the compressed files. UNIX performs these two tasks with separate programs and in opposite order—first you archive the files and then you compress the archive.

The `tar` Command

`tar` is the original archive program for UNIX. Its name means "tape archiver." Originally intended to create a large file on a backup tape, `tar` can be directed to send its output to any file (device or regular) that you specify. This means you can create a tape archive, a floppy disk archive, or a regular file archive. Here are its several syntaxes:

```
tar -c[vwf target b num L[#s]] file1 file2 ...
tar -r[vwf target b num L[#s]] file1 file2 ...
tar -t[vf target L[#s]] file1 file2 ...
tar -u[vwf target b num L[#s]] file1 file2 ...
tar -x[lmovwf target L[#s]] [file1 file2 ...]
```

The major option character—`crtux`—specifies which of five different tasks you want `tar` to do.

-c	Create an archive
-r	Replace *file* in the archive

9

`-t`	List the "table of contents" of the archive
`-u`	Update the archive
`-x`	Extract `file` from the archive; that is, copy one or more files from the archive file into the current directory (or whatever directory is specified by the pathname of the file in the archive)

`fileN` can be a relative or absolute pathname or a directory name, or it can be omitted in some cases. If `fileN` is specified with `-x`, only those files will be extracted. If no file is indicated with `-x`, all files in the archive will be extracted. Unlike other UNIX commands, the minus sign (-) may be omitted from `tar` options.

The options in brackets are as follows:

`#s`	`#` specifies the number of the tape drive, and `s` specifies the tape density. Ordinarily, you omit this option.
`v`	Verbose—`tar` will print the name of each file as it is being processed. This is frequently used with t to print the equivalent of an `ls -nl` command.
`w`	Prompts the user before performing the specified archiving action.
`f target`	Causes `tar` to write to or read from a file named `target`. This is more convenient than using redirection.
`b`	Blocking factor—ignored when writing to a file.
`l`	Used only when extracting files. `tar` attempts to resolve links that were defined when the archive was created. Specifying l causes `tar` to print an error message if it cannot resolve a link.
`m`	Changes each file's modification time to the time it is being extracted.
`o`	Changes the owner and group of each file to that of the person running the `tar` command.
`L`	Follows symbolic links, if any.

Here are some examples of using `tar` to create an archive file. Specifically, you want to create a file, names.tar, of certain files in the current directory—specifically, all of the files having filenames that begin with na.

9

```
$ ls -l na*
```

```
-rw-r--r--    1 pjh        root        113 Nov   9 12:57 na
-rw-r--r--    1 pjh        root        100 Nov   9 16:40 na.1
-rw-r--r--    1 pjh        root         95 Nov   9 12:58 na.2
-rw-r--r--    1 pjh        root        190 Sep  19 15:05 names
-rw-r--r--    1 pjh        root        177 Nov   3 18:26 names.1
-rw-r--r--    1 pjh        root        172 Nov   3 18:26 names.2
-rw-r--r--    1 pjh        root        186 Nov   6 15:06 names.3
-rw-r--r--    1 pjh        root       1000 Nov  10 11:28 names.scr
```

```
$ tar -cvf names.tar na*
```

```
a na 1 tape blocks
a na.1 1 tape blocks
a na.2 1 tape blocks
a names 1 tape blocks
a names.1 1 tape blocks
a names.2 1 tape blocks
a names.3 1 tape blocks
a names.scr 2 tape blocks
```

The a at the beginning of each line means that tar is adding the file to the archive:

```
$ ls -l na*
```

```
-rw-r--r--    1 pjh        root        113 Nov   9 12:57 na
-rw-r--r--    1 pjh        root        100 Nov   9 16:40 na.1
-rw-r--r--    1 pjh        root         95 Nov   9 12:58 na.2
-rw-r--r--    1 pjh        root        190 Sep  19 15:05 names
-rw-r--r--    1 pjh        root        177 Nov   3 18:26 names.1
-rw-r--r--    1 pjh        root        172 Nov   3 18:26 names.2
-rw-r--r--    1 pjh        root        186 Nov   6 15:06 names.3
-rw-r--r--    1 pjh        root       1000 Nov  10 11:28 names.scr
-rw-r--r--    1 pjh        root       9728 Nov  10 11:59 names.tar
```

Notice the size of names.tar. It's much larger than just the sum of the file sizes of all the tar'd files! tar has added a lot of "archiving" information to each file and has assigned an integral number of blocks to each file. Let's be sure that all the files are actually archived.

```
$ tar -tf names.tar
```

```
na
na.1
na.2
names
names.1
names.2
names.3
names.scr
```

The following shows even more detail:

```
$ tar -tvf names.tar

tar: blocksize = 19
rw-r--r--102/0      113 Nov  9 12:57 1991 na
rw-r--r--102/0      100 Nov  9 16:40 1991 na.1
rw-r--r--102/0       95 Nov  9 12:58 1991 na.2
rw-r--r--102/0      190 Sep 19 15:05 1991 names
rw-r--r--102/0      177 Nov  3 18:26 1991 names.1
rw-r--r--102/0      172 Nov  3 18:26 1991 names.2
rw-r--r--102/0      186 Nov  6 15:06 1991 names.3
rw-r--r--102/0     1000 Nov 10 11:28 1991 names.scr
```

This looks very much like the output of an `ls -ln` command in a directory.

You can use `tar` to copy a group of files or even an entire directory structure from one place to another. Suppose you want to copy all the na* files to a new subdirectory. You could, of course, simply say

```
$ cp na* tar
```

and be done with it, but here's how to do it with `tar`:

```
$ (tar cf - na* ) ¦ (cd tar; tar xf - )
```

Note that the target in both cases is stdin, represented by the `-`! The commands are in parentheses so that they are executed in a subshell, and the `cd`s also would not change the current working directory.

More useful than this is an interesting property of `tar`. This property comes into play when you create an archive and *file1* is a directory name: `tar` will archive all the files in the specified directory and all of its subdirectories as well. For example, the following is the command that will copy the directory hierarchy under *dir1* to *dir2*:

```
$ (cd dir1; tar cf - . ) ¦ (cd dir2; tar xf - )
```

Here's an example that shows how to archive a directory tree. The name of the current directory is . and I will create an archive file named /usr/pjh/tools/comm.tar (assuming that the value of the shell environment variable HOME is /usr/pjh):

```
$ tar -cvf $HOME/tools/comm.tar .

a ./chat/chat/chat-2.8.sh 97 tape blocks
a ./chat/chat/Makefile 2 tape blocks
a ./chat/chat/README 9 tape blocks
a ./chat/multiuser/m.u.chat-1.2 56 tape blocks
a ./chat/multiuser/chat.c 19 tape blocks
a ./chat/multiuser/chatter.c 8 tape blocks
```

9

```
a ./chat/magpie/Chat.Doc 24 tape blocks
a ./chat/magpie/Makefile 2 tape blocks
a ./chat/magpie/chat.c 30 tape blocks
a ./talk/multi/multitalk1.2.s 104 tape blocks
a ./talk/multi/Readme.1st 10 tape blocks
a ./talk/multi/cmds.txt 3 tape blocks
a ./talk/two/talk.SV.c 10 tape blocks
a ./party/u.partyline.c 47 tape blocks
a ./phone/phone.sh.Z 18 tape blocks
a ./phone/phone.doc 7 tape blocks
a ./gossip/gossip 200 tape blocks
a ./kermit/Makefile 88 tape blocks
a ./kermit/ckcasc.h 3 tape blocks
a ./kermit/ckcdeb.h 18 tape blocks
a ./tutor/tutor.sh 18 tape blocks
a ./tutor/script.c 15 tape blocks
```

Here is what's in the archive:

```
$ tar -tvf /usr/pjh/tools/comm.tar

tar: blocksize = 20
rw-rw-rw-  0/0      49274 Jan 31 17:09 1991 ./chat/chat/chat-2.8.sh
rw-r--r--  0/0        832 Feb  5 21:41 1991 ./chat/chat/Makefile
rw-r--r--  0/0       4455 Feb  5 21:41 1991 ./chat/chat/README
rw-rw-rw-  0/0      28439 Jan 31 16:54 1991 ./chat/multiuser/m.u.chat-1.2
rw-r--r--  0/0       9540 Feb  5 22:01 1991 ./chat/multiuser/chat.c
rw-r--r--  0/0       4071 Feb  5 22:01 1991 ./chat/multiuser/chatter.c
rw-r--r--  0/0      12203 Feb  5 21:47 1991 ./chat/magpie/Chat.Doc
rw-r--r--  0/0       1008 Feb  5 21:51 1991 ./chat/magpie/Makefile
rw-r--r--  0/0      15313 Feb  5 21:47 1991 ./chat/magpie/chat.c
rw-rw-rw-  0/0      53091 Jan 31 17:13 1991 ./talk/multi/multitalk1.2.s
rw-r--r--  0/0       5104 Feb  5 22:10 1991 ./talk/multi/Readme.1st
rw-r--r--  0/0       1506 Feb  5 22:10 1991 ./talk/multi/cmds.txt
rw-rw-rw-  0/0       5080 Feb  5 22:06 1991 ./talk/two/talk.SV.c
rw-rw-rw-  0/0      23647 Jan 31 17:14 1991 ./party/u.partyline.c
rw-rw-rw-  0/0       8894 Jan 31 17:14 1991 ./phone/phone.sh.Z
rw-r--r--  0/0       3444 Feb  5 22:12 1991 ./phone/phone.doc
rw-rw-rw-  0/0     102035 Jan 31 17:12 1991 ./gossip/gossip
rw-r--r--102/0      44917 Apr 30 20:26 1991 ./kermit/Makefile
rw-r--r--102/0       1139 Apr 30 20:26 1991 ./kermit/ckcasc.h
rw-r--r--102/0       9164 Apr 30 20:26 1991 ./kermit/ckcdeb.h
rw-rw-rw-102/0       9036 Oct  7 12:18 1991 ./tutor/tutor.sh
rw-r--r--102/0       7226 Oct  7 13:24 1991 ./tutor/script.c
```

Note that each file has a relative pathname, which is desirable when you extract files from the archive. If a file has an absolute pathname, it can only be extracted to that directory. However, if that directory doesn't exist on your system, tar will create it for you.

9

The `cpio` Command

The `cpio` command means "copy in and out" and is used to create and manipulate archive files for transfer or backups, just like `tar`. `cpio` normally operates in either *input mode*, where it creates an archive, or *output mode*, where it extracts files from a previously created `cpio` archive. A third mode of `cpio` enables files to be copied in and out in a single pass. This is helpful when moving directory structures. `cpio` has one advantage over `tar`—it produces smaller archive files.

The three syntaxes are

```
cpio -o[aABcLvV] [-C size] [-H header] [-O file [-M message]]

cpio -i[bBcdfkmrsStuvV6] [-C size] [-E file] [-H header]
     [-I file [-M message]] [-R ID][file(s)]

cpio -p[adlLmuvV] [-R ID] directory
```

The following examples illustrate the common options of `cpio`. For more information about `cpio`, refer to Chapter 11, "UNIX System V Release 4 Command Reference."

You can use `cpio` to create an archive using the `-o` option. Pipe a list of the names of the files to be archived to `cpio` by using any UNIX command that prints filenames (`ls`, `echo`, `find`, and so on). For example, to create a `cpio` archive of the files in your current directory, enter

```
$ ls ¦ cpio -o
```

`cpio` writes the archive to stdout, so that the output of the command comes on your screen. You may instead redirect `cpio`'s output to a regular file:

```
$ ls ¦ cpio -oc > my.cpio
```

Note that I've added `.cpio` to the filename so that I'll recognize the file as a `cpio` archive. The `c` option tells `cpio` to write archiving header information in text form, for better portability between different computers.

Of course, the output file can be a special file, such as a floppy disk or tape. In this case, if you have write permission, you can redirect output to the device, as follows:

```
$ ls ¦ cpio -oc > /dev/rdsk/fd096
```

Your system administrator's guide will tell you the names of the tape and floppy disk devices on your system.

9

If an archive is too large to fit on one disk or tape, cpio prompts with the following message:

```
If you want to go on, type device/file name when ready.
```

Changing the disk or tape and entering the same device name that you used in the original cpio command will continue creating the archive. When you have two floppy disk drives of the same size (5.25-inch or 3.5-inch) and (high density or medium density), type the name of the second drive so that cpio continues while you are changing the first floppy disk.

There are many options that you can use with cpio in the output mode. As stated earlier, full descriptions of these options can be found in Chapter 11. However, you will use the following option quite often. The -v (verbose) option prints the filename to the screen as it adds the file to the archive. Actually, the filenames are printed to stderr rather than stdout. If you wish to save the names, you can redirect stderr to a file, as follows:

```
$ ls ¦ cpio -oc > my.cpio 2> filenames
```

Use the find command to provide the list of filenames to cpio when you want to archive a directory hierarchy.

```
$ find $HOME -print ¦ cpio -ocv > home.cpio 2> filenames
```

This find command archives all the files in your home directory as well as all files in subdirectories under HOME. The archived files are placed in a file called home.cpio and their names—they will be absolute pathnames—are placed in a file called filenames. You should cd to the desired directory and use . (dot) as the directory name in the find command, so that the files in the archive will have relative pathnames.

You can extract any number, or all, of the files from a cpio archive by using cpio in the "input" mode. The format is

```
$ cpio -i < archivefile-or-device
```

In this mode, cpio reads the archive and extracts each file. If you use the -r option, cpio stops at each file and asks whether you want to rename it. Typing a . (dot) causes cpio to use the name in the archive. If you press Enter, cpio won't extract that file.

If you used the -c option to create the archive, be sure to specify it when extracting files. If you don't, you might see the following message:

```
Out of sync
Perhaps the -c option should be used.
```

This message indicates that cpio cannot read the header information correctly.

cpio does not create needed directories and subdirectories unless you specify the -d option.

When there is a regular file in existence with the same or newer age than a file of the same name in the archive, cpio does not extract it unless you specify the -u (copy unconditionally) option.

When you want to maintain the original file/directory modification times for extracted files, you need to specify the -m option. Otherwise, each extracted file will have a modification date and time corresponding to the instant it was extracted. In order to extract files in an archive, create directories and subdirectories, overwrite existing files of the same name, and keep the same modification times, you enter

```
$ cpio -icvdum < archivefile-or-device
```

If you are logged in as "root" and are extracting files from a cpio archive, you may use the -r *ID* option to change the owner and group ID of the file being extracted to *ID* (as long as *ID* is a user ID that is currently in /etc/passwd).

If you would like to see a table of contents of a cpio archive, use the -t or -tv options. These are quite like the -t and -tv options of tar.

You may use cpio to move entire directory hierarchies. The -p (pass) option tells cpio to copy files without creating an archive file. For example, suppose you want to move tom's home directory from /usr/tom to /usr2/tom. The following sequence of commands accomplishes this:

```
$ cd /usr
```

```
$ find tom -print ¦ cpio -pdvum /usr2
```

The find command will print a list of the names of all the files in the tom directory hierarchy, and pipe them to cpio. It, in turn, will "pass" (-p) them to /usr2. The other options tell cpio to: create subdirectories under usr2 as they were for tom under usr; display the names as they're being copied; overwrite any existing files under /usr2/tom; and do not change the modification times.

Notice that redirection to a file or device *is not* needed when using the -p option, because no archive file is created. cpio copies the files and directories to the new location. You would then remove the files and directories from the old location.

To save time, use the -l option only with the -p option, telling cpio to link files wherever possible rather than copy them. Of course, you can only use this when manipulating files on the same file system. When cpio cannot link the file, it copies the file. This is much faster than physically copying the contents of the file from one place on the disk to another, because cpio is merely writing new directory entries. See Chapter 1, "Overview of UNIX" to review the differences between copies and links.

9

- Creating temporary backups of a directory structure without consuming additional disk space

- Shrinking directories

Suppose you want to clean up a directory without accidentally removing any essential files. To play it safe, you can either back up the directory onto a disk or copy all the files into another directory. You then can remove the old directory, recreate a minimum-size directory with the same name as the one you deleted, and finally, copy the files back into that directory. Better still, you can use `cpio` to create a "clone" of the directory structure with linked files. (Remember, a file does not actually disappear from the disk where it is stored until it has no more links.)

Now assume that you are going to clean your reports directory. There are some files that you definitely *do not* want to remove, so you must first save them. `cpio` helps with the clean up.

1. First, create a temporary directory:

   ```
   $ mkdir reports.bk
   ```

2. Now, change to the reports directory:

   ```
   $ cd reports
   ```

3. Use `cpio` to link all the files into the backup directory:

   ```
   $ find . -print ¦ cpio -pdvlum ../reports.bk
   ```

4. Now go through reports and remove unwanted files. Remember, even if you `rm` a file by mistake, there is still a copy in reports.bk.

5. When you're finished removing all the files you don't want, remove the temporary directory:

   ```
   $ cd ..; rm -rf reports.bk
   ```

This process requires only minor additional disk space, and all files are "safe" against accidental removal.

The second use of the `-l` option enables you to shrink directories. Remember, under UNIX, directories grow but never shrink. When adding a file to a directory, the file creates a new directory entry. When removing a file, the i-number in the directory file changes to zero, but nothing is removed from the directory file. Consequently, directories can be large even if they contain no files. On some systems, you can increase your available disk space as much as 35 percent simply by shrinking directories.

The only way to shrink a directory is to archive its files, remove it, and then restore them. The `cpio -p` command with the `-l` option is helpful for shrinking directories. Follow these steps:

9

1. Use `cpio -plvdum` to clone the directory structure, as w .· did previously.

2. Remove the old directory structure.

3. Rename the new directory to the old directory name.

The following commands summarize how a system administrator might shrink tom's directory structure. (Be sure `tom` is not logged on!)

```
$ cd /usr

$ mkdir tom.new

$ cd tom

$ find . -print ¦ cpio -pdvlum ../tom.new

$ cd /usr

$ rm -rf tom

$ mv tom.new tom

$ chown tom tom
```

The system administrator first changes to the /usr directory and creates a new subdirectory called tom.new. Then, the administrator changes to /usr/tom and links all of tom's files and subdirectories to /usr/tom.new. Next, the administrator changes back to /usr and removes all traces of the tom directory structure. (The `-rf` option to `rm` means to wipe out everything in the current directory and in all subdirectories!) Finally, the administrator renames tom.new to tom and changes the directory ownership to tom.

File Compression: `compress`, `uncompress`, and `zcat`

While investigating storage techniques, some computer science researchers discovered that certain types of files are stored quite inefficiently in their natural form. Most common among these "offenders" is the text file, which is stored one ASCII character at a time. An ASCII character requires only seven bits, but almost all memory devices handle a minimum of eight bits at a time. Consequently, there is a 12.5 percent waste right off the bat! (A bit is a binary digit—the "famous" 1 or 0 found in electronic on/off switches the world over.) These researchers further studied the field of language patterns, where they found that characters could be coded into even smaller bit patterns according to how frequently they are used.

9

The result of this research was a programming technique that compresses text files to about 50% of their original lengths. While not as efficient with files having characters that use all eight bits, this technique is indeed able to achieve a substantial reduction in file size. Because the files are smaller, storage and file transfer can be much more efficient.

```
compress [ -cfv ] [ -b bits ] file(s)
```

```
uncompress [ -cv ] [ file(s) ]
```

```
zcat [ file(s)]
```

and the options are explained in the following:

-c	Writes to stdout instead of changing the file.
-f	Forces compression even if the compressed file is no smaller than the original.
-v	Tells the percent reduction for each compressed file.
-b bits	Tells compress how efficient to be. bits is 16 by default, but it can be reduced to as little as 9, if needed, for compatibility with computers that are not sufficiently powerful to handle full, 16-bit compression.

Normally, compress shrinks the file and replaces it with a file that has .Z appended to the filename. However, things could go wrong; for example, the original filename might have 13 or 14 characters, or the compressed file could be the same size as the original and you have not specified the -f option. uncompress expands the file and replaces the .Z file with the expanded file that has an appropriate name (usually the name is the name of the compressed file with the .Z removed).

zcat temporarily uncompresses a compressed file and prints it.

Incidentally, note that all three of these utilities can take their inputs from stdin via a pipe.

Encoding and Decoding:
uuencode and uudecode

I've mentioned file transfer several times without explanation; now, let's explore this a little further. Many UNIX computers are connected to other UNIX computers through what AT&T calls the *basic networking utilities* (BNU). But BNU is not, in fact, a "network" in the usual sense of machines being physically wired together. Instead, BNU is a suite of software that enables one UNIX system to call another UNIX system via modem and dial-up telephone lines. Under UNIX System V Release 4, AT&T has also provided true networking software—although that is beyond the scope of this discussion. The BNU software also is known as the UUCP (*UNIX-to-UNIX CoPy*) set of programs. UUCP is probably the most common way to send electronic mail and files from one UNIX machine to another.

Certain electronic mail programs on some UNIX systems can handle only files that use seven-bit characters. In other words, such systems can only handle text files. But compressed files, `cpio` archives, and `tar` archives are not text files. The most common "fix" for this situation is to convert a nontext (or binary) file to a text file by encoding each digit to an ASCII (that is, a seven-bit) character.

This conversion process is frequently done through a program called `uuencode`—although other programs do similar but incompatible conversions. The original file can then be restored through the "sister" program, `uudecode`. Any uuencoded file can be sent from one machine to another via electronic mail. An uuencoded file is about 35 percent bigger than its original binary file but, as in the case of compressed text files, we are still ahead of the game. For example, if you have a 10,000-byte text file and compress it to 5,000 bytes, the uuencoded version would still be less than 8,000 bytes.

The syntax for the two commands is simply

```
uuencode [ file ] uudecode-name > outfile
```

```
uudecode [ file ]
```

For example:

```
$ uuencode myfile newfile > myfile.uue
```

will encode myfile. When it is subsequently decoded by

```
$ uudecode myfile.uue
```

the decoded version will be called newfile.

The `split` and `csplit` Commands

Once you've uuencoded a binary file for transmission, you need to check its size, because many sites do not process electronic mail messages greater than some arbitrary size (usually 50 to 100Kbytes). If your file is bigger than that, you can split it into two or more files by using either `split` or `csplit`.

The syntax for `split` is

```
split [ -n ] [ in-file [ out-file ] ]
```

This command reads the text file *in-file* and splits it into a number of
files, each having *n* lines (except possibly the last file). If *-n* is omitted, split
will create 1000-line files. The names of the small files depend on whether or
not you specify *out-file*. If you do, these files will be called *out-file*aa, *out-
file*ab, *out-file*ac, and so on. If you have more than 26 output files, the 27th
will be called *out-file*ba; the 28th, *out-file*bb; and so forth. If you omit *out-
file*, split will use x in its place, and the files will be named xaa, xab, xac, and
so on.

Assuming that the size of each split output file is less than 50Kbytes, you
can mail them electronically to your intended recipient. When the files are
received, the original files can be rebuilt with

`$ **cat** out-file* > new-name`

On the receiving end, the problem with split is that you have no way
of telling—just by looking at the contents of the output files—the order they
should go in. This can be a problem if the mailed pieces do not arrive at the
recipient's site in the same order you sent them. To help overcome this
problem, UNIX offers a *context splitter*, called csplit. Its syntax is

`csplit [ -s ] [ -k ] [ -f out-file ] in-file arg(s)`

The *arg(s)* determine where each file is split. If you have *N* args, you will
have *N+1* output files, named *out-file*00, *out-file*01, and so on, through
*out-file*N (with a 0 in front of *N* if *N* is less than 10). *N* cannot be greater than
99. If you do not specify *out-file*s, csplit will name them xx00, xx01, and so
forth.

The -s option suppresses csplit's reporting of the number of characters in each output file, whereas -k prevents csplit from deleting all output
files if an error occurs.

Here's a simple example showing how to split the following file:

`$ **cat passwd**`
```
root:x:0:0:System Administrator:/usr/root:/bin/ksh
reboot:x:7:1:---:/:/etc/shutdown -y -g0 -i6
listen:x:37:4:x:/usr/net/nls:
slan:x:57:57:StarGROUP Software NPP Administration:/usr/slan:
lp:x:71:2:x:/usr/spool/lp:
_:-             :6:6:    ============================    :6:
_:-             :6:6:    ==   UUCP Logins                :6:
_:-             :6:6:    ============================    :6:
uucp:x:5:5:0000-uucp(0000):x:
nuucp:x:10:10:0000-uucp(0000):/usr/spool/uucppublic:/usr/lib/uucp/uucico
zzuucp:x:37:100:Bob Sorenson:/usr/spool/uucppublic:/usr/lib/uucp/uucico
asyuucp:x:38:100:Robert L. Wald:/usr/spool/uucppublic:/usr/lib/uucp/uucico
knuucp:x:39:100:Kris Knigge:/usr/spool/uucppublic:/usr/lib/uucp/uucico
```

```
_:-                   :6:6:     =============================     :6:
_:-                   :6:6:     ==   Special Users              :6:
_:-                   :6:6:     =============================     :6:
msnet:x:100:99:Server Program:/usr/net/servers/msnet:/bin/false
install:x:101:1:x:/usr/install:
pjh:x:102:0:Peter J. Holsberg:/usr/pjh:/bin/ksh
hohen:x:346:1:Michael Hohenshilt:/usr/home/hohen:/bin/ksh
reilly:x:347:1:Joan Reilly:/usr/home/reilly:/bin/ksh
_:-                   :6:6:     =============================     :6:
_:-                   :6:6:     ==   DP Fall 1991               :6:
_:-                   :6:6:     =============================     :6:
gordon:x:304:20:gordon gary g:/u1/fall91/dp168/gordon:/bin/csh
lewis:x:288:20:lewis prince e:/u1/fall91/dp168/lewis:/bin/ksh
metelit:x:265:20:metelitsa natalya:/u1/fall91/dp270/metelit:/bin/ksh
nadaraj:x:307:20:nadarajah kalyani:/u1/fall91/dp168/nadaraj:/bin/ksh
nado:x:266:20:nado conan j:/u1/fall91/dp270/nado:/bin/ksh
_:-                   :6:6:     =============================     :6:
_:-                   :6:6:     ===   NCR   =================     :6:
_:-                   :6:6:     =============================     :6:
antello:x:334:20:antello ronald f:/u1/fall91/ff437/antello:/bin/ksh
cilino:x:335:20:cilino michael a:/u1/fall91/ff437/cilino:/bin/ksh
emmons:x:336:20:emmons william r:/u1/fall91/ff437/emmons:/bin/ksh
foreste:x:337:20:forester james r:/u1/fall91/ff437/foreste:/bin/ksh
hayden:x:338:20:hayden richard:/u1/fall91/ff437/hayden:/bin/ksh
```

You can see that the passwd file is divided into sections: an unlabeled one at the beginning, followed by UUCP Logins, Special Users, DP Fall 1991, and NCR. It would be nice to have each section in its own file. To do this, you must specify appropriate arguments to csplit. Each takes the form of a text string surrounded by slash (/) marks. csplit will then copy from the current line up to—but not including—the argument. The following is the first attempt at splitting with csplit:

```
$ csplit -f PA passwd /UUCP/ /Special/ /Fall/ /NCR/

270
505
426
490
446
```

Five files are created: the first has 270 characters, the second has 505 characters, and so on. Now let's see what they look like:

```
$ cat PA00

root:x:0:0:System Administrator:/usr/root:/bin/ksh
reboot:x:7:1:--:/:/etc/shutdown -y -g0 -i6
listen:x:37:4:x:/usr/net/nls:
slan:x:57:57:StarGROUP Software NPP Administration:/usr/slan:
lp:x:71:2:x:/usr/spool/lp:
_:-                   :6:6:     =============================     :6:
```

```
$ cat PA01

_:-                   :6:6:      ==  UUCP Logins                :6:
_:-                   :6:6:      ==============================  :6:
uucp:x:5:5:0000-uucp(0000):x:
nuucp:x:10:10:0000-uucp(0000):/usr/spool/uucppublic:/usr/lib/uucp/uucico
zzuucp:x:37:100:Bob Sorenson:/usr/spool/uucppublic:/usr/lib/uucp/uucico
asyuucp:x:38:100:Robert L. Wald:/usr/spool/uucppublic:/usr/lib/uucp/uucico
knuucp:x:39:100:Kris Knigge:/usr/spool/uucppublic:/usr/lib/uucp/uucico
_:-                   :6:6:      ==============================  :6:

$ cat PA02

_:-                   :6:6:      ==  Special Users               :6:
_:-                   :6:6:      ==============================  :6:
msnet:x:100:99:Server Program:/usr/net/servers/msnet:/bin/false
install:x:101:1:x:/usr/install:
pjh:x:102:0:Peter J. Holsberg:/usr/pjh:/bin/ksh
hohen:x:346:1:Michael Hohenshilt:/usr/home/hohen:/bin/ksh
reilly:x:347:1:Joan Reilly:/usr/home/reilly:/bin/ksh
_:-                   :6:6:      ==============================  :6:

$ cat PA03

_:-                   :6:6:      ==  DP Fall 1991                :6:
_:-                   :6:6:      ==============================  :6:
gordon:x:304:20:gordon gary g:/u1/fall91/dp168/gordon:/bin/csh
lewis:x:288:20:lewis prince e:/u1/fall91/dp168/lewis:/bin/ksh
metelit:x:265:20:metelitsa natalya:/u1/fall91/dp270/metelit:/bin/ksh
nadaraj:x:307:20:nadarajah kalyani:/u1/fall91/dp168/nadaraj:/bin/ksh
nado:x:266:20:nado conan j:/u1/fall91/dp270/nado:/bin/ksh
_:-                   :6:6:      ==============================  :6:

$ cat PA04

_:-                   :6:6:      ===  NCR  ==================      :6:
_:-                   :6:6:      ==============================  :6:
antello:x:334:20:antello ronald f:/u1/fall91/ff437/antello:/bin/ksh
cilino:x:335:20:cilino michael a:/u1/fall91/ff437/cilino:/bin/ksh
emmons:x:336:20:emmons william r:/u1/fall91/ff437/emmons:/bin/ksh
foreste:x:337:20:forester james r:/u1/fall91/ff437/foreste:/bin/ksh
hayden:x:338:20:hayden richard:/u1/fall91/ff437/hayden:/bin/ksh
```

This is not bad, but each file ends and/or begins with one or more lines that you don't want. csplit enables you to adjust the *split point* by appending an offset to the argument. For example, /UUCP/-1 means that the split point is the line before the one on which UUCP appears for the first time. Let's apply the -1 to each argument. This should get rid of the unwanted line that ends each of the first four files.

```
$ csplit -f PB passwd /UUCP/-1 /Special/-1 /Fall/-1 /NCR/-1
```

```
213
505
426
490
503
```

You can see that the first file is smaller than the previous first file. Perhaps this is working!

```
$ cat PB00
```

```
root:x:0:0:System Administrator:/usr/root:/bin/ksh
reboot:x:7:1:---:/:/etc/shutdown -y -g0 -i6
listen:x:37:4:x:/usr/net/nls:
slan:x:57:57:StarGROUP Software NPP Administration:/usr/slan:
lp:x:71:2:x:/usr/spool/lp:
```

```
$ cat PB01
```

```
_:-            :6:6:     ============================    :6:
_:-            :6:6:     ==   UUCP Logins                :6:
_:-            :6:6:     ============================    :6:
uucp:x:5:5:0000-uucp(0000):x:
nuucp:x:10:10:0000-uucp(0000):/usr/spool/uucppublic:/usr/lib/uucp/uucico
zzuucp:x:37:100:Bob Sorenson:/usr/spool/uucppublic:/usr/lib/uucp/uucico
asyuucp:x:38:100:Robert L. Wald:/usr/spool/uucppublic:/usr/lib/uucp/uucico
knuucp:x:39:100:Kris Knigge:/usr/spool/uucppublic:/usr/lib/uucp/uucico
```

```
$ cat PB02
```

```
_:-            :6:6:     ============================    :6:
_:-            :6:6:     ==   Special Users              :6:
_:-            :6:6:     ============================    :6:
msnet:x:100:99:Server Program:/usr/net/servers/msnet:/bin/false
install:x:101:1:x:/usr/install:
pjh:x:102:0:Peter J. Holsberg:/usr/pjh:/bin/ksh
hohen:x:346:1:Michael Hohenshilt:/usr/home/hohen:/bin/ksh
reilly:x:347:1:Joan Reilly:/usr/home/reilly:/bin/ksh
```

```
$ cat PB03
```

```
_:-            :6:6:     ============================    :6:
_:-            :6:6:     ==   DP Fall 1991               :6:
_:-            :6:6:     ============================    :6:
gordon:x:304:20:gordon gary g:/u1/fall91/dp168/gordon:/bin/csh
lewis:x:288:20:lewis prince e:/u1/fall91/dp168/lewis:/bin/ksh
metelit:x:265:20:metelitsa natalya:/u1/fall91/dp270/metelit:/bin/ksh
nadaraj:x:307:20:nadarajah kalyani:/u1/fall91/dp168/nadaraj:/bin/ksh
nado:x:266:20:nado conan j:/u1/fall91/dp270/nado:/bin/ksh
```

9

```
$ cat PB04
```

```
_:-               :6:6:   =============================   :6:
_:-               :6:6:   ===   NCR   =================   :6:
_:-               :6:6:   =============================   :6:
antello:x:334:20:antello ronald f:/u1/fall91/ff437/antello:/bin/ksh
cilino:x:335:20:cilino michael a:/u1/fall91/ff437/cilino:/bin/ksh
emmons:x:336:20:emmons william r:/u1/fall91/ff437/emmons:/bin/ksh
foreste:x:337:20:forester james r:/u1/fall91/ff437/foreste:/bin/ksh
hayden:x:338:20:hayden richard:/u1/fall91/ff437/hayden:/bin/ksh
```

This is very nice indeed! Now, let's get rid of the unwanted lines at the beginning by having `csplit` *advance* its current line without copying anything. A pair of arguments, /UUCP/-1 %uucp%, tells `csplit` to skip over all the lines beginning with the one preceding the line containing UUCP through the one that precedes the line containing uucp. This will cause `csplit` to skip over the lines that begin with _:-. The following displays the full command:

```
$ csplit -f PC passwd /UUCP/-1 %uucp% /Special/-1 %msnet% \
/Fall/-1 %dp[12][67][80]% /NCR/1%ff437%
```

```
213
334
255
321
332
```

Note that any argument can be a regular expression. Here are the resulting files:

```
$ cat PC00
```

```
root:x:0:0:System Administrator:/usr/root:/bin/ksh
reboot:x:7:1:---:/:/etc/shutdown -y -g0 -i6
listen:x:37:4:x:/usr/net/nls:
slan:x:57:57:StarGROUP Software NPP Administration:/usr/slan:
lp:x:71:2:x:/usr/spool/lp:
```

```
$ cat PC01
```

```
uucp:x:5:5:0000-uucp(0000):x:
nuucp:x:10:10:0000-uucp(0000):/usr/spool/uucppublic:/usr/lib/uucp/uucico
zzuucp:x:37:100:Bob Sorenson:/usr/spool/uucppublic:/usr/lib/uucp/uucico
asyuucp:x:38:100:Robert L. Wald:/usr/spool/uucppublic:/usr/lib/uucp/uucico
knuucp:x:39:100:Kris Knigge:/usr/spool/uucppublic:/usr/lib/uucp/uucico
```

```
$ cat PC02
```

```
msnet:x:100:99:Server Program:/usr/net/servers/msnet:/bin/false
install:x:101:1:x:/usr/install:
pjh:x:102:0:Peter J. Holsberg:/usr/pjh:/bin/ksh
hohen:x:346:1:Michael Hohenshilt:/usr/home/hohen:/bin/ksh
reilly:x:347:1:Joan Reilly:/usr/home/reilly:/bin/ksh
```

9

```
$ cat PC03

gordon:x:304:20:gordon gary g:/u1/fall91/dp168/gordon:/bin/csh
lewis:x:288:20:lewi prince e:/u1/fall91/dp168/lewis:/bin/ksh
metelit:x:265:20:metelitsa natalya:/u1/fall91/dp270/metelit:/bin/ksh
nadaraj:x:307:20:nadarajah kalyani:/u1/fall91/dp168/nadaraj:/bin/ksh
nado:x:266:20:nado conan j:/u1/fall91/dp270/nado:/bin/ksh
```

```
$ cat PC04

antello:x:334:20:antello ronald f:/u1/fall91/ff437/antello:/bin/ksh
cilino:x:335:20:cilino michael a:/u1/fall91/ff437/cilino:/bin/ksh
emmons:x:336:20:emmons william r:/u1/fall91/ff437/emmons:/bin/ksh
foreste:x:337:20:forester james r:/u1/fall91/ff437/foreste:/bin/ksh
hayden:x:338:20:hayden richard:/u1/fall91/ff437/hayden:/bin/ksh
```

The program, therefore, has been a success.

In addition, an argument can be a line number (typed as an argument but without slashes) to indicate that the desired split should take place at the line before the number specified. You also can specify a repeat factor by appending {*number*} to a pattern. For example, /login/{8} means "use the first eight lines that contain login as split points."

File Information: `file` and `strings`

UNIX has two commands that give you information about the nature of a file itself. `file` attempts to classify what kind of file it is, and `strings` prints the text that is contained in a binary file.

Syntax for the `file` command can be in one of these two forms:

```
file [ -h ] [ -m magic ] [ -f file ] arg(s)
file [ -h ] [ -m magic ]   -f file
```

`file` reads the beginning of each one of the *arg* files and tries to classify it. If `file` is looking at a text file, it reads the first 512 bytes and, if it appears to be source code, tries to ascertain the programming language in which it is written. The `file` command uses /etc/magic to identify files that have a special numeric value—called the *magic number*—near their beginnings. You can specify a different magic number file by using the `-m` option. The `-h` option tells `file` to ignore symbolic links. If you have a long list of files to check, you can put the files in a listing file and supply the name of the listing file to the `-f` option.

The following are some examples of what you find by running `file` in several directories on a UNIX computer:

```
AWK:            ASCII cpio archive
Magic:          ascii text
at:             English text
awk:            directory
count.lines:    commands text
make.roster:    empty

/usr/local/bin/answer: iAPX 386 executable not stripped
/usr/local/bin/atob:   ELF 386 executable - Version 1
/usr/local/bin/crc:    Microsoft a.out segmented word-swapped 86 executable
/usr/local/bin/rb:     Microsoft a.out separate pure segmented word-swapped 86 executable
/bin/du:        iAPX 386 executable
/usr/bin/ct:    cannot open for reading
../c/10.10.c:   c program text
../c/fp4.exe:   DOS executable (EXE)
../c/fp4.obj:   8086 relocatable (Microsoft)
```

The `strings` command looks for runs of four or more ASCII characters in a binary file. Its syntax is

```
strings [ -a ] [ -o ] [-n num ¦ -num ] file(s)
```

You can specify the minimum number of ASCII characters as *num*. The `-a` option tells `strings` to examine the entire file. The `-o` causes `strings` to output the relative location of each string.

A binary file contains machine language code for a program's instructions, as well as text strings for prompts, error messages, identification, and so on. However, whereas text strings use only the 128 ASCII characters, machine language code may use all of the 256 possible values that can be contained in an eight-bit number—including all 128 ASCII characters. `strings` is not a very "smart" program, and much of its output will be "garbage"— strings formed by those consecutive machine language bytes that just so happen to match printable ASCII characters. For this reason, you will usually get much more output from `strings` than you might have imagined, and you should generally pipe the output to `more` or `pg`.

The following examples have been truncated to save space. You will surely discover more information just by experimenting with `strings` on your own UNIX computer:

$ strings /usr/local/bin/answer

```
@(#)$Id: answer.c,v 4.1 90/04/28 22:44:27 syd Exp $
@(#) Version 2.3, USENET supported version, released May 1990
----------------------------------------------------------------
Sorry, could not find '%s' [%s] in list!
** Fatal Error: could not open %s to write
Enter message for %s ending with a blank line.
((%s -s "While You Were Out" %s ; %s %s) & ) < %s > /dev/null
** Can't have more than 'FirstName LastName' as address!
** Fatal Error: Could not open %s!
```

9

```
Alias %s not found for group expansion!
Bad alias name: %s.  Too long.
Error: Get_token calls nested greated than %d deep!
@(#)$Id: opt_utils.c,v 4.1 90/04/28 22:43:37 syd Exp $
@(#)$Id: string2.c,v 4.1 90/04/28 22:44:14 syd Exp $
        (((((                    H
@(#)libc-port:stdio/stdio_def.c
remove_possible_trailing_spaces
/tmp/hst2HAAa05769.20ecf25d.1689
```

$ **strings /usr/local/bin/crc**

```
Deadlock situation detected/avoided
Value too large for defined data type
Cannot access a needed shared library
Accessing a corrupted shared library
.lib section in a.out corrupted
Attempting to link in more shared libraries than system limit
Cannot exec a shared library directly
Number of symbolic links encountered during pathname traversal exceeds MAXSYMLINKS
Socket operation on non-socket
Protocol wrong type for socket
Option not supported by protocol
Operation not supported on transport endpoint
Address family not supported by protocol family
Cannot assign requested address
Network dropped connection because of reset
Software caused connection abort
Transport endpoint is already connected
Transport endpoint is not connected
Cannot send after socket shutdown
Too many references: cannot splice
btoa End N %ld %lx E %lx S %lx R %lx
        (((((                    H
 !"#$%&´()*+,-
./0123456789:;<=>?@abcdefghijklmnopqrstuvwxyz[\]^_`ABCDEFGHIJKLMNOPQRSTUVWXYZ{¦}~
@(#)/usr/ccs/lib/crt1.o.sl 1.1 5.0-3 11/05/89 64628 AT&T-SF 0.0
@(#)/usr/ccs/lib/crti.o.sl 1.1 5.0-3 11/05/89 0 AT&T-SF 0.0
@(#)/usr/ccs/lib/values-Xt.o.sl 1.1 5.0-3 11/05/89 0 AT&T-SF 0.0
@(#)/usr/include/stdio.h.sl 1.1 5.0-3 11/05/89 31623 AT&T-SF 0.0
@(#)/usr/ccs/lib/libc.a/kill.o.sl 1.1 5.0-3 11/05/89 14042 AT&T-SF 0.0
@(#)/usr/ccs/lib/libc.a/fp_data.o.sl 1.1 5.0-3 11/05/89 0 AT&T-SF 0.0
@(#)/usr/ccs/lib/libc.a/ldexp.o.sl 1.1 5.0-3 11/05/89 23299 AT&T-SF 0.0
@(#)/usr/ccs/lib/crtn.o.sl 1.1 5.0-3 11/05/89 0 AT&T-SF 0.0
```

$ **strings /bin/du**

```
.text
.data
.bss
.fka000
.fka040
```

```
.comment
.lib
PWVS
Y[^_
usage: du [-ars] [name ...]
du: bad status < %s >
du: link table overflow.
Huge directory < %s >--call administrator
du: cannot open < %s >
du: cannot read < %s >
du: cannot read < %s >
bad dir entry <%s>
         (((((                        H
 !"#$%&'()*+,
-./0123456789:;<=>?@abcdefghijklmnopqrstuvwxyz[\]^_`ABCDEFGHIJKLMNOPQRSTUVWXYZ{¦}~
CHRCLASS
ascii
/lib/chrclass/
@(#)/bin/du.sl 1.1 3.2c 06/15/89 17985 AT&T-SF
/shlib/libc_s
```

As you can see, you can learn much about a binary file by running it through strings.

Summary

In this chapter, you have met some useful commands for dealing with files. Some of them compare files; others create archives, compress files, and encode files for electronic distribution; and still others tell you about the nature of the files' contents.

9

## Chapter 10

Putting It All Together

Y ou have met a number of different UNIX System V Release 4 commands and used them singly and with other commands in pipes and simple scripts. In this chapter, you'll see how to take a few of the commands and build some useful tools from them. I will use commands, awk and sed, shell scripts, aliases, and functions too. This will help you see the true meaning of tools, and perhaps even give you some incentive to learn more about shell programming.

Simple Pipes and Shell Scripts

I'll begin with one or two simple commands and then change them into scripts. Furthermore, you will see what to do with these scripts in order to make them more useful to you.

How Many Files?

The simplest way to count the number of files in the current directory is to give the command

```
$ ls -al ¦ wc -l
```

and ls -al will output the names of all files—hidden or not— to stdout, one per line. Then, wc -l will print a count of the number of lines it sees at stdin. This is very simple.

10

Suppose you want to count the number of files in another directory? This is also simple. Just use

```
$ ls -a1 directory | wc -l
```

where `directory` is the full pathname of the desired directory. Now, instead of memorizing this command, suppose you wanted to create a script called count.files that would do the job for you. You could create the following:

```
$ cat count.files

# count.files [directory]

DIR=$1
ls -a1 $DIR | wc -l
```

The first argument on the command line, `directory` (if it exists), will be assigned to `DIR`. If `directory` does not exist, `DIR` will be null, but that will have no negative affect on `ls -a1`.

```
$ count.files

    132

$ count.files $HOME

    143
```

This looks fine. You now have a tool called count.files that will count the number of files for you. You could add a "bell" or "whistle" or two—such as having count.files report the name of the directory whose files it is counting. Because count.files can count files in only one directory and you just typed its name, there is not much point in such an embellishment.

You may be thinking that it would be nice if count.files could report on several directories with one command. For example:

```
$ cat count.files

# count.files [directory]
#
DIR=$*

for dir in $DIR
    ls -a1 $dir | wc -l
done
```

You may recall that `*` is a special shell variable whose value is "all the arguments on the command line." Of course, you should also remember the `for` loop. So the shell expands

```
for dir in $DIR
```

into

```
for dir in /usr/local/bin /usr/local/lib /usr/local
```

for the command line

```
$ count.files /usr/local/bin /usr/local/lib /usr/local
```

This results in

```
$ count.files /usr/local/bin /usr/local/lib /usr/local

    141
     16
      7
```

But now the script should print the name of each directory:

```
$ cat count.files

# count.files [directory]
#
DIR=$*

for dir in $DIR
do
     echo "Files in $dir:\c"
     ls -a1 $dir ¦ wc -l
done

$ count.files /usr/local/bin /usr/local/lib /usr/local

Files in /usr/local/bin:    141
Files in /usr/local/lib:     16
Files in /usr/local:      7
```

The \c character (in the echo statements) prevents echo from printing a newline.

Where Did I Put That File?

Along the same lines as the previous example, you can write a script that looks for a given file and tells you the full pathname. Of course, you could use find, but that command takes a long time to execute. Instead, let's write a script whose search is limited to whatever directories are mentioned in the variable PATH, plus any that you choose to add to the script. The following script was inspired by one given to me by Lt. Michael McConaghy of the Chelsea, Massachusetts Police Department who revised what Jim Foy had originally written in November of 1989.

10

```
# Add the directories where you usually keep all your goodies --
# programs AND targets -- stashed to the end of the next statement:
PATH=$PATH:.

FILENAME=$1

IFS=":"
set $PATH

while true
do
    DIR=$1
    if [ -f ${DIR}/${FILENAME} ]
        then echo ${DIR}/${FILENAME}
        exit 0
    fi

    shift
    if [ $# -eq 0 ]
        then echo "Sorry: $FILENAME not in PATH"
        exit 1
    fi
done
```

In the PATH=$PATH:. statement, the current directory (.) is added to PATH, just for the time that whereis is running. Next, we've temporarily changed the IFS character to : from the default whitespace. This is necessary because each pathname in PATH is separated from the next one with a colon (:). The set command assigns the first pathname to shell positional parameter 1, the second to 2, and so on.

The loop that begins while true is an endless loop, because true is never false. To exit the loop, I included two if statements, each of which contains an exit command.

The first if statement tests for the presence of the file you're looking for in the first directory in PATH. If it is there, whereis echoes the pathname and exits. If not, it executes the shift command. This command assigns the present value of positional parameter 2 to 1, the present value of 3 to 2, and so on. (It certainly has an appropriate name!) shift does one other thing: it decrements the value of #, the number of arguments on the command line. When # reaches 0, whereis will have visited every directory in PATH but will not have found the file you're looking for. Thus, whereis will exit with a return code of 1 and print a "not found" message. If # is not 0, the while loop will be repeated, with a new value for DIR. Here are some sample runs:

```
$ whereis whereis

./whereis

$ whereis emacs

/usr/local/bin/emacs

$ whereis mkdir

/bin/mkdir

$ whereis echo

/bin/echo

$ whereis mksir

Sorry: mksir not in PATH
```

How Is It Spelled?

Many UNIX systems lack commands to check spelling of the words in a text file. If you have an on-line spelling dictionary (that is, only the correctly spelled words are contained, but no meanings), a script to check spelling is within reach. The dictionary I have contains all lowercase letters, one word per line. To get comm to compare the words in the target text file with the words in the dictionary, you need to make all letters lowercase, place the words one per line, sort them, and throw out any duplicates. Here's the script called spl:

```
$ cat spl

# Usage: spl file
#
file=$1
cat $file | tr -cs ´[a-z][A-Z]´ ´[\012*]´ |\
    tr ´[A-Z]´ ´[a-z]´ | sort  | uniq |\
    comm -23 - /usr/dict/dict
```

Impressively small, isn't it? But look at all the piping! Let's dissect it.

First, spl assigns the target filename to a variable with a meaningful name. Next, it cats that file to stdout where the first of two tr commands gets it. The first tr command changes all characters that are not letters to newline characters (and simultaneously squeezes out multiple consecutive newlines into a single newline). You then have the one word per line that you need.

Next, the stream of one word per line is fed to the second tr; it changes all uppercase letters to lowercase. The result is piped to sort and then to uniq and then to comm. The - tells comm that the first file is coming from stdin, and the -23 tells comm to print only the lines that are unique to the first file. This means that any word not in /usr/dict/dict will be printed, and thus will be displayed as a misspelled word. Of course, if you have the appropriate permissions, you can add new words to the dictionary. Be sure to sort it after every addition!

Did you notice that each of the first two lines of code ended with a \? Actually, each was terminated with \<newline>. The \ made the shell believe that you had one very long line, rather than three short lines. Although it is not necessary to use \ on lines that end with the pipe symbol (¦), it doesn't hurt and is a good habit to develop.

Scripts with awk and/or sed

Because awk and sed are themselves such powerful commands, scripts that employ them are even more powerful tools than the ones you've seen so far. However, the same principles hold: first, determine what commands you need to put together, and then use the shell's programming aspects to help you do it.

Finding a Word and Showing a Paragraph

Often when a user greps for a word in a file, grep's display of the line(s) in which that word appears does not give the user enough information. In those cases, the user wants to see a few lines above the one that grep shows and a few below. UNIX people frequently call this a "context grep."

Writing a Korn script for this is not terribly difficult. It requires using a loop to search the file for the word, and then using sed to print the target line and those surrounding it. Here's a script called look:

```
# Usage: look word file
#
file="$2"
word="$1"
lines=`wc -l $2`
for num in `grep -n $word $file ¦ cut -d":" -f1`
do
     ((above=$num-2))
     if [ $above -le 0 ]
     then above=1
     fi
```

10

```
((below=$num+2))
if [ $below -gt $lines ]
then below=$lines
fi

sed  -n "$above,$below p" $file ¦ nl -v$above

echo "\nTap any key to continue: \c:"
read key
done
```

Here are a couple of sample executions to look at before I explain how
look actually works. Let's use the auto file that you're familiar with from
earlier chapters. (The searched-for line will appear in boldface type.)

$ **cat auto**

ES	Arther	85	Honda	Prelude	49.412
BS	Barker	90	Nissan	300ZX	48.209
AS	Saint	88	BMW	M-3	46.629
ES	Straw	86	Honda	Civic	49.543
DS	Swazy	87	Honda	CRX-Si	49.693
ES	Downs	83	VW	GTI	47.133
ES	Smith	86	VW	GTI	47.154
AS	Neuman	84	Porsche	911	47.201
CS	Miller	84	Mazda	RX-7	47.291
CS	Carlson	88	Pontiac	Fiero	47.398
DS	Kegler	84	Honda	Civic	47.429
ES	Sherman	83	VW	GTI	48.489
DS	Arbiter	86	Honda	CRX-Si	48.628
DS	Karle	74	Porsche	914	48.826
ES	Shorn	87	VW	GTI	49.357
CS	Chunk	85	Toyota	MR2	49.558
CS	Cohen	91	Mazda	Miata	50.046
DS	Lisanti	73	Porsche	914	50.609
CS	McGill	83	Porsche	944	50.642
AS	Lisle	72	Porsche	911	51.030
ES	Peerson	86	VW	Golf	54.493

In the following examples, I've highlighted the lines that match the search.

$ **look Toyota auto**

14	DS	Karle	74	Porsche	914	48.826
15	ES	Shorn	87	VW	GTI	49.357
16	**CS**	**Chunk**	**85**	**Toyota**	**MR2**	**49.558**
17	CS	Cohen	91	Mazda	Miata	50.046
18	DS	Lisanti	73	Porsche	914	50.609

Tap any key to continue:

10

```
$ look Mazda auto

        7     ES    Smith     86    VW        GTI       47.154
        8     AS    Neuman    84    Porsche   911       47.201
        9     CS    Miller    84    Mazda     RX-7      47.291
       10     CS    Carlson   88    Pontiac   Fiero     47.398
       11     DS    Kegler    84    Honda     Civic     47.429

Tap any key to continue:
       15     ES    Shorn     87    VW        GTI       49.357
       16     CS    Chunk     85    Toyota    MR2       49.558
       17     CS    Cohen     91    Mazda     Miata     50.046
       18     DS    Lisanti   73    Porsche   914       50.609
       19     CS    McGill    83    Porsche   944       50.642

Tap any key to continue:

$ look Honda auto

        1     ES    Arther    85    Honda     Prelude   49.412
        2     BS    Barker    90    Nissan    300ZX     48.209
        3     AS    Saint     88    BMW       M-3       46.629

Tap any key to continue:
        2     BS    Barker    90    Nissan    300ZX     48.209
        3     AS    Saint     88    BMW       M-3       46.629
        4     ES    Straw     86    Honda     Civic     49.543
        5     DS    Swazy     87    Honda     CRX-Si    49.693
        6     ES    Downs     83    VW        GTI       47.133

Tap any key to continue:
        3     AS    Saint     88    BMW       M-3       46.629
        4     ES    Straw     86    Honda     Civic     49.543
        5     DS    Swazy     87    Honda     CRX-Si    49.693
        6     ES    Downs     83    VW        GTI       47.133
        7     ES    Smith     86    VW        GTI       47.154

Tap any key to continue:
        9     CS    Miller    84    Mazda     RX-7      47.291
       10     CS    Carlson   88    Pontiac   Fiero     47.398
       11     DS    Kegler    84    Honda     Civic     47.429
       12     ES    Sherman   83    VW        GTI       48.489
       13     DS    Arbiter   86    Honda     CRX-Si    48.628

Tap any key to continue:
       11     DS    Kegler    84    Honda     Civic     47.429
       12     ES    Sherman   83    VW        GTI       48.489
       13     DS    Arbiter   86    Honda     CRX-Si    48.628
       14     DS    Karle     74    Porsche   914       48.826
       15     ES    Shorn     87    VW        GTI       49.357

Tap any key to continue:
```

10

You see that not only does look display the line that grep finds plus the four lines that surround it, but it also prints the number of each line. The look script does this with nl.

The first thing I did was to assign the values of the command-line arguments to variables with meaningful names. This makes the script more understandable. Then I have look calculate the number of lines in the target file by using a backquoted wc command:

```
file="$2"
word="$1"
lines=`wc -l $2`
```

Next I set up a for loop that did several things: First, it extracted the number of the line on which grep -n found the target word, and assigned it to num. Recall that grep -n prints the line number, a colon, and then the line itself, so cutting the first field of that output results in the line number.

Inside the loop, look first calculates the line number of the first of the two lines above the grepped line, and then checks to see if in fact there are two lines above the grepped one. If not, it starts the display with the first line of the file. Similarly, it checks whether there are two lines after the target line, and then adjusts accordingly.

Now look knows where to start and where to end its display, so it calls on sed to select and output only those lines. Then sed pipes them to nl, so that a line number followed by a tab will precede each line of the file that gets printed.

Finally, the echo and read lines simply provide a way to pause the script.

Displaying Files According to Size

One thing that I had to do in the course of writing this book was to look at my book directory and subdirectories for good "sample" files. Good sample files are neither too short nor too long and contain certain needed information, or are formatted in a particular way so that they can be used to demonstrate commands and tools. In the beginning, I would just look at file contents and, when I found a good one, would often subsequently discover that it was too big or too small to be useful. So, I developed the following one-liner into a script. It displays the names of all ordinary files in a given directory that are between two sizes.

10

```
$ cat filesize

# filesize directory smallest largest
#
dir=$1
small=$2
large=$3
ls -l "$dir" | sort -n +4 |\
awk '$5 >= '"$small"' && $5 <= '"$large"'  && $1 !~ /d/ {print $0}'
```

You can see that the previous script uses some piping plus ls, sort, and awk. Here are some sample runs:

```
$ filesize . 100 200

-rw-r--r--   1 pjh       root        100 Nov  9 16:40 na.1
----------   1 pjh       root        103 Dec  9 15:25 filesize.scr
-rw-rw-rw-   1 pjh       root        105 Oct 17 16:15 nonprint
-rwxr-xr-x   1 pjh       root        106 Dec  9 13:11 cf-2
-rw-r--r--   1 pjh       root        113 Nov  9 12:57 na
-rw-r--r--   1 pjh       root        113 Nov  9 17:20 p12
-rwx--x--x   1 pjh       root        115 Dec  8 14:30 textfiles
-rwxr-xr-x   1 pjh       root        116 Dec  7 13:16 spl
-rw-r--r--   1 pjh       root        123 Nov  1 13:53 count.scr
-rwxr-xr-x   1 pjh       root        124 Dec  7 13:38 filesize
-rw-r--r--   1 pjh       root        145 Oct 18 14:47 draw.lines
-rw-r--r--   1 pjh       root        164 Nov  1 15:46 tests.0
-rw-r--r--   1 pjh       root        172 Nov  3 18:26 names.2
-rw-r--r--   1 pjh       root        177 Nov  3 18:26 names.1
-rw-r--r--   1 pjh       root        186 Nov  6 15:06 names.3
-rw-r--r--   1 pjh       root        190 Sep 19 15:05 names
-rw-r--r--   1 pjh       root        200 Nov  1 15:05 tests.2

$ filesize .. 100 300

-rwxr-xr-x   1 pjh       root        105 Nov  1 16:30 dump.TB
-rw-r--r--   1 pjh       root        121 Jul 18 12:36 ira.fuchs
-rw-r--r--   1 pjh       root        137 Nov 27 14:50 getfiles
-rw-r--r--   1 pjh       root        179 May 28  1991 reminder
-rw-r--r--   1 pjh       root        242 Sep 19 17:48 dp168
-rw-r--r--   1 pjh       root        298 Oct 29 17:39 HDSCAN.KEY

$ filesize . 10000 20000

-rw-r--r--   1 pjh       root      13275 Nov  9 13:10 diff.scr1
-rwxr-xr-x   1 pjh       root      15036 Nov 22 17:24 XYZ

$ filesize . 16000 20000
$
```

As usual, you copy the command-line parameter values into variables with meaningful names. Next, filesize sends a long listing of the visible files in the target directory to stdout where it is piped to sort. sort reads the listing, sorts it on the 5th field (the `filesize` field), and passes it to awk. awk reads each record (that is, each line of the listing) and tests the fifth field and the first field: the fifth field, the filesize, must both be greater than or equal to the value of small and (&&) be less than or equal to the value of large. The first field—the permissions field—must not contain a d. For every line that satisfies these three conditions, awk prints the entire line. If no lines satisfy all three, then filesize is silent, like a good UNIX tool should be.

Making Scripts Friendlier

One of the things that annoys new (and not-so-new UNIX users) is that commands generally display pretty cryptic messages when they cannot do what you want them to do. For that reason, some script writers insist that their scripts "fail gracefully" when they have to fail. This means, for example, that if a certain script needs three command-line arguments and the user types but two, the script will not sit there forever waiting for the third, but will instead display the correct syntax.

Counting Command-Line Arguments

You know that the special variable # contains the number of arguments actually typed. If you know exactly how many arguments a command should have, you can easily test for that. For example, the correct syntax of filesize is

```
$ filesize dir small large
```

This has three arguments. For testing purposes, you can add the following to the top of the script:

```
if [ $# -ne 3 ]
then echo "Syntax: filesize directory small large"
        exit 1
fi
```

If the user types too many or not enough arguments, filesize will respond with the Syntax message and terminate.

Some people don't like to use if but instead use the "short-circuit" properties of AND (&&) and OR (¦¦). That is, if two expressions are connected with && and the first expression evaluates as "false," the second expression will not be evaluated at all. Similarly, if two expressions are connected with ¦¦ and the first one is "true," the second will not be evaluated at all. Thus, the previous if statement can be rewritten as

```
[ $# -ne 3 ] && { echo "Syntax: filesize small large"; exit 1; }
```

10

The braces make the two commands they enclose look like one to the shell. Here's the new version of filesize:

```
$ cat filesize

[ $# -ne 3 ] && { echo "Syntax: filesize dir small large"; exit 1; }
dir=$1
small=$2
large=$3
ls -l "$dir" | sort -n +4 |\
awk '$5 >= '"$small"' && $5 <= '"$large"' && $1 !~ /d/ {print $0}'
```

Setting Default Values for Arguments

Perhaps you think that users most often want filesize to search the current directory, and you want to save them the "burden" of having to type its name (or .). You can specify that filesize should either accept three arguments—directory, minimum file size, and maximum file size—or accept only two arguments—the two file size values. If the user enters only two arguments, filesize must use the current directory. This requires two steps: change the dir assignment, and then change the test involving $#.

Something like this would be nice:

```
if there are 2 arguments,
    dir=.
otherwise if there are not 3 arguments,
    print the syntax message and quit
```

You also must consider that if there are only two parameters, small should get its value from positional parameter 1 and large from 2.

```
if there are 2 arguments,
    dir=.
    small=$1
    large=$2
otherwise if there are not 3 arguments,
    print the syntax message and quit
otherwise
    dir=$1
    small=$2
    large=$3
```

Here's the new version of filesize:

```
$ cat filesize

if [ $# -eq 2 ]
then
```

```
        dir=.
        small=$1
        large=$2
elif [ $# -ne 3 ]
then
        echo "Syntax: filesize dir small large"
        exit 1
else
        dir=$1
        small=$2
        large=$3
fi

ls -ll "$dir" | sort -n +4 |\
awk '$5 >= '"$small"'  && $5 <= '"$large"' && $1 !~ /d/ {print $0}'
```

Here are some sample runs:

$ filesize

```
Syntax: filesize dir small large
```

$ filesize 100 130

```
-rw-r--r--    1 pjh       root           100 Nov  9 16:40 na.1
-rw-rw-rw-    1 pjh       root           105 Oct 17 16:15 nonprint
-rwxr-xr-x    1 pjh       root           106 Dec  9 13:11 cf-2
-rw-r--r--    1 pjh       root           113 Nov  9 12:57 na
-rw-r--r--    1 pjh       root           113 Nov  9 17:20 p12
-rwx--x--x    1 pjh       root           115 Dec  8 14:30 textfiles
-rwxr-xr-x    1 pjh       root           116 Dec  7 13:16 spl
-rw-r--r--    1 pjh       root           123 Nov  1 13:53 count.scr
-rwxr-xr-x    1 pjh       root           124 Dec  7 13:38 filesize
```

$ filesize .. 100 130

```
-rwxr-xr-x    1 pjh       root           105 Nov  1 16:30 dump.TB
-rw-r--r--    1 pjh       root           121 Jul 18 12:36 ira.fuchs
```

$ filesize .. 100 130 xx

```
Syntax: filesize dir small large
```

$ filesize 100 130 xx

```
100: No such file or directory
```

Look at the last example. You should also check one more thing. If there are three arguments, the first had better not be a number! But what if there is a directory whose name is a number (perfectly legal!)? You could test the value of 1 to see whether indeed it is a directory filename (recall the [-d *dir*] test?).

10

You can probably tell from this last example that you have barely scratched the surface of shell programming. UNIX includes many additional commands in the shell that are special to the shell and exist just for use in scripts. These are beyond the scope of this book, but they are covered very nicely in John Valley's *UNIX Desktop Guide to the Korn Shell*.

Writing Aliases and Functions

Let's not forget the roles played by functions and by Korn shell aliases in building tools as you learned in Chapter 1. Recall that both get loaded into memory when you log in and are thus faster to execute than scripts. However, *always* loading them into memory can have negative effects—a certain amount of time is taken to do the loading, and a certain amount of memory is no longer available for your other processes. So you should only make aliases and functions of your most often-used tools.

The major difference between aliases and functions is that an alias cannot accept any command-line parameters, but a function can.

Writing Simple Aliases

Here's a simple alias you can use to list the names of subdirectories (including hidden ones) in the current directory:

```
alias dir="ls -al ¦ grep ´^d´ ¦ cut -c55-70"
```

You might want to add a pipe to pr for multicolumn display.

The next alias lists all the files in the directory I use to keep track of user logins, and pipes them to the pager I use—a public domain program called less (as in "less is more," an abysmal pun!):

```
alias log="ls -al /usr/spool/Log ¦ less"
```

I can quickly glance at the screen to see the date and time a user last logged in.

System administration is an area that I've avoided, but there are a very large number of shell scripts in existence to make the administrator's job less dependent on remembering cryptic and rarely-used commands. I wrote this alias because I could never remember the syntax for shutdown, a command which can power down a UNIX computer (on the AT&T 3B2/400, this command with the right arguments even turns the power switch off!) or reboot it into any one of several different operating modes. The alias reboots to normal multiuser operation and must be used after installing new software.

```
alias reboot="cd /;shutdown -i6 -y -g0"
```

Writing a Useful Korn Shell Function

To illustrate functions, I'm going to show you a combination of shell script, alias definition, and function definition that causes my system to have a customized command-line prompt. First, I define a variable PS0 to be the name of my machine. I can do this with the assignment

```
PS0="`uname`"
```

uname is a command that returns the name of the computer on which uname is executed.

Next I define the function cd that will replace the cd that's built into the Korn shell:

```
function _cd {
        `cd` $1
        PS1="$PS0 [$LOGNAME] $PWD> "
}
```

Note that this function executes cd to change the current directory to whatever the first command-line argument is. Then it assigns a value to PS1, the command-line prompt (the default, as you know, is $), based on three shell variables, PS0, LOGNAME, and PWD. LOGNAME gets its value when you log in. It is your login name (ours is pjh). PWD gets its value from the current directory. Every time you change directories, PWD gets an appropriate value automatically. I defined PS0 in the preceding paragraph.

Now I redefine cd as

```
alias -x cd=_cd
```

The -x means that this definition will be exported so that it is available to other shell scripts (except those that cause a new invocation of the Korn shell). This new definition for cd will replace the built-in command.

Finally, I provide a definition for PS1 that will be used only when I log in:

```
PS1="$PS0 [$LOGNAME] $PWD> "
```

10

Thus, when pjh logs in on a computer named mccc, he sees

```
mccc [pjh] /usr/pjh>
```

as his prompt. You can place all of these lines in your .profile file or in your Korn shell .env file so that this customized prompt will appear automatically. Here's what it would look like, embedded in a .env file:

```
PS0="`uname`"
#
function _cd {
        'cd' $1
        PS1="$PS0 [$LOGNAME] $PWD> "
}
#
alias -x cd=_cd
PS1="$PS0 [$LOGNAME] $PWD> "
export PS1
```

Exporting PS1 guarantees that the customized prompt will be appear if you use a subshell.

A final example of function definitions uses two command-line arguments. The first argument is a directory name and the second a word (or regular expression). This function greps for the word in all regular files in the specified directory:

```
function fgrpl {
    dir=$1
    word=$2
    find "$dir" -type f -print ¦ xargs grep "$word" ¦ less
}
```

The find command produces a list of all regular files in the specified directory, and pipes them to xargs. It invokes grep "$word" on each filename piped to it. Again, I have piped the output to my favorite pager, less. You may use more or pg.

Summary

In this chapter, you have seen UNIX System V Release 4 commands turned into tools through piping and by placing them into shell scripts. In addition, you saw some aliases and functions. This only opens the door into the world of UNIX tools, a world in which you create what you need to make your life with UNIX as pleasant as possible.

Part

Reference

Chapter **11**

UNIX System V Release 4

Command Reference

This chapter presents a brief description of each UNIX command mentioned in Parts I and II of this book. My goal is to provide you with something more readable than what you find in the printed (and on-line) UNIX documentation.

Options are listed alphabetically unless the order makes a difference to the command.

The suffix *(s)* means *one or more*. For example:

- *file(s)* means *one or more files*.

- *arg(s)* means *one or more arguments*.

- *path(s)* means *one or more absolute or relative pathnames*.

Note: I use the UNIX convention of referring to ordinary and regular files, directory files, and device files as simply *files*. However, when necessary, I use the appropriate adjectives for clarity.

---

awk

"Classic" awk produces reports from structured text, ordinary files, and patterns. One such source of structured text is the log files produced by certain UNIX background commands. awk can identify lines based on the patterns they contain, and can break lines into fields that can be processed by its built-in text operators, numeric operators, and functions.

Note: See Chapter 7 for details on using awk. See also nawk.

Note: Two versions of awk—old (*oawk*) and new (*nawk*)—are included with UNIX System V Release 4, with awk existing as a link to nawk. This is a temporary step to provide time for users with awk scripts developed under old awk to convert them to new awk. The following examples apply equally well to both versions.

```
awk [ -Fc ] [ commands ¦ -f file ] [ parameter assignments ][ file(s) ]
```

-Fc	Change the field separator from any whitespace character to the character *c*.
commands	One or more awk commands.
-f *file*	Read the awk command script from the ordinary file *file*.
parameter assignments	Define awk variables and their initial values in the form *name1=value1* [*name2=value2*].
file(s)	Read data from one or more ordinary file(s). Use - to read standard input.

Examples:

Emulate the cat command:

```
$ awk {print} names
```

```
allen christopher
babinchak david
best betty
bloom dennis
```

```
boelhower joseph
bose anita
cacossa ray
chang liang
crawford patricia
crowley charles
cuddy michael
czyzewski sharon
delucia joseph
```

Print all lines that contain the pattern `joseph` in the filenames:

$ awk ´/joseph/ {print}´ names

```
boelhower joseph
delucia joseph
```

Print fields 1 and 2 of each line that contains the pattern `jos` in the filenames:

$ awk ´/jos/ {print $1 $2}´ names

```
boelhowerjoseph
deluciajoseph
```

Print the string `hello`, (including a blank space after the comma), followed by field 2 of each line of the filenames:

$ awk ´{print "hello, " $2}´ names

```
hello, christopher
hello, david
hello, betty
hello, dennis
hello, joseph
hello, anita
hello, ray
hello, liang
hello, patricia
hello, charles
hello, michael
hello, sharon
hello, joseph
```

cat

cat prints files on the standard output.

```
cat [ -s ] [ -u ] [ -v[te] ] [ file(s) ]
```

-s   Suppress error messages about missing files.

-u   Cause cat's output to be unbuffered. (Not implemented in all versions of cat.)

-v   Print nonprinting characters in a visual format, but do not print whitespace characters in that format unless one or both of the following modifiers is used:

    -t   Print tabs as ^I and formfeeds as ^L

    -e   Display newline characters as $

The format for *control characters* (ASCII codes \000 through \037) is ^N, where N is the corresponding printing character from the range \100 through \137. Other nonprinting characters are printed as M-x, where x is a printing character from the range \100 through \137.

cat is a filter and as such can take its input from stdin. To cause this to occur, simply omit filenames from the command line, or use a - in place of a filename.

Examples:

Print the contents of the file cal:

```
$ cat cal

The cal command in UNIX is
very useful. It prints a
calendar of the month you
specify.
```

Echo what the user enters at stdin (in this case, stdin is the keyboard because no filename is given on the command line). Each line—terminated by tapping the enter key—is immediately printed:

```
$ cat

this is cat

this is cat

taking input from stdin and

taking input from stdin and

echoing it as soon as I hit <Enter>!

echoing it as soon as I hit <Enter>!

^d
```

cd

cd, a shell internal command, changes your working directory either to HOME or to the directory specified (if you have execute permission in that directory).

```
cd [ directory ]
```

> directory   Can be either a complete pathname (either absolute or relative) or an incomplete pathname relative to a path specified in CDPATH.

11

> **Note:** If you're using the Korn shell, use cd - to change to the previous directory.

Example:

Change from the current directory to any other directory:

$ pwd

```
/usr/pjh
```

$ cd /usr/spool/uucppublic/pjh/from/princeton

$ pwd

```
/usr/spool/uucppublic/pjh/from/princeton
```

chmod

chmod enables the owner to change permissions and other attributes of files. It has two modes: absolute, which uses a number to designate permissions, and symbolic, which uses a sequence of letters and symbols to specify permissions. Syntax for the absolute mode is

```
chmod [ -R ] perms file(s)
```

Syntax for the symbolic mode is

```
chmod [ugoa] {+|-|=} [rwxlstugo] file(s)
```

In absolute mode, the arguments are

-R   Recursively descend through directories and symbolic links, applying the change to all files.

perms   Permissions set as the sum of any of the following multidigit octal numbers:

4000	Set user ID (setuid)
20#0	Set group ID (setgid) if # is odd (either 1, 3, 5 or 7); otherwise (0, 2, 4 or 6), enable mandatory locking
1000	Turn on sticky bit
0400	Read by owner permitted
0200	Write by owner permitted
0100	Execute (search, if applied to a directory) by owner permitted
0040	Read by members of group permitted
0020	Write by members of group permitted
0010	Execute (search, if applied to a directory) by members of group permitted
0004	Read by others permitted
0002	Write by others permitted
0001	Execute (search, if applied to a directory) by others permitted

file(s)   List of files to be changed.

In chmod's symbolic mode:

- The first set of letters designates whose permissions are changed and are any combination of

u	User; the file's owner
g	Group; the file's group
o	Other; other users
a	All; all users

The default is to a (all).

- The next symbol is the operator, which specifies how permissions are to be changed. The symbol is any one of the following:

+	Add the permissions (relative to current permissions)
-	Remove the permissions (relative to current permissions)
=	Set the permissions (absolute change)

- The last string consists of symbols for the actual permissions, and can be any combination of the following:

r	Read permission
w	Write permission
x	Execute permission
l	Mandatory locking
s	Set ID on execution
t	Sticky bit
u	Use current permissions of owner
g	Use current permissions of group
o	Use current permissions of others
file(s)	List of files to be changed

Examples:

Remove read permission from all users on the file pjh-00:

```
$ ls -l

total 176
drwxr--r--   2 pjh       root            64 Oct  2 14:46 ch01
drwxr-xr-x   2 pjh       root            48 Sep 14 15:19 ch02
-rw-r--r--   1 pjh       root          3973 Nov  3 13:12 pjh-00
-rw-r--r--   1 pjh       root         82497 Nov  3 12:53 pjh-01

$ chmod -r pjh-00

$ ls -l

total 176
drwxr--r--   2 pjh       root            64 Oct  2 14:46 ch01
drwxr-xr-x   2 pjh       root            48 Sep 14 15:19 ch02
--w-------   1 pjh       root          3973 Nov  3 13:12 pjh-00
-rw-r--r--   1 pjh       root         82497 Nov  3 12:53 pjh-01
```

11

Change the permissions on pjh-00 to "read for everyone and write for the owner only":

```
$ chmod 644 pjh-00

$ ls -l

total 177
drwxr--r--   2 pjh      root             64 Oct  2 14:46 ch01
drwxr-xr-x   2 pjh      root             48 Sep 14 15:19 ch02
-rw-r--r--   1 pjh      root           3973 Nov  3 13:12 pjh-00
-rw-r--r--   1 pjh      root          82497 Nov  3 12:53 pjh-01
```

chown

chown enables one user to give files to another user by changing the ownership of the files. chown can be used only by the owner of the file(s).

chown [-R] [-h] *newowner file(s)*

-h   If one of *file(s)* is a symbolic link, change the owner of the link. Do not change the owner of the file referred to by the symbolic link.

-R   Change ownership of all files and subdirectories of *file(s)*, including files and subdirectories encountered when symbolic links are followed.

Examples:

Give ownership of the file pjh-01 to root:

```
$ ls -l

total 177
drwxr--r--   2 pjh      root             64 Oct  2 14:46 ch01
drwxr-xr-x   2 pjh      root             48 Sep 14 15:19 ch02
-rw-r--r--   1 pjh      root           3973 Nov  3 13:12 pjh-00
-rw-r--r--   1 pjh      root          82497 Nov  3 12:53 pjh-01

$ chown root pjh-01

$ ls -l

total 178
drwxr--r--9  2 pjh      root             64 Oct  2 14:46 ch01
drwxr-xr-x   2 pjh      root             48 Sep 14 15:19 ch02
-rw-r--r--   1 pjh      root           3973 Nov  3 13:12 pjh-00
-rw-r--r--   1 root     root          82497 Nov  3 12:53 pjh-01
```

Now give the ownership of pjh-01 back to pjh:

```
$ chown pjh pjh-01
```

```
pjh-01: Not owner
```

Oops! Giving away ownership cannot be reversed. Only the system administrator or the new owner can successfully execute chown.

11

cmp

cmp compares two files and, if they differ, reports the byte number of the first differing byte and the number of the line where it resides. If they are identical, cmp is silent.

cmp [-l] [-s] *file1 file2*

-l   Print the offset (the number of bytes from the beginning of the file) and values of differing bytes.

-s   Suppress all messages.

cmp always returns a result code:

0   Files are identical

1   Files are not identical

2   One or both files either do not exist or cannot be accessed

Example:

```
$ cat na.1
```

```
allen christopher
babinchak david
best betty
bloom dennis
boelhower joseph
bose anita
cacossa ray
delucia joseph
```

```
$ cat na.2
```

```
allen christopher
babinchak David
best betty
boelhower joseph
bose
cacossa ray
delucia joseph
```

```
$ cmp na.1 na.2
```

```
na.1 na.2 differ: char 29, line 2
```

The character count includes one for each end-of-line—that is, newline—character even though you cannot see it.

11

comm

comm prints lines common to two files in a three-column format, with lines unique to *file1* in column 1, lines unique to *file2* in column 2, and lines common to both in column 3.

comm [-123] *file1 file2*

-1	Print only lines unique to *file1*
-2	Print only lines unique to *file2*
-3	Print only lines that appear in both files

Note: stdin (-) may be used as one of the files.

Example:

```
$ cat na.1
```

```
allen christopher
babinchak david
best betty
bloom dennis
boelhower joseph
bose anita
cacossa ray
delucia joseph
```

```
$ cat na,2
```

```
allen christopher
babinchak David
best betty
boelhower joseph
bose
cacossa ray
delucia joseph
```

```
$ comm na.1 na.2
```

```
                                            allen christopher
                        babinchak David
babinchak david
                                            best betty
                                            bloom dennis
                                            boelhower joseph
                        bose
bose anita
                                            cacossa ray
                                            delucia joseph
```

11

---

compress

compress, a filter, reduces the size of ordinary files and replaces them with similarly named files, with the new names ending in .Z if possible. Maximum, or 16-bit, compression "efficiency" is the default, although a less efficient compression can be specified to accommodate systems that cannot handle 16-bit compression.

```
compress [ -cfv ] [ -b bits ] [ file(s) ]
```

-b *bits*	Change compression efficiency to bits (9 through 16)
-c	Write to standard output without creating a compressed file
-f	Force compression to occur, even if no reduction results or if a .Z file already exists for this file
-v	Verbose: print the percentage reduction ratio for each file

If no file is specified on the command line, compress takes its input from stdin.

Example:

```
$ ls -l no.blanks
```

```
-rw-r--r--  1 pjh     root          742 Sep 30 14:03 no.blanks
```

```
$ compress no.blanks
```

```
$ ls -l no.blanks*
```

```
-rw-r--r--  1 pjh     root          511 Sep 30 14:03 no.blanks.Z
```

Notice that the file no.blanks has been replaced by the compressed version, no.blanks.Z.

$ **cat no.blanks.Z**

When I executed this command, it printed a stream of characters that locked my keyboard! A compressed file is a binary file.

11

cp

cp copies an ordinary file to another ordinary file, or one or more ordinary files to a directory, or a directory and all of its files and subdirectories to another directory. If the target file exists, it is overwritten unless the -i option is used. cp is related to both ln and mv.

cp [-ipr] *file(s)* *target*

-i	Confirm before overwriting an existing file.
-p	Preserve file modification times and permissions.
-r	Must be specified if you want to copy a directory structure to another directory in the same file system.
files(s)	Files to be copied. If *target* is an ordinary file, only one *file(s)* argument is allowed and it must be the name of an ordinary file.
target	If *target* is the name of an ordinary file, it receives the contents of the original ordinary file. cp will create the target file if it does not exist, or will overwrite its contents if it does exist.
	If *target* is a directory and file(s) are the names of ordinary files, the contents of *file(s)* are copied to that directory and stored as originally named. However, if *file(s)* is the name of a directory, *target* must be a directory in the same physical file system for the copying to occur.

Example:

Make a copy of the file elmedit.c and call it xyzzy:

$ **ls -l**

```
total 8
-rw-r--r--  1 pjh      root       603 Jul  3  1990 SharFile.Headers
-rw-r--r--  1 pjh      root      6554 Jul  3  1990 elmedit.c
```

```
$ cp elmedit.c xyzzy

$ ls -l

total 15
-rw-r--r--  1 pjh        root         603 Jul  3  1990 SharFile.Headers
-rw-r--r--  1 pjh        root        6554 Jul  3  1990 elmedit.c
-rw-r--r--  1 pjh        root        6554 Jan 27 12:05 xyzzy
```

11

cpio

cpio manipulates file archives. That is, it can create an archive from a list of filenames, and extract the contents of an archive into individual files. It can also copy directory structures.

The syntax for "copy-out" mode is

```
cpio -o[aABcLvV] [-C size] [-H hdr] [-O file [-M mesg]]
```

The syntax for "copy-in" mode is

```
cpio -i[bBcdfkmrsStuvV6] [-C size] [-E file] [-H hdr]
     [-I file [-M mesg] ] [-R ID] [pattern(s)]
```

The syntax for "pass" mode is

```
cpio -p[adlLmuvV] [-R ID] directory
```

Copy-out mode creates an archive from a list of pathnames supplied to stdin. Select copy-out mode with the -o option.

The following modifiers are valid for the copy-out mode:

-a	Reset access times of copied files
-A	Append files to an archive
-B	Block records to 5,120 bytes when writing the archive directly to a character special device
-c	Write an ASCII header for portability
-C size	Use record blocks of size bytes when writing directly to a character special device
-H hdr	Write header information in one of the following hdr formats:
	crc or CRC ASCII header with checksum value for each file and expanded device numbers

11

odc	ASCII header with small device numbers
tar or TAR	tar header and format
ustar or USTAR	IEEE/P1003 Data Interchange Standard header and format

-L	Follow symbolic links
-M *mesg*	Define the message to prompt for media switching
-O *file*	Write output to file
-v	Verbose: print files written.
-V	Print a dot (.) for each file written

Copy-in mode extracts files from an archive created with cpio -o. Select copy-in mode with the -i option.

The following modifiers are valid for the copy-in mode:

-b	Reverse the order of the bytes within each word. This option is needed when the archive was created on a machine with a different byte order than that used for extraction.
-B	Block records to 5,120 bytes when reading the archive directly from a character special device.
-c	Read header information in ASCII character form.
-C *size*	Use record blocks of size bytes when reading directly from a character special device.
-d	Create directories as needed.
-E *file*	Read the list of filenames to be extracted from a file.
-f	Extract all files except those matching *pattern(s)*. Patterns are filename generation strings, so that -f *.c would tell cpio to extract all files having names that end in .c from the archive.
-H *hdr*	Read header information in one of the following *hdr* formats:

crc or CRC	ASCII header with checksum value for each file and expanded device numbers
ustar or USTAR	IEEE/P1003 Data Interchange Standard header and format

`tar` or `TAR`	tar header and format
`odc`	ASCII header with small device numbers
`-I` *file*	*file* contains the names of the files to be extracted from the archive, and is used when supplying patterns on the command line are onerous.
`-k`	Skip bad file headers and I/O errors, if possible. This enables you to extract the "good" files from a corrupted archive.
`-m`	Retain file modification times.
`-M` *mesg*	Define the message to prompt for media switching.
`-r`	Interactively rename files as they are being extracted.
`-R ID`	Assign file's owner and group to that of user ID.
`-s`	Swap bytes within each halfword.
`-S`	Swap halfwords within each word.
`-t`	Print a table of contents without extracting.
`-u`	Extract unconditionally. The default is to extract only if the modification time of the extracted file is newer than the existing file.
`-v`	Verbose: print files written. With `-t`, print a display that's like the output of an `ls -l` command.
`-V`	Print a dot (`.`) for each file written.
`-6`	Use UNIX Sixth Edition archive format.

Pass mode (`-p`) reads stdin and copies the files whose names appear there to directory. Select pass mode with the `-p` option.

The following modifiers are valid for the pass mode:

`-a`	Reset access times of copied files.
`-d`	Create directories as needed.
`-l`	Link files if possible instead of copying them.
`-L`	Follow symbolic links.
`-m`	Retain file modification times.
`-u`	Extract unconditionally. The default is to extract only if the modification time of the extracted file is newer than the existing file.

-V	Print a dot (.) for each file written.
-R ID	Assign file's owner and group to that of user ID.
-M *mesg*	Define the message to prompt for media switching.

Example:

The following commands illustrate how a system administrator would "shrink" tom's directory structure—/usr/tom and its subdirectories. (Be sure tom is not logged on before you try this). The system responses are not shown because they depend on what's in tom's directories. Directory shrinking is a reasonable activity because directories only grow with the addition of new files but never shrink when files are removed.

```
$ cd /usr

$ mkdir tom.new

$ cd tom

$ find . -print ¦ cpio -pdvlm ../tom.new

$ cd /usr

$ rm -rf tom

$ mv tom.new tom
```

The fourth command prints the relative pathnames of all files in the directory tree that begins at the current directory (/usr/tom.) The command then pipes the pathnames to cpio. Operating in pass mode, cpio links each file from the original tree to a corresponding file in the tree under /usr/tom.new, creating needed directories and preserving the file modification times of the original files.

crypt

crypt is a filter that is used to encode files so that no one else can read them. It is also used to decode encrypted files.

> **Note:** crypt cannot be purchased outside of the United States. It is available in the Security Administration Utilities package.

```
crypt [ password ]

crypt [ -k ]
```

    -k   Use the value of CRYPTKEY as the encryption key.

    password   An arbitrary string used as the encryption key.

Normally, you use `crypt` in the following manner:

$ crypt < *infile* > *outfile*

This causes `crypt` to prompt for an encryption key, much as login prompts for a password. This is the safest way to use `crypt`, because the key is never available to prying eyes. To make your system less vulnerable to an attacker, avoid using the same key for all encryptions. In *UNIX System Security* (Hayden, 1985), Patrick H. Wood and Stephen G. Kochan say

> The `crypt` command shouldn't be considered unbreakable, however, since the method it uses to encrypt text is not kept secret, and decryption methods are known...Anyone who is determined enough and has the time, patience, and computer facilities can crack the encrypted text.

Example:

$ ls -l mess

```
-rw-r--r--  1 pjh         root       294 Feb  5 13:48 mess
```

$ cat mess

```
This area is what's accumulated as I've gone around FTPing things for
installation locally.  (Well, most of it -- some things I've gotten
explicitly just to put in here.)  It's an independent effort, so I
can't promise it'll be maintained religiously: it's whenever I have
the time to check it.
```

$ crypt < mess > mess.crypt

```
Enter key:
```

$ ls -l mess*

```
-rw-r--r--  1 pjh         root       294 Feb  5 13:48 mess
-rw-r--r--  1 pjh         root       294 Feb  5 13:49 mess.crypt
```

Notice that both the original file and the encrypted file are the same size. However, the encrypted version is a binary file, so I cannot show you its contents.

csplit

csplit splits big files into little files, based on a set of regular expressions you provide. csplit scans your big file and cuts it up when it finds matches to the regular expressions.

csplit [-s] [-k] [-f *ofile*] *file arg(s)*

-f *ofile*	Name the new files *ofile*00, *ofile*01, and so on. The default is to name the new files xx00, xx01, and so on.
-k	Keep all generated files if csplit fails.
-s	Suppress printing of character counts.
arg(s)	A series of search strings identifying break points:

/*rexp*/	Break before regular expression *rexp*
%*rexp*%	Break before regular expression *rexp* and discard the section (do not write the section to an output file)
num	Break before line number *num*
arg{ct}	Repeat the previous argument *ct* times

file	Read from the file named *file*. Use - to read from standard input.

Example:

Split the passwd file into five pieces: the first will be everything up to but not including the first line that contains UUCP; the second, from UUCP up to but not including the first line that contains Special; and so on. Files will be named PA00, PA01, and so on.

```
$ csplit -f PA passwd /UUCP/ /Special/ /Fall/ /NCR/

270
505
426
490
446

$ cat PA00

root:x:0:0:System Administrator:/usr/root:/bin/ksh
reboot:x:7:1:---:/:/etc/shutdown -y -g0 -i6
listen:x:37:4:x:/usr/net/nls:
slan:x:57:57:StarGROUP Software NPP Administration:/usr/slan:
lp:x:71:2:x:/usr/spool/lp:
_:-              :6:6:   ==============================   :6:
```

```
$ cat PA01

_:-                    :6:6:    ==  UUCP Logins                    :6:
_:-                    :6:6:    ============================    :6:
uucp:x:5:5:0000-uucp(0000):x:
nuucp:x:10:10:0000-uucp(0000):/usr/spool/uucppublic:/usr/lib/uucp/uucico
zzuucp:x:37:100:Bob Sorenson:/usr/spool/uucppublic:/usr/lib/uucp/uucico
asyuucp:x:38:100:Robert L. Wald:/usr/spool/uucppublic:/usr/lib/uucp/uucico
knuucp:x:39:100:Kris Knigge:/usr/spool/uucppublic:/usr/lib/uucp/uucico
_:-                    :6:6:    ============================    :6:
```

11

cut

cut selects columns or fields from input lines.

cut -c*list* [*file(s)*]

cut -f*list* [-d*char*] [-s] [*file(s)*]

Note: Fields and columns are numbered beginning with 1.

-c*list*	Select columns. For a list, list one or more column ranges separated by commas, where a column range is one of the following:

15-18	Columns 15 through 18, inclusive
25-	Columns 25 through the last one on the line, inclusive
-12	Columns 1 through 12, inclusive
15-18,25-	Columns 15 through 18, inclusive, and columns 25 through the last one on the line, inclusive

-f*list*	Select fields. For a list, list one or more field ranges separated by commas; for example, 1-5,7,10. Field ranges are patterned after column ranges.
-d*char*	Field delimiter character is *char*. The default field delimiter character is the tab.
-s	Skip lines having no delimiter character.
file(s)	Input files. Use - to read standard input.

11

Examples:

Using the colon as a field separator, cut the first and fifth fields from the file Passwd:

```
$ cat Passwd

root:x:0:0:System Administrator:/usr/root:/bin/ksh
slan:x:57:57:StarGROUP Software NPP Administration:/usr/slan:
nuucp:x:10:10:0000-uucp(0000):/usr/spool/uucppublic:/usr/lib/uucp/uucico
labuucp:x:21:100:shevett's UPC:/usr/spool/uucppublic:/usr/lib/uucp/uucico
puucp:x:22:100:princeton:/usr/spool/uucppublic:/usr/lib/uucp/uucico
juucp:x:24:100:Jon LaBadie:/usr/spool/uucppublic:/usr/lib/uucp/uucico
couucp:x:25:100:Bill Michaelson:/usr/spool/uucppublic:/usr/lib/uucp/uucico
fanuucp:x:32:100:Jo Poplawski:/usr/spool/uucppublic:/usr/lib/uucp/uucico
pjh:x:102:0:Peter J. Holsberg:/usr/pjh:/bin/ksh
```

```
$ cut -d: -f1,5 Passwd

root:System Administrator
slan:StarGROUP Software NPP Administration
nuucp:0000-uucp(0000)
labuucp:shevett's UPC
puucp:princeton
juucp:Jon LaBadie
couucp:Bill Michaelson
fanuucp:Jo Poplawski
pjh:Peter J. Holsberg
```

Cut the 9th through 15th and the 40th through the end of the line from each line of the file magic.1:

```
$ cat magic.1

0        short       070707        cpio archive
0        string      070707        ASCII cpio archive
0        long        0177555       obsolete ar archive
0        long        0100554       apl workspace
0        short       017037        packed data
0        short       0407          pdp11/pre System V vax executable
0        short       0401          unix-rt ldp
0        short       0405          pdp11 overlay
0        short       0410          pdp11/pre System V vax pure executable
```

```
$ cut -c9-15,40- magic.1

short    cpio archive
string   ASCII cpio archive
long     obsolete ar archive
long     apl workspace
short    packed data
short    pdp11/pre System V vax executable
short    unix-rt ldp
short    pdp11 overlay
short    pdp11/pre System V vax pure executable
```

date

date prints the current date and time. If you have root privileges, date enables you to change the date and time.

```
date [-u] [+format]

date [-a nnn.nnn ] [-u] [ [mmdd]HHMM ¦ mmddHHMM[cc]yy]
```

-u	Use Greenwich Mean Time (GMT)
-a	Adjust the time by *nnn.nnn* seconds. (*nnn.nnn* can be positive or negative)
mm	Month number
dd	Day of the month
HH	Hour using a 24-hour clock
MM	Minute
cc	Century number minus 1; that is, the first two digits of the year
yy	Last two digits of the year
+*format*	Print the date and time according to one of the following format specifications:

	%a	Abbreviated weekday name; for example, Sat
	%A	Full weekday name; for example, Saturday
	%b	Abbreviated month name; for example, Sep
	%B	Full month name; for example, September
	%c	Country-specific date and time format
	%d	Day of month; for example, 28
	%D	Date in %m/%d/%y format; for example, 09/28/91
	%e	Day of month (in two columns); for example, "28" for the 28th but " 7" for the 7th

11

%h	Same as %b	
%H	Hour in 24-hour format; for example, 13 (for 1:00 p.m.)	
%I	Hour in 12-hour format; for example, 1 (for 1:00 a.m. or p.m.)	
%j	Day of year as a three-digit number; for example, 271 for the 271st day, and 012 for the 12th day	
%m	Month as a two-digit number; for example, 09 (for September)	
%M	Minute as a two-digit number; for example, 48	
%n	Print a newline character	
%p	Print AM or PM, as appropriate	
%r	Time as %I:%M:%S:%p; for example, 1:48:25 AM	
%R	Time as %H:%M; for example, 13:48	
%S	Second as a two-digit number; for example, 42	
%t	Print a tab character	
%T	Time as %H:%M:%S; for example, 13:48:51	
%U	Week as a two-digit number (00 to 53), with Sunday as the first day of the week	
%w	Day of week; Sunday = 0	
%W	Same as %U except that Monday is the first day of the week	
%x	Date in a country-specific format	
%X	Time in a country-specific format	
%y	Last two digits of the year; for example, 91	
%Y	Four-digit year	
%Z	Name of time zone; for example, EDT	

Examples:

Invoke date with no options:

$ **date**

Sat Sep 28 1:45:58 EDT 1991

> What time is it?

$ **date +%r**

1:48:25 AM

11

diff

diff prints the detailed differences between two files. The differences are displayed in a variety of formats, all of which indicate what must be changed in the two files to make them identical.

diff [-bitw] [-c ¦ -e ¦ -f ¦ -h ¦ -n] *file1 file2*

diff [-bitw] [-C *number*] *file1 file2*

diff [-bitw] [-D *string*] *file1 file2*

diff [-bitw] [-c ¦ -e ¦ -f ¦ -h ¦ -n] [-l] [-r] [-s][-S *name*] *dir1 dir2*

diff's major options include the following:

-b	Ignore whitespace (tabs and spaces) at the ends of lines, and treat other strings of blanks as equivalent
-i	Ignore case
-t	Expand tab characters in output lines to preserve the original indentations
-w	Ignore all whitespace, and treat other strings of blanks as equivalent

The following options are mutually exclusive:

-c	Print three context lines around each difference and use "context format" (see Chapter 9)
-C *number*	Print number context lines around each difference and use "context format" (described in the examples that follow)

-e	Print differences using ed commands (see the description of ed in this chapter)
-D *string*	Make a file that can generate either *file1* or *file2* using the C preprocessor and option -D*string*
-f	Same as -e, but in the opposite order and so cannot be used with ed (see the description of ed in this chapter)
-h	Fast diff, good for large files having short stretches of changes that are widely separated from each other; causes diff to use an algorithm for finding differences that is not as robust as usual
-n	Similar to -e, but reversed and with line counts

Use the following options when comparing directories:

-l	Print a long format report
-r	Recursively descend through directories
-s	Report identical files
-S *name*	Start a directory scan at filename *name*

Examples:

Show the differences between two files, file1 and file2:

```
$ cat file1
```

```
root:x:0:0:System Administrator:/usr/root:/bin/ksh
slan:x:57:57:StarGROUP Software NPP Administration:/usr/slan:
juucp:x:24:100:Jon LaBadie:/usr/spool/uucppublic:/usr/lib/uucp/uucico
couucp:x:25:100:Bill Michaelson:/usr/spool/uucppublic:/usr/lib/uucp/uucico
fanuucp:x:32:100:Jo Poplawski:/usr/spool/uucppublic:/usr/lib/uucp/uucico
pjh:x:102:0:Peter J. Holsberg:/usr/pjh:/bin/ksh
pete:x:200:1:PJH:/usr/home/pete:/bin/ksh
irv:x:257:1:Irv Ashkenazy:/usr/home/irv:/bin/ksh
ajh:x:258:1:Alan Pjh:/usr/home/ajh:/bin/ksh
mccollo:x:329:1:Carol McCollough:/usr/home/mccollo:/bin/ksh
rechter:x:293:20:rechter jay:/u1/fall91/dp168/rechter:/bin/ksh
reeve:x:308:20:reeve michael j:/u1/fall91/dp168/reeve:/bin/ksh
regh:x:331:20:regh jeff l:/u1/fall91/dp270/regh:/bin/ksh
sicigna:x:327:20:sicignano joseph p:/u1/fall91/dp168/sicigna:/bin/ksh
small:x:309:20:small thomas j:/u1/fall91/dp168/small:/bin/ksh
solarsk:x:294:20:solarski linda m:/u1/fall91/dp168/solarsk:/bin/ksh
steill:x:269:20:steill keith r:/u1/fall91/dp270/steill:/bin/ksh
temple:x:295:20:temple linda c:/u1/fall91/dp168/temple:/bin/ksh
varvar:x:270:20:varvar anthiny j:/u1/fall91/dp270/varvar:/bin/ksh
vaas:x:325:20:vaas eric:/u1/fall91/dp270/vaas:/bin/ksh
washing:x:310:20:washington reginald:/u1/fall91/dp168/washing:/bin/ksh
```

```
weiner:x:276:20:weiner sibylle u:/u1/fall91/dp270/weiner:/bin/ksh
wiedenh:x:311:20:wiedenhofer allen e:/u1/fall91/dp168/wiedenh:/bin/ksh
wight:x:296:20:wight charles n:/u1/fall91/dp168/wight:/bin/ksh
william:x:297:20:williams tony j:/u1/fall91/dp168/william:/bin/ksh
```

$ cat file2

```
root:x:0:0:System Administrator:/usr/root:/bin/ksh
slan:x:57:57:StarGROUP Software NPP Administration:/usr/slan:
nuucp:x:10:10:0000-uucp(0000):/usr/spool/uucppublic:/usr/lib/uucp/uucico
labuucp:x:21:100:shevett´s UPC:/usr/spool/uucppublic:/usr/lib/uucp/uucico
puucp:x:22:100:princeton:/usr/spool/uucppublic:/usr/lib/uucp/uucico
juucp:x:24:100:Jon LaBadie:/usr/spool/uucppublic:/usr/lib/uucp/uucico
couucp:x:25:100:Bill Michaelson:/usr/spool/uucppublic:/usr/lib/uucp/uucico
fanuucp:x:32:100:Jo Poplawski:/usr/spool/uucppublic:/usr/lib/uucp/uucico
pjh:x:102:0:Peter J. Holsberg:/usr/pjh:/bin/ksh
pete:x:200:1:PJH:/usr/home/pete:/bin/ksh
lkh:x:250:1:lkh:/usr/lkh:/bin/ksh
shevett:x:251:1:dave shevett:/usr/shevett:/bin/ksh
moser:x:252:1:sue moser:/usr/moser:/bin/ksh
irv:x:257:1:Irv Ashkenazy:/usr/home/irv:/bin/ksh
ajh:x:258:1:Alan Pjh:/usr/home/ajh:/bin/ksh
mccollo:x:329:1:Carol McCollough:/usr/home/mccollo:/bin/ksh
rechter:x:293:20:rechter jay:/u1/fall91/dp168/rechter:/bin/ksh
reeve:x:308:20:reeve michael j:/u1/fall91/dp168/reeve:/bin/ksh
regh:x:331:20:regh jeff l:/u1/fall91/dp270/regh:/bin/ksh
sicigna:x:327:20:sicignano joseph p:/u1/fall91/dp168/sicigna:/bin/ksh
small:x:309:20:small thomas j:/u1/fall91/dp168/small:/bin/ksh
solarsk:x:294:20:solarski linda m:/u1/fall91/dp168/solarsk:/bin/ksh
steill:x:269:20:steill keith r:/u1/fall91/dp270/steill:/bin/ksh
```

$ diff file1 file2

```
2a3,5
> nuucp:x:10:10:0000-uucp(0000):/usr/spool/uucppublic:/usr/lib/uucp/uucico
> labuucp:x:21:100:shevett´s UPC:/usr/spool/uucppublic:/usr/lib/uucp/uucico
> puucp:x:22:100:princeton:/usr/spool/uucppublic:/usr/lib/uucp/uucico
7a11,13
> lkh:x:250:1:lkh:/usr/lkh:/bin/ksh
> shevett:x:251:1:dave shevett:/usr/shevett:/bin/ksh
> moser:x:252:1:sue moser:/usr/moser:/bin/ksh
18,25d23
< temple:x:295:20:temple linda c:/u1/fall91/dp168/temple:/bin/ksh
< varvar:x:270:20:varvar anthiny j:/u1/fall91/dp270/varvar:/bin/ksh
< vaas:x:325:20:vaas eric:/u1/fall91/dp270/vaas:/bin/ksh
< washing:x:310:20:washington reginald:/u1/fall91/dp168/washing:/bin/ksh
< weiner:x:276:20:weiner sibylle u:/u1/fall91/dp270/weiner:/bin/ksh
< wiedenh:x:311:20:wiedenhofer allen e:/u1/fall91/dp168/wiedenh:/bin/ksh
< wight:x:296:20:wight charles n:/u1/fall91/dp168/wight:/bin/ksh
< william:x:297:20:williams tony j:/u1/fall91/dp168/william:/bin/ksh
```

Show the difference between two files in "context" format:

```
$ cat na.1

allen christopher
babinchak david
best betty
bloom dennis
boelhower joseph
bose anita
cacossa ray
delucia joseph

$ cat na,2

allen christopher
babinchak David
best betty
boelhower joseph
bose
cacossa ray
delucia joseph

$ diff -c na.1 na.2

*** na.1        Sat Nov  9 12:57:55 1991
--- na.2        Sat Nov  9 12:58:27 1991
***************
*** 1,8 ****
  allen christopher
! babinchak david
  best betty
- bloom dennis
  boelhower joseph
! bose anita
  cacossa ray
  delucia joseph
--- 1,7 ----
  allen christopher
! babinchak David
  best betty
  boelhower joseph
! bose
  cacossa ray
  delucia joseph
```

The portion of each file that surrounds a difference is printed so that you can see what the context of the possible change is.

echo

echo prints its arguments, separated from each other by one space, and ends by printing a newline. echo can print any character supplied as "\0n" or ´\0n´ or \\0n, where *n* is the three-digit octal value of the character's ASCII code.

```
echo [ -n ] [ arg(s) ]
```

   -n   Do not print the terminal newline (for csh and BSD
                         compatibility)

Note: echo may be built into your shell or may exist as /bin/echo.

11

Examples:

Print the value of a shell environment variable:

```
$ echo $LOGNAME
```

```
pjh
```

Print a literal string:

```
$ echo This                         is      fun!
```

```
This is fun
```

Notice that the shell "eats" the extraneous whitespace before it passes the command line to the command echo.

---

ed

ed is UNIX's standard line-oriented text editor. Its importance to tool users lies in

- How it deals with regular expressions (REs)
- How its commands can be used noninteractively

ed is rarely used.

```
ed [ -s ] [ -p string ] [ -x ] [ -C ] [ file ]
```

   -C   Indicate that the input file to be edited is in encrypted
                        form.

   -p string   Prompt for input with *string*. ed normally does not
                        prompt for commands.

-s	Suppress character counts, diagnostics, and the ! prompt.
-x	Encrypt; the input file may be plain text or encrypted.

ed uses the following metacharacters within regular expressions:

Dot (.)	Matches any one character except the newline.
Star (*)	Matches zero or more one-character REs that precede it.
Square brackets ([ ])	Enclose a one-character RE that matches any character in the string enclosed. For example, [aeiou] matches any vowel.
Backslash (\)	Causes the following character to become "ordinary" if it is special, and special if it was ordinary.
Caret (^)	When used at the beginning of an RE, indicates that the RE is the first thing on the line; when used as the first character within a pair of square brackets, indicates that the one-character RE matches any character except newline and the remaining characters between the square brackets.
Dollar sign ($)	When used as the last character of an RE, indicates that the line ends with that RE.
Slash (/)	The usual delimiter that surrounds an RE in an ed command.

A one-character RE may be followed by one of the following special notations to indicate repetition:

\(m\}	Exactly *m* occurrences
\{m,\}	At least *m* occurrences
\{m,n\}	Any number of occurrences between *m* and *n*

An RE enclosed in escaped parentheses—\(and \)—is saved in a numbered buffer for subsequent retrieval with the escaped number of the buffer: \n.

An RE preceded by an escaped left angle bracket (\<) means that the RE must follow a character that is not a digit, an underscore, or a letter. The RE, on the other hand, must begin with either a digit, an underscore, or a letter. Similarly, an RE followed by an escaped right angle bracket (\>) means that the RE must precede a character that is not a digit, an underscore, or a letter.

ed commands useful for scripts have the following general syntax:

`[ line [, line ]] operation [ parameter ]`

`line [, line]`	An optional address—either a line number or a range of lines
`operation`	A one-letter command
`parameter`	An optional parameter

You can specify addresses by line numbers, using one or more of the following:

`.`	The current line
`$`	The last line
`/RE/`	The line containing the regular expression

For example:

`/cat/,$ operation`

performs the specified operations on all lines between the first one that has `cat` on it and the last line of the file.

In the following list of `ed` commands, a 1 indicates that the operation accepts an optional, one-line address, a 2 indicates that it accepts an optional, two-line address, and 1, 2 indicates that it accepts either option. `ed` commands include the following:

`a text`	1	Append `text` after the line specified
`i text`	1	Insert `text` before the line specified
`p`	1, 2	Print the indicated lines
`n`	1, 2	Print the indicated lines with line numbers
`r file`	1	Read `file` into the buffer after the specified line
`w file`	1, 2	Write all lines inclusive to `file`
`d`	1, 2	Delete all lines, inclusive
`c text`	1, 2	Delete all lines, inclusive, and append `text`
`q`		Quit
`/RE1/s/RE2/string/`		In the next line containing `RE1`, substitute `string` for the first occurrence of `RE2`

11

`g/RE1/s/RE2/string/`		In all lines containing RE1, substitute *string* for the first occurrence of RE2
`g/RE1/s/RE2/string/g`		In all lines containing RE1, substitute *string* for all occurrences of RE2
`/s/RE/string/`	1, 2	In all lines addressed, substitute *string* for the first occurrence of RE

> **Note:** For most noninteractive editing tasks, sed is better than ed. For interactive tasks, vi is better than ed. ed is rarely used.

---

egrep

egrep is a filter that performs searches much the same way as grep, but has more regular expressions.

egrep [-bcihlnv] [-e *string*] [-f *script*] *regexp* [*file(s)*]

-b	Print the block number containing each matched line
-c	Print only a count of the matching lines
-i	Ignore case distinctions
-h	Do not prefix output lines with the name(s) of the file(s) that contain the match(es)
-l	Print only the names of files containing matches
-n	Print the line number of each matched line
-v	Print all lines except those containing a match
-e *string*	Treat the next argument as a regular expression (used for an RE that begins with a -)
-f *script*	Read a list of regular expressions from a file named *script*
regexp	Search pattern as a full regular expression

egrep uses the following metacharacters in regular expressions:

Dot (.)	Matches any one character except newline.
Star (*)	Matches zero or more of the RE that precedes it.
Plus (+)	Matches one or more of the RE that precedes it.
Question mark (?)	Matches zero or one of the RE(s) that precede(s) it.
Vertical bar (¦)	Matches REs separated by ¦ with strings that match any of the REs. **Note:** Newline can be used in place of ¦.
Parentheses (( ))	Group REs to clarify the use of ¦. For example:

11

$ egrep ´Joe (Blow¦Montana)´ roster

matches Joe Blow or Joe Montana.

Square brackets ([ ])	Enclose a one-character RE that matches any character in the string enclosed. For example, [aeiou] matches any vowel.
Backslash (\)	Causes the following character to become "ordinary" if it is special, or special if it was ordinary.
Caret (^)	When used at the beginning of an RE, indicates that the RE is the first thing on the line; when used as the first character in a pair of square brackets, indicates that the one-character RE matches any character except newline and the remaining characters between the square brackets.
Dollar sign ($)	When used as the last character of an RE, indicates that the line ends with that RE.
Slash (/)	The usual delimiter that surrounds an RE in an ed command.

A one-character RE can be followed by one of the following special notations to indicate repetition:

\(m\}	Exactly *m* occurrences
\{m,\}	At least *m* occurrences
\{m,n\}	Any number of occurrences between *m* and *n*

An RE preceded by an escaped left angle bracket (\<) means that the RE must follow a character that is not a digit, an underscore, or a letter. The RE, on the other hand, must begin with either a digit, an underscore, or a letter. Similarly, an RE followed by an escaped right angle bracket (\>) means that the RE must precede a character that is not a digit, underscore, or letter.

As an example of OR, the following command searches the file roster for a line containing either the string Joe Blow or the string Montana:

```
$ egrep 'Joe Blow|Montana' roster
```

However, the following command illustrates grouping; it searches the file roster for a line containing either Joe Blow or Joe Montana:

```
$ egrep 'Joe (Blow|Montana)' roster
```

Examples:

Look for Joe Blow and Montana in the file roster:

```
$ cat roster

Marc Arturo:Trenton:NJ:08601:609-396-8765
Joe Blow:Wrightstown:NJ:08520:609-758-7057
William Jefferson:Trenton:NJ:08638:609-883-7799
Sidney Hoffman:Trenton:NJ:08638:609-298-1952
Jeremy Montana:Mercerville:08619:609-587-7041
Leon Franks:Trenton:NJ:08610:609-888-1352
Barbara Fire:Hamilton Square:NJ:08690:201-287-9015
Joe Montana:Bayonne:NJ:07002:201-823-6683
Thomas Large:Trenton:NJ:08629:215-596-0123
Richard Street:Mercerville:NJ:08619:609-587-1238

$ egrep 'Joe Blow|Montana' roster

Joe Blow:Wrightstown:NJ:08520:609-758-7057
Jeremy Montana:Mercerville:08619:609-587-7041
Joe Montana:Bayonne:NJ:07002:201-823-6683
```

Look for Joe Blow and Joe Montana in the file roster:

```
$ egrep 'Joe (Blow|Montana)' roster

Joe Blow:Wrightstown:NJ:08520:609-758-7057
Joe Montana:Bayonne:NJ:07002:201-823-6683
```

expr

expr evaluates expressions.

expr *arg(s)*

arg(s)   A list of arguments forming the following expression types:

expr1 \¦ *expr2*   Evaluates to *expr1* if neither expression is 0 or null; otherwise, evaluates to *expr2*. For example:

$ **VAR=`expr $XYZZY \¦ pjh`**

causes VAR to become the value of XYZZY if XYZZY's value is neither 0 nor null, or the value *pjh* otherwise.

expr1 \& *expr2*   Evaluates to *expr1* if neither expression is 0 or null; otherwise, evaluates to 0. For example:

$ **VAR=´expr $XYZZY \& pjh´**

causes VAR to become the value of XYZZY if XYZZY's value is neither 0 nor null (pjh is in fact a non-null string value), or the value 0 otherwise.

expr1 { =, \>, \>=, \<, \<=, != } *expr2*
Tests the values of the two expressions in a relational sense; that is, equal, greater than, greater than or equal, less than, less than or equal, and not equal. The result is 0 if the relationship is false, or 1 if it is true.

expr1 { +, -, *, /, % } *expr2*
Performs arithmetic operations— add, subtract, multiply, divide, and find the remainder.

expr1 : *expr2*   Checks whether the characters in *expr1* (a string) match those in *expr2* (an RE as in ed) and returns the number of characters matched.

Examples:

Calculate the value of an expression:

$ **expr 15 - 8**

7

Check on the number of characters matched:

$ **expr material : mat**

3

fgrep

fgrep, despite the re in its name, searches for character strings, not regular expressions. Reputed to be faster than other members of the grep family, it usually shows no speed advantage, so it is not used very often. fgrep does have one advantage over grep and egrep in that it can read a file to get the string or strings you want it to search for. Like the others, it too is a filter.

fgrep [-bchilnvx] [-e *stringfile*] [-f *script*] *string(s)* [*file(s)*]

-b	Print the block number containing each matched line
-c	Print only a count of the matching lines
-e *stringfile*	Treat the next argument as a search string (used for strings that begin with a -)
-f *script*	Read a list of strings from *script*
-h	Do not prefix output lines with the name(s) of file(s) that contain the match(es)
-i	Ignore case distinctions
-l	Print only the names of files containing matches
-n	Print the line number of each matched line
-v	Print all lines except those containing a match
-x	Print only lines that are matched in their entirety
string(s)	One or more strings separated by newline characters

Example:

Find all occurrences of the string print in the file elmedit.c:

```
$ fgrep print elmedit.c
        (void) fprintf(stderr,"\n%s: Cannot allocate %d bytes\n",
            (void) mvprintw(23,0,"%s: Cannot open \"%s\"",
                progname,filename);
        (void) mvprintw(23,10,
                (void) mvprintw(row,col,"%c",ch);
        fprintf(output,"%s\n",linebuf);
        (void) mvprintw(row,0,"%s",line);
        (void) fprintf(stderr,"\n%s: Bad argument
            count\n",progname);
```

Note that strings such as `fprint` and `mvprintw` were found.

However, any attempt to give `fgrep` a regular expression will fail:

```
$ fgrep "printf*" elmedit.c

$
```

11

file

`file` tries to determine the type of a file: text (with several variations), source code, data, executable (with several variations), and so on.

```
file [ -h ] [ -m mfile ] [ -f ffile ] [ file(s) ]

file -c [ -m mfile ]
```

-c	Check the magic file for format errors
-f *ffile*	Read a list of filenames from *ffile*
-h	Do not follow symbolic links
-m *mfile*	Use magic file *mfile* instead of /etc/magic

Example:

What kinds of files do I have in my current directory?

```
$ ls -l
```

```
total 26
-rw-r--r--  1 pjh        root       603 Jul  3  1990 SharFile.Headers
-rw-r--r--  1 pjh        root      9053 Jan 27 12:08 ee.c.uue
-rw-r--r--  1 pjh        root      6554 Jul  3  1990 elmedit.c
-rw-r--r--  1 pjh        root      9053 Jan 27 12:09 xaa
```

```
$ file *
```

```
SharFile.Headers:   c-shell commands
ee.c.uue:           uuencoded file
elmedit.c:          English text
xaa:                uuencoded file
```

As this example demonstrates, `file` can identify many different kinds of files.

find

find searches for files by criteria stated on the command line.

find *path(s)* *expr*

path(s)	One or more pathnames that indicate the starting point(s) for the search
expr	A combination of one or more of the following tests:

-atime [+¦-]*n*	Last access time was *n* days ago. -*n* means "less than *n* days ago"; +*n* means "more than *n* days ago."
-ctime [+¦-]*n*	Last time i-node was changed was *n* days ago.
-depth	Files in a directory are acted on before the directory file itself is acted on.
-exec *command*	Execute the command *command*. Use {} to represent the current path to *command*. Must be terminated with \;. For example: -exec rm {} \; means to remove all files that find located with one (or more) of its other tests.
-follow	Follow symbolic links.
-fstype *type*	All files on filesystem type *type*.
-group *group*	All files owned by group *group*.
-inum *n*	Files with i-node number *n*.
-links *n*	All files with *n* links.
-local	Search only filesystems on the local computer.
-mount	Search only mounted filesystems.
-mtime [+¦-]*n*	Last modification time was *n* days ago.

-name *pattern*	All filenames matching *pattern*. (You can use shell filename generation characters in *pattern*, but you cannot use regular expressions.)
-newer *file*	All files modified more recently than *file*.
-nogroup	All files without a valid group.
-nouser	All files without a valid user ID.
-ok *command*	Conditional exec. User must press y to execute *command*.
-perm [-]*octal*	All files with *octal* permissions (see chmod). If - is used, only the permission bits specified in *octal* are compared with the corresponding bits in each file's permission.
-print	Print found pathnames.
-prune *pattern*	Do not search below *pattern*.
-size *n*[c]	All files of size *n* times 512 bytes. If c is specified, all files of *n* bytes. *n* can be a signed or unsigned number. If *n* is unsigned, it means a file of exactly the specified size. If *n* is positive, it means a file larger than the value-specified and if *n* is negative, it means a file smaller than the specified size. For example:

-size -1000c

means a file smaller than 1000 bytes, and

-size +2

means a file larger than 1024 (2 times 512) bytes.

-type *x*	All files of type *x*, where *x* is one of the following options:

11

b	Block special files
c	Character special files
d	Directory files
f	Ordinary file
l	Symbolic links
p	"Named" pipes

-user *user*	All files owned by *user*.
\(*expr1* -o *expr2* \)	Combined options: logical OR of two expressions.
! *expr*	True if *expr* is false.

Examples:

Print the names of all files having names ending in .c in the directory tree that begins at /usr/pjh:

```
$ find /usr/pjh -name ´*.c´ -print

/usr/pjh/myfind.c
/usr/pjh/c/p4a.c
/usr/pjh/c/168q2p5.c
/usr/pjh/c/p333.c
/usr/pjh/c/side.c
/usr/pjh/c/gwyn.c
/usr/pjh/c/friedel.c
/usr/pjh/mg2a/echo.c
/usr/pjh/mg2a/help.c
/usr/pjh/mg2a/sys/bsd/fileio.c
/usr/pjh/mg2a/sys/bsd/ttyio.c
/usr/pjh/mg2a/termlib/tgoto.c
/usr/pjh/mg2a/fileio.c
/usr/pjh/mg2a/ttykbd.c
/usr/pjh/hello.c
```

Copy all files in the /u1/fall91/dp168 tree structure having names that begin with PR1A and end with .c to the current directory, but ask about each before making the copy:

```
$ find /u1/fall91/dp168 -name "PR1A*c" -ok cp {} . \;

< cp ... /u1/fall91/dp168/allen/PR1A-allen.c >?    y
< cp ... /u1/fall91/dp168/dintron/PR1A-dintron.c >?    y
< cp ... /u1/fall91/dp168/norcros/test/PR1A_norcros.c >?    n
< cp ... /u1/fall91/dp168/wight/PR1A-wight.c >?    n
< cp ... /u1/fall91/dp168/delucia/PR1A-delucia.c >?    n
< cp ... /u1/fall91/dp168/dimemmo/test/PR1A-dimemmo.c >?    n
< cp ... /u1/fall91/dp168/fuchs/PR1A-fuchs.c >?    y
```

```
< cp ... /u1/fall91/dp168/lane/PR1A-lane.c >?   y
< cp ... /u1/fall91/dp168/nadaraj/test/PR1A-nadaraj.c >?   n
< cp ... /u1/fall91/dp168/small/PR1A-small.c >?   y
```

11

fmt

fmt is a filter that provides simple formatting of text files by filling short lines from lines below and wrapping long lines.

fmt [-cs] [-w *wid*] [*file(s)*]

-c	Preserve indentation of first two lines in a paragraph. Align subsequent lines with the second line.
-s	Wrap lines only; do not fill.
-w *wid*	Set the "wrap margin" to *wid* columns. The default is 72.

Example:

Format the contents of the file info so that each line is no longer than 50 columns, and that "wrapping" occurs between words:

```
$ cat info

        Tickets are sold ONLY at the door, on Saturday, April 20 and
Sunday, April 21.  Each ticket has a stub that can be entered into the
door prize drawing.  Usually, a prize is awarded each hour the
festival is open.

$ fmt -50 info

        Tickets are sold ONLY at the door,
on Saturday, April 20 and Sunday, April 21.  Each
ticket has a stub that can be entered into the
door prize drawing.  Usually, a prize is awarded
each hour the festival is open.
```

fold

fold is a filter that wraps lines at a given column (default 80), rudely dividing words to achieve the specified wrap.

```
fold [ -w width ¦ -width ] [ file(s) ]
```

    -w *width*   Wrap lines at *width* column.

Example:

Format the contents of the file info so that each line is no longer than 50 columns:

```
$ fold -50 info

         Tickets are sold ONLY at the door, on Satu
rday, April 20 and
Sunday, April 21.  Each ticket has a stub that can
 be entered into the
door prize drawing.  Usually, a prize is awarded e
ach hour the
festival is open.
```

---

grep

grep is a filter that searches a file for a limited regular expression (as defined in ed).

```
grep [ -bcihlnsv ] RE [ file(s) ]
```

-b	Print block number containing each matched line
-c	Print only a count of the matching lines
-h	Do not prefix output lines with the name(s) of the file(s) that contain the match(es)
-i	Ignore case distinctions
-l	Print only the names of files containing matches
-n	Print the line number of each matched line
-s	Suppress error messages about nonexistent and unreadable files
-v	Print all lines except those containing a match
RE	Regular expression

grep uses the following metacharacters in regular expressions:

Dot (.)	Matches any one character except the newline.
Star (*)	Matches zero or more one-character REs that precede it.

11

Square brackets ([ ])	Enclose a one-character RE that matches any character in the string enclosed. For example, [aeiou] matches any vowel.
Backslash (\\)	Causes the following character to become "ordinary" if it is special, and special if it was ordinary.
Caret (^)	When used at the beginning of an RE, indicates that the RE is the first thing on the line; when used as the first character within a pair of square brackets, indicates that the one-character RE matches any character except newline and the remaining characters between the square brackets.
Dollar sign ($)	When used as the last character of an RE, indicates that the line ends with that RE.
Slash (/)	The usual delimiter that surrounds an RE in an ed command.

A one-character RE can be followed by one of the following special notations to indicate repetition:

\\(*m*\\}	Exactly *m* occurrences
\\{*m*,\\}	At least *m* occurrences
\\{*m*,*n*\\}	Any number of occurrences between *m* and *n*

An RE enclosed in escaped parentheses—\\(and \\)—is saved in a numbered buffer for subsequent retrieval with the escaped number of the buffer: *n*.

An RE preceded by an escaped left angle bracket (\\<) means that the RE must follow a character that is not a digit, an underscore, or a letter. The RE, on the other hand, must begin with either a digit, an underscore, or a letter. Similarly, an RE followed by an escaped right angle bracket (\\>) means that the RE must precede a character that is not a digit, an underscore, or a letter.

Example:

```
$ cat roster

Marc Arturo:Trenton:NJ:08601:609-396-8765
Joe Blow:Wrightstown:NJ:08520:609-758-7057
William Jefferson:Trenton:NJ:08638:609-883-7799
Sidney Hoffman:Trenton:NJ:08638:609-298-1952
Jeremy Montana:Mercerville:08619:609-587-7041
Leon Franks:Trenton:NJ:08610:609-888-1352
Barbara Fire:Hamilton Square:NJ:08690:201-287-9015
```

Joe Montana:Bayonne:NJ:07002:201-823-6683
Thomas Large:Trenton:NJ:08629:215-596-0123
Richard Street:Mercerville:NJ:08619:609-587-1238

$ **grep Montana roster**

Jeremy Montana:Mercerville:08619:609-587-7041
Joe Montana:Bayonne:NJ:07002:201-823-6683

11

---

head

head is a filter that prints the first 10 lines of a file.

head [*-num*] [*file(s)*]

      num   Number of lines in each file to print (if different from 10)

Example:

$ **cat names**

```
allen christopher
babinchak david
best betty
bloom dennis
boelhower joseph
bose anita
cacossa ray
chang liang
crawford patricia
crowley charles
```

$ **head -3 names**

```
allen christopher
babinchak david
best betty
```

---

id

id prints your login name, user ID, group, and group ID.

id [-a]

      -a   Report all groups to which the current user belongs

Example:

Who am I?

```
$ id
```

```
uid=102(pjh) gid=0(root)
```

11

join

`join` creates, on stdout, a new file from two related files. The relation is determined by a common field (the "join" field) on each line of the two files. The command is useful for merging line-oriented text database files.

```
join [-a num] [-e str] [-jn m] [-o list] [-t char] file1 file2
```

-a *num*	If an unpairable line is found in file *num*, output it anyway
-e *str*	Replace empty output fields with string *str*
-jn *m*	Use the *m*th field of file number *n* as the "join field"
-o *list*	Output these fields: *n.m, n.m, n.m, . . .*, where *n.m* means the *m*th field of file *n*
-t *char*	Input fields are separated by character *char* rather than whitespace (the default)

Example:

Join two files based on whatever lines have their first fields in common:

```
$ cat auto.1.1
```

```
AS   Neuman Saint
BS   Barker
CS   Carlson Miller
DS   Swazy
ES   Arther Downs Smith Straw
```

```
$ cat auto.2.1
```

```
AS   Lisle
CS   Chunk Cohen McGill
DS   Arbiter Karle Kegler Lisanti
ES   Peerson Sherman Shorn
```

```
$ join auto.1.1 auto.2.1

AS Neuman Saint Lisle
CS Carlson Miller Chunk Cohen McGill
DS Swazy Arbiter Karle Kegler Lisanti
ES Arther Downs Smith Straw Peerson Sherman Shorn
```

Notice that the output does not have a line that begins with BS because BS is not found in the first field of both files.

11

ln

ln creates hard or symbolic links by linking *fileN* to target. It is related to both cp and mv.

ln [-f] [-n] [-s] *file1* [*file(s)*] *target*

-f	Attempt to create the link regardless of permissions. Do not report errors.
-n	Do not overwrite an existing file.
-s	Create a symbolic instead of a hard link.
fileN	One or more existing files.
target	If only *file1* is specified, *target* may be a directory name or a new filename that becomes an alias of *file1*. If two more filenames are given, *target* must be a directory; new links are created in the target directory with the same filename as the original files.

Examples:

Link two files with an ordinary hard link:

```
$ ls -l

total 22
-rw-r--r--  1 pjh          root       603 Jul  3  1990 SharFile.Headers
-rw-r--r--  1 pjh          root      6554 Jul  3  1990 elmedit.c
-rw-r--r--  1 pjh          root      6554 Jan 27 12:05 xyzzy

$ ln xyzzy xyzzy.link

$ ls -l

total 22
-rw-r--r--  1 pjh          root       603 Jul  3  1990 SharFile.Headers
-rw-r--r--  1 pjh          root      6554 Jul  3  1990 elmedit.c
```

```
-rw-r--r--   2 pjh        root       6554 Jan 27 12:05 xyzzy
-rw-r--r--   2 pjh        root       6554 Jan 27 12:05 xyzzy.link
```

Notice that the link count of both xyzzy and xyzzy.link is 2.

Create a symbolic link for a file:

```
$ ln -s xyzzy xyzzy.sym
```

```
$ ls -l
```

```
total 23
-rw-r--r--   1 pjh        root        603 Jul  3  1990 SharFile.Headers
-rw-r--r--   1 pjh        root       6554 Jul  3  1990 elmedit.c
-rw-r--r--   2 pjh        root       6554 Jan 27 12:05 xyzzy
-rw-r--r--   2 pjh        root       6554 Jan 27 12:05 xyzzy.link
lrwxrwxrwx   1 pjh        root          5 Jan 27 12:05 xyzzy.sym -> xyzzy
```

Notice that creating a symbolic link does not affect the link count. Also notice the l in the first column of the permissions and the unusual name of the new file.

logname

logname prints the name of the user.

logname

Example:

```
$ logname
```

```
pjh
```

ls

ls prints the contents of directory files in various formats.

ls [-abcCdfFgilLmnopqrRstux1] [*file(s)*]

-a	List all filenames (even those beginning with .)
-b	Display unprintable characters as *nnn*, according to their ASCII codes
-c	Sort and print time of i-node change

-C   Arrange output in columns, with names sorted down the page (default unless the command is redirected to a file or piped to another command)

-d   List the directory name rather than its contents

-f   Forcibly process the named files as directories

-F   Append flag characters to the filename:

/	Directory
*	Executable
@	Symbolic link

-g   Omit the owner column from the long listing (-l) format

-i   Add the i-node number to the long listing (-l) format

-l   Long listing format; prints columns as follows per entry:

Entry type:

b	Block special file
c	Character special file
d	Directory
l	Symbolic link
m	XENIX "shared data" file
p	Named pipe special file
s	XENIX semaphore
-	Ordinary file

Permissions

Number of links

Owner's login name

Group name

Size in bytes, or, if special file, major and minor device numbers

Date and time of last modification

Filename (or, if a symbolic link, -) followed by the pathname of the referenced file

-L	List the target (the referenced file) of a symbolic link
-m	List files across the page, separated by commas
-n	Display owner and group numbers rather than names
-o	Omit the group column from the long listing format
-p	Print / after the name of a directory
-q	Show unprintable characters in filenames as ?
-r	Reverse the sort order of the listing
-R	List all subdirectories all the way down
-s	Add the size in blocks
-t	Sort the listing by date and time rather than name
-u	Sort and print using time of last access
-x	Arrange output in columns, sorted across the page
-1	Print one file per line of output

11

Example:

Print a long listing of the files in the current directory:

```
$ ls -l
```

```
total 12
-rw-r--r--   1 pjh      root          88 Feb  5 11:31 cal
-rw-r--r--   1 pjh      root         311 Feb  5 11:32 cat.eg
-rw-r--r--   1 pjh      root        1500 Feb  5 12:00 chmod-own.eg
-rw-r--r--   1 pjh      root         281 Feb  5 12:10 expr.eg
-rw-r--r--   1 pjh      root          58 Feb  5 12:07 file.022
-rw-------   1 pjh      root          41 Feb  5 12:08 file.077
----------   1 pjh      root          87 Feb  5 12:11 ls.eg
-rw-r--r--   1 pjh      root         713 Feb  5 12:08 umask
-rw-r--r--   1 pjh      root         229 Feb  5 12:05 umask.eg
```

mesg

mesg controls whether your terminal is writable by others (see write)

mesg [-n] [-y]

-n	Disable write commands to your terminal
-y	Enable write commands to your terminal

Example:

Is my terminal writable?

```
$ mesg

is_y
```

Make my terminal unwritable:

```
$ mesg n
```

Now check it:

```
$ mesg

is_n
```

mkdir

mkdir creates new directories and subdirectories in places where the user has the appropriate permissions. Newly created directories have permissions determined by the value of umask.

mkdir [-m *mode*] [-p] *path(s)*

   -m   Set access permissions to *mode* (see chmod
               [absolute mode])

   -p   Create all nonexistent parent directories

For example, suppose that you want to create a directory in your home directory's hierarchy with the full pathname $HOME/xyzzy/furball/dir, but neither xyzzy nor furball exist. Suppose further that you want dir to have 755 permission. You would enter

```
$ mkdir -m 755 -p $HOME/xyzzy/furball/dir
```

and create all three directories—$HOME/xyzzy, $HOME/xyzzy/furball, and $HOME/xyzzy/furball/dir—with each having 755 permissions.

Example:

```
$ ls -l

total 8
-rw-r--r--  1 pjh         root       603 Jul  3  1990 SharFile.Headers
-rw-r--r--  1 pjh         root      6554 Jul  3  1990 elmedit.c
```

```
$ mkdir stuff

$ ls -l

total 9
-rw-r--r--  1 pjh        root        603 Jul  3  1990 SharFile.Headers
-rw-r--r--  1 pjh        root       6554 Jul  3  1990 elmedit.c
drwxr-xr-x  2 pjh        root        512 Jan 27 12:06 stuff
```

11

more

more is a filter that prints the contents of a text file one screenful ("page") at a time. To get the next page, you must press the Spacebar in response to the prompt --More--.

more [-cdflrsuw] [-lines] [+lnum] [+/pattern] [file(s)]

-c	Clear the screen before displaying each page
-d	Display error messages instead of ringing the terminal bell
-f	Do not fold long lines
-l	Ignore formfeed ($^\wedge$L) characters, usually treated as page breaks
-r	Display control characters (such as $^\wedge$L) instead of ignoring them
-s	Display consecutive blank lines as one blank line
-u	Do not attempt to display underlining or boldface as may be specified in the file
-w	Wait for a keypress before quitting at end of file
-lines	Display lines lines per screen
+lnum	Start the display at line number lnum.
+/pattern	Start the display two lines above the first line containing pattern

more has several commands, most of which can be immediately preceded by a number (indicated in the following by N). These commands include the following:

11

*N*Spacebar	Print *N* full screens
*N*z	Same as *N*Spacebar, except that *N* becomes the default screen size
*N*Return	Print *N* additional lines
N^D	Scroll down (toward the end of the file) *N* (default 11) more lines
*N*d	Same as *N*^D
*N*s	Skip *N* lines and print a full screen
*N*f	Skip *N* full screens and print a full screen
N^B	Skip *N* full screens backwards and print a full screen
b	Same as ^B
q,Q	Quit
=	Print the current line number
v	Invoke the editor defined by the EDITOR environmental variable (default is ed) so that you can edit the file you have been reading
h	Print brief descriptions of all more commands
N/*RE*	Search for the *N*th occurrence of RE
*N*n	Search for the *N*th occurrence of the last RE
´	Jump to the place where the last search, if any, started, or to the beginning of the file
!*command*	Invoke a new shell that executes *command*

Note: You can use % as an argument to *command* to refer to the file being mored.

N:n	Skip to the *N*th file given on the command line
N:p	Skip to the *N*th previous file given on the command line
:f	Print the filename and current line number
:q, :Q	Same as q
.	Repeat the previous command

mv

mv moves files from one directory to another, or renames a file, if permissions are appropriate. mv is related to ln and cp.

```
mv [ -f ] [ -i ] file(s) target
```

-f   Ignore permissions and -i, and suppress error messages.

-i   Prompt for confirmation if a file would be overwritten.

target   New filename if only one file argument; otherwise directory name.

If *file* is a directory, *target* must be a directory on the same file system.

If *file* is an ordinary file and *target* is a file with a link count greater than 1, the links remain and *target* becomes a new file. However, if *file* and *target* are on different file systems, mv copies *file*, deletes the original, and severs all links.

Example:

Change the name of a file:

```
$ ls -l

total 23
-rw-r--r--  1 pjh        root       603 Jul  3  1990 SharFile.Headers
-rw-r--r--  1 pjh        root      6554 Jul  3  1990 elmedit.c
-rw-r--r--  2 pjh        root      6554 Jan 27 12:05 xyzzy
-rw-r--r--  2 pjh        root      6554 Jan 27 12:05 xyzzy.link
lrwxrwxrwx  1 pjh        root         5 Jan 27 12:05 xyzzy.sym -> xyzzy

$ mv xyzzy Xyzzy

$ ls -l

total 23
-rw-r--r--  1 pjh        root       603 Jul  3  1990 SharFile.Headers
-rw-r--r--  2 pjh        root      6554 Jan 27 12:05 Xyzzy
-rw-r--r--  1 pjh        root      6554 Jul  3  1990 elmedit.c
-rw-r--r--  2 pjh        root      6554 Jan 27 12:05 xyzzy.link
lrwxrwxrwx  1 pjh        root         5 Jan 27 12:05 xyzzy.sym -> xyzzy
```

11

nawk

nawk is an improved version of awk. Examples in this book were written and executed with nawk.

nawk [-F *RE*] [-v *name=value*] [´*prog*´ ¦ -f *script*] [*file(s)*]

-F *RE*	*RE* is a regular expression specifying the characters that separate fields (for example, [:,])
-v	Define variables before nawk starts
-f *script*	Name of a script containing nawk commands
prog	A nawk command script
file(s)	One or more input filenames. Use - to read standard input

nawk includes a number of built-in variables:

ARGC	The number of arguments on the command line
ARGV	An array of command-line arguments
ENVIRON	An array of environment variables that have names as subscripts
FILENAME	The name of the current file being processed
FNR	Ordinal number of the current record of the current file
FS	Input field separator RE (default is a space or tab character)
NF	Number of fields in the current record
NR	Ordinal number of the current record
OFMT	Output format for floating point numbers (default is %.6g—that is, the number will have six digits to the right of the decimal point and will be printed as, for example, either 0.001234 or 1.234000e-03, whichever requires fewer columns)
OFS	Output field separator (default is a space)
ORS	Output record separator (default is a newline)
RS	Input record separator (default is a newline)
SUBSEP	Character that separates multiple subscripts (beyond the scope of this book)

nawk includes a number of built-in functions:

close(*file*)	Close the indicated file.
command ¦ getline	Pipe the output of *command* into getline. Each succeeding use of getline retrieves the next line of output from *command*.
getline	Set $0 (an awk built-in variable) to the next record of the current input file.
getline < *file*	Set $0 to the next record of file.
getline *var*	Set *var* to the next record of the current input file.
getline *var* < *file*	Set *var* to the next record of file.
gsub(*RE*, *string*, *in*)	Substitute *string* for all occurrences of *RE* in string *in*, or in the current record.
index(*str1*, *str2*)	Return the position in string *str1* where string *str2* first occurs, or 0 if *str2* does not occur at all in *str1*.
int	Truncate to an integer.
length(*str*)	Return the length of *str*.
match(*str*, *RE*)	Return the position in string *str* where the regular expression *RE* occurs, or 0.
rand	Return a random number between 0 and 1.
split(*str*,*ra*,*RE*)	Split string *str* into array elements *ra*[1], *ra*[2], ..., *ra*[N] and return N. The separation occurs wherever *RE* occurs.
srand	Seed rand.
sprintf(*fmt*, *exp(s)*)	Format each *exp* using the format *fmt*, and return the resulting string.
sub(*RE*, *string*, *in*)	Substitute *string* for the first occurrence of *RE* in string *in*, or in the current record.
substr(*str*, *m*, *n*)	Return the *n*-character substring that begins at character number *m* of string *str*.
system(*command*)	Execute *command* and return its exit status.

11

nawk also enables users to write their own functions, using this pattern:

```
function name(arg(s))
{
        statement1
        statement2
        ...
        ...
        statementN
}
```

Examples:

See the examples for awk.

newform

newform, a filter, is a powerful formatter for text files.

```
newform [-s] [-itabspec] [-otabspec] [-bnum] [-enum] [-pnum] [-anum]
        [-f] [-cchar] [-lnum] [ file(s) ]
```

> **Note:** Options are processed in order from left to right, so that
> -e20-l40 produces a different result from -l40 -e20.

-anum	Prefix *n* characters to the beginning of each line that is not longer than length specified by -lnum (default length is 72)
-bnum	Truncate *num* characters from the beginning of the line if the line is longer than the length specified by -lnum (default length is 72)
-cchar	Set prefix/append character to *char* (default is a space)
-enum	Truncate *num* characters from the end of the line if the line is longer than the length specified by -lnum (default length is 72)
-f	Write tab specification format at the beginning of the output
-itabspec	Input tab specification: expand tabs to spaces (default is 8)
-lnum	Set effective line length to *num* characters (default is 72)

-o*tabspec*	Output tab specification: replace spaces with tabs (default is whatever is used for -i)
-p*num*	Prefix *n* characters to the beginning of each line that is not longer than length specified by -l*num* (default length is 72)
-s	Remove leading characters of each line up to the first tab, and append up to eight of them to the end of the line

11

Example:

Format the contents of the names file so that each line of the output is 50 characters long, the original contents of the line is right-justified, and leading blanks are replaced with plus signs:

```
$ cat names

allen christopher
babinchak david
best betty
bloom dennis
boelhower joseph
bose anita
cacossa ray
chang liang
crawford patricia
crowley charles


$ newform -l50 -c+ -p names

+++++++++++++++++++++++++++++++++++allen christopher
+++++++++++++++++++++++++++++++++++++babinchak david
+++++++++++++++++++++++++++++++++++++++++best betty
++++++++++++++++++++++++++++++++++++++++bloom dennis
+++++++++++++++++++++++++++++++++++++boelhower joseph
+++++++++++++++++++++++++++++++++++++++++++bose anita
++++++++++++++++++++++++++++++++++++++++++cacossa ray
++++++++++++++++++++++++++++++++++++++++++chang liang
+++++++++++++++++++++++++++++++++++crawford patricia
++++++++++++++++++++++++++++++++++++crowley charles
```

nl

nl is a filter that numbers lines on a "logical page." A logical page begins with \:\:\: followed by the header of that page, then \:\: precedes the body of the page, and \: precedes the page's footer. The footer is terminated by the next \:\:\:.

```
nl [-btype] [-ftype] [-htype] [-vstart] [-iinc] [-p] [-lnum] [-ssep]
   [-wwid] [-nfmt] [-ddelim] [file]
```

-b*type*	Body lines to be numbered, where *type* is one of the following:

	a	Number all lines
	n	No line numbering
	p*RE*	Number only lines containing the regular expression *RE*
	t	Number lines with printable text only

-d*delim*	Change the delimiter between logical page sections from the default of \: to *delim*
-f*type*	Same as -b except for footer lines (default type for footer is n)
-h*type*	Same as -b except for header lines (default type for header is n)
-i*inc*	Increment line numbers by *inc*
-l*num*	Count *num* blank lines as one
-p	Do not restart numbering at logical page breaks
-n*fmt*	Line numbering format, where *fmt* is one of the following:

	ln	Left-justified without leading zeroes
	rn	Right-justified without leading zeroes
	rz	Right-justified with leading zeroes

-s*sep*	Insert *sep* character between line number and text
-v*start*	Start numbering lines at *start*
-w*wid*	Width of line number field (default is 6)

Example:

$ **cat text**

```
NIC Mail Services                                           June 1990

This is an automated service provided by the DDN Network Information
Center.  It allows access to NIC documents and information via ordinary
electronic mail.  This is especially useful for people who do not have
access to the NIC via a direct Internet link, such as BITNET, CSNET
and UUCP sites.
```

$ **nl text**

```
1    NIC Mail Services                                  June 1990

2        This is an automated service provided by the DDN Network Information
3    Center.  It allows access to NIC documents and information via ordinary
4    electronic mail.  This is especially useful for people who do not have
5    access to the NIC via a direct Internet link, such as BITNET, CSNET
6    and UUCP sites.
```

11

passwd

passwd enables users to change their passwords, and also enables the system administrator to manage the password file. An ordinary user simply enters

$ **passwd**

The program prompts for the old password, and then prompts twice for the new one—the first time so that the user will enter it, and the second time to confirm the first entry. A system administrator would use passwd in one of the following forms:

passwd *name*

passwd [-l ¦ -d] [-f] [-n *min*] [-x *max*] [-w *warn*] *name*

passwd -s [-a]

passwd -s [*name*]

name	Change password information for user *name*
-a	Show password attributes (*min*, *max*, *warn*, and so on) for all users
-d	Delete password for *name*
-f	Force user to change the password at next login
-l	Lock password entry
-n *min*	Minimum days between password changes
-s	Show password attributes for name or current user
-w *warn*	Number of days before password expires that system should warn the user on logging in
-x *max*	Maximum days before user must change passwords

Example for an ordinary user:

```
$ passwd

Old password:
New password:
Re-enter new password:
```

Notice that none of the typed passwords appears on the screen.

paste

paste merges two (or more) files, line by line, treating the contents of each file as if they were a column of a table. It is not a filter.

```
paste [ -dlist ] file1 file(s)
```

```
paste [ -s ] [ -dlist ] file1 file(s)
```

-dlist	Use characters in list (rather than the default character tab) to concatenate lines.
-s	Merge adjacent lines of the same file. Makes a multicolumn file from the rest of the lines in a single column file.
file1 file(s)	Input filenames. Use - to read standard input.

Example:

```
$ cat f1

pjh
lkh
shevett
moser
irv
ajh
mccollo
rechter
reeve
regh

$ cat f3

102
250
251
252
```

```
257
258
329
293
308
331
```

```
$ cat f5
```

```
Peter J. Holsberg
lkh
dave shevett
sue moser
Irv Ashkenazy
Alan Pjh
Carol McCollough
rechter jay
reeve michael j
regh jeff l
```

```
$ paste f1 f3 f5
```

```
pjh       102  Peter J. Holsberg
lkh       250  lkh
shevett   251  dave shevett
moser     252  sue moser
irv       257  Irv Ashkenazy
ajh       258  Alan Pjh
mccollo   329  Carol McCollough
rechter   293  rechter jay
reeve     308  reeve michael j
regh      331  regh jeff l
```

pg

pg is a filter that browses through files one screenful ("page") at a time.

pg [*-lines*] [-p *string*] [-cefnrs] [+*lnum*] [+/*RE*/] [*file(s)*]

pg has the following command-line arguments:

-lines	Number of screen lines to use (the size of a "window")
-c	Clear the screen before each page.
-e	Do not pause at the end of each file.
-f	Do not fold lines.

-n	Accept commands without waiting for newline.
-p	Prompt string. Use %d for current page number.
-r	Disallow escaping to the shell.
-s	Display messages and prompts in "standout mode"— that is, either in brighter than normal screen characters or in inverse video.
+*lnum*	Start at line number *lnum*.
+/*RE*/	Start at the first line containing *RE*.
file(s)	Input files. Default is standard input.

pg has a number of browsing commands, most of which can be immediately preceded by an unsigned or a signed (that is, either positive or negative) number (indicated in the following example by *N*) to specify the starting point for the next display. A signed number specifies a relative starting point based on the current page or line; an unsigned number specifies an absolute starting point (that is, relative to the beginning of the current file). The commands include the following:

*N*Spacebar	Print a screenful.
*N*Return	Same as *N*Return.
*N*l	Signed: scroll the screen *N* lines.
	Unsigned: print a screenful beginning at line *N*.
N^D	Scroll half a screen.
*N*d	Same as *N*^D.
*N*f	Skip *N* full screens and print a screenful.
*N*w	Display the next window of the file. If a value is present, change the window size to *N* lines.
*N*z	Same as *N*Spacebar, except that *N* (if a value is given) becomes the default screen size.
.	Redraw the current page.
^L	Same as ..
$	Print the last page of the file.
N/*RE*/	Search for the *N*th occurrence of *RE*. (*N*, if given, must be a positive number.)
N^*RE*^	Search backwards for the *N*th occurrence of *RE*. (*N*, if given, must be a positive number.)

N?RE?	Same as *N* ^ *RE* ^
*N*n	Skip to the *N*th file given on the command line. (*N*, if given, must be a positive number.)
*N*p	Skip to the *N*th previous file given on the command line. (*N*, if given, must be a positive number.)
*N*w	Display another window.
!command	Invoke a new shell (as defined in the SHELL environment variable, or the default shell) that executes command.
q,Q	Quit.
h	Print brief descriptions of all pg commands.

11

pr

pr is a filter that formats files for printing in a variety of ways.

pr [*options*] [*file(s)*]

Here are pr's command-line options:

+num	Begin printing with page number *num*.
-cols	Print input lines in multiple columns where *cols* is the number of columns (default is 1).
-a	Print columns across the page rather than down if *cols* is greater than 1. Do not use this option with *-m*.
-d	Double-space the output lines.
-e[c]k	Expand tabs to character positions $k+1$, $2k+1$, and so on. Default is every eight columns. Use optional *c* as the tab character.
-f	Separate pages with form feeds instead of blank lines.
-F	Fold input lines to fit the column or page width.
-h header	Print string header at the top of each page.
-i[c]k	Convert whitespace to tabs, with tabs at $k+1$, $2k+1$, and so on. Use optional *c* as the tab character.
-ln	Set page length to *n* lines. Default is 66: 5 for header, 5 for footer, and 56 for body.

11

`-m`	Merge and print files, one per column, in up to eight columns across the page. Do not use with `-cols`.
`-n[c]k`	Number each line with a *k*-digit line number. Default for *k* is 5. Append *c* (if specified). to the number for spacing in place of the default tab.
`-on`	Offset each line by *n* character positions. Default is 0.
`-p`	Pause before printing each page and signal user.
`-r`	Suppress messages about files that can't be opened.
`-t`	Do not print page headings and footing lines. If used, `-t` overrides `-h` *header*.
`-ssep`	Separate columns with the single character *sep* instead of spaces.
`-wwid`	Use line width *wid* for multicolumn output (default is 72).

Examples:

> **Note:** To save space (and trees), multiple blank lines have been replaced in each instance by a single blank line.

Print the contents of the names file 17 lines per page:

```
$ pr -117 names

Sep 19 15:05 1991  names Page 1

allen christopher
babinchak david
best betty
bloom dennis
boelhower joseph
bose anita
cacossa ray

Sep 19 15:05 1991  names Page 2

chang liang
crawford patricia
crowley charles
```

Repeat, numbering each line and then printing the lines in two columns:

```
$ pr -l17 -n -2 names
```

```
Sep 19 15:05 1991   names Page 1
```

```
    1      allen christopher        8 chang liang
    2      babinchak david          9 crawford patricia
    3      best betty              10 crowley charles
    4      bloom dennis
    5      boelhower joseph
    6      bose anita
    7      cacossa ray
```

11

printf

`printf` provides for the display of formatted text strings.

`printf format [ arg(s) ]`

arg(s)	Zero or more strings to be substituted into the conversion specification.
format	A character string that contains (1) literal characters that are copied to the output, (2) zero or more conversion specifications, each requiring one *arg*, and (3) optional escape sequences.

A conversion specification consists of the character % followed by zero or more of the following items followed by the character s:

`[-]`*wid*	A number signifying the minimum number of characters to be displayed. If the actual number of characters is less than *wid*, the string is padded with blanks beginning on the left (right, if -*wid*). If the first digit of *wid* is 0, the string is padded with zeros rather than blanks.
.*max*	A number signifying the maximum number of characters to be printed.

Note: Both *wid* and *max* can each be replaced by an asterisk (*), in which case the next *arg* supplies the missing number.

Escape sequences include the following:

\n	Newline
\b	Backspace
\t	Tab
\nnn	An ASCII character having the octal code *nnn*

11

Examples:

Print a string of characters and leave the cursor at the beginning of the next line:

```
$ printf "01234567890123456789\n"
```

```
01234567890123456789
$
```

Print the value of a shell environment variable, using a format that puts the cursor on a new line:

```
$ printf "%s\n" $HOME
```

```
/usr/pjh
$
```

Print the value of a variable right-justified in a field that's 20 columns wide and leave the cursor on a new line:

```
$ printf "%20s\n" $HOME
```

```
            /usr/pjh
$
```

Print the same thing but left-justified:

```
$ printf "%-20s\n" $HOME
```

```
/usr/pjh
$
```

Print the first four characters of the value, right-justified in a 20-column field:

```
$ printf "%20.4s\n" $HOME
```

```
                /usr
$
```

ps

11

ps reports on the status of active processes. It is one of the few UNIX commands that prints a heading for each column of information. This makes it more difficult to use in a pipe.

```
ps [ -edalfcj ] [ -r sysname ] [ -t termlist ] [ -u uidlist ]
    [ -p proclist ] [ -g grplist] [ -s sidlist ]
```

With no options, ps reports on processes associated with the terminal that invoked ps; that is, the "controlling terminal." Items in a list can be either (1) separated by commas or (2) enclosed in double quotation marks and separated by spaces or commas.

The following are ps's options:

-a	List all processes associated with a terminal.
-c	Show scheduler properties.
-d	List all processes except session leaders.
-e	List all processes (the default is your processes only).
-f	Use full listing format.
-j	Show session-ID and process-group ID
-g *grplist*	List only processes in the process groups in *grplist*. **Note:** *grplist* is a list of numbers.
-l	Long listing format (more info than -f).
-p *proclist*	List only process-IDs given in *proclist*. **Note:** *proclist* is a list of numbers.
-s *sidlist*	List only session leaders in *sidlist*.
-t *termlist*	List only processes using the specified terminal. For *termlist*, give full terminal names or tty suffixes.
-u *uidlist*	List only processes owned by the specified users. For *uidlist*, give user names or IDs.

Column headings include the following:

ADDR	The address in memory of the process
C	The CPU utilization, used by the scheduler

CLS	The scheduling class of the process
COMMAND	The name of the command that the process came from
F	Flags associated with the process, in hexadecimal and computed additively:

00	Process has terminated
01	System process, always in primary memory
02	Parent is tracing the process
04	Parent has stopped process and is waiting
08	Process is in primary memory
10	Same as 08 and is waiting for an event to complete

NI	The "nice" value, used in computation of the priority
S	The state of the process; the process is one of the following states:

I	Being created ("idle")
O	Running
R	In the run queue ("runnable")
S	Waiting for an event to complete ("sleeping")
T	Stopped because the parent is tracing it ("traced")
X	Waiting for more memory to be given to it
Z	Terminated but the parent is not waiting ("zombie")

PID	The process's ID
PPID	The PID of the parent process
PRI	Priority of the process
STIME	The time the process started
SZ	The size of the process's image in main memory

TIME	The cumulative execution time (in CPU seconds) of the process
TTY	The controlling terminal of the process
UID	The user ID of the process owner
WCHAN	The address of the event that the process is waiting for

11

Example:

```
$ ps

  PID TTY      TIME COMMAND
 3084 slan04   0:00 ttysrv
 3085 slan04   0:02 ksh
 3125 slan04   0:00 ps
```

Notice that ps reports on itself.

rm

If you have the appropriate permissions, you can use rm to remove files. In general, there is no way in UNIX to "unremove" a file that has been acted on by rm, so use rm with caution.

```
rm [ -rfi ] file(s)
```

| -f | Unconditionally remove all files and suppress all error messages and warnings. |

> **Note:** If the directory is write-protected, files are not removed.

| -i | Inquire whether each file encountered should be deleted. Respond y or n as appropriate. |
| -r | Recursively remove subdirectories and files of each directory file specified. Symbolic links are not followed. |

Example:

Remove all files having names that begin with an *x* or an *X*:

```
$ ls -l

total 23
-rw-r--r--  1 pjh       root       603 Jul  3  1990 SharFile.Headers
```

```
-rw-r--r--  2 pjh        root         6554 Jan 27 12:05 Xyzzy
-rw-r--r--  1 pjh        root         6554 Jul  3  1990 elmedit.c
-rw-r--r--  2 pjh        root         6554 Jan 27 12:05 xyzzy.link
lrwxrwxrwx  1 pjh        root            5 Jan 27 12:05 xyzzy.sym ->
xyzzy

$ rm [Xx]*

$ ls -l

total 8
-rw-r--r--  1 pjh        root          603 Jul  3  1990 SharFile.Headers
-rw-r--r--  1 pjh        root         6554 Jul  3  1990 elmedit.c
```

rmdir

rmdir removes empty directories.

rmdir [-p] [-s] *path(s)*

-p   Remove all parent directories that become empty

-s   Suppress error messages caused by -p

Example:

```
$ ls -l

total 9
-rw-r--r--  1 pjh        root          603 Jul  3  1990 SharFile.Headers
-rw-r--r--  1 pjh        root         6554 Jul  3  1990 elmedit.c
drwxr-sr-x  2 pjh        root          512 Jan 27 12:06 stuff

$ rmdir stuff

$ ls -l

total 8
-rw-r--r--  1 pjh        root          603 Jul  3  1990 SharFile.Headers
-rw-r--r--  1 pjh        root         6554 Jul  3  1990 elmedit.c
```

sdiff

sdiff prints the differences between two files in a side-by-side format.

sdiff [-w *num*] [-l] [-s] [-o *output*] *file1 file2*

-l	Print only the left side of identical lines.
-o *output*	Build a user-controlled merge into file output. The user is prompted with % and responds with one of the following:

e	Edit a new file
e b	Edit the concatenation of left and right columns before sending to output
e l	Edit the left column before sending to output
e r	Edit the right column before sending to output
l	Append the left column to output
q	Exit
r	Append the right column to output
s	Do not print identical lines from this point on ("silent" mode)
v	Turn off silent mode

-s	Suppress identical lines.
-w *num*	Output line width (default is 130).

Example:

$ **cat na.1**

```
allen christopher
babinchak david
best betty
bloom dennis
boelhower joseph
bose anita
cacossa ray
delucia joseph
```

$ **cat na,2**

```
allen christopher
babinchak David
best betty
boelhower joseph
bose
cacossa ray
delucia joseph
```

11

```
$ sdiff -w80 na.1 na.2

allen christopher                       allen christopher
babinchak david                     |   babinchak David
best betty                              best betty
boelhower joseph                        boelhower joseph
bose anita                          |   bose
cacossa ray                             cacossa ray
delucia joseph                          delucia joseph
```

sed

sed, a filter, is the UNIX "stream" editor. That is, sed edits the input file by reading commands from another file—the script file—and applies the commands to the input file without human intervention. sed reads the input file, usually one line at a time, into an area of memory called the "pattern space"; the editor then applies all script commands having addresses that are in the pattern space to the contents of the pattern space, and then copies the modified pattern space to stdout.

Simple commands do not require a script file but may be written on the command line.

```
sed [ -n ] [ -e command ] [ -e command ] ... [ -f script ] [ file(s) ]

sed [ -n ] command command ... [ file(s) ]
```

-e	Needed only when there are multiple commands on the command line; each must be prefaced with -e
-n	Suppress default printing of result lines

A script consists of one or more commands, each having the general form

```
[ addr1 [ , addr2 ] ] command [ arg(s) ]
```

addrN is one of the following:

- An input file line number

- A $ to indicate the last line of the input file

- A regular expression

If both addresses are omitted, every pattern space is acted on. If one address is used, only the one pattern space that matches the address is acted on. If both addresses are used, all pattern spaces between the first one that matches the first address through the next one that matches the second address, inclusive, are acted on.

sed's regular expressions are like ed's except that

- \n matches a newline in the pattern space

- . matches any character except the terminal newline in the pattern space

commands and their *arg(s)*—where appropriate—are the following:

a\	
text	Send *text* to stdout before reading the next input line.
b *lbl*	Branch to the : command having the label *lbl*.
c\	
text	Delete the pattern space and send *text* to stdout.
d	Delete the pattern space.
D	Delete the pattern from its beginning to its first newline.
g	Replace the pattern space with the hold space (see h and H).
G	Append the hold space to the pattern space.
h	Destructively copy the pattern space to the hold space. (The hold space is another area of memory that sed uses as for temporary storage.)
H	Append the pattern space to the hold space.
i\	
text	Send *text* to stdout.
l	Print the pattern space with nonprinting characters replaced by their octal ASCII codes and with long lines folded.
n	Copy the pattern space to stdout and replace it with the next input line.
N	Append a newline and the next input line to the pattern space; increment the line count.
p	Copy the pattern space to stdout.
P	Copy the pattern from its beginning to its first newline to stdout.
q	Quit.

11

r *file*	Read *file* and place its contents in stdout before reading the next input line.
s/*RE*/*str*/*flag(s)*	Substitute *str* for *RE* in the pattern space, subject to the following flags:

	N	Substitute *str* for the *N*th occurrence of *RE*
	g	Substitute *str* for all occurrences of *RE*
	p	Print the pattern space if a substitution occurred
	w *file*	Append the pattern space to *file* if a substitution occurred

t *lbl*	Branch to the : command having the label *lbl* if any substitutions occurred since the most recent reading of an input line or execution of a t *lbl* command.
w *file*	Append the pattern space to file. **Note:** The first execution of w *file* clears *file* if it exists, or creates it if it does not.
x	Exchange the pattern and hold spaces.
y/*str1*/*str2*/	Replace characters in *str1* with the corresponding characters of *str2*.
! *command*	Apply command only to lines not matched by its address(es).
: *lbl*	Establishes a label *lbl* for the given line.
=	Print the number (and then a newline) of the current line in stdout.
{	Execute a group of commands (terminated with }) in a matching pattern space.
#	If the first character on a line, ignore the line, because it is a comment—unless the second character is an n. #n suppresses the default output and the rest of the characters on the line are ignored.

Examples:

Remove lines 3 through 6 from the file refile.1 (actually, the command means "print all lines except 3 through 6"):

```
$ cat refile.1
```

```
 1     A regular expression is a sequence of characters taken
 2     from the set of uppercase and lowercase letters, digits,
 3     punctuation marks, etc., plus a set of special regular
 4     expression operators. Some of these operators may remind
 5     you of file name matching, but be forewarned: in general,
 6     regular expression operators are different from the
 7     shell metacharacters we discussed in Chapter 1.
 8
 9     The simplest form of a regular expression is one that
10     includes only letters. For example, the would match only
11     the three-letter sequence t, h, e. This pattern is found
12     in the following words: the, therefore, bother. In other
13     words, wherever the regular expression pattern is found
14     -- even if it is surrounded by other characters --, it will
15     be matched.
```

```
$ sed '3,6d' refile.1
```

```
 1     A regular expression is a sequence of characters taken
 2     from the set of uppercase and lowercase letters, digits,
 7     shell metacharacters we discussed in Chapter 1.
 8
 9     The simplest form of a regular expression is one that
10     includes only letters. For example, the would match only
11     the three-letter sequence t, h, e. This pattern is found
12     in the following words: the, therefore, bother. In other
13     words, wherever the regular expression pattern is found
14     -- even if it is surrounded by other characters --, it will
15     be matched.
```

Remove all lines that contain the regular expression regu:

```
$ sed '/regu/d' refile.1
```

```
 2     from the set of uppercase and lowercase letters, digits,
 4     expression operators. Some of these operators may remind
 5     you of file name matching, but be forewarned: in general,
 7     shell metacharacters we discussed in Chapter 1.
 8
10     includes only letters. For example, the would match only
11     the three-letter sequence t, h, e. This pattern is found
12     in the following words: the, therefore, bother. In other
14     -- even if it is surrounded by other characters --, it will
15     be matched.
```

Remove all sets of lines that begin with a line that contains the regular expression char and end with the regular expression letter:

```
$ sed '/char/,/letter/d' refile.1
```

```
 3     punctuation marks, etc., plus a set of special regular
 4     expression operators. Some of these operators may remind
```

```
 5    you of file name matching, but be forewarned: in general,
 6    regular expression operators are different from the
11    the three-letter sequence t, h, e. This pattern is found
12    in the following words: the, therefore, bother. In other
13    words, wherever the regular expression pattern is found
```

11 sort

sort is a filter that sorts and/or merges *database* files. These are files having lines that are divided into fields by a specified delimiter character (sort's default is the Tab or Spacebar).

```
sort [-cmu] [-o output] [-y mem] [-z len] [-dfiMnr] [-b] [-t sep]
     [+pos1 [-pos2]] [file(s)]
```

-b	Ignore leading blanks in a field. Can attach to all fields or to individual fields.
-c	Test whether the input file is already sorted.
-d	Use dictionary order (only letters, digits, and blanks).
-f	Ignore case distinctions.
-i	Ignore nonprintable characters.
-m	Simply merge the already-sorted files.
-M	Compare as months, such as JAN, FEB, and MAR.
-n	Sort by numeric values in the fields (default is to sort as strings, which puts 329 before 35).
-o *output*	Write the sorted output to file output.
-r	Reverse the sort order.
-t *sep*	Use *sep* as the field separator character.
-u	Discard duplicate records.
-y *mem*	Start the sort with *mem* kilobytes of memory.
-z *len*	Longest line accepted from the input file(s).
+*pos1*	Starting position of field. +*pos1* means skip field *pos1*; therefore, to sort beginning with the second field, you would specify +1.
-*pos2*	Ending position of field. If omitted, the rest of the line is used. **Note:** Fields can be further subdivided by *m*.*n* to represent the *n*th character in the *m*th field.

Example:

Sort the file auto on the entire line:

$ cat auto

```
ES   Arther   85   Honda     Prelude   49.412
BS   Barker   90   Nissan    300ZX     48.209
AS   Saint    88   BMW       M-3       46.629
ES   Straw    86   Honda     Civic     49.543
DS   Swazy    87   Honda     CRX-Si    49.693
ES   Downs    83   VW        GTI       47.133
ES   Smith    86   VW        GTI       47.154
AS   Neuman   84   Porsche   911       47.201
CS   Miller   84   Mazda     RX-7      47.291
CS   Carlson  88   Pontiac   Fiero     47.398
DS   Kegler   84   Honda     Civic     47.429
ES   Sherman  83   VW        GTI       48.489
DS   Arbiter  86   Honda     CRX-Si    48.628
DS   Karle    74   Porsche   914       48.826
ES   Shorn    87   VW        GTI       49.357
CS   Chunk    85   Toyota    MR2       49.558
CS   Cohen    91   Mazda     Miata     50.046
DS   Lisanti  73   Porsche   914       50.609
CS   McGill   83   Porsche   944       50.642
AS   Lisle    72   Porsche   911       51.030
ES   Peerson  86   VW        Golf      54.493
```

$ sort auto

```
AS   Lisle    72   Porsche   911       51.030
AS   Neuman   84   Porsche   911       47.201
AS   Saint    88   BMW       M-3       46.629
BS   Barker   90   Nissan    300ZX     48.209
CS   Carlson  88   Pontiac   Fiero     47.398
CS   Chunk    85   Toyota    MR2       49.558
CS   Cohen    91   Mazda     Miata     50.046
CS   McGill   83   Porsche   944       50.642
CS   Miller   84   Mazda     RX-7      47.291
DS   Arbiter  86   Honda     CRX-Si    48.628
DS   Karle    74   Porsche   914       48.826
DS   Kegler   84   Honda     Civic     47.429
DS   Lisanti  73   Porsche   914       50.609
DS   Swazy    87   Honda     CRX-Si    49.693
ES   Arther   85   Honda     Prelude   49.412
ES   Downs    83   VW        GTI       47.133
ES   Peerson  86   VW        Golf      54.493
ES   Sherman  83   VW        GTI       48.489
ES   Shorn    87   VW        GTI       49.357
ES   Smith    86   VW        GTI       47.154
ES   Straw    86   Honda     Civic     49.543
```

11

split

split is a filter divides a file into pieces. The default is to create files that are each 1000 lines long.

```
split [ -n ] [ file [ name ] ]
```

-n	Output file size in lines.
file	Input file; use - to read standard input.
name	Prefix for output filenames (default is x). The suffixes for output filenames begin with aa, then ab, ac, ..., az, ba, bb, and so on.

Example:

Split the file ch10.asc into smaller files, each having no more than 1,000 lines:

```
$ wc -l ch10.asc

   1518 ch10.asc

$ ls -l ch10.asc

-rw-r--r--    1 pjh       root         68303 Feb  5 11:28 ch10.asc

$ split ch10.asc

$ ls -l xa[ab]

-rw-r--r--    1 pjh       root         45774 Feb  5 19:16 xaa
-rw-r--r--    1 pjh       root         22529 Feb  5 19:16 xab

$ wc -l xa[ab]
   1000 xaa
    518 xab
   1518 total
```

strings

strings prints strings that are four or more characters long that are found in a file. strings is mostly used on nontext files—that is, binary files—because better tools than strings are available for examining the contents of a text file.

```
strings [ -a ] [ -o ] [ -n number ¦ -number ] file(s)
```

-a   Look everywhere (default is initialized data area)

-n   Use number as minimum string length (default 4)

-o   Print the offset of each string found

Example:

Find the strings in the crypt program file (if you try this on your system, you may see output in a slightly different form):

```
$ strings /bin/crypt
```

```
.text
.data
.bss
.comment
An attempt was made to execute the
 program.  This program is installed as part of the
 package which you do not have on your system.  Please install
 this package before attempting to run this program again.
 Consult your 'Operations/System Administration Guide' for
 further assistance.
message -d "
Security Administration
" 1>&2
/bin/sh
         (((((                        H
 !"#$%&'()*+,-./0123456789:;<=>?@abcdefghijklmnopqrstuvwxyz[\]^_
`ABCDEFGHIJKLMNOPQRSTUVWXYZ{¦}~
CHRCLASS
ascii
/lib/chrclass/
@(#)/bin/crypt.nf.sl 1.1 3.2c 06/15/89 48387 AT&T-SF
```

You can see the warning message that's built into the program. Also, the last line gives you clues as to the version of crypt with which you're working.

tail

tail is a filter that prints the end of a file.

```
tail [ ±number [lbcf] ] [ file ]
```

```
tail [ -lbcf ] [ file ]
```

```
tail [ ±number [lbcr] ] [ file ]
```

```
tail [ -lbcr ] [ file ]
```

±*number*	The distance from the end (-*number*) or from the beginning (+*number*) to start copying the input file to stdout. The units for number are either blocks (-b), characters (-c), or lines (-l). The default is -l. The default value of number is -10.
-f	Follow the file. Read the contents of the file every second and print any lines that have been added to file while `tail` is being executed.
-r	Copy in reverse order, that is, from the starting point to the beginning of the file.

Example:

Print the last three lines of the names file:

```
$ cat names

allen christopher
babinchak david
best betty
bloom dennis
boelhower joseph
bose anita
cacossa ray
chang liang
crawford patricia
crowley charles
cuddy michael
czyzewski sharon
delucia joseph

$ tail -3 names

cuddy michael
czyzewski sharon
delucia joseph
```

tar

tar gathers up bunches of files and places them into one "archive" file. Originally, tar was intended for use with backup magnetic tape devices, so the name was derived from "*tape ar*chiver."

```
tar [-]c[vwf target b num L[Ns]]  file(s)

tar -r[vwf target b num L[Ns]]  file(s)

tar -t[vf target L[Ns]] [ file(s) ]

tar -u[vwf target b num L[Ns]]  file(s)

tar -x[lmovwf target L[Ns]] [ file(s) ]
```

11

tar has five major, mutually exclusive options:

[-]c	Create a new archive file
[-]r	Replace named files in the archive
[-]t	Print a table of contents of the archive
[-]u	Update the archive
[-]x	Extract named files from the archive

The options are modified by the following:

b num	Use num as the blocking factor. Significant for character special files but is usually omitted when dealing with ordinary files and directories.
f target	Use file target for reading or writing. target can be an ordinary file, a device file, or - (stdin or stdout, depending on whether an archive is being created or outputting its contents).
l	Report an error when unable to resolve all links.
L	Follow symbolic links.
m	Do not restore original file modification times.
Ns	Read or write tape drive N at speed s (1 = low, m = medium, h = high); for example, specify 5h to read /dev/mt/5h.
o	Set file owner and group to that of the user.
v	List each file processed.
w	User confirmation required for each action.

Example:

Collect all files having names beginning with na into an archive called names.tar:

```
$ ls -l na*
```

```
-rw-r--r--   1 pjh       root        113 Nov  9 12:57 na
-rw-r--r--   1 pjh       root        100 Nov  9 16:40 na.1
-rw-r--r--   1 pjh       root         95 Nov  9 12:58 na.2
-rw-r--r--   1 pjh       root        190 Sep 19 15:05 names
-rw-r--r--   1 pjh       root        177 Nov  3 18:26 names.1
-rw-r--r--   1 pjh       root        172 Nov  3 18:26 names.2
-rw-r--r--   1 pjh       root        186 Nov  6 15:06 names.3
-rw-r--r--   1 pjh       root       1000 Nov 10 11:28 names.scr
```

Create a tar archive from the files called na*, printing each name as it is copied into names.tar, the archive file:

```
$ tar -cvf names.tar na*
```

```
a na 1 tape blocks
a na.1 1 tape blocks
a na.2 1 tape blocks
a names 1 tape blocks
a names.1 1 tape blocks
a names.2 1 tape blocks
a names.3 1 tape blocks
a names.scr 2 tape blocks
```

The a at the beginning of each line means that tar is adding the file to the archive.

```
$ ls -l na*
```

```
-rw-r--r--   1 pjh       root        113 Nov  9 12:57 na
-rw-r--r--   1 pjh       root        100 Nov  9 16:40 na.1
-rw-r--r--   1 pjh       root         95 Nov  9 12:58 na.2
-rw-r--r--   1 pjh       root        190 Sep 19 15:05 names
-rw-r--r--   1 pjh       root        177 Nov  3 18:26 names.1
-rw-r--r--   1 pjh       root        172 Nov  3 18:26 names.2
-rw-r--r--   1 pjh       root        186 Nov  6 15:06 names.3
-rw-r--r--   1 pjh       root       1000 Nov 10 11:28 names.scr
-rw-r--r--   1 pjh       root       9728 Nov 10 11:59 names.tar
```

Notice how big names.tar is—much bigger than just the sum of the file size of the tared files! tar has added much "archiving" information to each file and has assigned each file an integral number of blocks.

The following command displays the names of the files in the names.tar archive file:

```
$ tar -tf names.tar
```

```
na
na.1
na.2
names
names.1
names.2
names.3
names.scr
```

The following command provides more detail:

```
$ tar -tvf names.tar
```

```
tar: blocksize = 19
rw-r--r--102/0      113 Nov  9 12:57 1991 na
rw-r--r--102/0      100 Nov  9 16:40 1991 na.1
rw-r--r--102/0       95 Nov  9 12:58 1991 na.2
rw-r--r--102/0      190 Sep 19 15:05 1991 names
rw-r--r--102/0      177 Nov  3 18:26 1991 names.1
rw-r--r--102/0      172 Nov  3 18:26 1991 names.2
rw-r--r--102/0      186 Nov  6 15:06 1991 names.3
rw-r--r--102/0     1000 Nov 10 11:28 1991 names.scr
```

tee

tee is a filter that sits between elements of a pipe and passes all information from stdin to stdout without any processing. It also siphons off a copy of what is passing through to one or more files.

```
tee [ -i ] [ -a ] [ file(s) ]
```

-a	Append output to *file(s)* instead of overwriting
-i	Ignore interrupts
file(s)	Files in which to receive the siphoned-off input

Example:

Count the number of users now logged on and save the output of the who command in the file called users:

```
$ who ¦ tee users ¦ wc -l
```

```
3
```

```
$ cat users
```

```
juucp      tty00       Sep 28 11:13
joe        ttyaB       Sep 28 12:04
pjh        slan05      Sep 28 12:08
```

test

test evaluates conditional expressions and returns an appropriate exit status.

```
test expr
[ expr ]
```

   expr may be one or more of the following classes of expressions. There are three classes of these expressions: file tests, string tests, and numerical tests. The explanation indicates the condition for which test returns 0 (true).

-b *file*	*file* is a block-special file
-c *file*	*file* is a character-special file
-d *file*	*file* is a directory
-f *file*	*file* is an ordinary file
-g *file*	*file* has the set-group-ID bit set
-h *file*	*file* is a symbolic link
-k *file*	*file* has the sticky bit set
-p *file*	*file* is a named pipe
-r *file*	*file* is readable by you
-s *file*	*file* has a size greater than zero
-t [*fd*]	*file* descriptor *fd* (the default is 1) is a terminal
-u *file*	*file* has the set-user-ID bit set
-w *file*	*file* is writable by you
-x *file*	*file* has execute (search, if it is a directory file) permission for you
-n *s1*	String *s1* has nonzero length
-z *s1*	String *s1* is zero length
s1 = *s2*	Strings *s1* and *s2* are identical
s1 != *s2*	Strings *s1* and *s2* are not identical
s1	String *s1* is not null
n1 -eq *n2*	Integer *n1* is equal to *n2*
n1 -ne *n2*	Integer *n1* is not equal to *n2*
n1 -lt *n2*	Integer *n1* is less than *n2*
n1 -le *n2*	Integer *n1* is less than or equal to *n2*

n1 -gt *n2*   Integer *n1* is greater than *n2*

n1 -ge *n2*   Integer *n1* is greater than or equal to *n2*

The following are operators for combining tests:

!   Unary negation

-              Binary *and*

-o   Binary *or*

(expr)   Grouping parentheses

The following example shows how these operators can be used:

```
[ -c file -o -b file ]
```

This example determines whether `file` is a special file of either type.

Example:

test is normally used in a shell script as part of an `if` statement. Here is a sample script (if you try this on your computer, replace x with the name of an ordinary file; xx with a name that doesn't exist in the current directory; and xxx with the name of a subdirectory):

```
$ cat tests
```

```
if [ -d "$1" ]
then
     echo "$1 is a directory"
elif [ -f "$1" ]
then
     echo "$1 is a regular file"
elif [ -c "$1" -o -b "$1" ]
then
     echo "$1 is a special file"
else
     echo "I don't know what $1 is!"
fi
```

```
$ chmod +x tests
```

```
$ tests x
```

```
x is a regular file
```

```
$ tests xx
```

```
I don't know what xx is!
```

```
$ tests xxx
```

```
xxx is a directory
```

tr

tr is a filter that changes characters.

tr [-cds] [*search* [*subst*]]

-c	Complement the set of characters in *search*
-d	Delete all input characters in *search*
-s	Delete repetitions of characters in *subst*
search	Characters to look for in the input
subst	Corresponding output for each character in *search*

Two special abbreviations are allowed in both *search* and *subst*:

[*char1-char2*]	Represents the string of consecutive ASCII characters that range from *char1* to *char2*. **Note:** The ASCII code for *char1* must be smaller than the ASCII code for *char2*. That is, [A-M], [a-z], [2-6], and [C-F] are all acceptable, but [Z-A], [9-7], and [m-d] are not.
[*char*n*]	Repeats *char n* times. **Note:** If *n* begins with 0, tr interprets *n* as an octal number rather than a base ten value.

A nonprinting character can be represented by using its escaped octal ASCII code, or its shell escape sequence. For example, a newline can be represented to tr as either \012 or \n.

Examples:

Perform a simple encryption on the names file by switching letters (a becomes n, b becomes o, and so on):

```
$ cat names

allen christopher
babinchak david
best betty
bloom dennis
boelhower joseph
bose anita
cacossa ray
chang liang
crawford patricia
crowley charles
```

```
cuddy michael
czyzewski sharon
delucia joseph
```

```
$ tr ´[a-z]´ ´vnopqrstuvwxyzabcdefghijklm´ < names
```

```
nyyra puevfgbcure
onovapunx qnivq
orfg orggl
oybbz qraavf
obryubjre wbfrcu
obfr navgn
pnpbffn enl
punat yvnat
penjsbeq cngevpvn
pebjyrl puneyrf
phqql zvpunry
pmlmrjfxv funeba
qryhpvn wbfrcu
```

Delete all uppercase letters from a file:

```
$ cat some.caps
```

```
AllEn ChristophEr
BABinChAk DAviD
BEst BEtty
Bloom DEnnis
BoElhowEr josEph
BosE AnitA
CACossA rAy
ChAng liAng
CrAwforD pAtriCiA
CrowlEy ChArlEs
CuDDy miChAEl
CzyzEwski shAron
DEluCiA josEph
```

```
$ tr -d ´[A-Z]´ < some.caps
```

```
lln hristophr
inhk vi
st tty
loom nnis
olhowr josph
os nit
oss ry
hng ling
rwfor ptrii
rowly hrls
uy mihl
zyzwski shron
lui josph
```

11

Delete everything except uppercase letters and newlines from a file:

```
$ tr -dc '\012[A-Z]' < some.caps
```

```
AECE
BABCADAD
BEBE
BDE
BEEE
BEAA
CACAA
CAA
CADACA
CECAE
CDDCAE
CEA
DECAE
```

umask

umask sets the default permissions for newly created files.

umask [*UGO*]

If *UGO* is omitted, the system prints the current value of umask.

UGO   The inverse of the "read-write-execute/search" permission number for each of user, group, and others. In other words, umask's value indicates "denials" rather than permissions. The values are the following:

0   Nothing is denied

1   Execute/search permission is denied

2   Write permission is denied

4   Read permission is denied

Thus a umask value of 022 denies write permission to all but the owner.

> **Note:** If umask is 000, ordinary files are created with 666 permissions, and directory files with 777 permissions.

Example:

Create an ordinary file with the default value of umask, change that value, and create another ordinary file:

```
$ umask

022

$ cat > file.022

Four score and seven years ago, I was much younger!
^d

$ ls -l file.022

-rw-r--r--  1 pjh       root            58 Feb  5 12:07 file.022

$ umask 077

$ cat > file.077

To be or not to be is just one of my questions.
^d

$ ls -l file.0*

-rw-r--r--  1 pjh       root            58 Feb  5 12:07 file.022
-rw-------  1 pjh       root            41 Feb  5 12:08 file.077
```

---

uncompress

```
uncompress [ -cv ] file(s)
```

-c	Write to standard output
-v	Print the percent reduction of each file
file(s)	Files to be uncompressed

Example:

Compress and then uncompress the file no.blanks:

```
$ ls -l no.blanks*

-rw-r--r--  1 pjh       root           742 Sep 30 14:03 no.blanks

$ compress no.blanks
```

```
$ ls -l no.blanks*

-rw-r--r--   1 pjh       root           511 Sep 30 14:03 no.blanks.Z

$ uncompress no.blanks.Z

$ ls -l no.blanks*

-rw-r--r--   1 pjh       root           742 Sep 30 14:03 no.blanks
```

uniq

uniq is a filter that removes duplicate lines from a sorted text file.

uniq [-udc [+n] [-n]] [infile [outtfile]]

-c	Print unique lines with a count of how many times each appeared in the input.
-d	Output one copy of just the repeated lines.
+n	Ignore the first *n* characters of each line.
-n	Ignore the first *n* fields of each line. Tabs and spaces separate fields.
-u	Output only the lines that were not repeated.

Example:

Print each unique line in the sorted file ngs and prefix each with a count of how many times it appeared:

$ **cat ngs**

```
comp.archives
comp.bugs.sys5
comp.databases
comp.databases.informix
comp.lang.c
comp.lang.c
comp.lang.c
comp.lang.c
comp.lang.c++
comp.lang.c++
comp.lang.postscript
comp.laserprinters
comp.mail.maps
```

```
comp.sources.3b
comp.sources.3b
comp.sources.3b
comp.sources.bugs
comp.sources.d
comp.sources.misc
comp.sources.reviewed
comp.sources.unix
comp.sources.unix
comp.sources.wanted
comp.std.c
comp.std.c
comp.std.c++
comp.std.c++
comp.std.unix
comp.std.unix
comp.sys.3b
comp.sys.att
comp.sys.att
comp.unix.questions
comp.unix.shell
comp.unix.sysv386
comp.unix.wizards
```

$ uniq -c ngs

```
   1 comp.archives
   1 comp.bugs.sys5
   1 comp.databases
   1 comp.databases.informix
   4 comp.lang.c
   2 comp.lang.c++
   1 comp.lang.postscript
   1 comp.laserprinters
   1 comp.mail.maps
   3 comp.sources.3b
   1 comp.sources.bugs
   1 comp.sources.d
   1 comp.sources.misc
   1 comp.sources.reviewed
   2 comp.sources.unix
   1 comp.sources.wanted
   2 comp.std.c
   2 comp.std.c++
   2 comp.std.unix
   1 comp.sys.3b
   2 comp.sys.att
   1 comp.unix.questions
   1 comp.unix.shell
   1 comp.unix.sysv386
   1 comp.unix.wizards
```

uudecode

uudecode, a filter, is the opposite of uuencode: it converts a uuencoded file to its original form (most likely, binary). The name of the uudecoded file is taken from information on the first line of the uuencoded file.

uudecode [*file*]

    file   File to be uudecoded

Example:

Decode the file ee.c.uue that was previously encoded with uuencode:

```
$ ls -l ee.c*
```

```
-rw-r--r--  1 holsberg     9053 Jan 27 12:08 ee.c.uue
```

Let's look at the beginning of the encoded file:

```
$ more ee.c.uue
```

```
begin 644 ee.c
M("\J"B @@*B!E;&UE9&ET+F,@"B @@*B!-87)K(%=;=%;;G-0<B F($$$;;@4VEE
M9V5L"B @@*B!4:&ES(&ES(&EN=&5N9&5$(&$%S(&$$@5D5$5262!S:6UP;&4@05-#
M24D@961I=&]R(&90<B!T:&41Q-(&UA:6QE<BX*(" J($%E(&%%L;&]W<R!N
M86EV92!U<V5R<R!T;R!U<V4@14@@-(&&=&A%O86EN86@5A<FYI;F<;F<@@5W<R!&10
M("?5S92!A;B!E9&ET;W;W(N"B @@*B!)="'[S(&FY(0;;;AFY1L97,L(&EN97?%,@@@
.
.      (Many lines omitted.)
.
end
```

```
$ uudecode ee.c.uue
```

```
$ ls -l ee.c*
```

```
-rw-r--r--  1 holsberg     6554 Jan 27 12:09 ee.c
-rw-r--r--  1 holsberg     9053 Jan 27 12:08 ee.c.uue
```

Note that the name of the decoded file, ee.c, was obtained from the first line of encoded file.

uuencode

uuencode converts a binary file into one that contains only ASCII characters, so that it can be electronically mailed to another UNIX computer. Although uuencode writes to stdout, I show the syntax with redirection so that you will have an encoded file to mail to someone else.

```
uuencode [ file ] label > outfile
```

`file`	Filename to process (default is standard input)
`label`	Filename that is inserted into the uuencoded file by uuencode, will become the name of the file that uudecode writes its output to.
`outfile`	Filename of the encoded file.

11

Example:

uuencode the file elmedit.c so that it will be named ee.c.uue by the encoding process, and be called ee.c when it is decoded:

```
$ ls -l

total 8
-rw-r--r--  1 holsberg      603 Jul  3  1990 SharFile.Headers
-rw-r--r--  1 holsberg     6554 Jul  3  1990 elmedit.c

$ uuencode elmedit.c ee.c > ee.c.uue

$ ls -l

total 17
-rw-r--r--  1 holsberg      603 Jul  3  1990 SharFile.Headers
-rw-r--r--  1 holsberg     9053 Jan 27 12:08 ee.c.uue
-rw-r--r--  1 holsberg     6554 Jul  3  1990 elmedit.c
```

Note that ee.c.uue is about 35 percent larger than elmedit.c.

Let's look at the beginning of the encoded file. In the first line—begin 644 ee,c—the name at the end of the line—ee.c—is the name that the decoding program will give to the decoded file.

```
$ more ee.c.uue

begin 644 ee.c
M("\J"B @@*B!E;&UE9&ET+F,N@"B @@*B!-87)K(%=I;&O<B F($$$$$SUA<F,@$4VEE
M9V5L"B @@*B!4:&ES(&ES(&EN=&5N9&5D(&%S(&$$@@5D5262I S:6UP;&4$4@05-#
M24D@961I=&R(&9O<B!T:&4$14Q-(&UA:6P=(&UA:6QE<BX*(")J ($ET(&%L W<R!N
M86EV92!U<V5R<R!T;R!U<V4$V8R14Q-(6FED=&]R<@&5A;F0$&AA<FED;"!W(10
M("'5S92!A;B!E9&ET;W(@("B-"B @@*B!)="!=="!!0U)0;97!0;;Y(;F<E%5497,@@6
```

.
.
.

```
end
```

WC

wc is a filter that counts characters, words, and lines of a file.

wc [-lwc] [*file(s)*]

-l	Print only a line count
-w	Print only a word count
-c	Print only a character count

Note: If *file(s)* are specified on the command line, the names are printed along with the count(s) that wc produces.

Example:

$ cat REfile

```
A regular expression is a sequence of characters taken
from the set of uppercase and lowercase letters, digits,
punctuation marks, etc., plus a set of special regular
expression operators. Some of these operators may remind
you of file name matching, but be forewarned: in general,
regular expression operators are different from the
shell metacharacters we discussed in Chapter 1.

The simplest form of a regular expression is one that
includes only letters. For example, the would match only
the three-letter sequence t, h, e. This pattern is found
in the following words: the, therefore, bother. In other
words, wherever the regular expression pattern is found
-- even if it is surrounded by other characters --, it will
be matched.
```

$ wc REfile

```
    10      87     555 REfile
```

$ wc -l REfile auto

```
    10 REfile
    21 auto
    31 total
```

who

who reports on the users currently using the system.

who [-uTlHqpdbrtas] [*file*]

who -qn *num* [*file*]

who am i

who am I

who takes the following options:

-a	Use all options.
-b	Show the time and date of the most recent system reboot.
-d	List expired processes that were not respawned by init.
-H	Print column headings as appropriate to the options selected. For -a, they are as follows: NAME LINE TIME IDLE PID COMMENT
-l	List only those input lines waiting for login.
-n *num*	List *num* users per line (the default is 1).
-p	List active processes spawned by /etc/init.
-q	List only user names and the number of users logged in. All other options are overridden.
-r	Show the current run level.
-s	Show standard report (default): user name, line logged in on, and time.
-t	Show when the last change to the system clock was made.
-T	Show standard report that indicates whether or not the terminal is writable by everyone. Places a + just before the name of the terminal if it is writable, and - if it is not.
-u	List only users currently logged in.
file	Usually /var/adm/wtmp, the log file for all logins since this file was created. Otherwise, wc reads from /var/adm/utmp, the file of current logins.

who am i and who am I (for the "correct English" crowd) are useful if you are logged in on several terminals and want to know the correct designation of the one you're currently using.

Example:

```
$ who

juucp      tty00       Sep 28 11:13
pjh        slan05      Sep 28 12:08
```

This shows that that juucp, who logged in at 11:13, and pjh, who logged in at 12:08, are currently logged in.

write

write sends a "real-time" message from your terminal to another user's terminal, if that user's terminal is writable (who -T).

write *user* [*line*]

user	User login name.
line	Terminal name. Use this name (determined from who -u) if *user* is logged in on more than one terminal.

Example:

My Terminal Displays
```
$ write lkh
hi -o-
Message from lkh on mccc ...
hi! -o-
how's your class? -o-
ok -o-
good. talk to you later. -oo-
^c
$ bye! -oo-
<EOT>
```

***lkh*'s Terminal Displays**
```
Message from pjh on mccc  [ Wed Feb  5 20:25:53 ] ...
hi -o-
$ write pjh
hi! -o-
how's your class? -o-
ok -o-
 good, talk to you later. -oo-
<EOT>
bye! -oo-
^c
```

xargs

xargs is a filter that transforms the output of one command into a series of commands. This overcomes the shell's limits on the number of command-line arguments and the size of the command line.

xargs [*options*] [*command* [*arg(s)*]]

The options include the following:

-e *eof*	Stop reading stdin when *eof* (the default is underscore) is read.
-i *str*	Replace every occurrence of *str* with the next input word (the default *str* is {}).
-l *linct*	Process *linct* nonempty lines from standard input.
-n *argct*	Limit the number of stdin arguments to *argct*.
-p	Prompt the user before executing a generated command. y executes the command; anything else skips the command.
-s *size*	*size* is the maximum number of characters in each argument list (the limit is 470).
-t	Print each generated command before executing it.
-x	Terminate whether a generated command exceeds *size* characters. See -s.

Examples:

Print exactly what the shell does with the output of the command piped into xargs:

$ date ¦ xargs -t

```
/bin/echo Tue May 28 08:37:06 EDT 1991
Tue May 28 08:37:06 EDT 1991
```

Notice that the shell uses /bin/echo to send the output of date through the pipeline.

Execute the mv command on the stream piped into xargs, two lines at a time, and ask for verification before doing the actual mv:

$ cat sources

```
book.part1
table_of_contents
database
```

```
$ cat destination

chapt1
toc
dbase

$ paste sources destination ¦ xargs -n2 -p mv

mv book.part1 chapt1 ?...y<enter>
mv table_of_contents toc ?...y<enter>
mv database dbase ?...n<enter>
```

Copy files whose names are being piped to xargs to the directory old. In the cp command, file is used as a placeholder for each name coming from the pipe.

```
$ ls

REs          ksh.prompts  no.blanks    xargs.2
UNIX.times   ksh.strings  x

$ ls ¦ xargs -ifile echo cp file old

cp REs old
cp UNIX.times old
cp ksh.prompts old
cp ksh.strings old
cp no.blanks old
cp x old
cp xargs.2 old
```

zcat

zcat is a filter that prints compressed files without having to uncompress them first.

```
zcat [ file(s) ]
```

    file(s)   Files to be uncompressed. If omitted, zcat reads from stdin.

Example:

cat the contents of a compressed file:

```
$ ls -l no.blanks

-rw-r--r--   1 pjh       root        742 Sep 30 14:03 no.blanks

$ cat no.blanks
```

A regular expression is a sequence of characters taken
from the set of uppercase and lowercase letters, digits,
punctuation marks, etc., plus a set of special regular
expression operators. Some of these operators may remind
you of file name matching, but be forewarned: in general,
regular expression operators have different means from the
shell metacharacters we discussed in Chapter 1.
The simplest form of a regular expression is one that
includes only letters. For example, the would match only
the three-letter sequence t, h, e. This pattern is found
in the following words: the, therefore, bother. In other
words, wherever the regular expression pattern is found
-- even if it is surrounded by other characters --, it will
be matched.

$ **compress no.blanks**

$ **ls -l no.blanks***

-rw-r--r--   1 pjh   root   511 Sep 30 14:03 no.blanks.Z

$ **zcat no.blanks.Z**

A regular expression is a sequence of characters taken
from the set of uppercase and lowercase letters, digits,
punctuation marks, etc., plus a set of special regular
expression operators. Some of these operators may remind
you of file name matching, but be forewarned: in general,
regular expression operators have different means from the
shell metacharacters we discussed in Chapter 1.
The simplest form of a regular expression is one that
includes only letters. For example, the would match only
the three-letter sequence t, h, e. This pattern is found
in the following words: the, therefore, bother. In other
words, wherever the regular expression pattern is found
-- even if it is surrounded by other characters --, it will
be matched.

The ASCII Code Table

Char	Name	Dec.	Hex.	Octal
^@	NUL	0	00	000
^A	SOH	1	01	001
^B	STX	2	02	002
^C	ETX	3	03	003
^D	EOT	4	04	004
^E	ENQ	5	05	005
^F	ACK	6	06	006
^G	BEL	7	07	007
^H	BS	8	08	010
^I	TAB	9	09	011
^J	LF	10	0A	012
^K	VT	11	0B	013
^L	FF	12	0C	014
^M	CR	13	0D	015
^N	SO	14	0E	016
^O	SI	15	0F	017
^P	DLE	16	10	020
^Q	DC1	17	11	021
^R	DC2	18	12	022
^S	DC3	19	13	023

Char	Name	Dec.	Hex.	Octal
^T	DC4	20	14	024
^U	NAK	21	15	025
^V	SYN	22	16	026
^W	ETB	23	17	027
^X	CAN	24	18	030
^Y	EM	25	19	031
^Z	SUB	26	1A	032
^[	ESC	27	1B	033
^\	FS	28	1C	034
^]	GS	29	1D	035
^^	RS	30	1E	036
^_	US	31	1F	037

Char	Dec.	Hex.	Octal
SP	32	20	040
!	33	21	041
"	34	22	042
#	35	23	043
$	36	24	044
%	37	25	045
&	38	26	046
'	39	27	047
(	40	28	050
)	41	29	051
*	42	2A	052
+	43	2B	053
,	44	2C	054
-	45	2D	055
.	46	2E	056
/	47	2F	057
0	48	30	060
1	49	31	061
2	50	32	062

Char	Dec.	Hex.	Octal
3	51	33	063
4	52	34	064
5	53	35	065
6	54	36	066
7	55	37	067
8	56	38	070
9	57	39	071
:	58	3A	072
;	59	3B	073
<	60	3C	074
=	61	3D	075
>	62	3E	076
?	63	3F	077
@	64	40	100
A	65	41	101
B	66	42	102
C	67	43	103
D	68	44	104
E	69	45	105
F	70	46	106
G	71	47	107
H	72	48	110
I	73	49	111
J	74	4A	112
K	75	4B	113
L	76	4C	114
M	77	4D	115
N	78	4E	116
O	79	4F	117
P	80	50	120
Q	81	51	121
R	82	52	122
S	83	53	123

A

Char	Dec.	Hex.	Octal
T	84	54	124
U	85	55	125
V	86	56	126
W	87	57	127
X	88	58	130
Y	89	59	131
Z	90	5A	132
[	91	5B	133
\	92	5C	134
]	92	5D	135
^	93	5E	136
_	94	5F	137
`	96	60	140
a	97	61	141
b	98	62	142
c	99	63	143
d	100	64	144
e	101	65	145
f	102	66	146
g	103	67	147
h	104	68	150
i	105	69	151
j	106	6A	152
k	107	6B	153
l	108	6C	154
m	109	6D	155
n	110	6E	156
o	111	6F	157
p	112	70	160
q	113	71	161
r	114	72	162
s	115	73	163
t	116	74	164

A

Char	Dec.	Hex.	Octal
u	117	75	165
v	118	76	166
w	119	77	167
x	120	78	170
y	121	79	171
z	122	7A	172
{	123	7B	173
|	124	7C	174
}	125	7D	175
~	126	7E	176
DEL	127	7F	177

Legend:

Char = the keystrokes. ^T means Ctrl-T.
Name = ASCII name if different from Char
Dec. = ASCII code in decimal (base 10)
Hex. = ASCII code in hexadecimal (base 16)
Octal = ASCII code in octal (base 8)

A

Index

Symbols

I

I

I

D

I

I

I

I

I

I

I

How to Get the Files Used in This Book

There are several ways for you to save yourself the chore of typing all the data files I use to illustrate UNIX tools. The easiest way is via anonymous FTP. Please see the introduction for detailed instructions.

You can also order the files on an MS-DOS disk by sending to the following address $20 (money order or check in U.S. funds drawn on a U.S. bank, please) and the desired MS-DOS disk type/size. Payment must accompany your order.

P.C.L.A.B. Computing
44 Lopatcong Drive
Trenton, New Jersey 08638-1326

If you prefer, you can simply copy this page, fill in the blanks, and send with the check or money order to the preceding address.

Cost Including Shipping and Handling:

$20.00   U.S. orders
$25.00   Foreign orders

Disk Preference:

5.25-inch high-density (1.2M)   ___   3.5-inch high-density (1.44M)   ___
5.25-inch medium-density (360K)   ___   3.5-inch low-density (720K)   ___

Payment Method:

Check   _____
Money order   _____

Name: _____

Street Address: _____

City: _____

State: _____ **Zip:** _____

Check or money orders should be made to: **Peter J. Holsberg**

Note: Allow four weeks for delivery.

This offer is made by P.C.L.A.B. Computing. SAMS assumes no responsibility for this offer. This is solely an offer of P.C.L.A.B. Computing, and not of SAMS.